HEGEL
The Essential Writings

HEGEL
The Essential Writings

EDITED AND WITH INTRODUCTIONS BY
Frederick G. Weiss

Foreword by J. N. Findlay

HARPER TORCHBOOKS
Harper & Row, Publishers
New York, Hagerstown, San Francisco, London

This book is dedicated to my father,
who never read a word of Hegel, but without whose example nothing I read would
have held any meaning.

Published under the editorship of Charles M. Sherover.

HEGEL: THE ESSENTIAL WRITINGS. Copyright © 1974 by Frederick G. Weiss. All
rights reserved. Printed in the United States of America. No part of this book
may be used or reproduced in any manner without written permission except
in the case of brief quotations embodied in critical articles and reviews. For
information address Harper & Row, Publishers, Inc., 10 East 53d Street, New
York, N.Y. 10022. Published simultaneously in Canada by Fitzhenry & White-
side Limited, Toronto.

First HARPER & ROW PAPERBACK edition published 1974

LIBRARY OF CONGRESS CATALOG CARD NUMBER: 74-3521

STANDARD BOOK NUMBER: 06-131831-0

05 RRD H 30 29 28 27

Time was when man had a heaven, decked and fitted out with endless wealth of thoughts and pictures. The significance of all that is, lay in the thread of light by which it was attached to heaven; instead of dwelling in the present as it is here and now, the eye glanced away over the present to the Divine, away, so to say, to a present that lies beyond. The mind's gaze had to be directed under compulsion to what is earthly, and kept fixed there; and it has needed a long time to introduce that clearness, which only celestial realities had, into the crassness and confusion shrouding the sense of things earthly, and to make attention to the immediate present as such, which was called Experience, of interest and of value. Now we have apparently the opposite of all this; man's mind and interest are so deeply rooted in the earthly that we require a like power to have them raised above that level. His spirit shows such poverty of nature that it seems to long for the mere pitiful feeling of the divine in the abstract, and to get refreshment from that, like a wanderer in the desert craving for the merest mouthful of water. By the little which can thus satisfy the needs of the human spirit we can measure the extent of its loss.

—Hegel's *Phenomenology*

Contents

Foreword

It is not generally the case that a philosopher is best approached, on first encounter, through a carefully chosen set of selections; it is in general much better to start one's study of a philosopher by plunging straight into one of his main works, and going through it in great depth and detail. Thus the *Republic*, studied with immense minuteness, long did duty as a gateway to the study of Plato at Oxford, and not only to the study of Plato, but of philosophy generally. In the case of Hegel, however, such a minute, representative method does not readily work, and well-chosen selections, duly meditated upon, and seen in their mutual relevance, are the best way of introducing someone to the philosophy as a whole. The reason for this peculiarity of approach lies in two facts about Hegel as a philosopher: (a) the supreme importance of grasping the *general* drift and character of his reasoning, both in each section of the system and in the system as a whole—Hegel deprecates all advance accounts of where he is tending, but without some advance intimation of his general direction even the quite subtle reader will often be at a loss; (b) the almost superhuman difficulty of achieving complete clearness in regard to the content and the cogency of a large number of Hegel's transitions —a lifetime will not suffice in some cases. Hegel has in fact to be studied like some monumental inscription in which there are many defaced and broken-off portions, which can only be satisfactorily filled in when *all* the rest of the inscription has been called in to help. Those who refuse to arrive at the sense of the whole except by an orderly, piecemeal progression through the parts, and who never take a leap from one salient thought-position to the next, much less leap back from a later eminence to an earlier one, may have their justification in what Hegel *says* of the gapless, unilineal necessity of his method, but will probably never advance beyond the opening phases of any part of the system, which, as a rudiment, will be almost certainly misinterpreted. Philosophical departments are full of exponents and critics of Hegel whose knowledge of the *Phenomenology of Spirit* becomes arrested at the stage of the Scientific Understanding or of Master and Slave, by no means crucial nodes in the work, or whose conceptions of Hegel's logical dialectic is entirely based on his first, famous triad of Being, Nothing, and Becoming, which, so far from being typical of the system, really represents only the abstract nonsense whose clearing away allows the system to begin. Such arrested knowledge of the beginnings of Hegel, with almost total ignorance of his immensely subtle, iridescent conclusions, is almost totally worthless: it can lead only to misdirected animadversions against what is basically misunderstood. And, apart from this, there are parts of Hegel's system, such as the *Philosophy of Nature*, which are only too readily ignored—on account of the necessarily dated, highly questionable character of much of their detail—but which nonetheless occupy such a centrally important place in Hegel's thought, and put forward conceptions (e.g., alienation) so crucial for its interpretation, that such ignoring can only be disastrous. The need, therefore, to introduce students to Hegel by well-chosen extracts, carefully garnered from every part of the system, by those who after long years know their way about it, becomes a prime desideratum.

It may further be argued that many of Hegel's claims for the seamless continuity of his dialectic, and the impossibility of helping on its self-development by irrelevant "external reflections," rather represent an ideal which Hegel aimed at than anything that he actually achieved. The seamless Dialectic that he talks of may be the Dialectic as "known to Nature"; it is not, however, the Dialectic as known to us or to him. Like all of us when we write philosophical essays, Hegel knew where he was tending before he saw precisely how he could get there, and there is often much more that is deeply persuasive in what arises out of his thought-movements, than in the highly tangled course of those movements themselves. Hegel's reasonings at times bear only too close a resemblance to the embarrassed pleadings of some cornered politician, whose hope is to steer his audience towards some desirable conclusion, in the face of difficulties that obstruct it or from premises that do not entail it. He does not, whatever he says, invariably follow the drift of "the things themselves," in whatever direction this may lead. Hegel has also not realized, what to us has become painfully familiar, that the most rigorous "musts" are also the most trivial and empty, and that the truly significant "musts" are the moral necessities, to which there are indeed alternatives, but only idly entertainable ones.

This book of Hegelian selections by Professor Weiss is, for all these reasons, very valuable. The passages incorporated are quite excellently chosen. Professor Weiss has included a long excerpt from the introductory chapters of the *Encyclopaedia*, which are Hegel's own, most successful attempt to introduce his system. He has also included some colorful sections from the *Phenomenology*, some weighty sections from the *Science of Logic*, as also the magnificently revealing paragraphs on the Absolute Idea at the end of the *Encyclopaedia Logic*. There are also good excerpts from the *Philosophy of Nature* and the *Philosophy of Right*. And, since the translations are good, a great deal of the difficult, self-revisionary thought of Hegel comes across, helped on by Professor Weiss's own valuable comments.

A last question remains. Is there really any point in trying to resuscitate and rehabilitate the thought of Hegel in our day and age? Is it not perhaps so difficult, so esoteric, so open to controversy, at many points so ill-stated and ill-reasoned, that, despite its immense historical and contemporary political significance, it would be better to let it be forgotten altogether, or be studied only by specialists? I should reply without hesitation, after fifty years of steady work on Hegel, that his is beyond doubt a supreme thought-treasure, and one that is always yielding new and surprising thought-dividends. Its detail may become more and more questionable at countless points, but it leaves one with a stock of invaluable methodological principles by which one's own thought may be guided. Of these I shall set down only three. It makes one see, first of all, that a merely descriptive view of the world, which never plunges beneath the surface or raises the question "Why?" but which is content to explore the boundless proliferation of empty, non-self-contradictory "logical possibilities," or to record empirical facts, which are never more than such facts, is really untenable. The mere possibilities of analytic thought, and the mere facts of radical empiricism, are both abstractions, which, taken as they are, can neither be nor be thought. Science, of course, recognizes the necessity of a dimension of depth beneath the descriptive surface of phenomena, and employs various categories of Law, Kind, Disposition, Cause, and so forth, which positivistic philosophies of science are always trying to explain away.

But the second principle that we learn from Hegel is that the endless explanatory regress favored by science cannot be intellectually satisfactory, but that its "bad infinity" requires emendation and supplementation by the "true infinity" of reentrant concepts, concepts which do indeed specify themselves in a round of difference, but which, throughout that round of difference, only reiterate and are more impressively themselves. Such concepts show their self-sufficiency and their independence of external justification simply by turning up again and again, however much we vary the context. To flee from them is but to find them in another form. There are of course thinkers who profess to be free of any such absolutistic commitments; but it is arguable that they do not really succeed in being so. They merely opt for ill-considered, indefensible Absolutes, for example, logically possible worlds, the four-dimensional Space-Time continuum, simple ideas, sense-data, and so forth, rather than well-considered and truly viable ones.

This brings me to the third methodological principle that one learns from Hegel: that one's Absolute must not be without something which contrasts with it, but that it also only can be an Absolute if what contrasts with it has no true independence from it, but exists only as providing the contrast in question. One's Absolute, in short, cannot merely be "above the battle," something which really is beneath mere illusion, or a scientific image merely underlying a manifest image, or a self-existent source having no real relation to contingent creatureliness, or an ideal essence irrelevantly distorted in its instances, or an order of things-in-themselves misread by mere subjectivity, or any similar case of the merely so-and-so contrasted with something equally "mere." Hegel has taught us that *this* sort of independence is in fact a case of dependence, and that the true independence is to be so thoroughly involved with and expended upon everything that, by a sudden inversion of perspective, everything becomes no more than a dependency of what one is oneself. To use Hegelian language, a true Absolute is essentially the Negation of the Negation, and can only be what it is by a sort of return from self-alienation.

These Hegelian concepts are no doubt always "on the blink," always on the verge of becoming vulgarly self-contradictory, but it is possible with some skill and subtlety to maintain their difficult, iridescent poise. It can be argued that Plato, in such works as the *Parmenides* and the *Timaeus*, Plotinus and Proclus, in their respective systems, and even Aquinas, in his view of the profoundly simple God who knows and makes all things without stepping an inch beyond His essence, were attempting much the same task as Hegel. Hegel, however, in his conceptions of the Infinite End, of the Absolute Idea and of Absolute Spirit, performed this task very much better than his predecessors, and in a fuller consciousness of its nature. Hegel's thought, properly understood, further has a place for all the nominalisms, pluralisms, formalisms, materialisms, subjectivisms, mechanisms, structuralisms, and so forth, to which it might seem opposed, so that there is indeed some sense, and not mere absurdity, in identifying it with philosophy itself, rather than with a special philosophy. The fact, at least, that it is not wholly unreasonable to regard it in this manner, as it would be in the case of much less cloudy, tidier systems, certainly makes it worthy of continued study.

J. N. FINDLAY

Boston University

Preface

What is and is not "essential" in the philosophy of Hegel may well
be a matter of debate among the enlightened savants, but such debate
is of little use to the thousands of students in the English-speaking
world who have, until only recently, been systematically deprived of
access to Hegel's thought. Given the contents of most of the introductory texts and books of readings in the various areas of philosophy
widely used today, it is possible and even probable that a college or
university student might graduate with a major in philosophy never
having even heard of Hegel.

On the other hand, the extant Hegel anthologies have become
dated both by new and vitally important translations, and by a fresh
understanding of Hegel generated by these translations and the wide-
spread and vigorous resurgence of interest in his work, especially in
America. Hegel is a systematic thinker, which means that whatever
the initial difficulties his work must be approached as the living whole
that it is—each part receiving an organic interpretation. It has been
the attempt to "salvage" certain portions of the Hegelian system in
blatant disregard of its integrity, that has led to many of the intellectual and political grotesqueries fathered on Hegel.

My chief concern in this text has been to present Hegel's mature
philosophy in the form in which Hegel himself thought it could alone
be understood, to offer, within a necessarily limited scope, a volume
of selections from which Hegel can be adequately *taught*, and not just
an assemblage of his more "interesting," provocative, or historically
important passages.

The word "writings" in the title pretty well dictates our choice of texts. Although the new Critical German Edition of Hegel's works will, on completion, comprise some forty volumes, Hegel published only four major books in his lifetime. The rest are lectures, letters, and minor, immature or incomplete treatises published posthumously by Hegel's editors. This material is extremely interesting, and especially valuable both for an understanding of Hegel's intellectual development and as a richly *supplemental* source of insight into Hegel's own and often terse mature speculations. But one first needs to face Hegel as he presented himself. Therefore the selections are taken from the works written and published by Hegel himself: the *Phenomenology of Spirit* (1807), *Science of Logic* (1812–1816), *Encyclopaedia of the Philosophical Sciences* (1st ed., 1817; 2d enl. and rev. ed., 1827; 3d edition, 1830), and *Philosophy of Right* (1821). The *Encyclopaedia* is the heart of Hegel's system, and in the words of William Wallace, "the only complete, matured, and authentic statement" of it.[1] It is that system, however, largely in outline form, and thus I have employed it not only for its specific content, but for the organizational structure it provides for our selections from the other three treatises, which expand upon and bring that content to life. The *Encyclopaedia* and the *Philosophy of Right* also contain valuable *Zusätze*, or additions, supplied by Hegel's editors from his own notes and lectures, and these are included in our text.

What I have tried to do in the general Introduction, given the limitations of space, is to provide a brief interpretation of Hegel's concept of dialectical development with some emphasis upon the problem of a beginning, an understanding of which is essential to even the most rudimentary grasp of what Hegel is doing. It is one of Hegel's most emphatic teachings that true or philosophic knowledge requires the identity of form and content, of method and result, and any attempt to embrace the one without the other is doomed to miss the mark that philosophy aims at, and is, in Hegel's view, alone capable of fully achieving. In the relatively brief span of pages I had at my disposal, I have chosen to approach the exposition largely via the method, allowing Hegel's own texts to demonstrate how this method brings to birth its content and vice versa. The Introduction is based largely upon Hegel's famous Preface to the *Phenomenology*, but the Preface itself will not be found among our selections. While it has been said that "Whoever has understood the Preface to the *Phenomenology* has understood Hegel," it is still no substitute for a full reading of Hegel, and there is nothing in it that is not elaborated elsewhere in our selections. In the lesser introductions or headnotes for the major sections, I have sought to indicate the function of these sections within Hegel's thought as a whole. These headnotes complement each other and the general Introduction, and it is suggested that they be read with it.

In defense of my liberal use of quotations from Hegel, I shall here invoke the remarks of two such diverse Hegel commentators as J. N. Findlay and Emil Fackenheim, who in this regard speak almost as one: "One must use [Hegel's] language, and the characteristic logic it embodies, if one is fully to understand or to communicate what he is maintaining."[2] "For as one tries to say differently exactly what Hegel says one often ends up either by saying much less, or else reverting to his own words."[3] Hegel is often a difficult writer, but he is dealing with difficult matters, and there is little point in making perfectly clear something Hegel never said or meant; we are after Hegel's meaning *(Bedeutung)*, not ours *(Meinung)*. I have, however, taken every opportunity in my discussion to lighten the burden with bracketed terms in the quotations and as simplified a commentary as possible surrounding them.

Finally, in defense of the absence in these pages of the usual biographical account of Hegel's life, I cannot better express what G. R. G. Mure has already said on this subject, in his *An Introduction to Hegel:*

The biography of a philosopher gains importance only so far as he fails to express himself fully in his writings, and it then serves to explain his failure rather than his philosophy. The half-philosopher, the empiricist in whom the philosophic interest is never, or for a period only, dominant, can to some extent be legitimately interpreted through the facts of his life; but the great thinker, so far as a man may, goes whole into his thoughts. In him the order of connexion is reversed—I might say restored—and his philosophy explains the rest of his life.[4]

Like all of us, Hegel was born, he suffered, and he died; but he also lived, and unlike most of us he thought life through and through. What is therefore most significant for us about his life is set out in this book. This is not to say that his private and public life is not in many respects quite fascinating, and the reader may, if he wishes, consult one or more of the volumes addressed to this subject, listed in our bibliography.

It remains only to thank those who have in one way or another made this volume possible. I am grateful to Charles Sherover, the general editor of the Harper & Row *Essential Writings* series, for putting me up to it in the first place. I owe a special debt for their valuable advice to J. N. Findlay, G.R.G. Mure, and Henry Paolucci, three of the greatest Hegelian philosophers we are ever likely to see. Finally I must thank my undergraduate students at Florida State University, particularly Ileana de la Torriente, the "little Hegelian." Contrary to the conventional wisdom of academia, they have been the real boon to my thinking, and make teaching the incomparably fruitful and enjoyable experience that it is.

A last word on approaching this text: If the material in chapters II and III on Hegel's *Phenomenology* and *Science of Logic* are found rough going, the reader is advised to proceed directly from chapter I (Introduction: The Philosophy of Hegel) to chapter IV (Toward a Concrete Metaphysics), where Hegel's relaxed, almost common-sense interpretation and criticism of familiar problems in modern thought both accustom us to his manner of thinking, and develop the need for a *Phenomenology* and *Logic*. Chapters II and III may then be returned to, followed by chapter V on Nature and Spirit, without loss of continuity.

FREDERICK G. WEISS

Notes. Preface

1. *Logic*, Wallace, p. ix.
2. *Philosophy of Nature*, p. x.
3. Emil L. Fackenheim, *The Religious Dimension in Hegel's Thought* (Bloomington: Indiana University Press, 1967), p. 6.
4. G.R.G. Mure, *An Introduction to Hegel* (Oxford: At the Clarendon Press, 1940), p. xvii.

Abbreviations and Credits

Logic, Miller | *Hegel's Science of Logic.* Translated by A. V. Miller. Foreword by J. N. Findlay. New York: Humanities Press, 1969. The selection on pp. 102–113 is taken from pp. 67–78 of this edition, and is reprinted by permission of Humanities Press, New York, and George Allen & Unwin Ltd., London.

Logic, Wallace | *The Logic of Hegel.* Translated by William Wallace from the *Encyclopaedia of the Philosophical Sciences.* 2d ed. rev. and aug. Oxford: Oxford University Press, 1892. The selections on pp. 19–36, 92–102, 113–123, 127–189 are taken from pp. 3–29, 143–155, 156–169, 57–75, 76–110, 115–120, 352–375, 378–379 of this edition.

Phenomenology | *The Phenomenology of Mind.* Translated, introduced, and edited by J. B. Baille. 2d ed. New York: Macmillan, 1931. The selections on pp. 44–85 are taken from pp. 131–145, 149–160, 162–163, 218–227, 229–240, 374–382 of this edition, and are reprinted by permission of George Allen & Unwin Ltd., London.

Philosophy of Mind | *Hegel's Philosophy of Mind.* Being Part III of the *Encyclopaedia of the Philosophical Sciences* (1830). Translated by William Wallace, together with *Zusätze* in Boumann's edition (1845), translated by A. V. Miller. Foreword by J. N. Findlay. Oxford: At the Clarendon Press, 1971. The selections on pp. 225–252, 269–278, 284–290, 317–338 of this edition are taken from pp. 1–24, 249–253, 253–258, 263–270 and are reprinted by permission of the Clarendon Press, Oxford.

Philosophy of Nature   *Hegel's Philosophy of Nature.* Being Part II of the *Encyclopaedia of the Philosophical Sciences* (1830). Translated by A. V. Miller from Nicolin and Pöggeler's edition (1959) and from the *Zusätze* in Michelet's edition (1847). Foreword by J. N. Findlay. Oxford: At the Clarendon Press, 1970. The selection on pp. 196–225 is taken from pp. 1–27 of this edition, and is reprinted by permission of the Clarendon Press, Oxford.

Philosophy of Right   *Hegel's Philosophy of Right.* Translated and edited by T. M. Knox. Oxford: At the Clarendon Press, 1942. Paperback ed., 1967. The selections on pp. 256–269, 278–284, 290–313 are taken from pp. 3–13, 14–20, 37–39, 73–74, 147–152, 154–155, 179–185, 208–223, and are reprinted by permission of the Clarendon Press, Oxford.

HEGEL
The Essential Writings

I

Introduction:
The Philosophy of Hegel

It has become customary in the introduction and exposition of Hegel to begin by bemoaning the difficulty of the task and, especially, of making a beginning at all. Many of Hegel's commentators have been compelled to go through a sort of personal catharsis before plunging into the labyrinthine abyss of Hegel's system and its expression. But if it is true, as Goethe says (and Hegel repeats), that there is no remedy but love against the great superiorities of others, then a purging of one's complacency and conceit may indeed be the best way to approach Hegel—or any other great thinker.

His entire philosophy is itself a spiritual bath, a baptism, which ravishes everything in its path and leaves nothing on earth or in heaven untouched. It is a religion built upon a profound faith, which teaches that we must die in order to live, and which regards man as natural, and points out how he may be born anew—how his first nature may be changed into a second, spiritual nature. It is a philosophy of education, a dialectical *paideia*, which calls upon us to obey that absolute commandment: *know thyself;* and a Promethean attempt to show that this summons is not an arbitrary law imposed from without, but the free and essential act of the God within, our innermost self. But in no other philosophy does the word "self" appear more often, yet more selflessly, than in that of Hegel, for the self that gradually and painfully emerges from its struggle with a protean world (which is, in truth, an inversion of its own nature) is like a phoenix risen from the ashes of its own funeral pyre, a subject become substance, creating out of itself by transforming itself and canceling within itself a myriad of inadequate forms of its own truth.

Hegel's philosophy is the suffering, death, and if we believe and can follow him, resurrection of everything incomplete, unknowing, and disconnected. It is the most ambitious, and at once impassioned and objective, endeavor to construe the inner and outer worlds of human experience rationally, and to systematize this construal into a "Science" of philosophic logic: "To help to bring philosophy nearer to the form of science [*Wissenschaft*]—that goal where it can lay aside the name of *love* of knowledge and be actual *knowledge*—that," Hegel says, "is what I have set before me."[1] But above all, Hegel's is a philosophy of freedom, where each human effort to discern the work of reason in all the processes of reality—in the animate and inanimate, in the intentional and unintentional, in the motions of atoms and stars, and in the labors and contests of men and nations—is at the same time a phase or moment of an eternal self-activity through which Spirit wins its independence from every form of externality by sensing, imagining, willing, and finally thinking this manifold otherness into an organic totality, in which the whole alone is true, and the consciousness of this, freedom:

Everything that from eternity has happened in heaven and earth, the life of God and all the deeds of time simply are the struggles for Spirit to know itself, to make itself objective to itself, to find itself, be for itself, and finally unite itself to itself; it is alienated and divided, but only so as to be able thus to find itself and return to itself. Only in this manner does Spirit attain its freedom, for that is free which is not connected with or dependent on another.[2]

Spirit *is* the truth, says Hegel, and the sole truth of Spirit is freedom. But he adds, elsewhere, that this freedom is won only through a "stern strife" against our own naive subjectivity, against the immediacy of arbitrary desire and passion. This stern strife makes many turn back, but it is only through this battle that culture is attained.

"The truth is the whole," Hegel says. But this whole is only the process of Spirit's own development, realized in the world and comprehended in thought, and the whole truth about Hegel is likewise a result, which can only be had by traversing and sharing the full range of the development of his thinking. While it is impossible for us in the brief compass of this Introduction to discuss the wealth of this development that Hegel's philosophy recounts, we can at least try to bring into focus prime aspects of the notion of development itself. For the notion of development is crucial. Its importance for understanding Hegel is paramount, and in his *History of Philosophy* he states explicitly that "we could, indeed, embrace the whole in the single principle of development [*Entwicklung*]; if this were clear, all else would result and follow of its own accord."[3] There is, however, no "secret" of Hegel, in the sense that by employing some sort of magic formula, one could bypass the labor and difficulty of reaching one's goal. Success in this case is a journey, and failure largely a fear of undertaking it. The persevering student will find that Hegel's "difficulty" is not external and contrived, but essential and necessary, the difficulty, as one writer puts it, of permanent and universal intelligibility, and that if the obstacles that his thought presents seem extraordinary, they are so only in proportion to the goals which overcoming them permits us to attain.

As to the question of "beginning," Hegel would have us believe that this is really no problem at all, or rather, that it is only a pedagogical one. "To speak of a beginning of philosophy," he writes, "has a meaning only in relation to a person who proposes to commence the study, and not in relation to the science as such."[4] Beginnings have no place in "Science," by which Hegel means fully developed truth, because they are gratuitous and abstract; they are there only to be done away with. As in the case of life itself, every beginning is a gift, and they are everywhere to be found. But while we cannot do without them, neither can we rest in them, and it is a homely but fundamental insight of all Hegel's thinking that the "gift" of life, and of all human experience, must ultimately be earned, if it is ever to be truly or fully possessed. A beginning, Hegel will say, in the sense of something primary and underived, not only makes an assumption but *is* an assumption, and its fate is to be abolished as such. Any proper, self-respecting beginning, he holds, suffers this fate at its own hands, its negation being the result of an immanent dialectic that abhors the vacuous abstraction of immediacy and converts its promise into a performance.

This point, one of the most important yet least understood in Hegel, is central to his concept of development, and we might best make our own beginning by quoting at length and commenting upon this pregnant passage from Hegel's Preface to the *Phenomenology:*

A so-called fundamental proposition or first principle of philosophy, even if it is true, is yet nonetheless false just because and insofar as it is merely a fundamental proposition, merely a first principle. It is for that reason easily refuted. The refutation consists in bringing out its defective character; and it *is* defective because it is merely the universal, merely a principle, the beginning. If the refutation is complete and thorough, it is derived and developed from the nature of the principle itself, and not [from without]. . . . The really positive working out of the beginning is at the same time just as much the very reverse, it is a negative attitude toward the principle we start from, negative, that is to say, of its one-sided form, which consists in being primarily immediate, a mere purpose. It may therefore be regarded as a refutation of what constitutes the basis of the system; but more correctly it should be looked at as a demonstration that the *basis* or principle of the system is in point of fact merely its *beginning*.[5]

The demand for a beginning is the work of thought, the universal, and the search for it reason's effort to find in the chaos and contingency of "everything" the embodiment of its own identity, dispersed and thus submerged there in the form of externality, otherness. The notion of a beginning itself entails some process of development that has begun, and some end or purpose in terms of which that beginning and its development come to have meaning. For Hegel, a genuine beginning has thus got to be an end in germ form, a purpose. It must involve the end in itself, though only implicitly or "ideally," together with the means of accomplishing it. Every cause, except the first and last, reveals itself as but an aspect of the cosmic *process* by which this first and last are united. The true beginning of things, their cause or origin, is the reason for their existence, but this is *par excellence* their end, that *for* which they come into being. What they "come from" is therefore actually where they are going, and what they "are" is a more or less arbitrary measure of the distance they have traveled toward this end. Their beginning is their destination, and they are not pushed blindly and indiscriminately, but drawn teleologically. If nothing "ends" or is realized, then nothing can be truly said either to begin or become, and thus everything disintegrates into what Hegel calls a "bad infinity." This ultimate collapse of the whole into mere finitude is averted only in the unity of beginning-and-end as fulfilled purpose; it is unity that does away with both as such, and constitutes thereby a true infinity, which Hegel likens to a circle closing with itself, any point of which is at once beginning and end. "The result is the same as the beginning solely because the beginning is purpose. . . . The realized purpose, or concrete actuality, is movement and development unfolded."[6] The development or working out of the principle is "negative," and constitutes a "refutation" of it only in the sense that, as abstract or immediate, this beginning or purpose is itself negative, i.e., lacking realization, and its unfolding is thus a negation of that initial negativity. It is complete and thorough when all that was implicit in the beginning has come forth, not as something *other* than it, but as a determinateness "posited" or implied by the principle itself, which, in turn, is authenticated in its rational articulation:

For the real subject-matter is not exhausted in its purpose, but in working the matter out; nor is the mere result attained the concrete whole itself, but the result along with the process of arriving at it. The purpose by itself is a lifeless universal, just as the general drift is a mere activity in a certain direction, which is still without its concrete realization; and the naked result is the corpse of the system which has left its guiding tendency behind it.[7]

The abstract reason *(Verstand)* of things is thus not by itself enough; the unending series of "hows" provided by the special sciences come to a bad end, i.e., *no* end. Reason *(Vernunft)* must gather and assimilate to itself everything requisite for its actualization, and this ability is alone the true measure of what Hegel means by "reason," the *concrete* universal.

The basis or principle of Hegel's system—and in light of the above, therefore, also its beginning, middle, and end—is *Geist*, variously translated "Mind" or "Spirit," and often also referred to by Hegel as the Notion, Concept *(Begriff)*, or Absolute Idea. This highest reality, he contends, in order to maintain its status as the Absolute, must be regarded not only as substance, i.e., as that which *is*, but also as subject or self. This requirement—of subject or self—is easily misunderstood, for what is meant is not that the Absolute is some sort of personal being, in the subjective or limited sense of "person," but that the supreme principle and truth of the universe is *one*, an undivided unity of differences, which is enriched rather than dissipated by the multitude of its manifestations. What it means is that the changing world and all its history is none other than this principle's *own* manifestation, the revelation of itself in various modes of consciousness or stages of unity culminating in philosophic thought, which alone adequately exhibits the full development of Spirit as nothing other than the raising of *itself* to truth. "Truth," Hegel says, "aware of what it is, is Spirit."[8] And again: "Spirit, which, when thus developed, knows itself to be Spirit, is science."[9]

The self-conscious truth, which is Spirit, cannot be something abstract, for "if the truth is abstract, it must be untrue."[10] What Hegel means by this is that the truth or explanation of anything cannot in the end be something other than what it is the truth *of*, or is supposed to explain, for to explain is simply to eradicate the difference between *explicans* and *explicandum*. An abstract truth is still "false" simply because it is cut off from or appears in opposition to its object, in the sense that it raises questions about itself which the factors that brought it into existence cannot of themselves answer. Something else, something *other* must be called into play which, as long as it remains other, places this truth in a position of dependency upon it, qualifies it externally, and thus limits its claim to truth. In Hegel's view, as nothing is simply false, neither is anything simply true. The truth must contain the false as a vanishing element in itself, or suffer limitation at the hands of what it cannot grasp. The false, however immature and distorted, must reveal itself as a prefiguration of something to come, without which its very deformity could not exist, but within which the negative aspect of that deformity is transmuted into a positive function of the larger whole. Hegel equates falsity with otherness, self-discordance, and holds that "the terms true and false must no longer be used where their otherness has been canceled and superseded." Similarly,

the expressions "unity of subject and object," of "finite and infinite," of "being and thought," etc., are clumsy when subject and object, etc., are taken to mean what they are *outside* their unity, and are thus in that unity not meant to be what its very expression conveys; in the same way falsehood is not, *qua* false, any longer a moment of truth.[11]

Genuine or philosophic truth is thus to be conceived as a *result* which consummates rather than transcends the process of arriving at it, i.e., the process must be construed as its own. For Hegel, philosophic truth *is* genuineness, not the correspondence of one thing with another, of *our* idea with the thing (mere correctness), but the correspondence of a thing with itself, of its being or objectivity with its notion.[12] Every ordinary form of experience amounts to an approximation of this truth, and all sub-philosophical experience is only abstract to the extent that its form (the mode of apprehension) and its content (the object apprehended) do not fully penetrate and explicate each other. What is called the merely "phenomenal" character of experience is precisely this dissonance or incongruity in the subject-object relation. Thinking begins in the wonder at this, i.e., arises out of this contradiction, and does not rest satisfied until it enters into and transforms the whole realm of appearance (*Schein*), abrogating its mere show and establishing its authenticity. This it does by reducing the various levels of experience, each of which exhibits both a unity and a difference, i.e., a truth and a falsehood, to what Hegel calls "ideal" moments of a developing whole, the relative absence of which at each such stage being at once what places it there and forces it beyond itself. Each moment or part lives only by participating in and eventually giving itself up to the whole, in and through which it alone or first becomes a part. The "self" or identity which is given up, however, is only the claim on the part of a fragment to be the whole, *a* truth claiming to be truer than it is, a being which is not Being, which must go beyond itself and reach out for another to support itself, thus affirming its own lack of a genuine, self-contained and self-sufficient identity. But this having to go outside itself, this requiring an other, is what constitutes its lack of full self-identity: "The subsistence or substance of anything that exists is its self-identity; for its want of identity, or oneness with itself, would be its dissolution."[13] What it loses in this dissolution is therefore only its own initial state of being lost, its otherness, alienation and abstraction, which the whole, as its truth, nullifies. Spirit thus displaces nothing, but places everything as a determination within itself, and without which it would be equally false and abstract. A true whole is constituted of parts each of which and in varying degrees "mirrors" that whole *negatively*; each is a microcosm, but not literally, i.e., we do not have here the box-within-box thesis. Rather, the whole is "there" by implication, in the sense that any attempt that is made to grasp fully the being of any part leads in the process to the whole which is its truth.[14] The whole is thus, as it were, the *non*being of its parts: all determination is thus negation, but all negation is equally determination. If, as Hegel says, each category in his Logic may be taken as a definition of the Absolute, each mode of existence, i.e., the being and life of each individual, may be construed as an attempt to make that definition work.

In the Preface to the *Phenomenology*, Hegel illustrates this dialectical advance toward self-identity by means of an analogy from the natural realm:

> The bud disappears when the blossom breaks through, and we might say that the former is refuted by the latter; in the same way when the fruit comes, the blossom may be explained to be a false form of the plant's existence, for the fruit appears as its true nature in place of the blossom. These stages are not merely differentiated; they supplant one another as being incompatible with one another. But the ceaseless activity of their own inherent nature makes them at the same time moments of an organic unity, where they not merely do not contradict one another, but where one is as necessary as the other; and this equal necessity of all moments constitutes alone and thereby the life of the whole.[15]

The difficult but crucial point to grasp here is that the apparently "positive" coming forth and existence of things is, for Hegel, also and essentially the operation of a negative dialectic, or better yet, a dialectic of negativity, whereby this coming-to-be of things is a passing away, a denial or development of a mere capacity in something else, and their passing away is, in turn, a coming-to-be of yet some truer, because more complete, i.e., self-identical, existence, the appearance of which embraces and requires the refutation of its earlier phases qua false, each of which is sublated (*aufgehoben*) in the next. "Appearance is the process of arising into being and passing away again, a process that itself does not arise and pass away, but is per se, and constitutes reality and the life-movement of truth."[16] The truth of this process is not to be found in any of its single phases, but in the totality (which is no mere plurality), the rational rhythm of the organic whole. The singularly perceived and individual aspects of this movement initially present themselves as solely positive and quietly self-abiding, with change a mere possibility and not a consequence of their inherent nature. But change, Hegel insists, lies within the very nature of existence (*Dasein*); its being is to perish, and development is its reality and truth. "Individuals" are far from indivisible as their name implies, and "experience confirms what the Concept teaches."

Hegel's "*aufheben*" has three distinct but related meanings, which the English verb "develop" does as much justice to as any. It means (1) to cancel or suspend, (2) to raise up, and (3) to preserve or maintain. The key to this triadic development, however, is what Hegel calls the negativity of the finite, a fact which defines and so pervades the experienced world that we take it for granted, and the "three" moments actually resolve themselves into a two-fold negation. The finite is *itself* the first negation, and the process of canceling or abrogating this negativity is the second. Hegel also speaks of "absolute negativity" by which he means the resultant (but not therefore static) truth which is this double negation itself.

Absolute negativity is infinite *self*-affirmation, while simple negativity, i.e., finitude, rather represents self-*suppression* or self-abnegation. "For anything to be finite," Hegel remarks, "is just to suppress itself and put itself aside."[17] And again: "The finite *is not*, i.e., is not the truth, but merely a transition and emergence to something higher."[18] It is this capacity for change, this implicit ideality of the finite, which both condemns it and through this condemnation makes possible its redemption: "The hand which inflicts the wound is also the hand which heals it."[19] For Hegel, finitude is synonymous with contingency, immediacy, and the immediate is simply the undeveloped. This contingency of things, whether of abstract philosophic principles or finite beings, is a function of their limitation or determinateness, a condition that organizes their very individuality for a larger enterprise. When the conditions that *render* a thing contingent are stipulated and seen to be a function of that thing's very nature, its contingency is at once suspended and preserved, actualized, reduced to a moment and raised, thereby, to the level of necessity. In this sense, the initial negativity of things is their *own* dialectic, revealed only by entering into their positive content, taking them for what they are, discovering the contradiction therein, and allowing them to "pass over" into their opposites. "All finite things involve an untruth: they have a notion [an essence, calling, kind, or end] and an existence." But the latter does not meet the requirements of the former.[20] Thus, the universal is the *truth* of the individual, actuality the *truth* of possibility, necessity the *truth* of contingency, and in the "death" of this contingent existence the universal (the subject or self) liberates itself and establishes its being. This, Hegel says, is the "portentous power of the negative, the energy of thought":

Death, as we may call that unreality, is the most terrible thing. . . . But the life of Mind is not one that shuns death, and keeps clear of destruction; it endures death, and in death maintains its being. It only wins to its truth when it finds itself utterly torn asunder. It is this mighty power, not by being a positive which turns away from the negative, as when we say of anything it is nothing or it is false, and, being then done with it, pass off to something else: on the contrary, Spirit is this power only by looking the negative in the face, and dwelling with it . . . the magic power that converts the negative into being . . . is just what we spoke of above as subject, which by giving determinacy a place in its substance, cancels abstract immediacy, i.e., immediacy which merely *is*, and, by so doing, becomes the true substance.[21]

Hegel's philosophy, by its very nature, is prohibited from being transcendently metaphysical. The dialectic only manifests itself when we enter fully into all the existential forms presented in experience. Nor is his "idealism" abstract and in a world beyond. "The ideality of the finite is the first maxim of philosophy," Hegel writes, "and thus all philosophy is idealism."[22] But the ideality of Mind or Spirit, its infinitude or freedom, consists only in its triumph over the externality, the "asunderness" and self-exclusion of a gratuitous world. It achieves its purpose, not by abandoning it, but by overcoming it. In the words of one of Hegel's ablest commentators, Mind represents "the world's deep unity asserting itself over the world's attempted dispersion, an attempted dispersion as essential to the deep unity as the latter is essential to the former."[23] Finitude may be a shadow cast by the mind's own light, but without this illusion to overcome, Spirit would itself be cast into utter darkness:

Hegel holds that the existence of a natural order, with its blindness, rigidity, contingency and mechanism, is a necessary pre-condition or pre-supposition of the existence of self-conscious Spirit. It is only if the world sets us a *task*, that our theorizing and practical activities will be called forth by it. . . . The Spirit, as Hegel calls it, is nothing without an Other to overcome: like the God of the German mystics . . . it would have to give up the ghost if it had neither world nor men to raise up and redeem.[24]

Hegel's own words are here precisely to the point:

Ideality only has meaning when it is the ideality of something: but this something is not a mere indefinite this or that, but existence characterized as reality, which, if retained in isolation, possesses no truth. The distinction between Nature and Mind is not improperly conceived, when the former is traced back to reality, and the latter to ideality as a fundamental category. Nature, however, is far from being so fixed and complete, as to subsist even without Mind: in Mind it first, as it were, attains its goal and its truth. And similarly, Mind on its part is not merely a world beyond Nature and nothing more: it is really, and with full proof, seen to be Mind only when it involves Nature as absorbed in itself.[25]

Elsewhere Hegel writes: "Spirit is the existent truth of matter—the truth that matter itself [*an sich*] has no truth."[26] And again: "The external world is the truth, if it could but know it [*an sich*]."[27] For Hegel, Mind is only implicit in Nature, slumbering there. Nature produces Mind out of itself, and our knowing this Nature is Nature's own coming to know itself, in Hegel's phrase, Mind's "returning to itself" out of this estranged state. But when we take the world for granted, i.e., qua natural, it is literally beside itself, and not unlike a neglected and unappreciated person, produces symptoms of stubbornness, intransigence, irreconcilability, irrationality, and even violent hostility. Those levels of consciousness that display this manifold disintegration suffer a like misfortune, but this pain, this negation of Mind's individuality and immediacy, is one which consciousness endures as a necessary precondition for its ultimate concrete unity. The "world" thus commands attention, and demands an explanation, because it is not, qua natural or undeveloped, really a world, a unity or totality at all. But neither is the natural realm so impotent and inert as to remain in this condition. "God does not remain petrified and dead," says Hegel, "the very stones cry out and raise themselves to Spirit."[28] Only when we abstract ourselves and the variety of ways in which, qua knowers and doers, we subdue this Proteus and make it our own, do we "make this Nature, which is an Other than we, into an Other than she is."[29] The nisus for development, which everything natural displays, represents in all the ways in which Mind mediates its world an attempt on its part to grasp itself. But in the grasp *(begreifen)* of lower-level forms of consciousness—sensuous intuition *(Anschauung)*, materialized conception *(Vorstellung)*, and abstract understanding *(Verstand)*—this full selfhood or unity of *the* Concept *(Begriff)* is only inadequately presaged, begging articulation at a higher linguistic level, where the fixity and mutual exclusion of its determinations can be broken down to reveal instead their fluid, interdependent and mutually determining character:

Thus we say of sensible things, that they are changeable: that is, they *are*, but it is equally true that they are *not*. We show [even] more obstinacy in dealing with the categories of the understanding. These are terms which we believe to be somewhat firmer, or even absolutely firm and fast. We look upon them as separated from each other by an infinite chasm, so that opposite categories can never get at each other. The battle of reason [*Vernunft*] is the struggle to break up the rigidity to which the understanding has reduced everything.[30]

Hegel is supposed to have scandalized logic and language by denying the validity of the principles of identity and noncontradiction, and riding roughshod over the common usages of words, "torturing language," as one critic has put it, "to make it say at once what must be said at once."[31] But Hegel denies only the *ultimate* or universal validity of the principles of formal logic; they have their place, and indeed, nothing further can be achieved without them. Regarding the abuse of language, Hegel actually delights in the agonies of *Verstand*, which now and then produce terms (like *aufheben*) with double meanings: "This double usage of language, which gives to the same word a positive and negative meaning, is not an accident, and gives no ground for reproaching language as a cause of confusion. We should rather recognize in it the speculative spirit of our language rising above the mere 'Either-or' of understanding."[32] For Hegel, this uniquely philosophical content escapes the logic and language of *Verstand*, which is characteristic of the empirical sciences and their handmaiden: positivist philosophy. "This content," he says, "is called a mystery, because it is something hidden from the understanding; for the latter does not get the length of the process, which this unity is, and thus it is that everything speculative, everything philosophical, is for the understanding a mystery."[33]

If Spirit is the truth, then it must absorb the world in itself, and it does this by absorbing itself in the world. But this mutual penetration is always and everywhere the work of the thing itself (*die Sache selbst*), the self-active Concept (*Begriff*) whose life and being is dialectic:

The Concept's moving principle, which alike engenders and dissolves the particularizations of the universal, I call "dialectic." . . . [But] this dialectic is not an activity of subjective thinking applied to some matter externally, but is rather the matter's very soul putting forth its branches and fruit organically. . . . To consider a thing rationally means not to bring reason to bear on the object from the outside and so to tamper with it, but to find that the object is rational on its own account. . . . The sole task of philosophic science is to bring into consciousness this proper work of the reason of the thing itself.[34]

To say that the Concept "alike engenders and dissolves the particularizations of the universal" means for Hegel that the very being of particular objects is a measure both of their success and failure to mirror the universal, which is their truth. But this contradiction is not, as G. R. G. Mure remarks, "a disaster to be shunned, an undiagnosed disease not in things but in us"[35]; that is, the finitude of cognition is not a mere subjective limitation, but also a deficiency of the object, and the one is a reflection of the other. Consciousness is the truth of its object only insofar as that object is *itself*, i.e., when it is *self-consciousness*. To the extent that the object is other than it, that object is finite and external, and the consciousness merely subjective. "We make ourselves finite by receiving an other into our consciousness," says Hegel, "but in knowing it, we transcend [sublate] this limitation."[36] And elsewhere:

This dialectic process which consciousness executes on itself—on its knowledge as well as on its object—in the sense that out of it the new and true object arises, is precisely what is termed Experience.[37]

It should by now be apparent that Hegel's dialectical thought defies presentation in terms solely of an epistemology on the one hand, and an ontology on quite another. The inseparability of the method and its results cannot be overemphasized. As with Plato, the way of knowing and the object known, the process and result, must be seen to be united in varying degrees along the rungs of a ladder, which is, as it were, drawn up, cast away, sublated in the ascent. The significance of the object, from the point of view of Science (*Wissenschaft*) or absolute knowledge (*das absolute Wissen*), is purely a function of the process by which knowledge of that object is reached. But this does not mean that we, as finite minds, create the substantial objects or beings of our world, because knowing, validating and vindicating are not and cannot be functions of *private* centers of finite consciousness. Indeed, Hegel remarks, it is meaningless to say "there *are* finite minds; mind qua mind is not finite," i.e., it is the true infinite, the negation of all finitude; "it *has* finitude within itself, but only as a finitude which is to be, and has been, reduced to a moment."[38] True being, *Wirklichkeit*, is not psychologically but logically arrived at, and this truth which also *is* can be arrived at in no other way. The process of knowledge, which for Hegel must be identical with its result, is not physical, mental, or neurological; true knowledge is rather a presupposition for the very existence of these processes themselves. The manner of thinking and the product of thought must mutually justify each other, else the method fails or the result is meaningless. Hegel's central idea, that of the concrete, is precisely that point of synthesis in which the object and its explanation coincide, the so-called identity of opposites, of knowing and being. If the derivation of the concrete from the abstract, of the true from the false, of Nature from logic, and of Spirit from Nature seems incomprehensible and absurd, it is, for Hegel, only because we have failed to grasp the logic of derivation.

Hegel's system is throughout an attempt to explicate this derivation as a dialectical logic of development, a logic which demonstrates the Nothingness of being, and the Being of nothingness. "In a system," he says, "it is the most abstract term which is the first, and the truth of each sphere is the last."[39] Hegel thus begins with the false, the abstract, the untrue. Why? He raises the question himself, and answers it thus:

Why then, it may be asked, begin with the false and not at once with the true? To which we answer that truth, to deserve the name, must authenticate its own truth. . . . We cannot begin with the truth, because the truth, when it forms the beginning, must rest on mere assertion.[40]

The truth, he adds elsewhere, is not "like stamped coin that is issued ready from the mint and so can be taken up and used."[41] Again: "Impatience asks for the impossible, wants to reach the goal without the means of getting there. The length of the journey has to be borne with, for every moment is necessary."[42] And finally: "That the truth is only realized in the form of system, that substance is essentially subject, is expressed in the idea which represents the Absolute as Spirit."[43] If we yet ask what *is* this Spirit, this freedom, this goal to which everything tends, Hegel gives three answers which are still one: (1) The Absolute Idea is LOGIC, "a realm of shadows" in itself, but as "positing" or presupposing Nature and Spirit as its being and truth, respectively, it is the whole, *das Ganze*, and therefore the truth; (2) The Absolute is equally NATURE, which, in itself, is the epitome of finitude and unfreedom, the very antithesis of the Idea, but as again presupposing or developing out of itself Spirit "which cognizes the Logical Idea in Nature and thus raises Nature to its essence," it is the whole; and (3) the Absolute is SPIRIT, but Spirit only is Spirit when it is mediated through Nature, and so forth. Each of these three moments of Hegel's great triad, when taken in isolation from the others, may form the beginning, and as such becomes abstract and untrue. Each, on the other hand, when complemented by the others, may equally be regarded as the end, and as presupposing their mediation, the truth, the Absolute. We can perhaps now see how it is both that there are no "beginnings" in Science, and equally that any point in this whole may be taken as a beginning.

Hegel sees the entire development of Mind as a *Geistesodyssey*, representing Spirit's freeing of itself from all its existential forms that do not accord with its notion. "As existing in an individual form, this liberation is called 'I'; as developed to its totality, it is free Spirit; as feeling, it is Love; and as enjoyment, it is Blessedness."[44] At one point in the Preface to the *Phenomenology*, Hegel makes what seems to be a concession to the romanticism he there polemicizes, saying: "The life of God and divine intelligence may be spoken of as *love* disporting with itself."[45] It is the pain of mortality's self-renunciation, and the joy of immortality's self-affirmation, and the only way from the one to the other. Love, he might have said, is life, for life is a dying of finitude and at the same time a birth in beauty and truth. Love is thus a dying of death, and in Shakespeare's words, "death once dead, there's no more dying then" (Sonnet 146, line 14). But Hegel quickly adds that this idea "falls into edification, and even sinks into insipidity, if it lacks the seriousness, the suffering, the patience, and the labor of the negative."[46] God's purpose with the world is not to provide for us a "flight of abstraction" from it, but to have us learn through a hard, infinite struggle against it that "the real is rational, and the rational real (*Was wirklich ist, ist vernünftig, und was vernünftig ist, ist wirklich*),"[47] that "to him who looks upon the world rationally, the world in turn presents a rational aspect."[48] Even to the intelligent observer, Hegel remarks, there seems to be much that fails to meet the requirements of reason. "But such acuteness," he continues, "is mistaken in the conceit that, when it examines these objects and pronounces what they ought to be, it is dealing with questions of philosophic science.''[49] Ultimately, Hegel would say, the only thing the *philosopher* has to be dissatisfied with is himself. But Hegel's polemic against romantic dissatisfaction is not to be interpreted as a denial of the importance of *praxis*. On the contrary, he holds that without the will, man's individual interest and activity, nothing would be carried into effect at all: "And if 'interest' be called 'passion' . . . we may affirm absolutely that nothing great in the world has been accomplished without [it]."[50] But again, and characteristically, Hegel adds that "It is the cunning of reason [*die List der Vernunft*] to have the passions work for its aims."[51]

At the close of his *Lectures on the Philosophy of History*, Hegel says:

That the history of the world, with all the changing scenes which its annals present, is this process of development and the realization of Spirit—this is the true Theodicy, the justification of God in history. Only *this* insight can reconcile Spirit with the history of the world—that what has happened, and is happening every day, is not only not "without God." but is essentially His work.[52]

If we are still tempted to ask what this cunning Reason, this God is in itself [*an sich*], we should have to answer that it is what it does, and that what it does is timelessly do away with the illusion that it has not yet accomplished it. "The Good," Hegel says, "the absolutely Good, is eternally accomplishing itself in the world; and the result is that it needs not wait upon us [qua individuals, in whose ascent the vision of the whole is still obscured by finite perspectives], but is already by implication, as well as in full actuality, accomplished."[53] This last "consolidating, quietistic" step that Hegel takes, is, in the words of Professor Findlay, "one which achieves its goal by suddenly coming to see its goal in what previously seemed only an infinite, hopeless struggle towards it":

It is by the capacity to understand and accept this last type of dialectical transformation that the true Hegelian is marked off from his often diligent and scholarly, but still profoundly misguided misinterpreter, who still yearns after the showy spectacular climax, the Absolute coming down in a machine accompanied by a flock of doves, when a simple arrest and return to utter ordinariness is in place. Finite existence in the here and the now, with every limitation of quality and circumstance, is, Hegel teaches, when rightly regarded and accepted, identical with the infinite existence which is everywhere and always. To live in Main Street is, if one lives in the right spirit, to inhabit the Holy City, a view that will be deeply shocking to many of Hegel's transcendental interpreters. The content of the Absolute Idea, the goal of the dialectic, is simply said to be "the system of which we have been hitherto studying the development," i.e., the dialectic itself, where the end of the journey is simply seen to be the journey itself, and the method that has been followed on [it]. The astringent realism of Hegel's final solution is, however, precisely what renders it acceptable to many who find flights of transcendental otherworldliness nothing but a nauseous opiate.[54]

Some have recoiled in utter disbelief at this, calling the whole thing a monstrous hoax. But the hoax is ours, Hegel would say, if we can seriously maintain the unthinkable and unarguable position that human reason and the experiential world it articulates is a mere delusion.

In any case, nothing short of a full reading of Hegel will enable us to properly judge both the validity of his claims and those of his critics, who are many. In this brief Introduction, and in the readings, we have a beginning, but only that. It remains to see Hegel's notion of dialectical development come to life in the rich texture of his voluminous writings and lectures on logic and law, ethics and aesthetics, history and nature, religion and science. Few men have penetrated so deeply or perceptively into our vast experience of the lived world, and fewer yet have been aware that Hegel's aim is throughout that of Greek science, ΣΩΖΕΙΝ ΤΑ ΦΑΙΝΟΜΕΝΑ, to save the appearances.

It is always easier, it seems, to damn Hegel's logic for the crushing effect it has upon our precious and pompous individuality, than to follow out that logic, from beginning to end, and to try to see our own predicament emerge in its true light. "Only one man has understood me," Hegel said, "and even he has not." Perhaps we are still too close to Hegel, and therefore too far, to see him as we should; perhaps, on the other hand, we have today so lost ourselves in the external and abstract that this is impossible. But if "the owl of Minerva spreads its wings only with the falling of the dusk," perhaps it is Hegel's time after all.

Notes. Introduction: The Philosophy of Hegel

1. *Phenomenology*, p. 70.
2. *Hegel's Lectures on the History of Philosophy*, trans. E. S. Haldane and

Frances H. Simson (New York: Humanities Press, 1963), vol. 1, p. 23.

3. Ibid., p. 20.

4. *Logic*, Wallace, p. 28.

5. *Phenomenology*, p. 85. It is ironically instructive that most attempts to "refute" Hegel's system have largely served to further its validity.

6. Ibid., p. 83.

7. Ibid., p. 69.

8. *Philosophy of Mind*, p. 178.

9. *Phenomenology*, p. 86.

10. *History of Philosophy*, p. 24.

11. *Phenomenology*, p. 99.

12. "Thus we speak of a true friend; by which we mean a friend whose manner of conduct accords with the notion of friendship. In the same way we speak of a true work of Art. Untrue in this sense means the same as bad, or self-discordant. In this sense a bad state is an untrue state; and evil and untruth may be said to consist in the contradiction subsisting between the function or notion and the existence of the object. Of such a bad object we may form a correct representation, but the import of such representation is inherently false." *Logic*, Wallace, p. 52.

13. Ibid., p. 113.

14. See Tennyson's "Flower in the Crannied Wall":

> Flower in the crannied wall,
> I pluck you out of the crannies,
> I hold you here, root and all, in my hand,
> Little flower—but if I could understand
> What you are, root and all, and all in all,
> I should know what God and man is.

15. *Phenomenology*, p. 68.

16. Ibid., p. 105.

17. *Logic*, Wallace, p. 147.

18. *Philosophy of Mind*, p. 23.

19. *Logic*, Wallace, p. 55.

20. Ibid., p. 52.

21. *Phenomenology*, pp. 93–94.

22. *Logic*, Wallace, p. 178.

23. J. N. Findlay, *Ascent to the Absolute* (New York: Humanities Press, 1970), p. 246.

24. J. N. Findlay, "Some Merits of Hegelianism," *Proceedings of the Aristotelian Society* 56 (1955–1956): 20–21.

25. *Logic*, Wallace, p. 180.

26. *Philosophy of Mind*, p. 30.

27. *Logic*, Wallace, p. 79. Wallace here shows his grasp of Hegel, if not his fidelity to the text.

28. *Philosophy of Nature*, p. 15.

29. Ibid., p. 8.

30. *Logic*, Wallace, p. 67

31. Emil L. Fackenheim, *The Religious Dimension in Hegel's Thought* (Bloomington: Indiana University Press, 1967), p. 6.

32. *Logic*, Wallace, p. 180.

33. *Lectures on the Philosophy of Religion, Together with a Work on the Proofs of the Existence of God*, trans. E. B. Speirs and J. B. Sanderson (London: Routledge & Kegan Paul, 1962), vol. 3, p. 367.

34. *Philosophy of Right*, pp. 34–35.

35. G.R.G. Mure, *The Philosophy of Hegel* (London: Oxford University Press, 1965), p. 17.

36. *Philosophy of Mind*, p. 24.

37. *Phenomenology*, p. 142.

38. *Philosophy of Mind*, p. 23.

39. *Philosophy of Nature*, p. 21.

40. *Logic*, Wallace, pp. 155, 285.

41. *Phenomenology*, p. 98.

42. Ibid., p. 90.

43. Ibid., p. 85.

44. *Logic*, Wallace, p. 285.

45. *Phenomenology*, p. 81.

46. Ibid.

47. *Philosophy of Right*, p. 10; *Logic*, Wallace, p. 10.

48. *The Philosophy of History*, trans. J. Sibree and introd. C. Friedrich (New York: Dover, 1956), p. 11.

49. *Logic*, Wallace, p. 11.

50. *Philosophy of History*, p. 23.

51. Ibid., p. 33.

52. Ibid., p. 457.

53. *Logic*, Wallace, p. 352.

54. Findlay, *Ascent to the Absolute*, pp. 135, 141.

WHAT IS PHILOSOPHY?

1. Philosophy misses an advantage enjoyed by the other sciences. It cannot like them rest the existence of its objects on the natural admissions of consciousness, nor can it assume that its method of cognition, either for starting or for continuing, is one already accepted. The objects of philosophy, it is true, are upon the whole the same as those of religion. In both the object is Truth, in that supreme sense in which God and God only is the Truth. Both in like manner go on to treat of the finite worlds of Nature and the human Mind, with their relation to each other and to their truth in God. Some *acquaintance* with its objects, therefore, philosophy may and even must presume, that and a certain interest in them to boot, were it for no other reason than this: that in point of time the mind makes general *images* of objects, long before it makes *notions* of them, and that it is only through these mental images, and by recourse to them, that the thinking mind rises to know and comprehend *thinkingly*.

But with the rise of this thinking study of things, it soon becomes evident that thought will be satisfied with nothing short of showing the *necessity* of its facts, of demonstrating the existence of its objects, as well as their nature and qualities. Our original acquaintance with them is thus discovered to be inadequate. We can assume nothing, and assert nothing dogmatically; nor can we accept the assertions and assumptions of others. And yet we must make a beginning: and a beginning, as primary and underived, makes an assumption, or rather is an assumption. It seems as if it were impossible to make a beginning at all.

2. This *thinking study of things* may serve, in a general way, as a description of philosophy. But the description is too wide. If it be correct to say, that thought makes the distinction between man and the lower animals, then everything human is human, for the sole and simple reason that it is due to the operation of thought. Philosophy, on the other hand, is a peculiar mode of thinking—a mode in which thinking becomes knowledge, and knowledge through notions. However great therefore may be the identity and essential unity of the two modes of thought, the philosophic mode gets to be different from the more general thought which acts in all that is human, in all that gives humanity its distinctive character. And this difference connects itself

SOURCE: *Logic*, Wallace, pp. 3-29.

with the fact that the strictly human and thought-induced phenomena
of consciousness do not originally appear in the form of a thought,
but as a feeling, a perception, or mental image—all of which aspects
must be distinguished from the form of thought proper.

According to an old preconceived idea, which has passed into a
trivial proposition, it is thought which marks the man off from the
animals. Yet trivial as this old belief may seem, it must, strangely
enough, be recalled to mind in presence of certain preconceived
ideas of the present day. These ideas would put feeling and thought
so far apart as to make them opposites, and would represent them as
so antagonistic, that feeling, particularly religious feeling, is supposed to be contaminated, perverted, and even annihilated by
thought. They also emphatically hold that religion and piety grow out
of, and rest upon something else, and not on thought. But those who
make this separation forget meanwhile that only man has the capacity
for religion, and that animals no more have religion than they have
law and morality.

Those who insist on this separation of religion from thinking usually have before their minds the sort of thought that may be styled
after-thought. They mean "reflective" thinking, which has to deal with
thoughts as thoughts, and brings them into consciousness. Slackness
to perceive and keep in view this distinction which philosophy definitely draws in respect of thinking is the source of the crudest objections and reproaches against philosophy. Man—and that just because
it is his nature to think—is the only being that possesses law, religion,
and morality. In these spheres of human life, therefore, thinking,
under the guise of feeling, faith, or generalised image, has not been
inactive: its action and its productions are there present and therein
contained. But it is one thing to have such feelings and generalised
images that have been moulded and permeated by thought, and
another thing to have thoughts about them. The thoughts, to which
after-thought upon those modes of consciousness gives rise, are what
is comprised under reflection, general reasoning, and the like, as well
as under philosophy itself.

The neglect of this distinction between thought in general and the
reflective thought of philosophy has also led to another and more
frequent misunderstanding. Reflection of this kind has been often
maintained to be the condition, or even the only way, of attaining a
consciousness and certitude of the Eternal and True. The (now somewhat antiquated) metaphysical proofs of God's existence, for example, have been treated, as if a knowledge of them and a conviction of

their truth were the only and essential means of producing a belief and conviction that there is a God. Such a doctrine would find its parallel, if we said that eating was impossible before we had acquired a knowledge of the chemical, botanical, and zoological characters of our food; and that we must delay digestion till we had finished the study of anatomy and physiology. Were it so, these sciences in their field, like philosophy in its, would gain greatly in point of utility; in fact, their utility would rise to the height of absolute and universal indispensableness. Or rather, instead of being indispensable, they would not exist at all.

3. The *Content*, of whatever kind it be, with which our consciousness is taken up, is what constitutes the qualitative character of our feelings, perceptions, fancies, and ideas; of our aims and duties; and of our thoughts and notions. From this point of view, feeling, perception, &c. are the *forms* assumed by these contents. The contents remain one and the same, whether they are felt, seen, represented, or willed, and whether they are merely felt, or felt with an admixture of thoughts, or merely and simply thought. In any one of these forms, or in the admixture of several, the contents confront consciousness, or are its *object*. But when they are thus objects of consciousness, the modes of the several forms ally themselves with the contents; and each form of them appears in consequence to give rise to a special object. Thus what is the same at bottom, may look like a different sort of fact.

The several modes of feeling, perception, desire, and will, so far as we are *aware* of them, are in general called ideas (mental representations): and it may be roughly said, that philosophy puts thoughts, categories, or, in more precise language, adequate *notions*, in the place of the generalised images we ordinarily call ideas. Mental impressions such as these may be regarded as the metaphors of thoughts and notions. But to have these figurate conceptions does not imply that we appreciate their intellectual significance, the thoughts and rational notions to which they correspond. Conversely, it is one thing to have thoughts and intelligent notions, and another to know what impressions, perceptions, and feelings correspond to them.

This difference will to some extent explain what people call the unintelligibility of philosophy. Their difficulty lies partly in an incapacity—which in itself is nothing but want of habit—for abstract thinking; *i.e.*, in an inability to get hold of pure thoughts and move about in them. In our ordinary state of mind, the thoughts are clothed upon and made one with the sensuous or spiritual material of the hour; and in reflection, meditation, and general reasoning, we introduce a blend of thoughts into feelings, percepts, and mental images. (Thus, in propositions where the subject-matter is due to the senses—*e.g.*, "This leaf is green"—we have such categories introduced, as being and individuality.) But it is a very different thing to make the thoughts pure and simple our object.

But their complaint that philosophy is unintelligible is as much due to another reason; and that is an impatient wish to have before them as a mental picture that which is in the mind as a thought or notion. When people are asked to apprehend some notion, they often complain that they do not know what they have to think. But the fact is that in a notion there is nothing further to be thought than the notion itself. What the phrase reveals, is a hankering after an image with which we are already familiar. The mind, denied the use of its familiar ideas, feels the ground where it once stood firm and at home taken away from beneath it, and, when transported into the region of pure thought, cannot tell where in the world it is.

One consequence of this weakness is that authors, preachers, and orators are found most intelligible, when they speak of things which their readers or hearers already know by rote—things which the latter are conversant with, and which require no explanation.

4. The philosopher then has to reckon with popular modes of thought, and with the objects of religion. In dealing with the ordinary modes of mind, he will first of all, as we saw, have to prove and almost to awaken the need for his peculiar method of knowledge. In dealing with the objects of religion, and with truth as a whole, he will have to show that philosophy is capable of apprehending them from its own resources; and should a difference from religious conceptions come to light, he will have to justify the points in which it diverges.

5. To give the reader a preliminary explanation of the distinction thus made, and to let him see at the same moment that the real import of our consciousness is retained, and even for the first time put in its proper light, when translated into the form of thought and the notion of reason, it may be well to recall another of these old unreasoned beliefs. And that is the conviction that to get at the truth of any object or event, even of feelings, perceptions, opinions, and mental ideas, we must think it over. Now in any case to think things over is at least to transform feelings, ordinary ideas, &c., into thoughts.

Nature has given every one a faculty of thought. But thought is all that philosophy claims as the form proper to her business: and thus the inadequate view which ignores the distinction stated in § 3, leads to a new delusion, the reverse of the complaint previously mentioned about the unintelligibility of philosophy. In other words, this science must often submit to the slight of hearing even people who have never taken any trouble with it talking as if they thoroughly understood all about it. With no preparation beyond an ordinary education they do not hesitate, especially under the influence of religious sentiment, to philosophise and to criticise philosophy. Everybody allows that to know any other science you must have first studied it, and that you can only claim to express a judgment upon it in virtue of such knowledge. Everybody allows that to make a shoe you must have learned and practised the craft of the shoemaker, though every man has a model in his own foot, and possesses in his hands the natural endowments for the operations required. For philosophy alone, it seems to be imagined, such study, care, and application are not in the least requisite.

This comfortable view of what is required for a philosopher has recently received corroboration through the theory of immediate or intuitive knowledge.

6. So much for the form of philosophical knowledge. It is no less desirable, on the other hand, that philosophy should understand that its content is no other than *actuality*, that core of truth which, originally produced and producing itself within the precincts of the mental life, has become the *world*, the inward and outward world, of consciousness. At first we become aware of these contents in what we call Experience. But even Experience, as it surveys the wide range of inward and outward existence, has sense enough to distinguish the mere appearance, which is transient and meaningless, from what in itself really deserves the name of actuality. As it is only in form that philosophy is distinguished from other modes of attaining an acquaintance with this same sum of being, it must necessarily be in harmony with actuality and experience. In fact, this harmony may be viewed as at least an extrinsic means of testing the truth of a philosophy. Similarly it may be held the highest and final aim of philosophic science to bring about, through the ascertainment of this harmony, a reconciliation of the self-conscious reason with the reason which *is* in the world—in other words, with actuality.

In the preface to my Philosophy of Law, p. xix, are found the propositions:

> What is reasonable is actual; and,
> What is actual is reasonable.

These simple statements have given rise to expressions of surprise and hostility, even in quarters where it would be reckoned an insult to presume absence of philosophy, and still more of religion. Religion at least need not be brought in evidence; its doctrines of the divine government of the world affirm these propositions too decidedly. For their philosophic sense, we must pre-suppose intelligence enough to know, not only that God is actual, that He is the supreme actuality, that He alone is truly actual; but also, as regards the logical bearings of the question, that existence is in part mere appearance, and only in part actuality. In common life, any freak of fancy, any error, evil and everything of the nature of evil, as well as every degenerate and transitory existence whatever, gets in a casual way the name of actuality. But even our ordinary feelings are enough to forbid a casual (fortuitous) existence getting the emphatic name of an actual; for by fortuitous we mean an existence which has no greater value than that of something possible, which may as well not be as be. As for the term Actuality, these critics would have done well to consider the sense in which I employ it. In a detailed Logic I had treated amongst other things of actuality, and accurately distinguished it not only from the fortuitous, which, after all, has existence, but even from the cognate categories of existence and the other modifications of being.

The actuality of the rational stands opposed by the popular fancy that Ideas and ideals are nothing but chimeras, and philosophy a mere system of such phantasms. It is also opposed by the very different fancy that Ideas and ideals are something far too excellent to have actuality, or something too impotent to procure it for themselves. This divorce between idea and reality is especially dear to the analytic understanding which looks upon its own abstractions, dreams though they are, as something true and real, and prides itself on the imperative "ought," which it takes especial pleasure in prescribing even on the field of politics. As if the world had waited on it to learn how it ought to be, and was not! For, if it were as it ought to be, what would come of the precocious wisdom of that "ought"? When understanding turns this "ought" against trivial external and transitory objects, against social regulations or conditions, which very likely possess a great relative importance for a certain time and special circles, it may often be right. In such a case the intelligent observer may meet much that fails to satisfy the general requirements of right; for who is not acute enough to see a great deal in his own surroundings which is really far from being as it ought to be? But such acuteness is mistaken in the conceit that, when it examines these objects and pronounces what they ought to be, it is dealing with questions of philosophic science. The object of philosophy is the Idea; and the Idea is not so impotent as merely to have a right or an obligation to exist without actually existing. The object of philosophy is an actuality of which those objects, social regulations and conditions, are only the superficial outside.

7. Thus reflection—thinking things over—in a general way involves the principle (which also means the beginning) of philosophy. And when the reflective spirit arose again in its independence in modern times, after the epoch of the Lutheran Reformation, it did not, as in its beginnings among the Greeks, stand merely aloof, in a world of its own, but at once turned its energies also upon the apparently illimitable material of the phenomenal world. In this way the name philosophy came to be applied to all those branches of knowledge, which are engaged in ascertaining the standard and Universal in the ocean of empirical individualities, as well as in ascertaining the Necessary element, or Laws, to be found in the apparent disorder of the endless masses of the fortuitous. It thus appears that modern philosophy derives its materials from our own personal observations and perceptions of the external and internal world, from nature as well as from the mind and heart of man, when both stand in the immediate presence of the observer.

This principle of Experience carries with it the unspeakably important condition that, in order to accept and believe any fact, we must be in contact with it; or, in more exact terms, that we must find the fact united and combined with the certainty of our own selves. We must be in touch with our subject-matter, whether it be by means of our external senses, or, else, by our profounder mind and our intimate self-consciousness. This principle is the same as that which has in the present day been termed faith, immediate knowledge, the revelation in the outward world, and, above all, in our own heart.

Those sciences, which thus got the name of philosophy, we call *empirical* sciences, for the reason that they take their departure from experience. Still the essential results which they aim at and provide, are laws, general propositions, a theory—the thoughts of what is found existing. On this ground the Newtonian physics was called Natural Philosophy. Hugo Grotius, again, by putting together and comparing the behaviour of states towards each other as recorded in history, succeeded, with the help of the ordinary methods of general reasoning, in laying down certain general principles, and establishing a theory which may be termed the Philosophy of International Law. In England this is still the usual signification of the term philosophy. Newton continues to be celebrated as the greatest of philosophers; and the name goes down as far as the price-lists of instrument-makers. All instruments, such as the thermometer and barometer, which do not come under the special head of magnetic or electric apparatus, are styled philosophical instruments.* Surely thought, and not a mere combination of wood, iron &c., ought to be called the instrument of philosophy! The recent science of Political Economy in particular, which in Germany is known as Rational Economy of the State, or intelligent national economy, has in England especially appropriated the name of philosophy.†

8. In its own field this empirical knowledge may at first give satisfaction; but in two ways it is seen to come short. In the first place there is another circle of objects which it does not embrace. These are Freedom, Spirit, and God. They belong to a different sphere, not because it can be said that they have nothing to do with experience; for though they are certainly not experiences of the senses, it is quite an identical proposition to say that whatever is in consciousness is

---

*The journal, too, edited by Thomson is called "Annals of Philosophy; or Magazine of Chemistry, Mineralogy, Mechanics, Natural History, Agriculture, and Arts." We can easily guess from the title what sort of subjects are here to be understood under the term "philosophy." Among the advertisements of books just published, I lately found the following notice in an English newspaper: "The Art of Preserving the Hair, on Philosophical Principles, neatly printed in post 8vo, price seven shillings." By philosophical principles for the preservation of the hair are probably meant chemical or physiological principles.

†In connexion with the general principles of Political Economy, the term "philosophical" is frequently heard from the lips of English statesmen, even in their public speeches. In the House of Commons, on the 2nd Feb. 1825, Brougham, speaking on the address in reply to the speech from the throne, talked of "the statesman-like and philosophical principles of Free-trade—for philosophical they undoubtedly are—upon the acceptance of which his majesty this day congratulated the House." Nor is this language confined to members of the Opposition. At the shipowners' yearly dinner in the same month, under the chairmanship of the Premier Lord Liverpool, supported by Canning the Secretary of State, and Sir C. Long the Paymaster-General of the Army, Canning in reply to the toast which had been proposed said: "A period has just begun, in which ministers have it in their power to apply to the administration of this country the sound maxims of a profound philosophy." Differences there may be between English and German philosophy; still, considering that elsewhere the name of philosophy is used only as a nickname and insult, or as something odious, it is a matter of rejoicing to see it still honoured in the mouth of the English Government.

experienced. The real ground for assigning them to another field of cognition is that in their scope and *content* these objects evidently show themselves as infinite.

There is an old phrase often wrongly attributed to Aristotle, and supposed to express the general tenor of his philosophy. *"Nihil est in intellectu quod non fuerit in sensu"*: there is nothing in thought which has not been in sense and experience. If speculative philosophy refused to admit this maxim, it can only have done so from a misunderstanding. It will, however, on the converse side no less assert: *"Nihil est in sensu quod non fuerit in intellectu."* And this may be taken in two senses. In the general sense it means that νοῦς or spirit (the more profound idea of νοῦς in modern thought) is the cause of the world. In its special meaning (see § 2) it asserts that the sentiment of right, morals, and religion is a sentiment (and in that way an experience) of such scope and such character that it can spring from and rest upon thought alone.

9. But in the second place in point of *form* the subjective reason desires a further satisfaction than empirical knowledge gives; and this form, is, in the widest sense of the term, Necessity (§ 1). The method of empirical science exhibits two defects. The first is that the Universal or general principle contained in it, the genus, or kind, &c., is, on its own account, indeterminate and vague, and therefore not on its own account connected with the Particulars or the details. Either is external and accidental to the other; and it is the same with the particular facts which are brought into union: each is external and accidental to the others. The second defect is that the beginnings are in every case data and postulates, neither accounted for nor deduced. In both these points the form of necessity fails to get its due. Hence reflection, whenever it sets itself to remedy these defects, becomes speculative thinking, the thinking proper to philosophy. As a species of reflection, therefore, which, though it has a certain community of nature with the reflection already mentioned, is nevertheless different from it, philosophic thought thus possesses, in addition to the common forms, some forms of its own, of which the Notion may be taken as the type.

The relation of speculative science to the other sciences may be stated in the following terms. It does not in the least neglect the empirical facts contained in the several sciences, but recognises and adopts them: it appreciates and applies towards its own structure the universal element in these sciences, their laws and classifications; but besides all this, into the categories of science it introduces, and gives currency to, other categories. The difference, looked at in this way, is only a change of categories. Speculative Logic contains all previous Logic and Metaphysics: it preserves the same forms of thought, the same laws and objects,—while at the same time remodelling and expanding them with wider categories.

From *notion* in the speculative sense we should distinguish what is ordinarily called a notion. The phrase, that no notion can ever comprehend the Infinite, a phrase which has been repeated over and over again till it has grown axiomatic, is based upon this narrow estimate of what is meant by notions.

10. This thought, which is proposed as the instrument of philosophic knowledge, itself calls for further explanation. We must understand in what way it possesses necessity or cogency; and when it claims to be equal to the task of apprehending the absolute objects (God, Spirit, Freedom), that claim must be substantiated. Such an explanation, however, is itself a lesson in philosophy, and properly falls within the scope of the science itself. A preliminary attempt to make matters plain would only be unphilosophical, and consist of a tissue of assumptions, assertions, and inferential pros and cons, *i.e.*, of dogmatism without cogency, as against which there would be an equal right of counter-dogmatism.

A main line of argument in the Critical Philosophy bids us pause before proceeding to inquire into God or into the true being of things, and tells us first of all to examine the faculty of cognition and see whether it is equal to such an effort. We ought, says Kant, to become acquainted with the instrument, before we undertake the work for which it is to be employed; for if the instrument be insufficient, all our trouble will be spent in vain. The plausibility of this suggestion has won for it general assent and admiration; the result of which has been to withdraw cognition from an interest in its objects and absorption in the study of them, and to direct it back upon itself; and so turn it to a question of form. Unless we wish to be deceived by words, it is easy to see what this amounts to. In the case of other instruments, we can try and criticise them in other ways than by setting about the special work for which they are destined. But the examination of knowledge can only be carried out by an act of knowledge. To examine this so-called instrument is the same thing as to know it. But to seek to know before we know is as absurd as the wise resolution of Scholasticus, not to venture into the water until he had learned to swim.

Reinhold saw the confusion with which this style of commencement is chargeable, and tried to get out of the difficulty by starting with a hypothetical and problematical stage of philosophising. In this way he supposed that it would be possible, nobody can tell how, to get along, until we found ourselves, further on, arrived at the primary truth of truths. His method, when closely looked into, will be seen to be identical with a very common practice. It starts from a substratum of experiential fact, or from a provisional assumption which has been brought into a definition; and then proceeds to analyse this starting-point. We can detect in Reinhold's argument a perception of the truth, that the usual course which proceeds by assumptions and anticipations is no better than a hypothetical and problematical mode of procedure. But his perceiving this does not alter the character of this method; it only makes clear its imperfections.

11. The special conditions which call for the existence of philosophy may be thus described. The mind or spirit, when it is sentient or perceptive, finds its object in something sensuous: when it imagines, in a picture or image; when it wills, in an aim or end. But in contrast to, or it may be only in distinction from, these forms of its existence and of its objects, the mind has also to gratify the cravings of its highest and most inward life. That innermost self is thought. Thus the mind renders thought its object. In the best meaning of the phrase, it comes to itself; for thought is its principle, and its very unadulterated self. But while thus occupied, thought entangles itself in contradictions, *i.e.*, loses itself in the hard-and-fast non-identity of its thoughts, and so, instead of reaching itself, is caught and held in its counterpart. This result, to which honest but narrow thinking leads the mere understanding, is resisted by the loftier craving of which we have spoken. That craving expresses the perseverance of thought, which continues true to itself, even in this conscious loss of its native rest and independence, "that it may overcome" and work out in itself the solution of its own contradictions.

To see that thought in its very nature is dialectical, and that, as understanding, it must fall into contradiction,—the negative of itself, will form one of the main lessons of logic. When thought grows hopeless of ever achieving, by its own means, the solution of the contradiction which it has by its own action brought upon itself, it turns back to those solutions of the question with which the mind had learned to pacify itself in some of its other modes and forms. Unfortunately, however, the retreat of thought has led it, as Plato noticed even in his time, to a very uncalled-for hatred of reason (misology); and it then takes up against its own endeavours that hostile attitude of which an example is seen in the doctrine that "immediate" knowledge, as it is called, is the exclusive form in which we become cognisant of truth.

12. The rise of philosophy is due to these cravings of thought. Its point of departure is Experience: including under that name both our immediate consciousness and the inductions from it. Awakened, as it were, by this stimulus, thought is vitally characterised by raising itself above the natural state of mind, above the senses and inferences from the senses into its own unadulterated element, and by assuming, accordingly, at first a stand-aloof and negative attitude towards the point from which it started. Through this state of antagonism to the phenomena of sense its first satisfaction is found in itself, in the Idea of the universal essence of these phenomena: an Idea (the Absolute, or God) which may be more or less abstract. Meanwhile, on the other hand, the sciences, based on experience, exert upon the mind a stimulus to overcome the form in which their varied contents are presented, and to elevate these contents to the rank of necessary truth. For the facts of science have the aspect of a vast conglomerate, one thing coming side by side with another, as if they were merely given and presented—as in short devoid of all essential or necessary connexion. In consequence of this stimulus thought is dragged out of its unrealised universality and its fancied or merely possible satisfaction, and impelled onwards to a development from itself. On one hand this development only means that thought incorporates the contents of science, in all their speciality of detail as submitted. On the other it makes these contents imitate the action of the original creative thought, and present the aspect of a free evolution determined by the logic of the fact alone.

On the relation between "immediacy" and "mediation" in consciousness we shall speak later, expressly and with more detail. Here it may be sufficient to premise that, though the two "moments'" or factors present themselves as distinct, still neither of them can be absent, nor can one exist apart from the other. Thus the knowledge of God, as of every supersensible reality, is in its true character an exaltation above sensations or perceptions: it consequently involves a negative attitude to the initial data of sense, and to that extent implies mediation. For to mediate is to take something as a beginning and to go onwards to a second thing; so that the existence of this second thing depends on our having reached it from something else contradistinguished from it. In spite of this, the knowledge of God is no mere sequel, dependent on the empirical phase of consciousness:

in fact, its independence is essentially secured through this negation and exaltation.—No doubt, if we attach an unfair prominence to the fact of mediation, and represent it as implying a state of conditioned-ness, it may be said—not that the remark would mean much—that philosophy is the child of experience, and owes its rise to *a posteriori* fact. (As a matter of fact, thinking is always the negation of what we have immediately before us.) With as much truth however we may be said to owe eating to the means of nourishment, so long as we can have no eating without them. If we take this view, eating is certainly represented as ungrateful: it devours that to which it owes itself. Thinking, upon this view of its action, is equally ungrateful.

But there is also an *a priori* aspect of thought, where by a mediation, not made by anything external but by a reflection into self, we have that immediacy which is universality, the self-complacency of thought which is so much at home with itself that it feels an innate indifference to descend to particulars, and in that way to the development of its own nature. It is thus also with religion, which, whether it be rude or elaborate, whether it be invested with scientific precision of detail or confined to the simple faith of the heart, possesses, throughout, the same intensive nature of contentment and felicity. But if thought never gets further than the universality of the Ideas, as was perforce the case in the first philosophies (when the Eleatics never got beyond Being, or Heraclitus beyond Becoming), it is justly open to the charge of formalism. Even in a more advanced phase of philosophy, we may often find a doctrine which has mastered merely certain abstract propositions or formulae, such as, "In the absolute all is one," "Subject and object are identical"—and only repeating the same thing when it comes to particulars. Bearing in mind this first period of thought, the period of mere generality, we may safely say that experience is the real author of *growth* and *advance* in philosophy. For, firstly, the empirical sciences do not stop short at the mere observation of the individual features of a phenomenon. By the aid of thought, they are able to meet philosophy with materials prepared for it, in the shape of general uniformities, *i.e.*, laws, and classifications of the phenomena. When this is done, the particular facts which they contain are ready to be received into philosophy. This, secondly, implies a certain compulsion on thought itself to proceed to these concrete specific truths. The reception into philosophy of these scientific materials, now that thought has removed their immediacy and made them cease to be mere data, forms at the same time a development of thought out of itself. Philosophy, then, owes its development to the empirical sciences. In return it gives their contents what is so vital to them, the freedom of thought—gives them, in short, an *a priori* character. These contents are now warranted necessary, and no longer depend on the evidence of facts merely, that they were so found and so experienced. The fact as experienced thus becomes an illustration and a copy of the original and completely self-supporting activity of thought.

13. Stated in exact terms, such is the origin and development of philosophy. But the History of Philosophy gives us the same process from an historical and external point of view. The stages in the evolution of the Idea there seem to follow each other by accident, and to present merely a number of different and unconnected principles, which the several systems of philosophy carry out in their own way. But it is not so. For these thousands of years the same Architect has directed the work: and that Architect is the one living Mind whose nature is to think, to bring to self-consciousness what it is, and, with its being thus set as object before it, to be at the same time raised above it, and so to reach a higher stage of its own being. The different systems which the history of philosophy presents are therefore not irreconcilable with unity. We may either say, that it is one philosophy at different degrees of maturity, or that the particular principle, which is the groundwork of each system, is but a branch of one and the same universe of thought. In philosophy the latest birth of time is the result of all the systems that have preceded it, and must include their principles; and so, if, on other grounds, it deserves the title of philosophy, will be the fullest, most comprehensive, and most adequate system of all.

The spectacle of so many and so various systems of philosophy suggests the necessity of defining more exactly the relation of Universal to Particular. When the universal is made a mere form and co-ordinated with the particular, as if it were on the same level, it sinks into a particular itself. Even common sense in every-day matters is above the absurdity of setting a universal *beside* the particulars. Would any one, who wished for fruit, reject cherries, pears, and grapes, on the ground that they were cherries, pears, or grapes, and not fruit? But when philosophy is in question, the excuse of many is that philosophies are so different, and none of them is *the* philosophy,— that each is only *a* philosophy. Such a plea is assumed to justify any amount of contempt for philosophy. And yet cherries too are fruit. Often, too, a system, of which the principle is the universal, is put on a level with another of which the principle is a particular, and with theories which deny the existence of philosophy altogether. Such systems are said to be only different views of philosophy. With equal justice, light and darkness might be styled different kinds of light.

14. The same evolution of thought which is exhibited in the history of philosophy is presented in the System of Philosophy itself. Here, instead of surveying the process, as we do in history, from the outside, we see the movement of thought clearly defined in its native medium. The thought, which is genuine and self-supporting, must be intrinsically concrete, it must be an Idea; and when it is viewed in the whole of its universality, it is the Idea, or the Absolute. The science of this Idea must form a system. For the truth is concrete; that is, whilst it gives a bond and principle of unity, it also possesses an internal source of development. Truth, then, is only possible as a universe or totality of thought; and the freedom of the whole, as well as the necessity of the several sub-divisions, which it implies, are only possible when these are discriminated and defined.

Unless it is a system, a philosophy is not a scientific production. Unsystematic philosophising can only be expected to give expression to personal peculiarities of mind, and has no principle for the regulation of its contents. Apart from their interdependence and organic union, the truths of philosophy are valueless, and must then be treated as baseless hypotheses, or personal convictions. Yet many philosophical treatises confine themselves to such an exposition of the opinions and sentiments of the author.

The term *system* is often misunderstood. It does not denote a philosophy, the principle of which is narrow and to be distinguished from others. On the contrary, a genuine philosophy makes it a principle to include every particular principle.

15. Each of the parts of philosophy is a philosophical whole, a circle rounded and complete in itself. In each of these parts, however, the philosophical Idea is found in a particular specificality or medium. The single circle, because it is a real totality, bursts through the limits imposed by its special medium, and gives rise to a wider circle. The whole of philosophy in this way resembles a circle of circles. The Idea appears in each single circle, but, at the same time, the whole Idea is constituted by the system of these peculiar phases, and each is a necessary member of the organisation.

16. In the form of an Encyclopaedia, the science has no room for a detailed exposition of particulars, and must be limited to setting forth the commencement of the special sciences and the notions of cardinal importance in them.

How much of the particular parts is requisite to constitute a partic-ular branch of knowledge is so far indeterminate, that the part, if it is to be something true, must be not an isolated member merely, but itself an organic whole. The entire field of philosophy therefore really forms a single science; but it may also be viewed as a total, composed of several particular sciences.

The encyclopaedia of philosophy must not be confounded with ordinary encyclopaedias. An ordinary encyclopaedia does not pre-tend to be more than an aggregation of sciences, regulated by no principle, and merely as experience offers them. Sometimes it even includes what merely bear the name of sciences, while they are noth-ing more than a collection of bits of information. In an aggregate like this, the several branches of knowledge owe their place in the ency-clopaedia to extrinsic reasons, and their unity is therefore artificial: they are *arranged*, but we cannot say they form a *system*. For the same reason, especially as the materials to be combined also depend upon no one rule or principle, the arrangement is at best an experiment, and will always exhibit inequalities.

An encyclopaedia of philosophy excludes three kinds of partial science. (I) It excludes mere aggregates of bits of information. Philology in its *prima facie* aspect belongs to this class. (II) It rejects the quasi-sciences, which are founded on an act of arbitrary will alone, such as Heraldry. Sciences of this class are positive from begin-ning to end. (III) In another class of sciences, also styled positive, but which have a rational basis and a rational beginning, philosophy claims that constituent as its own. The positive features remain the property of the sciences themselves.

The positive element in the last class of sciences is of different sorts. (I) Their commencement, though rational at bottom, yields to the influence of fortuitousness, when they have to bring their univer-sal truth into contact with actual facts and the single phenomena of experience. In this region of chance and change, the adequate notion of science must yield its place to reasons or grounds of explanation. Thus, *e.g.*, in the science of jurisprudence, or in the system of direct and indirect taxation, it is necessary to have certain points precisely and definitively settled which lie beyond the competence of the abso-lute lines laid down by the pure notion. A certain latitude of settle-ment accordingly is left; and each point may be determined in one way on one principle, in another way on another, and admits of no definitive certainty. Similarly the Idea of Nature, when parcelled out in detail, is dissipated into contingencies. Natural history, geography, and medicine stumble upon descriptions of existence, upon kinds and distinctions, which are not determined by reason, but by sport and adventitious incidents. Even history comes under the same category. The Idea is its essence and inner nature; but, as it appears, everything is under contingency and in the field of voluntary action. (II) These sciences are positive also in failing to recognise the finite nature of what they predicate, and to point out how these categories and their whole sphere pass into a higher. They assume their statements to possess an authority beyond appeal. Here the fault lies in the finitude of the form, as in the previous instance it lay in the matter. (III) In close sequel to this, sciences are positive in consequence of the inadequate grounds on which their conclusions rest: based as these are on detached and casual inference, upon feeling, faith, and authority, and, generally speaking, upon the deliverances of inward and outward perception. Under this head we must also class the philosophy which proposes to build upon "anthropology," facts of consciousness, inward sense, or outward experience. It may happen, however, that empirical is an epithet applicable only to the form of scientific exposition; whilst intuitive sagacity has arranged what are mere phenomena, according to the essential sequence of the notion. In such a case the contrasts between the varied and numerous phenomena brought together serve to eliminate the external and accidental circumstances of their conditions, and the universal thus comes clearly into view. Guided by such an intuition, experimental physics will present the rational science of Nature—as history will present the science of human affairs and actions—in an external picture, which mirrors the philosophic notion.

17. It may seem as if philosophy, in order to start on its course, had, like the rest of the sciences, to begin with a subjective presupposition. The sciences postulate their respective objects, such as space, number, or whatever it be; and it might be supposed that philosophy had also to postulate the existence of thought. But the two cases are not exactly parallel. It is by the free act of thought that it occupies a point of view, in which it is for its own self, and thus gives itself an object of its own production. Nor is this all. The very point of view, which originally is taken on its own evidence only, must in the course of the science be converted to a result—the ultimate result in which philosophy returns into itself and reaches the point with which it began. In this manner philosophy exhibits the appearance of a circle which closes with itself, and has no beginning in the same way as the other sciences have. To speak of a beginning of philosophy has a meaning

only in relation to a person who proposes to commence the study, and not in relation to the science as science. The same thing may be thus expressed. The notion of science—the notion therefore with which we start—which, for the very reason that it is initial, implies a separation between the thought which is our object, and the subject philosophising which is, as it were, external to the former, must be grasped and comprehended by the science itself. This is in short the one single aim, action, and goal of philosophy—to arrive at the notion of its notion, and thus secure its return and its satisfaction.

18. As the whole science, and only the whole, can exhibit what the Idea or system of reason is, it is impossible to give in a preliminary way a general impression of a philosophy. Nor can a division of philosophy into its parts be intelligible, except in connexion with the system. A preliminary division, like the limited conception from which it comes, can only be an anticipation. Here however it is premised that the Idea turns out to be the thought which is completely identical with itself, and not identical simply in the abstract, but also in its action of setting itself over against itself, so as to gain a being of its own, and yet of being in full possession of itself while it is in this other. Thus philosophy is subdivided into three parts:

I. Logic: the science of the Idea in and for itself.

II. The Philosophy of Nature: the science of the Idea in its otherness.

III. The Philosophy of Mind: the science of the Idea come back to itself out of that otherness.

As observed in § 15, the differences between the several philosophical sciences are only aspects or specialisations of the one Idea or system of reason, which and which alone is alike exhibited in these different media. In Nature nothing else would have to be discerned, except the Idea: but the Idea has here divested itself of its proper being. In Mind, again, the Idea has asserted a being of its own, and is on the way to becoming absolute. Every such form in which the Idea is expressed, is at the same time a passing or fleeting stage: and hence each of these subdivisions has not only to know its contents as an object which has being for the time, but also in the same act to expound how these contents pass into their higher circle. To represent the relation between them as a division, therefore, leads to misconception; for it co-ordinates the several parts or sciences one beside another, as if they had no innate development, but were, like so many species, really and radically distinct.

II

Dialectic and Human Experience:
The Phenomenology of Spirit

In the *Phenomenology of Spirit* I have exhibited consciousness in its movement onwards from the first immediate opposition of itself and the object to absolute knowing. The path of this movement goes through every form of the *relation of consciousness to the object* and has the Notion of science [*Wissenschaft*] for its result. This Notion . . . cannot be justified in any other way than by this emergence in consciousness, all the forms of which are resolved into this Notion as into their truth . . .

The Notion of pure science and its deduction is therefore presupposed [in the *Science of Logic*] in so far as the *Phenomenology of Spirit* is nothing other than the deduction of it. Absolute knowing is the *truth* of every mode of consciousness because, as the course of the *Phenomenology* showed, it is only in absolute knowing that the separation of the *object* from the *certainty of itself* is completely eliminated: truth [object, content] is now equated with certainty [subject, form] and this certainty with truth.

Thus, pure science presupposes liberation from the opposition of consciousness. It contains *thought in so far as this is just as much the object in its own self, or the object in its own self in so far as it is equally pure thought*. As science, truth is pure self-consciousness in its self-development and has the shape of the Self, so that the absolute truth of being is the known Notion and the Notion as such is the absolute truth of being.[1]

In these brief passages from the Introduction to his *Science of Logic*, Hegel provides for us a terse answer to the puzzling and much-debated question of the place and function of the *Phenomenology* in his system. We have already seen that for Hegel, the truth which philosophic science alone represents cannot be had at the outset, "as if shot out of a pistol." It is rather

the reward which comes after a chequered and devious course of development, and after much struggle and effort. It is a whole which, after running
its course and laying bare all its content, returns again to itself; it is the
resultant abstract notion of the whole. But the actual realization of this abstract whole is only found when those previous shapes and forms, which are
now reduced to ideal moments of the whole, are developed anew again, but
developed and shaped within this new medium [of pure thought], and with the
meaning they have thereby acquired.[2]

The *Phenomenology* thus represents this "devious course of development" on the part of the individual mind. "The series of shapes
[*Gestalten des Bewusstseins*], which consciousness traverses on this road.
is . . . the detailed history of the process of training and educating
consciousness itself up to the level of science."[3] The individual has
the right to demand that science show him the way to this standpoint,
and in this sense the *Phenomenology* is the "deduction" of the concept
of science. But the way described by the *Phenomenology* is for the
fragmented individual no royal road to absolute knowing: "What is
a realization of the notion of knowledge means for it [the unscientific
consciousness] rather the ruin and overthrow of itself; for on this
road it loses its own truth. Because of that, the road can be looked
on as the path of doubt, or more properly a highway of despair."[4]
Like salmon in their life and death struggle upstream, driven toward
the serenity of their source, there to spawn and die, by an unconscious instinct and against seemingly insurmountable obstacles, the
individual mind must navigate the turbulent waters of experience to
reach the stage of genuine knowledge, truth, which both consummates and perforce implies the agonizing ascent to it. This truth "is
thus the bacchanalian revel, where not a member is sober; and because every member no sooner becomes detached than it *eo ipso*
collapses straightway, the revel is just as much a state of transparent
unbroken calm."[5] As we noted in our Introduction (p. 6), this turbu-
lence is due to the dialectical strife of the subject–object relation,
which *is* experience, the life of Spirit qua individual but less than
absolute. The aim of Hegel's *Phenomenology* is therefore the gradual
dissolution of the self-suppressing opposition between knowing and
being, the gradual dying of finitude and birth of infinity. "The terminus is at that point where knowledge is no longer compelled to go
beyond itself, where it finds its own self, and the notion corresponds
to the object and the object to the notion. The progress towards this
goal is consequently without a halt, and at no earlier stage is satisfaction to be found."[6] This process of the finite's self-diremption is
characteristic (though not necessarily in just Hegel's own order or

choice of experiences) of Mind's ascent to true selfhood via an auto-da-fé. But "the process by which [the mind's ways of appearing] are developed into an organically connected whole is Logic or Speculative Philosophy," set out in Hegel's *Science of Logic.*[7]

For some, the *Phenomenology* is the alpha and omega of Hegel's philosophy; but the vision attained only at the close of the book, *Das absolute Wissen,* where "being is entirely mediated and has the character of self, is notion," has yet to be worked out in the logic of the *Encyclopaedia of the Philosophical Sciences,* which follows. "The truth [of scientific, systematic, speculative philosophy] it contains," Hegel says, "is not to be found in this [phenomenological] exposition, which is in part historical [contingent, external] in character."[8] The *Phenomenology* is not logos, but rather, to borrow a term from Viktor Frankl, "logotherapy."

As to the content of the *Phenomenology,* we cannot attempt here to even outline it, for it covers the vast range of human experience of the world, and embraces most of the material systematically articulated in the *Encyclopaedia* and lectures. Some indication of its richness is provided in Josiah Royce's comparison of it to William James's *Varieties of Religious Experience.* It may also be likened in important respects to St. Bonaventura's *Itinerarium Mentis ad Deum,* to Spinoza's *Tractatus de intellectus emendatione,* and even to St. Augustine's *Confessions.* Regarding its argument and structure there are a number of problems that have been and continue to be debated by Hegel scholars, and it would be out of place here to go into them.

We might, however, attempt to clarify one very important issue that is most likely to be problematic for the student approaching Hegel's *Phenomenology*[9] for the first time, and this is the relation between the single consciousness and universal mind. Perhaps the easiest way to grasp this relation is to employ an analogy from current biological theory. The development of the single consciousness may be said to be related to that of the universal mind in the way that ontogenesis (the history of the individual development of an organized being) is believed to be related to phylogenesis (the history of the group or species of which the individual is a member). In biology, most of the evidence for phylogeny is afforded by ontogeny. Individuals of different species are quite diverse in their adult stages; but they appear very like in most of the preadult phases of embryonic development. Hegel would say that this concept of the biologists who associate phylogeny and ontogeny illustrates, rather naively, the objectivization of thought processes. Thought is read into the geological record and

into the embryological record, and the objectified thought—that projected thought—is taken for a mass of facts from which to induce the
thought of an evolution of the species or universal, which is recapitulated in the development of the individual.

This inducing of an evolutionary thought that has been projected
is fraught with epistemological difficulties which the naturalist can
avoid only by ignoring them. But, if the naturalist can understand that
the universal pattern of biological development is recapitulated in
each individual animal or plant, he should have no difficulty in understanding what Hegel means when he says that the individual consciousness, on each of the historical levels of human intellectual development, recapitulates the universal development of experience up
to his time. The forms of consciousness traced in the *Phenomenology*
are thus a sort of geological record, on each level of which are found
fossils of once-living organisms, each of which was a living whole, but
a whole which was to become a part of the "whole" of the next level.
This does not, of course, imply steady, linear progress. Even phylo-
genetic evolution recognizes retrograde development, degeneration
or degradation.

In the light of this analogy, we may now quote at length the following paragraph from Hegel's Preface to the *Phenomenology:*

The task of conducting the individual mind from its unscientific standpoint to
that of science had to be taken in its general sense; we had to contemplate the
formative development (*Bildung*) of the universal [or general] individual, of
self-conscious spirit. As to the relation between these two [the particular and
general individual], every moment, as it gains concrete form and its own
proper shape and appearance, finds a place in the life of the universal individual. The particular individual is incomplete mind, a concrete shape in whose
existence, taken as a whole, one determinate characteristic predominates,
while the others are found only in blurred outline. In that mind which stands
higher than another the lower concrete form of existence has sunk into an
obscure moment; what was formerly an objective fact (*die Sache selbst*) is now
only a single trace: its definite shape has been veiled, and become simply a
piece of shading. The individual, whose substance is mind at the higher level,
passes through these past forms, much in the way that one who takes up a
higher science goes through those preparatory forms of knowledge, which he
has long made his own, in order to call up their content before him; he brings
back the recollection of them without stopping to fix his interest upon them.
The particular individual, so far as content is concerned, has also to go
through the stages through which the general mind has passed, but as shapes
once assumed by mind and now laid aside, as stages of a road which has been
worked over and levelled out. Hence it is that, in the case of various kinds
of knowledge, we find that what in former days occupied the energies of men

of mature mental ability sinks to the level of information, exercises, and even pastimes, for children; and in this educational progress we can see the history of the world's culture delineated in faint outline. This bygone mode of existence has already become an acquired possession of the general mind, which constitutes the substance of the individual, and, by thus appearing externally to him, furnishes his inorganic nature. In this respect culture or development of mind *(Bildung)*, regarded from the side of the individual [ontogeny in our analogy], consists in his acquiring what lies at his hand ready for him, in making its inorganic nature organic to himself, and taking possession of it for himself. Looked at, however, from the side of universal mind *qua* general spiritual substance [phylogeny in our analogy], culture means nothing else than that this substance gives itself its own self-consciousness, brings about its own inherent process and its own reflection into self.[10]

Hegel remarks elsewhere that the diversity of the historical record of experiences must not be regarded as fixed and stationary, and composed of what is mutually exclusive; the differences are thoughts, and the various levels, frozen or petrified biographically, like fossils, constitute a development. What that development was like we can see by examining our own individual intellectual development.

Thomas H. Huxley, to return to our analogy, when he attempted to suggest a fitting image of the actual development from simple to complex organisms found fossilized, layer upon layer in the geological record, said:

the whole might be compared to that wonderful operation of development which may be seen going on every day under our eyes, in virtue of which there arises, out of the simi-fluid comparatively homogeneous substance which we call an egg, the complicated organisation of one of the higher animals. That, in a few words, is what is meant by the hypothesis of evolution.[11]

Hegel says, very acutely, that if we are willing to read a pattern of orderly movement into the phenomena of nature, where accidents and monstrosities abound—where contingency has its proper scope —how can we deny that such a pattern is to be read in the historical movement of thought itself. "As the best of what is in the world is that which Thought produces," he writes, "it is unreasonable to believe that reason only is in Nature, and not in Mind."[12]

Mind reads order into the phenomena of celestial mechanics and biological development; the historical development of Mind (the universal) embraces the activity of particular minds. The synthesis of these is the "whole," the Idea of ideas, thought thinking thought. "The chalice of this realm of spirits/Foams forth to God His own Infinitude."[13]

The influence of the *Phenomenology* on subsequent philosophy is difficult to overemphasize. Karl Marx, who borrowed heavily from many parts of Hegel's system, was especially affected by the dialectic of "Lordship and Bondage" *(Herrschaft und Knechtschaft)* and the concept of alienation *(Entfremdung)*. The existentialists Kierkegaard and Sartre were likewise profoundly influenced by Hegel's portrayal of the "Unhappy Consciousness" *(Das Unglückliche Bewusstsein)* in the *Phenomenology*. Similarly, the work of the American Pragmatists, especially James and Dewey, reveals the pervasive impact of Hegel's phenomenological and richly empirical analysis of experience. And finally, Husserl and Heidegger, in their emphasis upon the intentionality of consciousness as the "primal fact" and starting point of their own phenomenologies, reflect their debt to Hegel's voyage of discovery and its legacy. Much of this influence is only now being traced and explicated,[14] but the erudite student will discern in many of the pages that follow not only the positive foundations and inspiration of much contemporary philosophy, but also some anticipatory criticism of the most darling doctrines of the positivists and linguistic analysts. The *Phenomenology* is a feast for all seasons of the spirit, and a philosophical ode to the west wind, which "drive[s] . . . dead thoughts over the universe/Like withered leaves to quicken a new birth!"[15]

The selections that follow in this chapter take us along a single major line of development of the *Phenomenology*. The first, from the Introduction, is self-explanatory; but what it explains is a highly complex concept of what "knowing" really is. Hegel there distinguishes three levels of knowing: consciousness, self-consciousness, and that synthesis of the two, which Hegel calls Reason *(Vernunft)* as distinguished from understanding *(Verstand)*.

The next selection, which is headed "Consciousness: Sense-certainty and Perception," by no means exhausts that complex subject. Its purpose is to validate the "evidence of things seen"—the objects of knowledge of the empirical sciences, for instance—while at the same time to explore the reasons why our minds are not satisfied in the long run with the dogmatic assertion that "seeing is believing." When we doubt the evidence of things seen (as Descartes, Hume, and Kant force us to do by their rigorous analyses) we pass out of the realm of mere consciousness into that of the Lordship and Bondage of Self-consciousness, as Hegel calls it, where we struggle with ourselves for a sense of Self-certainty. That struggle, often intellectually painful, is the substance of the selection "Self-certainty and the Lordship and Bondage of Self-consciousness" which, from the point of view of historical influence, is perhaps most important through its impact on Karl Marx.

The last selection in this chapter, which we call the "Realization of Rational Self-consciousness," resolves the opposition of mere consciousness (evidence of things seen) and self-consciousness (the quest for inner certainty to which we are driven by doubt) in a higher synthesis. Is it possible to know and to doubt simultaneously? That, Hegel tells us, is what knowing in the fullest possible sense really is.

Notes. Dialectic and Human Experience:
The Phenomenology of Spirit

1. *Logic*, Miller, pp. 48–49.
2. *Phenomenology*, p. 76.
3. Ibid., p. 136. See also the headnote on p. 86f.
4. Ibid., p. 135.
5. Ibid., p. 105.
6. Ibid., pp. 137–138.
7. Ibid., p. 97.
8. Ibid., p. 116.
9. See also *Hegel's Lectures on the History of Philosophy*, trans. E. S. Haldane and Frances H. Simson (New York: Humanities Press, 1963), vol. 1, pp. 32–36.
10. *Phenomenology*, pp. 89–90.
11. T. H. Huxley, "Lectures on Evolution," in *Science and Hebrew Tradition Essays* (New York: D. Appleton, 1914), pp. 55–56.
12. *History of Philosophy*, vol. 1, p. 35.
13. *Phenomenology*, p. 808. The lines are adapted from Schiller.
14. See especially, Richard J. Bernstein, *Praxis and Action: Contemporary Philosophies of Human Activity* (Philadelphia: University of Pennsylvania Press, 1971).
15. Percy Bysshe Shelley, "Ode to the West Wind," lines 63–64.

INTRODUCTION

It is natural to suppose that, before philosophy enters upon its subject proper—namely, the actual knowledge of what truly is—it is necessary to come first to an understanding concerning knowledge, which is looked upon as the instrument by which to take possession of the Absolute, or as the means through which to get a sight of it. The apprehension seems legitimate, on the one hand that there may be various kinds of knowledge, among which one might be better adapted than another for the attainment of our purpose—and thus a wrong choice is possible; on the other hand again that, since knowing is a faculty of a definite kind and with a determinate range, without the more precise determination of its nature and limits we might take hold on clouds of error instead of the heaven of truth.

This apprehensiveness is sure to pass even into the conviction that the whole enterprise which sets out to secure for consciousness by means of knowledge what exists *per se*, is in its very nature absurd; and that between knowledge and the Absolute there lies a boundary which completely cuts off the one from the other. For if knowledge is the instrument by which to get possession of absolute Reality, the suggestion immediately occurs that the application of an instrument to anything does *not* leave it as it is for itself, but rather entails in the process, and has in view, a moulding and alteration of it. Or, again, if knowledge is not an instrument which we actively employ, but a kind of passive medium through which the light of the truth reaches us, then here, too, we do not receive it as it is in itself, but as it is through and in this medium. In either case we employ a means which immediately brings about the very opposite of its own end; or, rather, the absurdity lies in making use of any means at all. It seems indeed open to us to find in the knowledge of the way in which the *instrument* operates, a remedy for this parlous state; for thereby it becomes possible to remove from the result the part which, in our idea of the Absolute received through that instrument, belongs to the instrument, and thus to get the truth in its purity. But this improvement would, as a matter of fact, only bring us back to the point where we were before. If we take away again from a definitely formed thing that which the instrument has done in the shaping of it, then the thing (in this case the Absolute) stands before us once more just as it was

SOURCE: *Phenomenology*, pp. 131–145. Reprinted by permission of George Allen & Unwin Ltd., London.

previous to all this trouble, which, as we now see, was superfluous. If the Absolute were only to be brought on the whole nearer to us by this agency, without any change being wrought in it, like a bird caught by a limestick, it would certainly scorn a trick of that sort, if it were not in its very nature, and did it not wish to be, beside us from the start. For a trick is what knowledge in such a case would be, since by all its busy toil and trouble it gives itself the air of doing something quite different from bringing about a relation that is merely immediate, and so a waste of time to establish. Or, again, if the examination of knowledge, which we represent as a medium, makes us acquainted with the law of its refraction, it is likewise useless to eliminate this refraction from the result. For knowledge is not the divergence of the ray, but the ray itself by which the truth comes in contact with us; and if this be removed, the bare direction or the empty place would alone be indicated.

Meanwhile, if the fear of falling into error introduces an element of distrust into science, which without any scruples of that sort goes to work and actually does know, it is not easy to understand why, conversely, a distrust should not be placed in this very distrust, and why we should not take care lest the fear of error is not just the initial error. As a matter of fact, this fear presupposes something, indeed a great deal, as truth, and supports its scruples and consequences on what should itself be examined beforehand to see whether it is truth. It starts with ideas of knowledge as an instrument, and as a medium; and presupposes a distinction of ourselves from this knowledge. More especially it takes for granted that the Absolute stands on one side, and that knowledge on the other side, by itself and cut off from the Absolute, is still something real; in other words, that knowledge, which, by being outside the Absolute, is certainly also outside truth, is nevertheless true—a position which, while calling itself fear of error, makes itself known rather as fear of the truth.

This conclusion comes from the fact that the Absolute alone is true or that the True is alone absolute. It may be set aside by making the distinction that a knowledge which does not indeed know the Absolute as science wants to do, is none the less true too; and that knowledge in general, though it may possibly be incapable of grasping the Absolute, can still be capable of truth of another kind. But we shall see as we proceed that random talk like this leads in the long run to a confused distinction between an absolute truth and a truth of some other sort, and that "absolute," "knowledge," and so on, are words which presuppose a meaning that has first to be got at.

With suchlike useless ideas and expressions about knowledge, as an instrument to take hold of the Absolute, or as a medium through which we have a glimpse of truth, and so on (relations to which all these ideas of a knowledge which is divided from the Absolute and an Absolute divided from knowledge in the last resort lead), we need not concern ourselves. Nor need we trouble about the evasive pretexts which create the incapacity of science out of the presupposition of such relations, in order at once to be rid of the toil of science, and to assume the air of serious and zealous effort about it. Instead of being troubled with giving answers to all these, they may be straightway rejected as adventitious and arbitrary ideas; and the use which is here made of words like "absolute," "knowledge," as also "objective" and "subjective," and innumerable others, whose meaning is assumed to be familiar to everyone, might well be regarded as so much deception. For to give out that their significance is universally familiar and that everyone indeed possesses their notion, rather looks like an attempt to dispense with the only important matter, which is just to give this notion. With better right, on the contrary, we might spare ourselves the trouble of taking any notice at all of such ideas and ways of talking which would have the effect of warding off science altogether; for they make a mere empty show of knowledge which at once vanishes when science comes on the scene.

But science, in the very fact that it comes on the scene, is itself a phenomenon; its "coming on the scene" is not yet *itself* carried out in all the length and breadth of its truth. In this regard, it is a matter of indifference whether we consider that it (science) is the phenomenon because it makes its appearance alongside another kind of knowledge, or call that other untrue knowledge its process of appearing. Science, however, must liberate itself from this phenomenality, and it can only do so by turning against it. For science cannot simply reject a form of knowledge which is not true, and treat this as a common view of things, and then assure us that itself is an entirely different kind of knowledge, and holds the other to be of no account at all; nor can it appeal to the fact that in this other there are presages of a better. By giving that assurance it would declare its force and value to lie in its bare existence; but the untrue knowledge appeals likewise to the fact that it *is*, and assures us that to it *science* is nothing. One barren assurance, however, is of just as much value as another. Still less can science appeal to the presages of a better, which are to be found present in untrue knowledge and are there pointing the way towards science; for it would, on the one hand, be appealing again in the same way to a merely existent fact; and, on the other, it would be appealing to itself, to the way in which it exists in untrue knowledge, *i.e.*, to a bad form of its own existence, to its appearance, rather than to its real and true nature *(an und für sich)*. For this reason we shall here undertake the exposition of knowledge as a phenomenon.

Now because this exposition has for its object only phenomenal knowledge, the exposition itself seems not to be science, free, self-moving in the shape proper to itself, but may, from this point of view, be taken as the pathway of the natural consciousness which is pressing forward to true knowledge. Or it can be regarded as the path of the soul, which is traversing the series of its own forms of embodiment, like stages appointed for it by its own nature, that it may possess the clearness of spiritual life when, through the complete experience of its own self, it arrives at the knowledge of what it is in itself.

Natural consciousness will prove itself to be only knowledge in principle or not real knowledge. Since, however, it immediately takes itself to be the real and genuine knowledge, this pathway has a negative significance for it; what is a realization of the notion of knowledge means for it rather the ruin and overthrow of itself; for on this road it loses its own truth. Because of that, the road can be looked on as the path of doubt, or more properly a highway of despair. For what happens there is not what is usually understood by doubting, a jostling against this or that supposed truth, the outcome of which is again a disappearance in due course of the doubt and a return to the former truth, so that at the end the matter is taken as it was before. On the contrary, that pathway is the conscious insight into the untruth of the phenomenal knowledge, for which that is the most real which is after all only the unrealized notion. On that account, too, this thoroughgoing scepticism is not what doubtless earnest zeal for truth and science fancies it has equipped itself with in order to be ready to deal with them—viz., the *resolve*, in science, not to deliver itself over to the thoughts of others on their mere authority, but to examine everything for itself, and only follow its own conviction, or, still better, to produce everything itself and hold only its own act for true.

The series of shapes, which consciousness traverses on this road, is rather the detailed history of the process of training and educating consciousness itself up to the level of science. That resolve presents this mental development *(Bildung)* in the simple form of an intended purpose, as immediately finished and complete, as having taken place; this pathway, on the other hand, is, as opposed to this abstract intention, or untruth, the actual carrying out of that process of development. To follow one's own conviction is certainly more than to hand oneself over to authority; but by the conversion of opinion held on authority into opinion held out of personal conviction, the content of what is held is not necessarily altered, and truth has not thereby taken the place of error. If we stick to a system of opinion and preju- dice resting on the authority of others, or upon personal conviction, the one differs from the other merely in the conceit which animates the latter. Scepticism, directed to the whole compass of phenomenal consciousness, on the contrary, makes mind for the first time qual- ified to test what truth is; since it brings about a despair regarding what are called natural views, thoughts, and opinions, which it is a matter of indifference to call personal or belonging to others, and with which the consciousness, that proceeds straight away to criticize and test, is still filled and hampered, thus being, as a matter of fact, incapable of what it wants to undertake.

The completeness of the forms of unreal consciousness will be brought about precisely through the necessity of the advance and the necessity of their connection with one another. To make this compre- hensible we may remark, by way of preliminary, that the exposition of untrue consciousness in its untruth is not a merely negative pro- cess. Such a one-sided view of it is what the natural consciousness generally adopts; and a knowledge, which makes this one-sidedness its essence, is one of those shapes assumed by incomplete conscious- ness which falls into the course of the inquiry itself and will come before us there. For this view is scepticism, which always sees in the result only pure nothingness, and abstracts from the fact that this nothing is determinate, is the nothing of *that out of which* it comes as a result. Nothing, however, is only, in fact, the true result, when taken as the nothing of what it comes from; it is thus itself a determinate nothing, and has a *content*. The scepticism which ends with the ab- straction "nothing" or "emptiness" can advance from this not a step farther, but must wait and see whether there is possibly anything new offered, and what that is—in order to cast it into the same abysmal void. When once, on the other hand, the result is apprehended, as it truly is, as *determinate* negation, a new form has thereby immediately arisen; and in the negation the transition is made by which the pro- gress through the complete succession of forms comes about of itself.

The goal, however, is fixed for knowledge just as necessarily as the succession in the process. The terminus is at that point where knowl- edge is no longer compelled to go beyond itself, where it finds its own self, and the notion corresponds to the object and the object to the notion. The progress towards this goal consequently is without a halt, and at no earlier stage is satisfaction to be found. That which is confined to a life of nature is unable of itself to go beyond its immediate existence; but by something other than itself it is forced beyond that; and to be thus wrenched out of its setting is its death. Consciousness, however, is to itself its own notion; thereby it immediately transcends what is limited, and, since this latter belongs to it, consciousness transcends its own self. Along with the particular there is at the same time set up the "beyond," were this only, as in spatial intuition, *beside* what is limited. Consciousness, therefore, suffers this violence at its own hands; it destroys its own limited satisfaction. When feeling of violence, anxiety for the truth may well withdraw, and struggle to preserve for itself that which is in danger of being lost. But it can find no rest. Should that anxious fearfulness wish to remain always in unthinking indolence, thought will agitate the thoughtlessness, its restlessness will disturb that indolence. Or let it take its stand as a form of sentimentality which assures us it finds everything good in its kind, and this assurance likewise will suffer violence at the hands of reason, which finds something *not* good just because and in so far as it is a *kind*. Or, again, fear of the truth may conceal itself from itself and others behind the pretext that precisely burning zeal for the very truth makes it so difficult, nay impossible, to find any other truth except that of which alone vanity is capable—that of being ever so much cleverer than any ideas, which one gets from oneself or others, could make possible. This sort of conceit which understands how to belittle every truth and turn away from it back into itself, and gloats over this its own private understanding, which always knows how to dissipate every possible thought, and to find, instead of all the content, merely the barren Ego—this is a satisfaction which must be left to itself; for it flees the universal and seeks only an isolated existence on its own account *(Fürsichseyn)*.

As the foregoing has been stated, provisionally and in general, concerning the manner and the necessity of the process of the inquiry, it may also be of further service to make some observations regarding the method of carrying this out. This exposition, viewed as a process of relating science to phenomenal knowledge, and as an inquiry and critical examination into the reality of knowing, does not seem able to be effected without some presupposition which is laid down as an ultimate criterion. For an examination consists in applying an accepted standard, and, on the final agreement or disagreement therewith of what is tested, deciding whether the latter is right or wrong; and the standard in general, and so science, were this the criterion, is thereby accepted as the essence or inherently real (*Ansich*). But, here, where science first appears on the scene, neither science nor any sort of standard has justified itself as the essence or ultimate reality; and without this no examination seems able to be instituted.

This contradiction and the removal of it will become more definite if, to begin with, we call to mind the abstract determinations of knowledge and of truth as they are found in consciousness. Consciousness, we find, *distinguishes* from itself something, to which at the same time it *relates* itself; or, to use the current expression, there is something *for* consciousness; and the determinate form of this process of relating, or of there being something for a consciousness, is knowledge. But from this being for another we distinguish being in itself or *per se*; what is related to knowledge is likewise distinguished from it, and posited as also existing outside this relation; the aspect of being *per se* or in itself is called Truth. What really lies in these determinations does not further concern us here; for since the object of our inquiry is phenomenal knowledge, its determinations are also taken up, in the first instance, as they are immediately offered to us. And they are offered to us very much in the way we have just stated.

If now our inquiry deals with the truth of knowledge, it appears that we are inquiring what knowledge is in itself. But in this inquiry knowledge is *our* object, it is *for us*; and the essential nature (*Ansich*) of knowledge, were this to come to light, would be rather its being *for us*: what we should assert to be its essence would rather be, not the truth of knowledge, but only our knowledge of it. The essence or the criterion would lie in us; and that which was to be compared with this standard, and on which a decision was to be passed as a result of this comparison, would not necessarily have to recognize that criterion.

But the nature of the object which we are examining surmounts this separation, or semblance of separation, and presupposition. Consciousness furnishes its own criterion in itself, and the inquiry will thereby be a comparison of itself with its own self; for the distinction, just made, falls inside itself. In consciousness there is one element *for* an other, or, in general, consciousness implicates the specific character of the moment of knowledge. At the same time this "other" is to consciousness not merely *for it*, but also outside this relation, or has a being in itself, i.e., there is the moment of truth. Thus in what consciousness inside itself declares to be the essence or truth we have the standard which itself sets up, and by which we are to measure its knowledge. Suppose we call knowledge the notion, and the essence or truth "being" or the object, then the examination consists in seeing whether the notion corresponds with the object. But if we call the *inner nature of the object*, or *what it is in itself*, *the notion*, and, on the other side, understand by object the notion *qua* object, i.e., the way the notion is *for* an other, then the examination consists in our seeing whether the object corresponds to its own notion. It is clear, of course, that both of these processes are the same. The essential fact, however, to be borne in mind throughout the whole inquiry is that both these moments, notion and object, "being for another" and "being in itself," themselves fall within that knowledge which we are examining. Consequently we do not require to bring standards with us, nor to apply *our* fancies and thoughts in the inquiry; and just by our leaving these aside we are enabled to treat and discuss the subject as it actually is in itself and for itself, as it is in its complete reality.

But not only in this respect, that notion and object, the criterion and what is to be tested, are ready to hand in consciousness itself, is any addition of ours superfluous, but we are also spared the trouble of comparing these two and of making an examination in the strict sense of the term; so that in this respect, too, since consciousness tests and examines itself, all we are left to do is simply and solely to look on. For consciousness is, on the one hand, consciousness of the object, on the other, consciousness of itself; consciousness of what to it is true, and consciousness of its knowledge of that truth. Since both are for the same consciousness, it is itself their comparison; it is the same consciousness that decides and knows whether its knowledge of the object corresponds with this object or not. The object, it is true, appears only to be in such wise for consciousness as consciousness knows it. Consciousness does not seem able to get, so to say, behind it as it is, not for consciousness, but in itself, and consequently seems also unable to test knowledge by it. But just because consciousness has, in general, knowledge of an object, there is already present the distinction that the inherent nature, what the object is in itself, is one thing to consciousness, while knowledge, or the being of the object *for* consciousness, is another moment. Upon this distinction, which is present as a fact, the examination turns. Should both, when thus compared, not correspond, consciousness seems bound to alter its knowledge, in order to make it fit the object. But in the alteration of the knowledge, the object itself also, in point of fact, is altered; for the knowledge which existed was essentially a knowledge of the object; with change in the knowledge, the object also becomes different, since it belonged essentially to this knowledge. Hence consciousness comes to find that what formerly to it was the essence is not what is *per se*, or what was *per se* was only *per se for consciousness*. Since, then, in the case of its object consciousness finds its knowledge not corresponding with this object, the object likewise fails to hold out; or the standard for examining is altered when that, whose criterion this standard was to be, does not hold its ground in the course of the examination; and the examination is not only an examination of knowledge, but also of the criterion used in the process.

This dialectic process which consciousness executes on itself—on its knowledge as well as on its object—in the sense that out of it the new and true object arises, is precisely what is termed Experience. In this connection, there is a moment in the process just mentioned which should be brought into more decided prominence, and by which a new light is cast on the scientific aspect of the following exposition. Consciousness knows something; this something is the essence or what is *per se*. This object, however, is also the *per se*, the inherent reality, *for consciousness*. Hence comes ambiguity of this truth. Consciousness, as we see, has now two objects; one is the first *per se*, the second is the existence *for consciousness* of this *per se*. The last object appears at first sight to be merely the reflection of consciousness into itself, i.e., an idea not of an object, but solely of its knowledge of that first object. But, as was already indicated, by that very process the first object is altered; it ceases to be what is *per se*, and becomes consciously something which is *per se* only *for consciousness*. Consequently, then, what this real *per se* is for consciousness is truth; which, however, means that this is the essential reality, or the object which consciousness has. This new object contains the nothingness of the first; the new object is the *experience* concerning that first object.

In this treatment of the course of experience, there is an element in virtue of which it does not seem to be in agreement with what is ordinarily understood by experience. The transition from the first object and the knowledge of it to the other object, in regard to which we say we have had experience, was so stated that the knowledge of the first object, the existence *for consciousness* of the first *ens per se*, is itself to be the second object. But it usually seems that we learn by experience the untruth of our first notion by appealing to some other object which we may happen to find casually and externally; so that, in general, what we have is merely the bare and simple apprehension of what is in and for itself. On the view above given, however, the new object is seen to have come about by a transformation or conversion of consciousness itself. This way of looking at the matter is *our* doing, what *we* contribute; by its means the series of experiences through which consciousness passes is lifted into a scientifically constituted sequence, but this does not exist for the consciousness we contemplate and consider. We have here, however, the same sort of circumstance, again, of which we spoke a short time ago when dealing with the relation of this exposition to scepticism, viz., that the result which at any time comes about in the case of an untrue mode of knowledge cannot possibly collapse into an empty nothing, but must necessarily be taken as the negation of that of which it is a result—a result which contains what truth the preceding mode of knowledge has in it. In the present instance the position takes this form: since what at first appeared as object is reduced, when it passes into consciousness, to what knowledge takes it to be, and the implicit nature, the real in itself, becomes what this entity *per se* is *for consciousness;* this latter is the new object, whereupon there appears also a new mode or embodiment of consciousness, of which the essence is something other than that of the preceding mode. It is this circumstance which carries forward the whole succession of the modes or attitudes of consciousness in their own necessity. It is only this necessity, this origination of the new object—which offers itself to consciousness without consciousness knowing how it comes by it—that to us, who watch the process, is to be seen going on, so to say, behind its back. Thereby there enters into its process a moment of being *per se* or of being for us, which is not expressly presented to that consciousness which is in the grip of experience itself. The *content,* however, of what we see arising, exists for it, and we lay hold of and comprehend merely its formal character, i.e., its *bare* origination; *for it,* what has thus arisen has merely the character of object, while, *for us,* it appears at the same time as a process and coming into being.

In virtue of that necessity this pathway to science is itself *eo ipso* science, and is, moreover, as regards its content, Science of the Experience of Consciousness.

The experience which consciousness has concerning itself can, by its essential principle, embrace nothing less than the entire system of consciousness, the whole realm of the truth of mind, and in such wise that the moments of truth are set forth in the specific and peculiar character they here possess—i.e., not as abstract pure moments, but as they are for consciousness, or as consciousness itself appears in its relation to them, and in virtue of which they are moments of the whole, are embodiments or modes of consciousness. In pressing forward to its true form of existence, consciousness will come to a point at which it lays aside its semblance of being hampered with what is foreign to it, with what is only for it and exists as an other; it will reach a position where appearance becomes identified with essence, where, in consequence, its exposition coincides with just this very point, this very stage of the science proper of mind. And, finally, when it grasps this its own essence, it will connote the nature of absolute knowledge itself.

CONSCIOUSNESS: SENSE-CERTAINTY AND PERCEPTION

The knowledge, which is at the start or immediately our object, can be nothing else than just that which is immediate knowledge, knowledge of the immediate, of what *is*. We have, in dealing with it, to proceed, too, in an immediate way, to accept what is given, not altering anything in it as it is presented before us, and keeping mere apprehension (*Auffassen*) free from conceptual comprehension (*Begreifen*).

The concrete content, which sensuous certainty furnishes, makes this *prima facie* appear to be the richest kind of knowledge, to be even a knowledge of endless wealth—a wealth to which we can as little find any limit when we traverse its *extent* in space and time, where that content is presented before us, as when we take a fragment out of the abundance it offers us and by dividing and dividing seek to penetrate its *intent*. Besides that, it seems to be the truest, the most authentic knowledge: for it has not as yet dropped anything from the object; it has the object before itself in its entirety and completeness. This bare fact of *certainty*, however, is really and admittedly the abstractest and the poorest kind of *truth*. It merely says regarding what it knows: it *is*; and its truth contains solely the *being* of the fact it knows. Consciousness, on its part, in the case of this form of certainty, takes the shape merely of pure Ego. In other words, I in such a case am merely *qua* pure This, and the object likewise is merely *qua* pure This. I, *this* particular conscious I, am certain of *this* fact before me, not because I *qua* consciousness have developed myself in connection with it and in manifold ways set thought to work about it: and not, again, because the fact, the thing, of which I am certain, in virtue of its having a multitude of distinct qualities, was replete with possible modes of relation and a variety of connections with other things. Neither has

SOURCE: *Phenomenology*, pp. 149–160, 162–163, 180. Reprinted by permission of George Allen & Unwin Ltd., London.

anything to do with the truth sensuous certainty contains: neither the I nor the thing has here the meaning of a manifold relation with a variety of other things, of mediation in a variety of ways. The I does not contain or imply a manifold of ideas, the I here does not *think:* nor does the thing mean what has a multiplicity of qualities. Rather, the thing, the fact, *is;* and it *is* merely because it *is.* It *is*—that is the essential point for sense-knowledge, and that bare fact of *being,* that simple immediacy, constitutes its truth. In the same way the certainty *qua relation,* the certainty "of" something, is an immediate pure relation; consciousness is I—nothing more, a pure *this;* the *individual* consciousness knows a pure *this,* or knows what is *individual.*

But, when we look closely, there is a good deal more implied in that bare pure being, which constitutes the kernel of this form of certainty, and is given out by it as its truth. A concrete actual certainty of sense is not merely this pure immediacy, but an example, an instance, of that immediacy. Amongst the innumerable distinctions that here come to light, we find in all cases the fundamental difference—viz. that in sense-experience pure being at once breaks up into the two "thises," as we have called them, one this as I, and one as object. When *we* reflect* on this distinction, it is seen that neither the one nor the other is merely immediate, merely *is* in sense-certainty, but is at the same time *mediated:* I have the certainty through the other, viz., through the actual fact; and this, again, exists in that certainty through an other, viz., through the I.

It is not only we who make this distinction of essential truth and particular example, of essence and instance, immediacy and mediation; we *find* it in sense-certainty itself, and it has to be taken up in the form in which it exists there, not as we have just determined it. One of them is put forward in it as existing in simple immediacy, as the essential reality, the *object.* The other, however, is put forward as the non-essential, as *mediated,* something which is not *per se* in the certainty, but there through something else, ego, a state of knowledge which only knows the object because the *object* is, and which can as well be as *not* be. The object, however, is the real truth, is the essential reality; it *is,* quite indifferent to whether it is known or not; it remains and stands even though it is not known, while the knowledge does not exist if the object is not there.

We have thus to consider as to the object, whether in point of fact it does exist in sense-certainty itself as such an essential reality as that

*I.e., for the purposes of philosophical analysis.

certainty gives it out to be; whether its meaning and notion, which is to be essential reality, corresponds to the way it is present in that certainty. We have for that purpose not to reflect about it and ponder what it might be in truth, but to deal with it merely as sense-certainty contains it.

Sense-certainty itself has thus to be asked: What is the This? If we take it in the two-fold form of its existence, as the *Now* and as the *Here*, the dialectic it has in it will take a form as intelligible as the This itself. To the question, What is the Now? we reply, for example, the Now is night-time. To test the truth of this certainty of sense, a simple experiment is all we need: write that truth down. A truth cannot lose anything by being written down, and just as little by our preserving and keeping it. If we look again at the truth we have written down, look at it *now, at this noon-time*, we shall have to say it has turned stale and become out of date.

The Now that is night is kept fixed, i.e., it is treated as what it is given out to be, as something which *is;* but it proves to be rather a something which is *not.* The Now itself no doubt maintains itself, but as what is *not* night; similarly in its relation to the day which the Now is at present, it maintains itself as something that is also not day, or as altogether something negative. This self-maintaining Now is therefore not something immediate but something mediated; for, *qua* something that remains and preserves itself, it is determined through and *by means* of the fact that something else, namely day and night, is *not.* Thereby it is just as much as ever it was before, Now, and in being this simple fact, it is indifferent to what is still associated with it; just as little as night or day is its being, it is just as truly *also* day and night; it is not in the least affected by this otherness through which it is what it is. A simple entity of this sort, which is by and through negation, which is neither this nor that, which is a *not-this*, and with equal indifference this as well as that—a thing of this kind we call a Universal. The Universal is therefore in point of fact the truth of sense-certainty, the true content of sense-experience.

It is as a universal, too, that we* give utterance to sensuous fact. What we say is: "This," i.e., the universal this; or we say: "it is," i.e., being in general. Of course we do not present before our mind in saying so the universal this, or being in general, but we *utter* what is universal; in other words, we do not actually and absolutely say what in this sense-certainty we really *mean*. Language, however, as we see,

*I.e., the naïve consciousness here analysed.

is the more truthful; in it we ourselves refute directly and at once our own "meaning"; and since universality is the real truth of sense-certainty, and language merely expresses *this* truth, it is not possible at all for us even to express in words any sensuous existence which we "mean."

The same will be the case when we take the *Here*, the other form of the This. The Here is, e.g., the tree. I turn about and this truth has disappeared and has changed round into its opposite: the Here is not a tree, but a house. The Here itself does not disappear; it *is* and remains in the disappearance of the house, tree, and so on, and is indifferently house, tree. The This is shown thus again to be *mediated simplicity*, in other words, to be *universality*.

Pure being, then, remains as the essential element for this sense-certainty, since sense-certainty in its very nature proves the universal to be the truth of its object. But that pure being is not in the form of something immediate, but of something in which the process of negation and mediation is essential. Consequently it is not what we *intend* or "mean" by being, but being with the characteristic that it is an abstraction, the purely universal; and our intended "meaning," which takes the truth of sense-certainty to be *not* something universal, is alone left standing in contrast to this empty, indifferent Now and Here.

If we compare the relation in which knowledge and the object first stood with the relation they have come to assume in this result, it is found to be just the reverse of what first appeared. The object, which professed to be the essential reality, is now the non-essential element of sense-certainty; for the universal, which the object has come to be, is no longer such as the object essentially was to be for sense-certainty. The certainty is now found to lie in the opposite element, namely in knowledge, which formerly was the non-essential factor. Its truth lies in the object as my *(meinem)* object, or lies in the "meaning" *(Meinen)*, in what I "mean"; it *is*, because *I* know it. Sense-certainty is thus indeed banished from the object, but it is not yet thereby done away with; it is merely forced back into the I. We have still to see what experience reveals regarding its reality in this sense.

The force of its truth thus lies now in the I, in the immediate fact of my seeing, hearing, and so on; the disappearance of the particular Now and Here that we "mean" is prevented by the fact that *I* keep hold on them. The Now is daytime, because *I* see it; the Here is a tree for a similar reason. Sense-certainty, however, goes through, in this connection, the same dialectic process as in the former case. I, *this* I, see the tree, and assert the tree to be the Here; *another* I, however, sees the house and maintains the Here is not a tree but a house. Both truths have the same authenticity—the immediacy of seeing and the certainty and assurance both have as to their specific way of knowing; but the one certainty disappears in the other.

In all this, what does not disappear is the I *qua* universal, whose seeing is neither the seeing of this tree nor of this house, but just seeing *simpliciter*, which is mediated through the negation of this house, etc., and, in being so, is all the same simple and indifferent to what is associated with it, the house, the tree, and so on. I is merely universal, like Now, Here, or This in general. No doubt I "mean" an individual I, but just as little as I am able to say what I "mean" by Now, Here, so it is impossible in the case of the I too. By saying "this Here," "this Now," "an individual thing," I say all Thises, Heres, Nows, or Individuals. In the same way when I say "I," "this individual I," I say quite generally "all I's," every one is what I say, every one is "I," this individual I. When philosophy is requested, by way of putting it to a crucial test—a test which it could not possibly sustain —to "deduce," to "construe," "to find *a priori*," or however it is put, a so-called *this thing*, or *this particular man*,*it is reasonable that the person making this demand should say *what* "this thing," or *what* "this I," he means: but to say this is quite impossible.

Sense-certainty discovers by experience, therefore, that its essential nature lies neither in the object nor in the I; and that the immediacy peculiar to it is neither an immediacy of the one nor of the other. For, in the case of both, what I "mean" is rather something non-essential; and the object and the I are universals, in which that Now and Here and I, which I "mean," do not hold out, do not exist. We arrive in this way at the result, that we have to put the *whole* of sense-certainty as its essential reality, and no longer merely one of its moments, as happened in both cases, where first the object as against the I, and then the I, was to be its true reality. Thus it is only the whole sense-certainty itself which persists therein as immediacy, and in consequence excludes from itself all the opposition which in the foregoing had a place there.

This pure immediacy, then, has nothing more to do with the fact of otherness, with Here in the form of a tree passing into a Here that is not a tree, with Now in the sense of day-time changing into a Now that is night-time, or with there being an other I to which something

*Cf., *Encyclo.* § 250.

else is object. Its truth stands fast as a self-identical relation making no distinction of essential and non-essential, between I and object, and into which, therefore, in general, no distinction can find its way. I, *this* I, assert, then, the Here as tree, and do not turn round so that for me Here might become *not* a tree, and I take no notice of the fact that another I finds the Here as not-tree, or that I myself at some other time take the Here as not-tree, the Now as not-day. I am directly conscious, I intuit and nothing more, I am pure intuition; I *am—seeing, looking.* For myself I stand by the fact, the Now is day-time, or, again, by the fact the Here is tree, and, again, do not compare Here and Now themselves with one another; I take my stand on *one* immediate relation: the Now is day.

Since, then, this certainty wholly refuses to come out if we direct its attention to a Now that is night or an I to whom it is night, we will go to it and let ourselves point out the Now that is asserted. We must let ourselves *point it out* for the truth of this immediate relation is the truth of *this ego* which restricts itself to *a* Now or *a* Here. Were we to examine this truth *afterwards*, or stand at a distance from it, it would have no meaning at all; for that would do away with the immediacy, which is of its essence. We have therefore to enter the same point of time or of space, indicate them, point them out to ourselves, i.e., we must let ourselves take the place of the very same I, the very same This, which is the subject knowing with certainty. Let us, then, see how that immediate is constituted, which is *shown* to us.

The Now is pointed out; this Now. "Now"; it has already ceased to be when it is pointed out. The Now that is, is other than the one indicated, and we see that the Now is just this—to be no longer the very time when it is. The Now as it is shown to us is one that *has been*, and that is its truth; it does not have the truth of being, of something that *is*. No doubt this is true, that it *has* been; but what *has* been is in point of fact not genuinely real, it is *not*, and the point in question concerned what is, concerned being.

In thus pointing out the Now we see then merely a process which takes the following course: *First* I point out the Now, and it is asserted to be the truth. I point it out, however, as something that *has been*, or as something cancelled and done away with. I thus annul and pass beyond that first truth and in the *second* place I now assert as the second truth that it *has* been, that it is superseded. But, *thirdly*, what *has* been *is not*; I then supersede, cancel, its *having* been, the fact of its being *annulled*, the second truth, negate thereby the negation of the Now and return in so doing to the first position: that *Now is*. The

Now and pointing out the Now are thus so constituted that neither the one nor the other is an immediate simple fact, but a process with diverse moments in it. A *This* is set up; it is, however, rather an *other* that is set up; the *This* is superseded: and this otherness, this cancelling of the former, is itself again annulled, and so turned back to the first. But this first, reflected thus into itself, is not exactly the same as it was to begin with, namely something immediate: rather it is a something reflected-into-self, a simple entity which remains in its otherness, what it is: a Now which is any number of Nows. And that is the genuinely true Now; the Now is simple day-time which has many Nows within it—hours. A Now of that sort, again—an hour—is similarly many minutes; and this Now—a minute—in the same way many Nows and so on. Showing, indicating, pointing out [the Now] is thus itself the very process which expresses what the Now in truth really *is:* namely a result, or a plurality of Nows all taken together. And the pointing out is the way of getting to know, of *experiencing, that Now is a universal.*

The Here pointed out, which I keep hold of, is likewise a *this* Here which, in fact, is not *this Here*, but a Before and Behind, an Above and Below, a Right and Left. The Above is itself likewise this manifold otherness—above, below, etc. The Here, which was to be pointed out, disappears in other Heres, and these disappear similarly. What is pointed out, held fast, and is permanent, is a negative This, which only is so when the Heres are taken as they should be, but therein cancel one another; it is a simple complex of many Heres. The Here that is "meant" would be the point. But it *is* not: rather, when it is pointed out as *being*, as having existence, that very act of pointing out proves to be not immediate knowledge, but a process, a movement from the Here "meant" through a plurality of Heres to the universal Here, which is a simple plurality of Heres, just as day is a simple plurality of Nows.

It is clear from all this that the dialectic process involved in sense-certainty is nothing else than the mere history of its process—of its experience; and sense-certainty itself is nothing else than simply this history. The naïve consciousness, too, for that reason, is of itself always coming to this result, which is the real truth in this case, and is always having experience of it: but is always forgetting it again and beginning the process all over. It is therefore astonishing when, in defiance of this experience, it is announced as "universal experience" —nay, even as a philosophical doctrine, the outcome, in fact, of scepticism—that the reality or being of external things in the sense of "Thises," particular sense objects, has absolute validity and truth for consciousness. One who makes such an assertion really does not know what he is saying, does not know that he is stating the opposite of what he wants to say. The truth for consciousness of a "This" of sense is said to be universal experience; but the very opposite is universal experience. Every consciousness of itself cancels again, as soon as made, such a truth as, e.g., the Here is a tree, or the Now is noon, and expresses the very opposite: the Here is not a tree but a house. And similarly it straightway cancels again the assertion which here annuls the first, and which is also just such an assertion of a sensuous This. And in all sense-certainty what we find by experience is in truth merely, as we have seen, that "This" is a universal, the very opposite of what that assertion maintained to be universal experience.

We may be permitted here, in this appeal to universal experience, to anticipate with a reference to the practical sphere. In this connection we may answer those who thus insist on the truth and certainty of the reality of objects of sense, by saying that they had better be sent back to the most elementary school of wisdom, the ancient Eleusinian mysteries of Ceres and Bacchus; they have not yet learnt the inner secret of the eating of bread and the drinking of wine. For one who is initiated into these mysteries not only comes to doubt the being of things of sense, but gets into a state of despair about it altogether; and in dealing with them he partly himself brings about the nothingness of those things, partly he sees these bring about their own nothingness. Even animals are not shut off from this wisdom, but show they are deeply initiated into it. For they do not stand stock still before things of sense as if these were things *per se*, with being in themselves: they despair of this reality altogether, and in complete assurance of the nothingness of things they fall-to without more ado and eat them up. And all nature proclaims, as animals do, these open secrets, these mysteries revealed to all, which teach what the truth of things of sense is.

Those who put forward such assertions really themselves say, if we bear in mind what we remarked before, the direct opposite of what they mean: a fact which is perhaps best able to bring them to reflect on the nature of the certainty of sense-experience. They speak of the "existence" of external objects, which can be more precisely characterized as actual, absolutely particular, wholly personal, individual things, each of them not like anything or anyone else; this is the existence which they say has absolute certainty and truth. They "mean" this bit of paper I am writing on, or rather *have* written on: but they do not say what they "mean." If they really wanted to *say* this bit of paper which they "mean," and they wanted to *say* so, that is impossible, because the This of sense, which is "meant," cannot be reached by language, which belongs to consciousness, i.e., to what is inherently universal. In the very attempt to say it, it would, therefore, crumble in their hands; those who have begun to describe it would not be able to finish doing so: they would have to hand it over to others, who would themselves in the last resort have to confess to speaking about a thing that has no being. They "mean," then, doubt-less this bit of paper here, which is quite different from that bit over there; but they speak of actual things, external or sensible objects, absolutely individual, real, and so on; that is, they say about them what is simply universal. Consequently what is called unspeakable is nothing else than what is untrue, irrational, something barely and simply "meant."

If nothing is said of a thing except that it is an actual thing, an external object, this only makes it the most universal of all possible things, and thereby we express its likeness, its identity, with every-thing, rather than its difference from everything else. When I say "an individual thing," I at once state it to be really quite a universal, for everything is an individual thing: and in the same way "this thing" is everything and anything we like. More precisely, as this bit of paper, each and every paper is a "this bit of paper," and I have thus said all the while what is universal. If I want, however, to help out speech— which has the divine nature of directly turning the mere "meaning" right round about, making it into something else, and so not letting it ever come the length of words at all—by pointing out this bit of paper, then I get the experience of what is, in point of fact, the real truth of sense-certainty. I point it out as a Here, which is a Here of other Heres, or is in itself simply many Heres together, i.e., is a universal. I take it up then, as in truth it is; and instead of knowing something immediate, I "take" something "truly," I *per-ceive* (*wahr-nehme, per-cipio*).

Immediate certainty does not make the truth its own, for its truth is something universal, whereas certainty wants to deal with the This. Perception, on the other hand, takes what exists for it to be a univer-sal. Universality being its principle in general, its moments immedi-ately distinguished within it are also universal; *I* is a universal, and the *object* is a universal. That principle has *arisen* and come into being for *us* who are tracing the course of experience; and our process of apprehending what perception is, therefore, is no longer a contingent series of acts of apprehension, as is the case with the apprehension of sense-certainty; it is a logically necessitated process. With the origination of the principle, both the moments, which as they appear merely fall apart as happenings, have at once together come into being: the one, the process of pointing out and indicating, the other the same process, but as a simple fact—the former the process of perceiving, the latter the object perceived. The object is in its essential nature the same as the process; the latter is the unfolding and distinguishing of the elements involved; the object is these same elements taken and held together as a single totality. *For us* (tracing the process) or, in itself,*the universal, *qua* principle, is the essence of perception; and as against this abstraction, both the moments distinguished—that which perceives and that which is perceived—are what is non-essential. But in point of fact, because both are themselves the universal, or the essence, they are both essential: but since they are related as opposites, only one can in the relation (constituting perception) be the essential moment; and the distinction of essential and non-essential has to be shared between them. . . . Consciousness has found "seeing" and "hearing," etc., pass away in the dialectic process of sense-experience, and has, at the stage of perception, arrived at thoughts which, however, it brings together in the first instance in the unconditioned universal. . . .

---

*This expression refers to the distinction already made in the Introduction, between the point of view of the *Phenomenology* and that of the actual consciousness whose procedure is being analysed in the *Phenomenology*. That is "for us" which we (i.e., the philosophical "we") are aware of by way of anticipation, but which has not yet been evolved objectively and explicitly; it is intelligible, but not yet intellectually realized. That is "in itself" *(an sich)*, which is implicit, inherent, or potential, and hence not yet explicitly developed. The terms "for us" and "in itself" are thus strictly alternative: the former looks at the matter from the point of view of the philosophical subject, the latter from the point of view of the object discussed by the philosopher. The implicit nature of the object can only be "for us" who are thinking about the object; and what *we* have in mind can only be *implicitly* true of the object. The alternative disappears when the explicit nature of the object is what "we" explicitly take the object to be.

SELF-CERTAINTY AND THE LORDSHIP AND BONDAGE OF SELF-CONSCIOUSNESS

In the kinds of certainty hitherto considered, the truth for consciousness is something other than consciousness itself. The conception, however, of this truth vanishes in the course of our experience of it. What the object immediately was *in itself*—whether mere being in sense-certainty, a concrete thing in perception, or force in the case of understanding—it turns out, in truth, not to be this really; but instead, this inherent nature *(Ansich)* proves to be a way in which it is for an other. The abstract conception of the object gives way before the actual concrete object, or the first immediate idea is cancelled in the course of experience. Mere certainty vanishes in favour of the truth. There has now arisen, however, what was not established in the case of these previous relationships, viz., a certainty which is on a par with its truth, for the certainty is to itself its own object, and consciousness is to itself the truth. Otherness, no doubt, is also found there; consciousness, that is, makes a distinction; but what is distinguished is of such a kind that consciousness, at the same time, holds there is no distinction made. If we call the movement of knowledge conception, and knowledge, *qua* simple unity or Ego, the object, we see that not only for us [tracing the process], but likewise for knowledge itself, the object corresponds to the conception; or, if we put it in the other form and call conception what the object is in itself, while applying the term object to what the object is *qua* object or *for an other*, it is clear that being "in-itself" and being "for an other" are here the same. For the inherent being *(Ansich)* is consciousness; yet it is still just as much that for which an other (viz., what is "in-itself") is. And it is *for* consciousness that the inherent nature *(Ansich)* of the object, and its "being for an other" *are* one and the same. Ego is the content of the relation, and itself the process of relating. It is Ego itself which is opposed to an other and, at the same time, reaches out beyond this other, which other is all the same taken to be only itself.

With self-consciousness, then, we have now passed into the native land of truth, into that kingdom where it is at home. We have to see how the form or attitude of self-consciousness in the first instance appears. When we consider this new form and type of knowledge, the knowledge of self, in its relation to that which preceded, namely, the

SOURCE: *Phenomenology*, pp. 218–227, 229–240. Reprinted by permission of George Allen & Unwin Ltd., London.

knowledge of an other, we find, indeed, that this latter has vanished, but that its moments have, at the same time, been preserved; and the loss consists in this, that those moments are here present as they are implicitly, as they are in themselves. The being which "meaning" dealt with, particularity and the universality of perception opposed to it, as also the empty, inner region of understanding—these are no longer present as substantial elements *(Wesen)*, but as moments of self-consciousness, i.e., as abstractions or differences, which are, at the same time, of no account for consciousness itself, or are not differences at all, and are purely vanishing entities *(Wesen)*.

What seems to have been lost, then, is only the principal moment, viz., the simple fact of having independent subsistence for consciousness. But, in reality, self-consciousness is reflexion out of the bare being that belongs to the world of sense and perception, and is essentially the return out of otherness. As self-consciousness, it is movement. But when it distinguishes only its self as such from itself, distinction is straightway taken to be superseded in the sense of involving otherness. The distinction *is* not, and self-consciousness is only motionless tautology, Ego is Ego, I am I. When for self-consciousness the distinction does not also have the shape of *being*, it is *not* self-consciousness. For self-consciousness, then, otherness is a fact, it does exist as a distinct moment; but the unity of itself with this difference is also a fact for self-consciousness, and is a second distinct moment. With that first moment, self-consciousness occupies the position of consciousness, and the whole expanse of the world of sense is conserved as its object, but at the same time only as related to the second moment, the unity of self-consciousness with itself. And, consequently, the sensible world is regarded by self-consciousness as having a subsistence which is, however, only appearance, or forms a distinction from self-consciousness that *per se* has no being. This opposition of its appearance and its truth finds its real essence, however, only in the truth—in the unity of self-consciousness with itself. This unity must become essential to self-consciousness, i.e., self-consciousness is the state of *Desire* in general. Consciousness has, *qua* self-consciousness, henceforth a twofold object—the one immediate, the object of sense-certainty and of perception, which, however, is here found to be marked by the character of negation; the second, viz., itself, which is the true essence, and is found in the first instance only in the opposition of the first object to it. Self-consciousness presents itself here as the process in which this opposition is removed, and oneness or identity with itself established.

For us or implicitly, the object, which is the negative element for self-consciousness, has on its side returned into itself, just as on the other side consciousness has done. Through this reflexion into self, the object has become *Life.* What self-consciousness distinguishes as having a being distinct from itself, has in it too, so far as it is affirmed to *be,* not merely the aspect of sense-certainty and perception; it is a being reflected into itself, and the object of immediate desire is something living. For the inherent reality *(Ansich),* the general result of the relation of the understanding to the inner nature of things, is the distinguishing of what cannot be distinguished, or is the unity of what is distinguished. This unity, however, is, as we saw, just as much its recoil from itself; and this conception breaks asunder into the opposition of self-consciousness and life: the former is the unity *for which* the absolute unity of differences exists, the latter, however, *is* only this unity itself, so that the unity is not at the same time *for itself.* Thus, according to the independence possessed by consciousness, is the independence which its object in itself possesses. Self-consciousness, which is absolutely *for itself,* and characterizes its object directly as negative, or is primarily desire, will really, therefore, find through experience this object's independence.

The determination of the principle of life, as obtained from the conception or general result with which we enter this new sphere, is sufficient to characterize it, without its nature being evolved further out of that notion. Its circuit is completed in the following moments. The essential element *(Wesen)* is infinitude as the supersession of all distinctions, the pure rotation on its own axis, itself at rest while being absolutely restless infinitude, the very self-dependence in which the differences brought out in the process are all dissolved, the simple reality of time, which in this self-identity has the solid form and shape of space. The differences, however, all the same hold as differences in this simple universal medium; for this universal flux exercises its negative activity merely in that it is the sublation of them; but it could not transcend them unless they had a subsistence of their own. Precisely this flux is itself, as self-identical independence, their subsistence or their substance, in which they accordingly are distinct members, parts which have being in their own right. Being no longer has the significance of mere abstract being, nor has their naked essence the meaning of abstract universality: their being now is just that simple fluent substance of the pure movement within itself. The difference, however, of these members *inter se* consists, in general, in no other characteristic than that of the moments of infinitude, or of the mere movement itself.

The independent members exist for themselves. To be thus for themselves, however, is really as much their reflexion directly into the unity, as this unity is the breaking asunder into independent forms. The unity is sundered because it is absolutely negative or infinite unity; and because it is subsistence, difference likewise has independence only in *it*. This independence of the form appears as a determinate entity, as what is for another, for the form is something disunited; and the cancelling of diremption takes effect to that extent through another. But this sublation lies just as much in the actual form itself. For just that flux is the substance of the independent forms. This substance, however, is *infinite, and hence the form itself* in its very subsistence involves diremption, or sublation of its existence for itself.

If we distinguish more exactly the moments contained here, we see that we have as first moment the subsistence of the independent forms, or the suppression of what distinction inherently involves, viz., that the forms have no being *per se*, and no subsistence. The second moment, however, is the subjection of that subsistence to the infinitude of distinction. In the first moment there is the subsisting, persisting mode, or form; by its being in its own right, or by its being in its determinate shape an infinite substance, it comes forward in opposition to the universal substance, disowns this fluent continuity with that substance, and insists that it is not dissolved in this universal element, but rather on the contrary preserves itself by and through its separation from this its inorganic nature, and by the fact that it consumes this inorganic nature. Life in the universal fluid medium, quietly, silently shaping and moulding and distributing the forms in all their manifold detail, becomes by that very activity the movement of those forms, or passes into life *qua Process*. The mere universal flux is here the inherent being; the outer being, the "other," is the distinction of the forms assumed. But this flux, this fluent condition, becomes itself the other in virtue of this very distinction; because now it exists "for" or in relation to that distinction, which is self-conditioned and self-contained *(an und für sich)*, and consequently is the endless, infinite movement by which that stable medium is consumed —is life as living.

This inversion of character, however, is on that account again invertedness in itself as such. What is consumed is the essential reality: the Individuality, which preserves itself at the expense of the universal and gives itself the feeling of its unity with itself, precisely thereby cancels its contrast with the other, by means of which it exists for itself. The unity with self, which it gives itself, is just the fluent continuity of differences, or universal dissolution. But, conversely, the cancelling of individual subsistence at the same time produces the subsistence. For since the essence of the individual form—universal life—and the self-existent entity *per se* are simple substance, the essence, by putting the other within itself, cancels this its own simplicity or its essence, i.e., it sunders that simplicity; and this disruption of fluent undifferentiated continuity is just the setting up, the affirmation, of individuality. The simple substance of life, therefore, is the diremption of itself into shapes and forms, and at the same time the dissolution of these substantial differences; and the resolution of this diremption is just as much a process of diremption, of articulating. Thus both the sides of the entire movement which were before distinguished, viz., the *setting up of individual forms* lying apart and undisturbed in the universal medium of independent existence, and the *process* of life—collapse into one another. The latter is just as much a formation of independent individual shapes, as it is a way of cancelling a shape assumed; and the former, the setting up of individual forms, is as much a cancelling as an articulation of them. The fluent, continuous element is itself only the abstraction of the essential reality, or it is actual only as a definite shape or form; and that it articulates itself is once more a breaking up of the articulated form, or a dissolution of it. The *entire* circuit of this activity constitutes Life. It is neither what is expressed to begin with, the immediate continuity and concrete solidity of its essential nature; nor the stable, subsisting form, the discrete individual which exists on its own account; nor the bare process of this form; nor again is it the simple combination of all these moments. It is none of these; it is the *whole* which develops itself, resolves its own development, and in this movement simply preserves itself.

Since we started from the first immediate unity, and returned through the moments of form-determination, and of process, to the unity of both these moments, and thus again back to the first simple substance, we see that this *reflected* unity is other than the first. As opposed to that immediate unity, the unity expressed as a mode of being, this second is the universal unity, which holds all these moments sublated within itself. It is the simple genus, which in the movement of life itself does not exist in this simplicity for itself; but in this result points life towards what is other than itself, namely, towards Consciousness for which life exists as this unity or as genus.

This other life, however, for which the genus as such exists and which is genus for itself, namely, self-consciousness, exists in the first instance only in the form of this simple, essential reality, and has for object itself *qua* pure Ego. In the course of its experience, which we are now to consider, this abstract object will grow in richness, and will be unfolded in the way we have seen in the case of life.

The simple ego is this genus, or the bare universal, for which the differences are insubstantial, only by its being the negative essence of the moments which have assumed a definite and independent form. And self-consciousness is thus only assured of itself through sublating this other, which is presented to self-consciousness as an independent life; self-consciousness is *Desire*. Convinced of the nothingness of this other, it definitely affirms this nothingness to be for itself the truth of this other, negates the independent object, and thereby acquires the certainty of its own self, as *true* certainty, a certainty which it has become aware of in objective form.

In this state of satisfaction, however, it has experience of the independence of its object. Desire and the certainty of its self obtained in the gratification of desire, are conditioned by the object; for the certainty exists through cancelling this other; in order that this cancelling may be effected, there must be this other. Self-consciousness is thus unable by its negative relation to the object to abolish it; because of that relation it rather produces it again, as well as the desire. The object desired is, in fact, something other than self-consciousness, the essence of desire; and through this experience this truth has become realized. At the same time, however, self-consciousness is likewise absolutely for itself, exists on its own account; and it is so only by sublation of the object; and it must come to feel its satisfaction, for it is the truth. On account of the independence of the object, therefore, it can only attain satisfaction when this object itself effectually brings about negation within itself. The object must *per se* effect this negation of itself, for it is inherently *(an sich)* something negative, and must be for the other what it is. Since the object is in its very self negation, and in being so is at the same time independent, it is Consciousness. In the case of life, which is the object of desire, the negation *either* lies in an other, namely, in desire, *or* takes the form of determinateness standing in opposition to an other external individuum indifferent to it, *or* appears as its inorganic general nature. The above general independent nature, however, in the case of which negation takes the form of *absolute* negation, is the genus as such, or as self-consciousness. Self-consciousness attains its satisfaction only in another self-consciousness.

It is in these three moments that the notion of self-consciousness first gets completed: (a) pure undifferentiated ego is its first immediate object; (b) this immediacy is itself, however, thoroughgoing mediation. It has its being only by cancelling the independent object, in other words it is Desire. The satisfaction of desire is indeed the reflexion of self-consciousness into itself, is the certainty which has passed into objective truth. But (c) the truth of this certainty is really twofold reflexion, the reduplication of self-consciousness. Consciousness has an object which implicates its own otherness or affirms distinction as a void distinction, and therein is independent. The individual form distinguished, which is only a living form, certainly cancels its independence also in the process of life itself; but it ceases along with its distinctive difference to be what it is. The object of self-consciousness, however, is still independent in this negativity of itself; and thus it is for itself genus, universal flux or continuity in the very distinctiveness of its own separate existence; it is a living self-consciousness.

A self-consciousness has before it a self-consciousness. Only so and only then *is* it self-consciousness in actual fact; for here first of all it comes to have the unity of itself in its otherness. Ego which is the object of its notion, is in point of fact not *"object."* The object of desire, however, is only independent, for it is the universal, ineradicable substance, the fluent self-identical essential reality. When a self-consciousness is the object, the object is just as much ego as object.

With this we already have before us the notion of *Mind* or *Spirit.* What consciousness has further to become aware of, is the experience of what mind is—this absolute substance, which is the unity of the different self-related and self-existent self-consciousnesses in the perfect freedom and independence of their opposition as component elements of that substance: Ego that is "we," a plurality of Egos, and "we," that is, a single Ego. Consciousness first finds in self-consciousness—the notion of mind—its turning-point, where it leaves the parti-coloured show of the sensuous immediate, passes from the dark void of the transcendent and remote super-sensuous, and steps into the spiritual daylight of the present.

Lordship and Bondage

Self-consciousness exists in itself and for itself, in that, and by the fact that it exists for another self-consciousness; that is to say, it *is* only by being acknowledged or "recognized." The conception of this its unity in its duplication, of infinitude realizing itself in self-consciousness, has many sides to it and encloses within it elements of varied significance. Thus its moments must on the one hand be strictly kept apart in detailed distinctiveness, and, on the other, in this distinction must, at the same time, also be taken as not distinguished, or must always be accepted and understood in their opposite sense. This double meaning of what is distinguished lies in the nature of self-consciousness—of its being infinite, or directly the opposite of the determinateness in which it is fixed. The detailed exposition of the notion of this spiritual unity in its duplication will bring before us the process of Recognition.

Self-consciousness has before it another self-consciousness; it has come outside itself. This has a double significance. First it has lost its own self, since it finds itself as an *other* being; secondly, it has thereby sublated that other, for it does not regard the other as essentially real, but sees its own self in the other.

It must cancel this its other. To do so is the sublation of that first double meaning, and is therefore a second double meaning. First, it must set itself to sublate the other independent being, in order thereby to become certain of itself as true being, secondly, it thereupon proceeds to sublate its own self, for this other is itself.

This sublation in a double sense of its otherness in a double sense is at the same time a return in a double sense into its self. For, firstly, through sublation, it gets back itself, because it becomes one with itself again through the cancelling of *its* otherness; but secondly, it likewise gives otherness back again to the other self-consciousness, for it was aware of being in the other, it cancels this its own being in the other and thus lets the other again go free.

This process of self-consciousness in relation to another self-consciousness has in this manner been represented as the action of one alone. But this action on the part of the one has itself the double significance of being at once its own action and the action of that other as well. For the other is likewise independent, shut up within itself, and there is nothing in it which is not there through itself. The first does not have the object before it only in the passive form characteristic primarily of the object of desire, but as an object existing independently for itself, over which therefore it has no power to do anything for its own behoof, if that object does not *per se* do what the first does to it. The process then is absolutely the double process of both self-consciousnesses. Each sees the other do the same as itself; each itself does what it demands on the part of the other, and for that reason does what it does, only so far as the other does the same. Action from one side only would be useless, because what is to happen can only be brought about by means of both.

The action has then a *double entente* not only in the sense that it is an act done to itself as well as to the other, but also in the sense that the act *simpliciter* is the act of the one as well as of the other regardless of their distinction.

In this movement we see the process repeated which came before us as the play of forces; in the present case, however, it is found in consciousness. What in the former had effect only for us [contemplating experience], holds here for the terms themselves. The middle term is self-consciousness which breaks itself up into the extremes; and each extreme is this interchange of its own determinateness, and complete transition into the opposite. While *qua* consciousness, it no doubt comes outside itself, still, in being outside itself, it is at the same time restrained within itself, it exists for itself, and its self-externalization is for consciousness. *Consciousness* finds that it immediately is and is not another consciousness, as also that this other is for itself only when it cancels itself as existing for itself, and has self-existence only in the self-existence of the other. Each is the mediating term to the other, through which each mediates and unites itself with itself; and each is to itself and to the other an immediate self-existing reality, which, at the same time, exists thus for itself only through this mediation. They recognize themselves as mutually recognizing one another.

This pure conception of recognition, of duplication of self-consciousness within its unity, we must now consider in the way its process appears for self-consciousness. It will, in the first place, present the aspect of the disparity of the two, or the break-up of the middle term into the extremes, which, *qua* extremes, are opposed to one another, and of which one is merely recognized, while the other only recognizes.

Self-consciousness is primarily simple existence for self, self-identity by exclusion of every other from itself. It takes its essential nature and absolute object to be Ego; and in this immediacy, in this bare fact of its self-existence, it is individual. That which for it is other stands as unessential object, as object with the impress and character of negation. But the other is also a self-consciousness; an individual makes its appearance in antithesis to an individual. Appearing thus in their immediacy, they are for each other in the manner of ordinary objects. They are independent individual forms, modes of consciousness that have not risen above the bare level of life (for the existent object here has been determined as life). They are, moreover, forms of consciousness which have not yet accomplished for one another the process of absolute abstraction, of uprooting all immediate existence, and of being merely the bare, negative fact of self-identical consciousness; or, in other words, have not yet revealed themselves to each other as existing purely for themselves, i.e., as self-consciousness. Each is indeed certain of its own self, but not of the other, and hence its own certainty of itself is still without truth. For its truth would be merely that its own individual existence for itself would be shown to it to be an independent object, or, which is the same thing, that the object would be exhibited as this pure certainty of itself. By the notion of recognition, however, this is not possible, except in the form that as the other is for it, so it is for the other; each in its self through its own action and again through the action of the other achieves this pure abstraction of existence for self.

The presentation of itself, however, as pure abstraction of self-consciousness consists in showing itself as a pure negation of its objective form, or in showing that it is fettered to no determinate existence, that it is not bound at all by the particularity everywhere characteristic of existence as such, and is *not* tied up with life. The process of bringing all this out involves a twofold action—action on the part of the other and action on the part of itself. In so far as it is the other's action, each aims at the destruction and death of the other. But in this there is implicated also the second kind of action, self-activity; for the former implies that it risks its own life. The relation of both self-consciousnesses is in this way so constituted that they prove themselves and each other through a life-and-death struggle. They must enter into this struggle, for they must bring their certainty of themselves, the certainty of being for themselves, to the level of objective truth, and make this a fact both in the case of the other and in their own case as well. And it is solely by risking life that freedom is obtained; only thus is it tried and proved that the essential nature of self-consciousness is not bare existence, is not the merely immediate form in which it at first makes its appearance, is not its mere absorption in the expanse of life. Rather it is thereby guaranteed that there is nothing present but what might be taken as a vanishing moment—that self-consciousness is merely pure self-existence, being-for-self. The individual, who has not staked his life, may, no doubt, be recognized as a Person; but he has not attained the truth of this recognition as an independent self-consciousness. In the same way each must aim at the death of the other, as it risks its own life thereby; for that other is to it of no more worth than itself; the other's reality is presented to the former as an external other, as outside itself; it must cancel that externality. The other is a purely existent consciousness and entangled in manifold ways; it must view its otherness as pure existence for itself or as absolute negation.

This trial by death, however, cancels both the truth which was to result from it, and therewith the certainty of self altogether. For just as life is the natural "position" of consciousness, independence without absolute negativity, so death is the natural "negation" of consciousness, negation without independence, which thus remains without the requisite significance of actual recognition. Through death, doubtless, there has arisen the certainty that both did stake their life, and held it lightly both in their own case and in the case of the other; but that is not for those who underwent this struggle. They cancel their consciousness which had its place in this alien element of natural existence; in other words, they cancel themselves and are sublated as terms or extremes seeking to have existence on their own account. But along with this there vanishes from the play of change the essential moment, viz., that of breaking up into extremes with opposite characteristics; and the middle term collapses into a lifeless unity which is broken up into lifeless extremes, merely existent and not opposed. And the two do not mutually give and receive one another back from each other through consciousness; they let one another go quite indifferently, like things. Their act is abstract negation, not the negation characteristic of consciousness, which cancels in such a way that it preserves and maintains what is sublated, and thereby survives its being sublated.

In this experience self-consciousness becomes aware that *life* is as essential to it as pure self-consciousness. In immediate self-consciousness the simple ego is absolute object, which, however, is for us or in itself absolute mediation, and has as its essential moment substantial and solid independence. The dissolution of that simple unity is the result of the first experience; through this there is posited a pure self-consciousness, and a consciousness which is not purely for itself, but for another, i.e., as an existent consciousness, consciousness in the form and shape of thinghood. Both moments are essential, since, in the first instance, they are unlike and opposed, and their reflexion into unity has not yet come to light, they stand as two opposed forms or modes of consciousness. The one is independent, and its essential nature is to be for itself; the other is dependent, and its essence is life or existence for another. The former is the Master, or Lord, the latter the Bondsman.

The master is the consciousness that exists *for itself*; but no longer merely the general notion of existence for self. Rather, it is a consciousness existing on its own account which is mediated with itself through an other consciousness, i.e., through an other whose very nature implies that it is bound up with an independent being or with thinghood in general. The master brings himself into relation to both these moments, to a thing as such, the object of desire, and to the consciousness whose essential character is thinghood. And since the master, is *(a)* qua notion of self-consciousness, an immediate relation of self-existence, but *(b)* is now moreover at the same time mediation, or a being-for-self which is for itself only through an other—he [the master] stands in relation *(a)* immediately to both *(b)* mediately to each through the other. The master relates himself to the bondsman mediately through independent existence, for that is precisely what keeps the bondsman in thrall; it is his chain, from which he could not in the struggle get away, and for that reason he proved himself to be dependent, to have his independence in the shape of thinghood. The master, however, is the power controlling this state of existence, for he has shown in the struggle that he holds it to be merely something negative. Since he is the power dominating existence, while this existence again is the power controlling the other [the bondsman], the master holds, *par consequence,* this other in subordination. In the same way the master relates himself to the thing mediately through the bondsman. The bondsman being a self-consciousness in the broad sense, also takes up a negative attitude to things and cancels them; but the thing is, at the same time, independent for him, and, in consequence, he cannot, with all his negating, get so far as to annihilate it outright and be done with it; that is to say, he merely works on it. To the master, on the other hand, by means of this mediating process, belongs the immediate relation, in the sense of the pure negation of it, in other words he gets the enjoyment. What mere desire did not attain, he now succeeds in attaining, viz., to have done with the thing, and find satisfaction in enjoyment. Desire alone did not get the length of this, because of the independence of the thing. The master, however, who has interposed the bondsman between it and himself, thereby relates himself merely to the dependence of the thing, and enjoys it without qualification and without reserve. The aspect of its independence he leaves to the bondsman, who labours upon it.

In these two moments, the master gets his recognition through an other consciousness, for in them the latter affirms itself as unessential, both by working upon the thing, and, on the other hand, by the fact of being dependent on a determinate existence; in neither case can this other get the mastery over existence, and succeed in absolutely negating it. We have thus here this moment of recognition, viz., that the other consciousness cancels itself as self-existent, and, *ipso facto*, itself does what the first does to it. In the same way we have the other moment, that this action on the part of the second is the action proper of the first; for what is done by the bondsman is properly an action on the part of the master. The latter exists only for himself, that is his essential nature; he is the negative power without qualification, a power to which the thing is naught. And he is thus the absolutely essential act in this situation, while the bondsman is not so, he is an unessential activity. But for recognition proper there is needed the moment that what the master does to the other he should also do to himself, and what the bondsman does to himself, he should do to the other also. On that account a form of recognition has arisen that is one sided and unequal.

In all this, the unessential consciousness is, for the master, the object which embodies the truth of his certainty of himself. But it is evident that this object does not correspond to its notion; for, just where the master has effectively achieved lordship, he really finds that something has come about quite different from an independent consciousness. It is not an independent, but rather a dependent consciousness that he has achieved. He is thus not assured of self-existence as his truth; he finds that his truth is rather the unessential consciousness, and the fortuitous unessential action of that consciousness.

The truth of the independent consciousness is accordingly the consciousness of the bondsman. This doubtless appears in the first instance outside itself, and not as the truth of self-consciousness. But just as lordship showed its essential nature to be the reverse of what it wants to be, so, too, bondage will, when completed, pass into the opposite of what it immediately is: being a consciousness repressed within itself, it will enter into itself, and change round into real and true independence.

We have seen what bondage is only in relation to lordship. But it is a self-consciousness, and we have now to consider what it is, in this regard, in and for itself. In the first instance, the master is taken to be the essential reality for the state of bondage; hence, for it, the truth is the independent consciousness existing for itself, although this truth is not taken yet as inherent in bondage itself. Still, it does in fact contain within itself this truth of pure negativity and self-existence, because it has experienced this reality within it. For this consciousness was not in peril and fear for this element or that, nor for this or that moment of time, it was afraid for its entire being; it felt the fear of death, the sovereign master. It has been in that experience melted to its inmost soul, has trembled throughout its every fiber, and all that was fixed and steadfast has quaked within it. This complete perturbation of its entire substance, this absolute dissolution of all its stability into fluent continuity, is, however, the simple, ultimate nature of self-consciousness, absolute negativity, pure self-referrent existence, which consequently is involved in this type of consciousness. This moment of pure self-existence is moreover a fact for it; for in the master it finds this as its object. Further, this bondsman's consciousness is not only this total dissolution in a general way; in serving and toiling the bondsman actually carries this out. By serving he cancels in every particular aspect his dependence on and attachment to natural existence, and by his work removes this existence away.

The feeling of absolute power, however, realized both in general and in the particular form of service, is only dissolution implicitly; and albeit the fear of the lord is the beginning of wisdom, consciousness is not therein aware of being self-existent. Through work and labour, however, this consciousness of the bondsman comes to itself. In the moment which corresponds to desire in the case of the master's consciousness, the aspect of the non-essential relation to the thing seemed to fall to the lot of the servant, since the thing there retained its independence. Desire has reserved to itself the pure negating of the object and thereby unalloyed feeling of self. This satisfaction, however, just for that reason is itself only a state of evanescence, for it lacks objectivity or subsistence. Labour, on the other hand, is desire restrained and checked, evanescence delayed and postponed; in other words, labour shapes and fashions the thing. The negative relation to the object passes into the *form* of the object, into something that is permanent and remains; because it is just for the labourer that the object has independence. This negative mediating agency, this activity giving shape and form, is at the same time the individual existence, the pure self-existence of that consciousness, which now in the work it does is externalized and passes into the condition of permanence. The consciousness that toils and serves accordingly attains by this means the direct apprehension of that independent being as its self.

But again, shaping or forming the object has not only the positive significance that the bondsman becomes thereby aware of himself as factually and objectively self-existent; this type of consciousness has also a negative import, in contrast with its first moment, the element of fear. For in shaping the thing it only becomes aware of its own proper negativity, its existence on its own account, as an object, through the fact that it cancels the actual form confronting it. But this objective negative element is precisely the alien, external reality, before which it trembled. Now, however, it destroys this extraneous alien negative, affirms and sets itself up as a negative in the element of permanence, and thereby becomes for itself a self-existent being. In the master, the bondsman feels self-existence to be something external, an objective fact; in fear self-existence is present within himself; in fashioning the thing, self-existence comes to be felt explicitly as his own proper being, and he attains the consciousness that he himself exists in its own right and on its own account (*an und für sich*). By the fact that the form is objectified, it does not become something other than the consciousness moulding the thing through work; for just that form is his pure self-existence, which therein becomes truly realized. Thus precisely in labour where there seemed to be merely some outsider's mind and ideas involved, the bondsman becomes aware, through this re-discovery of himself by himself, of having and being a "mind of his own."

For this reflexion of self into self the two moments, fear and service in general, as also that of formative activity, are necessary: and at the same time both must exist in a universal manner. Without the discipline of service and obedience, fear remains formal and does not spread over the whole known reality of existence. Without the formative activity shaping the thing, fear remains inward and mute, and consciousness does not become objective for itself. Should consciousness shape and form the thing without the initial state of absolute fear, then it has a merely vain and futile "mind of its own"; for its form or negativity is not negativity *per se*, and hence its formative activity cannot furnish the consciousness of itself as essentially real. If it has endured not absolute fear, but merely some slight anxiety, the negative reality has remained external to it, its substance has not been through and through infected thereby. Since the entire content of its natural consciousness has not tottered and shaken, it is still inherently a determinate mode of being; having a "mind of its own" (*der eigene Sinn*) is simply stubbornness (*Eigensinn*), a type of freedom which does not get beyond the attitude of bondage. As little as the pure form can become its essential nature, so little is that form, considered as extending over particulars, a universal formative activity, an absolute notion; it is rather a piece of cleverness which has mastery within a certain range, but not over the universal power nor over the entire objective reality.

THE REALIZATION OF RATIONAL SELF-CONSCIOUSNESS

Self-consciousness found the "thing" in the form of itself, and itself in the form of a thing; that is to say, self-consciousness is explicitly aware of being in itself the objective reality. It is no longer the *immediate* certainty of being all reality; it is rather a kind of certainty for which the immediate in general assumes the form of something sublated, so that the objectivity of the immediate is regarded now merely as something superficial whose inner core and essence is self-conscious consciousness.

The object, therefore, to which self-consciousness is positively related, is a self-consciousness. The object has the form and character of thinghood, i.e., is independent: but self-consciousness has the conviction that this independent object is not alien to itself; it knows herewith that itself is inherently *(an sich)* recognized by the object. Self-consciousness is mind, which has the assurance of having, in the duplication of its self-consciousness and in the independence of both, its unity with its own self. This certainty has to be brought out now before the mind in all its truth; what self-consciousness holds as a fact, viz., that implicitly *in* itself and in its *inner* certainty it *is*, has to enter into its consciousness and become explicit *for* it.

What the general stages of this actualization will be can be indicated in a general way by reference to the road thus far traversed. Just as reason, when exercised in observation, repeated in the medium of the category the movement of "consciousness" as such, namely, sense-certainty,* perception,† and understanding,‡ the course of reason here, too, will again traverse the double movement of "self-consciousness," and from independence pass over into its freedom. To begin with, this active reason is aware of itself merely as "an individual," and must, being such, demand and bring forth its reality in an "other." Thereafter, however, its consciousness being lifted into universality, it becomes *universal* reason, and is consciously aware of itself as reason, as something already recognized in and for

SOURCE: *Phenomenology.* pp. 374-382. Reprinted by permission of George Allen & Unwin Ltd., London.

*Viz., in descriptive observation of nature as such.

†Viz., in observation of living nature, the "organic."

‡Viz., in observation of nature as the external reality of mind, laws of thought, psychology, physiognomy, phrenology.

itself, which within its pure consciousness unites all self-consciousness. It is the simple ultimate spiritual realty *(Wesen)*, which, by coming at the same time to consciousness, is the real substance, into which preceding forms return and in which they find their ground, so that they are, as contrasted with reference to the latter, merely particular moments of the process of its coming into being, moments which indeed break loose and appear as forms on their own account, but have in fact only existence and actuality when borne and supported by it, and only retain their truth in so far as they are and remain in it.

If we take this final result of the process as it is when really accomplished—this end, which is the notion that has already become manifest before us, viz., recognized self-consciousness, which has the certainty of itself in the other free self-consciousness and finds its truth precisely there; in other words, if we bring this still inward and unevolved mind to light as the substance that has developed into its concrete existence—we shall find that in this notion there is opened up the realm of the Social Order, the Ethical World *(Sittlichkeit)*. For this latter is nothing else than the absolute spiritual unity of the essential substance *(Wesen)* of individuals in their independent reality; it is an inherently universal self-consciousness, which is aware of being so concrete and real in an other consciousnes₃, that this latter has complete independence, is looked on as a "thing," and the universal self-consciousness is aware precisely therein of its unity with that "thing," and is only then self-consciousness, when thus in unity with this objective being *(Wesen)*. This ethical substance when taken in its abstract universality is only the conception of law, thought-constituted law; but just as much it is immediately actual self-consciousness, it is Custom *(Sitte)*. The single individual conversely is only a "this," a given existent unit, in so far as he is aware of the universal consciousness as his own being in his own particular individuality, seeing that his action and existence are the universal custom.

In point of fact the notion of the realization of self-conscious reason—of directly apprehending complete unity with another in his independence: of having for my object an other in the fashion of a "thing" found detached and apart from me, and the negative of myself, and of taking this as my own self-existence *(Fürmichseyn)*—finds its complete reality in fulfilment in the life of a nation. Reason appears here as the fluent universal substance, as unchangeable simple thinghood which yet breaks up into many entirely independent

beings, just as light bursts asunder into stars as innumerable lumi-
nous points, each giving light on its own account, and whose absolute
self-existence (*Fürsichseyn*) is dissolved, not merely implicitly (*an sich*),
but explicitly for themselves (*für sich*), within the simple independent
substance. They are conscious within themselves of being these individual independent beings through the fact that they surrender and
sacrifice their particular individuality, and that this universal substance is their soul and essence—as this universal again is the action
of themselves as individuals, and is the work and product of their own
activity.

The purely particular activity and business of the individual refer
to needs which he has as a part of nature, i.e., as a mere existent
particular. That even these, its commonest functions, do not come to
nothing, but have reality, is brought about by the universal sustaining
medium, the might of the entire nation.

It is not merely, however, this *form* of subsistence for his activity in
general that the individual gets in the universal substance, but likewise also his *content;* what he does is what all are capable of doing, is
the custom all follow. This content, in so far as it is completely
particularized, is, in its concrete reality, confined within the limits of
the activity of all. The labour of the individual for his own wants is
just as much a satisfaction of those of others as of himself, and the
satisfaction of his own he attains only by the labour of others.

As the individual in his own particular work *ipso facto* accomplishes
unconsciously a universal work, so again he also performs the universal task as his *conscious* object. The whole becomes *in its entirety* his
work, for which he sacrifices himself, and precisely by that means
receives back his own self from it.

There is nothing here which may not be reciprocal, nothing in
regard to which the independence of the individual may not, in dis-
sipating its existence on its own account (*Fürsichseyn*), in negating
itself, give itself its positive significance of existing for itself. This
unity of existing for another, or making self a "thing," and of existence for self, this universal substance, utters its universal language
in the *customs* and *laws* of a* nation. But this existent unchangeable
nature (*Wesen*) is nothing else than the expression of the particular
individuality which seems opposed to it: the laws give expression to
that which each individual is and does; the individual knows them not

*The first and succeeding editions read "*seines*" Volks: Lasson proposes
"*eines.*" This seems correct in the context.

merely to be what constitutes his universal objective nature as a "thing," but knows himself, too, in that form, or knows it to be particularized in his own individuality and in each of his fellow-citizens. In the universal mind, therefore, each has the certainty only of himself, the certainty of finding in the actual reality nothing but himself; he is as certain of the others as of himself. I apprehend and see in all of them that they are in their own eyes (für sich selbst) only these independent beings just as I am. I see in their case the free unity with others in such wise that just as this unity exists through me, so it exists through the others too—I see them as myself, myself as them.

In a free nation, therefore, reason is in truth realized. It is a present living spirit, where the individual not only finds his destiny (Bestimmung), i.e., his universal and particular nature (Wesen), expressed and given to him in the fashion of a thing, but himself is this essential being, and has also attained his destiny. The wisest men of antiquity for that reason declared that wisdom and virtue consist in living in accordance with the customs of one's own nation.

From this happy state, however, of having attained its destiny, and of living in it, the self-consciousness, which in the first instance is only immediately and in principle spirit, has broken away; or perhaps it has not yet attained it; for both can be said with equal truth.

Reason must pass out of and leave this happy condition. For only implicitly or immediately is the life of a free nation the real objective ethical order (Sittlichkeit). In other words, the latter is an existent social order, and in consequence this universal mind is also an individualized mind. It is the totality of customs and laws of a particular people, a specifically determinate ethical substance, which casts off this limitation only when it reaches the higher moment, namely, when it becomes conscious regarding its own nature; only with this knowledge does it get its absolute truth, and not as it is immediately in its bare existence. In this latter form it is, on the one hand, a restricted ethical substance, on the other, absolute limitation consists just in this that mind is in the form of existence.

Hence, further, the individual, as he immediately finds his existence in the actual objective social order, in the life of his nation, has a solid imperturbable confidence; the universal mind has not for him resolved itself into its abstract moments, and thus, too, he does not think of himself as existing in singleness and independence. When however he has once arrived at this knowledge, as indeed he must, this immediate unity with mind, this undifferentiated existence in the substance of mind, his naïve confidence, is lost. Isolated by himself he is himself now the central essential reality—no longer universal mind. The *element* of *this* singleness of self-consciousness is no doubt in universal mind itself, but merely as a vanishing quantity, which, as it appears with an existence of its own, is straightway resolved within the universal, and only becomes consciously felt in the form of that confidence. When the individual gets fixity in the form of singleness (and every moment, being a moment of the essential reality, must manage to reveal itself as essential), the individual has thereby set himself over against the laws and customs. These latter are looked on as merely a thought without absolutely essential significance, an abstract theory without reality; while he *qua* this particular ego is in his own view the living truth.

Or, again [we can say, as above stated, that] self-consciousness has *not yet attained* this happy state of being ethical substance, the spirit of a people. For, after leaving the process of rational Observation, mind, at first, is not yet as such actually realized through itself; it is merely affirmed as *inner* nature and essence, or as abstraction. In other words, mind is first immediate. As immediately existing, however, it is individualized. It is *practical consciousness*, which steps into the world it finds lying ready-made with the intention of duplicating itself in the determinate form of an individual, of producing itself as this particular individual, and creating this its own existential counterpart, and thus becoming conscious of this unity of its own actual reality with the objective world. Self-consciousness possesses the *certainty* of this unity; it holds that the unity is implicitly *(an sich)* already present, or that this union and agreement between itself and "thinghood" (objective existence) is already an accomplished fact, and has only to become expressly so for it through its own agency; or that its making that unity is at the same time and as much its finding the unity. Since this unity means happiness, the individual is thus sent forth into the world by his own spirit to seek his happiness.

If, then, we for our part find the truth of this rational self-consciousness to be ethical substance, that self-consciousness on its part finds here the beginning of its ethical experience of the world. From the point of view that it has not yet attained to its ethical substance, this movement presses onwards to that end, and what is cancelled in the process are the particular moments which self-consciousness takes as valid in isolation. They have the form of an immediate will-process, or impulse of nature, which attains its satisfaction, this satisfaction itself being the content of a new impulse. Looking at self-consciousness, however, as having lost the happiness of being in the substance, these natural impulses are bound up with a consciousness that their purpose is the true destiny and essential nature of self-consciousness. Ethical substance has sunk to the level of a floating selfless adjective, whose living subjects are individuals, which have to fill up their universality through themselves, and to provide for their destiny out of the same source.

Taken in the former sense, then, those forms and modes are the process by which the ethical substance comes to be, and precede this substance: in the latter they succeed it, and disclose for self-consciousness what its destined nature is. In the former aspect the immediacy or raw brute impulses get lost in the process of finding out what their truth is, and their content passes over to a higher. In the latter aspect, however, the false idea of consciousness, which puts its characteristic nature in those impulses, passes to a higher idea. In the former case the goal which they attain is the immediate ethical substance; while, in the latter, the end is the consciousness of that substance, such a consciousness as knows the substance to be its own essential being; and to that extent this process would be the development of morality (*Moralität*), a higher state or attitude than the former (*Sittlichkeit*). But these modes at the same time constitute only one side of the development of morality, that, namely, which belongs to self-existence, or in which consciousness cancels *its* purposes; they do not constitute the side where morality arises out of the substance itself. Since these moments cannot yet have the signification of being made into purposes in opposition to the lost social order (*Sittlichkeit*), they hold here no doubt in their simple uncriticized content, and the end towards which they work is the ethical substance; but since with our time is more directly associated that form of these moments in which they appear after consciousness has lost its ethical custom-constituted (*sittliches*) life, and in the search for it repeats those forms, they may be represented more after this latter manner of expression.

Self-consciousness, which is as yet merely the notion of mind, takes this path with the specific characteristic of being to itself the essential reality *qua* individual mind, and its purpose, therefore, is to give itself actualization as individual, and to enjoy itself, *qua* individual, in so doing.

In existing for itself it is aware of itself as the essentially real. In this character it is the negativity of the other. There arises, therefore, within its consciousness an opposition between itself *qua* positive and something which no doubt exists, but *for it* not in the sense of existing substantially. Consciousness appears sundered into this objective reality found lying at its hand, and the purpose, which it carries out by the process of cancelling that objectivity, and which it makes the actual fact instead of the given object. Its primary purpose, however, is its immediate abstract existence for itself, in other words seeing itself as this particular individual in another, or seeing another self-consciousness as itself. The experience of what the truth of this purpose is, places self-consciousness on a higher plane, and henceforth it is to itself purpose, in so far as it is at once universal, and has the law immediately within it. In carrying out this law of its heart, however, it learns that here the individual cannot preserve himself, but rather the good can only be performed through the sacrifice of the individual: and so it passes into *Virtue*. The experience which virtue goes through can be no other than that of finding that its purpose is already implicitly *(an sich)* carried out, that happiness lies immediately in action itself, and action itself is the good. The principle or notion of this entire sphere of experience—viz., that "thinghood" is the independent self-existence of mind—becomes in the course of this experience an objective fact *for* self-consciousness. In that self-consciousness has found this principle, it is aware of itself as reality in the sense of directly self-expressing *Individuality*, which no longer finds any resistance in a reality opposed to it, and whose object and purpose are merely this function of self-expression.

III

Dialectic and the Science of Logic

Hegel's *Science of Logic* is a work, which lacking an understanding of, no one can claim to be a true Hegelian. This perhaps explains why there are so few true Hegelians. Its difficulty among Hegelian texts is rivaled only by the *Phenomenology*, and in the latter, while the progress of the dialectic is often obscure, the terrain of human experience is at least recognizable. But in the *Logic*, which Hegel says "constitutes metaphysics proper or purely speculative philosophy,"[1] we take leave of the terra firma of earthly experience, and with the *Phenomenology* as a launching pad, enter a "realm of shadows, the world of simple essentialities freed from all sensuous concreteness."[2] But this liberation from the empirically real is no flight of abstraction; nor does its freedom from the phenomenal opposition of consciousness imply a retreat into a formalism lacking significant truth. The content of pure science, Hegel says, is objective thinking *par excellence*, a thinking which has not an other for its object, but its own self:

Consequently, far from it being formal, far from it standing in need of a matter to constitute an actual and true cognition, it is its content alone which has absolute truth, or, if one still wanted to employ the word matter, it is the veritable matter—but a matter which is not external to the form, since this matter is rather pure thought and hence the absolute form itself. Accordingly, logic is to be understood as the system of pure reason, as the realm of pure thought. This realm is truth as it is without veil and in its own absolute nature. It can therefore be said that this content is the exposition of God as he is in his eternal essence before the creation of nature and a finite mind.[3]

Hegel's *Logic* is thus abstract in the sense that it provides only the foundations of the absolute knowledge attained at the close of the

Phenomenology and only fully mediated in the *Philosophy of Nature* and the *Philosophy of Spirit*. Hegel's *Logic* thus compares in important respects with Aristotle's *Metaphysics*, Kant's *Critique of Pure Reason*, and Plato's *Parmenides*. It differs from the *Metaphysics* in that the categories are dialectically related and developed into a coherent whole, and from Kant in that these categories are transcendentally deduced as the a priori* conditions not only of our knowledge of the world, but of that world itself, i.e., of *true* knowledge, "the science of things set and held in thoughts."⁴ Kant's critical philosophy, Hegel remarks, had already turned metaphysics into logic:

but it . . . was overawed by the object, and so the logical determinations were given an essentially subjective significance with the result that [it] remained burdened with the object [it] had avoided and [was] left with the residue of a thing-in-itself, an infinite obstacle, as a beyond. . . . The Platonic Idea [on the other hand] is the universal, or more definitely the Notion of an object; only in its *Notion* does something possess actuality and to the extent that it is distinct from its Notion it ceases to be actual and is a non-entity.⁵

If the totality of the universe were viewed as a vast puzzle of inter-locking pieces, Hegel's *Logic* would be its pure form, the essential structure and method governing the articulation of the pieces qua organic parts and in such a way that they constitute that universe not as a puzzle, but as a whole. The *Phenomenology*, by contrast, describes the quasi-temporal process by which the typified individual, unmind-ful of that overall structure or form, receives the pieces and struggles to put them together. Of course, for Hegel, the individual is himself both one of the pieces and the whole, and thus his putting the puzzle together is his own construction of himself, his self-development, self-determination, and freedom. The initial fragmented "self" at first appears lost and merely contingent; it constructs its world about it and out of its own negativity, in more and more comprehensive (and thus less and less contingent) shapes, segments, or wholes. The absolute whole, however, does not come to be; it *is*. But it comes to be for us, i.e., it appears, but its ways of appearing are not for us, but only for itself, science, and from the standpoint of science they cease to be merely ways of appearing. "Pure knowing as concentrated into this unity has sublated all reference to an other and to mediation; it is without any distinction and as thus distinctionless, ceases itself to be knowledge; what is present is only *simple immediacy*. . . . This simple

*But "a priori" does not have the same significance here for Hegel as it does for Kant who, in the *Critique of Pure Reason*, is still laboring under the sense-thought dualism inherited from Hume.

immediacy, therefore, in its true expression is *pure being.*"[6] The category of pure being thus initiates Hegel's *scientific* reconstruction of the whole. "Hitherto *we* have had the Idea in development through its various grades as *our* object, but now the Idea comes to be its *own* object. This," Hegel adds significantly, "is the νόησις νοήσεως which Aristotle long ago termed the supreme form of the Idea."[7] The obliteration of the opposition of consciousness, however, results not in a new object, but rather in a transformation or reconstruction of the whole process culminating in this result. Hegel's tripartite system, the philosophical sciences of Logic, Nature, and Spirit, presents this transfigured whole, as the phrase is, *sub specie aeternitatis.*

With respect to our analogy of the puzzle, the individual, having completed it, now surveys the phenomenological, temporal, trial-and-error and mistake-ridden route in a new light, that of the design or εἶδος of the work, in terms of which its fragmentation and uncertainty are *no longer factors.* They are no longer factors because they are products of the rift between subjectivity and objectivity, form and content, which is overcome in absolute (philosophic) knowing. What *is* a factor is the *philosophical,* i.e., logical articulation of the whole in its absolute character, which "begins" at the absolute beginning, pure being, the first category or notion of the *Science of Logic,* and "ends" at the absolute end, philosophy, the last moment of Absolute Spirit at the close of the *Encyclopaedia,* "the one single aim, action and goal" of which is "to arrive at the notion of its notion, and thus secure its return and its satisfaction."[8] Philosophy, then, is nothing more than the reconstruction and *rational* articulation of the universe of experience by the philosophical sciences outlined in the *Encyclopaedia.*

Hegel's *Logic,* like that of Aristotle, is likely to remain unintelligible to the contemporary reader until the general character of this Hegelian universe comes into focus.[9] "It is only after profounder acquaintance with the other sciences [which are themselves, and after the manner of Plato's divided line "abstracted" from the fluxing content of the empirical world] that logic ceases to be for subjective spirit a merely abstract universal and reveals itself as the [concrete] universal that embraces within itself the wealth of the particular."[10]

When contrasted with the wealth of the world as pictorially conceived, with the apparently real content of the other sciences, and compared with the promise of absolute science to unveil the essential being of this wealth . . . then this science in its abstract shape, in the colourless, cold simplicity of its pure determinations looks as if it could achieve anything sooner than the fulfilment of its promise and seems to confront that richness as an empty, insubstantial form.[11]

But the business of logic, Hegel says, is to show that this content and the thoughts of it, "which as usually employed merely float before consciousness neither understood nor demonstrated, are really grades in the self-determination of thought."[12]

The aim of knowledge is to divest the objective world that stands opposed to us of its strangeness, and, as the phrase is, to find ourselves at home in it: which means no more than to trace the objective world back to the notion,— to our innermost self.[13]

It remains, of course, for Hegel's exposition of logic to show that his construal of things, indeed those things themselves, necessitates and justifies such an exposition. No part of Hegel's system stands on its own, and the notional skeleton of the *Logic* remains to be filled out by the second and third parts of the *Encyclopaedia*, the sciences of Nature and Spirit.

Hegel's *Logic* has had a less dramatic effect upon subsequent thought than his *Phenomenology*. The British Hegelians however, e.g., Bradley and Bosanquet, have emulated Hegel's ontologic in their own work. Sartre, again, was greatly concerned with the dialectic of "Being" (one of our selections) in his own *Being and Nothingness*.[14]

In the first selection here in chapter III, on "Understanding (*Verstand*) and Dialectic," from the "Smaller Logic,"* we have Hegel's briefest account of how doubtful thought (dialectic) forces us to abandon the standpoint of ordinary Understanding (*Verstand*) with its abstract either-or attitude. The second selection, from the "Larger Logic," is really a pioneering work, out of which has developed the whole analytical approach of modern existentialist scepticism. It is in Hegel's discussion of the question "With What Must Science Begin?" that a student usually discovers whether he can move comfortably forward into the rest of Hegel's philosophy. Some students of this part of Hegel have concluded that philosophical science not only begins where Hegel says it begins—in the dissolving dialectic of doubt—but also ends there.

For such students, the transition to the third selection in this chapter, "First Subdivision of Logic: The 'Doctrine of Being,' " is extremely difficult, if not impossible. But once one plunges into it (as

*"Smaller Logic" designates the first part of Hegel's *Encyclopaedia*; the "Larger Logic" is the *Science of Logic* of 1812–1816, an expanded version of the "Smaller (or Lesser) Logic." *Science of Logic* designates either.

we hope the reader of this book will) one is apt to be wrapped up in the highest kind of intellectual excitement. Hegel there explores with rigorous reasoning how our minds "eat up" and digest the fixed being of the objects of knowledge, almost in the same way that we eat and digest an apple to nourish ourselves. The ancient Eleatics, of whom the greatest was Parmenides, argued that Being, changeless and eternal, is the sole true object of knowledge, and that the ultimate common denominator of "all that is" is nothing. What abides? Parmenides asked. His answer was that nothing, insofar as there *is* such a thing as nothing, abides. Yet, Heraclitus came along to show that "nothing abides" has an obvious double sense. Hegel explores that double sense of Being, showing how Being, as a living thought, forces us by dialectic to identify it first with "nothing," and then with the synthesis of the two which is "becoming."

Notes. Dialectic and the *Science of Logic*

1. *Logic*, Miller, p. 27.
2. Ibid., p. 58.
3. Ibid., pp. 49–50.
4. *Logic*, Wallace, p. 45.
5. *Logic*, Miller, p. 51.
6. Ibid., p. 69.
7. *Logic*, Wallace, p. 374.
8. Ibid., p. 28.
9. G.R.G. Mure, *Aristotle* (New York: Oxford University Press, 1964), p. v.
10. *Logic*, Miller, p. 58.
11. Ibid., pp. 57–58. This passage and the whole of Hegel's *Logic* finds poetical expression in Keats's "Ode on a Grecian Urn" from which we quote:

> Thou still unravished bride of quietness,
>   Thou foster-child of Silence and slow Time,
> Sylvan historian, who canst thus express
>   A flowery tale more sweetly than our rhyme . . .
>
> Heard melodies are sweet, but those unheard
>   Are sweeter; therefore, ye soft pipes, play on;

Not to the sensual ear, but, more endeared,
  Pipe to the spirit ditties of no tone . . .

O Attic shape! Fair attitude! with brede
  Of marble men and maidens overwrought,
With forest branches and trodden weed;
  Thou, silent form! dost tease us out of thought
As doth eternity: Cold Pastoral!
  When old age shall this generation waste,
Thou shalt remain, in midst of other woe
  Than ours, a friend to man, to whom thou say'st,
"Beauty is truth, truth beauty,"—that is all
  Ye know on earth, and all ye need to know.

12. *Logic*, Wallace, p. 226.
13. Ibid., p. 335.
14. See especially, Klaus Hartmann, *Sartre's Ontology: A Study of Being and Nothingness in the Light of Hegel's Logic* (Evanston: Northwestern University Press, 1966).

UNDERSTANDING (*VERSTAND*) AND DIALECTIC

79. In point of form Logical doctrine has three sides: (α) the Abstract side, or that of understanding: (β) the Dialectical, or that of negative reason: (γ) the Speculative, or that of positive reason.

These three sides do not make three *parts* of logic, but are stages or "moments" in every logical entity, that is, of every notion and truth whatever. They may all be put under the first stage, that of understanding, and so kept isolated from each other; but this would give an inadequate conception of them. The statement of the dividing lines and the characteristic aspects of logic is at this point no more than historical and anticipatory.

80. (α) Thought, as *Understanding*, sticks to fixity of characters and their distinctness from one another: every such limited abstract it treats as having a subsistence and being of its own.

Zusatz. In our ordinary usage of the term thought and even notion, we often have before our eyes nothing more than the operation of Understanding. And no doubt thought is primarily an exercise of Understanding: only it goes further, and the notion is not a function of Understanding merely. The action of Understanding may be in general described as investing its subject-matter with the form of universality. But this universal is an abstract universal: that is to say, its opposition to the particular is so rigorously maintained, that it is at the same time also reduced to the character of a particular again. In this separating and abstracting attitude towards its objects, Understanding is the reverse of immediate perception and sensation, which, as such, keep completely to their native sphere of action in the concrete.

It is by referring to this opposition of Understanding to sensation or feeling that we must explain the frequent attacks made upon thought for being hard and narrow, and for leading, if consistently developed, to ruinous and pernicious results. The answer to these charges, in so far as they are warranted by their facts, is, that they do not touch thinking in general, certainly not the thinking of Reason, but only the exercise of Understanding. It must be added however, that the merit and rights of the mere Understanding should un-

SOURCE: *Logic*, Wallace, pp. 143–155.

hesitatingly be admitted. And that merit lies in the fact, that apart from Understanding there is no fixity or accuracy in the region either of theory or of practice.

Thus, in theory, knowledge begins by apprehending existing objects in their specific differences. In the study of nature, for example, we distinguish matters, forces, genera, and the like, and stereotype each in its isolation. Thought is here acting in its analytic capacity, where its canon is identity, a simple reference of each attribute to itself. It is under the guidance of the same identity that the process in knowledge is effected from one scientific truth to another. Thus, for example, in mathematics magnitude is the feature which, to the neglect of any other, determines our advance. Hence in geometry we compare one figure with another, so as to bring out their identity. Similarly in other fields of knowledge, such as jurisprudence, the advance is primarily regulated by identity. In it we argue from one specific law or precedent to another: and what is this but to proceed on the principle of identity?

But Understanding is as indispensable in practice as it is in theory. Character is an essential in conduct, and a man of character is an understanding man, who in that capacity has definite ends in view and undeviatingly pursues them. The man who will do something great must learn, as Goethe says, to limit himself. The man who, on the contrary, would do everything, really would do nothing, and fails. There is a host of interesting things in the world: Spanish poetry, chemistry, politics, and music are all very interesting, and if any one takes an interest in them we need not find fault. But for a person in a given situation to accomplish anything, he must stick to one definite point, and not dissipate his forces in many directions. In every calling, too, the great thing is to pursue it with understanding. Thus the judge must stick to the law, and give his verdict in accordance with it, undeterred by one motive or another, allowing no excuses, and looking neither left nor right. Understanding, too, is always an element in thorough training. The trained intellect is not satisfied with cloudy and indefinite impressions, but grasps the objects in their fixed character: whereas the uncultivated man wavers unsettled, and it often costs a deal of trouble to come to an understanding with him on the matter under discussion, and to bring him to fix his eye on the definite point in question.

It has been already explained that the Logical principle in general, far from being merely a subjective action in our minds, is rather the very universal, which as such is also objective. This doctrine is illustrated in the case of understanding, the first form of logical truths. Understanding in this larger sense corresponds to what we call the goodness of God, so far as that means that finite things are and subsist. In nature, for example, we recognise the goodness of God in the fact that the various classes or species of animals and plants are provided with whatever they need for their preservation and welfare. Nor is man excepted, who, both as an individual and as a nation, possesses partly in the given circumstances of climate, of quality and products of soil, and partly in his natural parts or talents, all that is required for his maintenance and development. Under this shape Understanding is visible in every department of the objective world; and no object in that world can ever be wholly perfect which does not give full satisfaction to the canons of understanding. A state, for example, is imperfect, so long as it has not reached a clear differentiation of orders and callings, and so long as those functions of politics and government, which are different in principle, have not evolved for themselves special organs, in the same way as we see, for example, the developed animal organism provided with separate organs for the functions of sensation, motion, digestion, &c.

The previous course of the discussion may serve to show, that understanding is indispensable even in those spheres and regions of action which the popular fancy would deem furthest from it, and that in proportion as understanding is absent from them, imperfection is the result. This particularly holds good of Art, Religion, and Philosophy. In Art, for example, understanding is visible where the forms of beauty, which differ in principle, are kept distinct and exhibited in their purity. The same thing holds good also of single works of art. It is part of the beauty and perfection of a dramatic poem that the characters of the several persons should be closely and faithfully maintained, and that the different aims and interests involved should be plainly and decidedly exhibited. Or again, take the province of Religion. The superiority of Greek over Northern mythology (apart from other differences of subject-matter and conception) mainly consists in this: that in the former the individual gods are fashioned into forms of sculpture-like distinctness of outline, while in the latter the figures fade away vaguely and hazily into one another. Lastly comes Philosophy. That Philosophy never can get on without the understanding hardly calls for special remark after what has been said. Its foremost requirement is that every thought shall be grasped in its full precision, and nothing allowed to remain vague and indefinite.

It is usually added that understanding must not go too far. Which is so far correct, that understanding is not an ultimate, but on the contrary finite, and so constituted that when carried to extremes it veers round to its opposite. It is the fashion of youth to dash about in abstractions: but the man who has learnt to know life steers clear of the abstract "either-or," and keeps to the concrete. End *Zusatz.*

81. (β) In the Dialectical stage these finite characterisations or formulae supersede themselves, and pass into their opposites.

(1) But when the Dialectical principle is employed by the understanding separately and independently, especially as seen in its application to philosophical theories, Dialectic becomes Scepticism; in which the result that ensues from its action is presented as a mere negation.

(2) It is customary to treat Dialectic as an adventitious art, which for very wantonness introduces confusion and a mere semblance of contradiction into definite notions. And in that light, the semblance is the nonentity, while the true reality is supposed to belong to the original dicta of understanding. Often, indeed, Dialectic is nothing more than a subjective seesaw of arguments *pro* and *con*, where the absence of sterling thought is disguised by the subtlety which gives birth to such arguments. But in its true and proper character, Dialectic is the very nature and essence of everything predicated by mere understanding—the law of things and of the finite as a whole. Dialectic is different from "Reflection." In the first instance, Reflection is that movement out beyond the isolated predicate of a thing which gives it some reference, and brings out its relativity, while still in other respects leaving it its isolated validity. But by Dialectic is meant the indwelling tendency outwards by which the one-sidedness and limitation of the predicates of understanding is seen in its true light, and shown to be the negation of them. For anything to be finite is just to suppress itself and put itself aside. Thus understood the Dialectical principle constitutes the life and soul of scientific progress, the dynamic which alone gives immanent connexion and necessity to the body of science; and, in a word, is seen to constitute the real and true, as opposed to the external, exaltation above the finite.

Zusatz. 1. It is of the highest importance to ascertain and understand rightly the nature of Dialectic. Wherever there is movement, wherever there is life, wherever anything is carried into effect in the actual world, there Dialectic is at work. It is also the soul of all knowledge which is truly scientific. In the popular way of looking at things, the refusal to be bound by the abstract deliverances of understanding appears as fairness, which, according to the proverb Live and let live, demands that each should have its turn; we admit the one, but we admit the other also. But when we look more closely, we find that the limitations of the finite do not merely come from without; that its own nature is the cause of its abrogation, and that by its own act it passes into its counterpart. We say, for instance, that man is mortal, and seem to think that the ground of his death is in external circumstances only; so that if this way of looking were correct, man would have two special properties, vitality and—also—mortality. But the true view of the matter is that life, as life, involves the germ of death, and that the finite, being radically self-contradictory, involves its own self-suppression.

Nor, again, is Dialectic to be confounded with mere Sophistry. The essence of Sophistry lies in giving authority to a partial and abstract principle, in its isolation, as may suit the interest and particular situation of the individual at the time. For example, a regard to my existence, and my having the means of existence, is a vital motive of conduct, but if I exclusively emphasise this consideration or motive of my welfare, and draw the conclusion that I may steal or betray my country, we have a case of Sophistry. Similarly, it is a vital principle in conduct that I should be subjectively free, that is to say, that I should have an insight into what I am doing, and a conviction that it is right. But if my pleading insists on this principle alone I fall into Sophistry, such as would overthrow all the principles of morality. From this sort of party-pleading Dialectic is wholly different; its purpose is to study things in their own being and movement and thus to demonstrate the finitude of the partial categories of understanding.

Dialectic, it may be added, is no novelty in philosophy. Among the ancients Plato is termed the inventor of Dialectic; and his right to the name rests on the fact, that the Platonic philosophy first gave the free scientific, and thus at the same time the objective, form to Dialectic. Socrates, as we should expect from the general character of his philosophising, has the dialectical element in a predominantly subjective shape, that of Irony. He used to turn his Dialectic, first against ordinary consciousness, and then especially against the Sophists. In his conversations he used to simulate the wish for some clearer knowledge about the subject under discussion, and after putting all sorts of questions with that intent, he drew on those with whom he conversed to the opposite of what their first impressions had pronounced correct. If, for instance, the Sophists claimed to be teachers, Socrates by a series of questions forced the Sophist Protagoras to confess that all learning is only recollection. In his more strictly scientific dialogues Plato employs the dialectical method to show the finitude of all hard and fast terms of understanding. Thus in the Parmenides he deduces the many from the one, and shows nevertheless that the many cannot but define itself as the one. In this grand style did Plato treat Dialectic. In modern times it was, more than any other, Kant who resuscitated the name of Dialectic, and restored it to its post of honour. He did it, as we have seen (§48),* by working out the Antinomies of the reason. The problem of these Antinomies is no mere subjective piece of work oscillating between one set of grounds and another; it really serves to show that every abstract proposition of understanding, taken precisely as it is given, naturally veers round into its opposite.

However reluctant Understanding may be to admit the action of Dialectic, we must not suppose that the recognition of its existence is peculiarly confined to the philosopher. It would be truer to say that Dialectic gives expression to a law which is felt in all other grades of consciousness, and in general experience. Everything that surrounds us may be viewed as an instance of Dialectic. We are aware that everything finite, instead of being stable and ultimate, is rather changeable and transient; and this is exactly what we mean by that Dialectic of the finite, by which the finite, as implicitly other than what it is, is forced beyond its own immediate or natural being to turn suddenly into its opposite. We have before this (§ 80) identified Understanding with what is implied in the popular idea of the goodness of God; we may now remark of Dialectic, in the same objective signification, that its principle answers to the idea of his power. All things, we say—that is, the finite world as such—are doomed; and in saying so, we have a vision of Dialectic as the universal and irresistible power before which nothing can stay, however secure and stable it may deem itself. The category of power does not, it is true, exhaust the depth of the divine nature or the notion of God; but it certainly forms a vital element in all religious consciousness.

Apart from this general objectivity of Dialectic, we find traces of its presence in each of the particular provinces and phases of the natural and the spiritual world. Take as an illustration the motion of the

*See below, pp. 157–160.

heavenly bodies. At this moment the planet stands in this spot, but implicitly it is the possibility of being in another spot; and that possibility of being otherwise the planet brings into existence by moving. Similarly the "physical" elements prove to be Dialectical. The process of meteorological action is the exhibition of their Dialectic. It is the same dynamic that lies at the root of every other natural process, and, as it were, forces nature out of itself. To illustrate the presence of Dialectic in the spiritual world, especially in the provinces of law and morality, we have only to recollect how general experience shows us the extreme of one state or action suddenly shifting into its opposite: a Dialectic which is recognised in many ways in common proverbs. Thus *summum jus summa injuria:* which means, that to drive an abstract right to its extremity is to do a wrong. In political life, as every one knows, extreme anarchy and extreme despotism naturally lead to one another. The perception of Dialectic in the province of individual Ethics is seen in the well-known adages. "Pride comes before a fall." "Too much wit outwits itself." Even feeling, bodily as well as mental, has its Dialectic. Every one knows how the extremes of pain and pleasure pass into each other: the heart overflowing with joy seeks relief in tears, and the deepest melancholy will at times betray its presence by a smile.

2. Scepticism should not be looked upon merely as a doctrine of doubt. It would be more correct to say that the Sceptic has no doubt of his point, which is the nothingness of all finite existence. He who only doubts still clings to the hope that his doubt may be resolved, and that one or other of the definite views, between which he wavers, will turn out solid and true. Scepticism properly so called is a very different thing: it is complete hopelessness about all which understanding counts stable, and the feeling to which it gives birth is one of unbroken calmness and inward repose. Such at least is the noble Scepticism of antiquity, especially as exhibited in the writings of Sextus Empiricus, when in the later times of Rome it had been systematised as a complement to the dogmatic systems of Stoic and Epicurean. Of far other stamp, and to be strictly distinguished from it, is the modern Scepticism already mentioned (§ 39),* which partly preceded the Critical Philosophy, and partly sprung out of it. That later Scepticism consisted solely in denying the truth and certitude of the super-sensible, and in pointing to the facts of sense and of immediate sensations as what we have to keep to.

*See below, p. 145.

Even to this day Scepticism is often spoken of as the irresistible enemy of all positive knowledge, and hence of philosophy, in so far as philosophy is concerned with positive knowledge. But in these statements there is a misconception. It is only the finite thought of abstract understanding which has to fear Scepticism, because unable to withstand it: philosophy includes the sceptical principle as a subordinate function of its own, in the shape of Dialectic. In contradistinction to mere Scepticism, however, philosophy does not remain content with the purely negative result of Dialectic. The sceptic mistakes the true value of his result, when he supposes it to be no more than a negation pure and simple. For the negative, which emerges as the result of dialectic, is, because a result, at the same time the positive: it contains what it results from, absorbed into itself, and made part of its own nature. Thus conceived, however, the dialectical stage has the features characterising the third grade of logical truth, the speculative form, or form of positive reason. End *Zusatz.*

82. (γ)The Speculative stage, or stage of Positive Reason, apprehends the unity of terms (propositions) in their opposition—the affirmative, which is involved in their disintegration and in their transition.

(1) The result of Dialectic is positive, because it has a definite content, or because its result is not empty and abstract nothing, but the negation of certain specific propositions which are contained in the result—for the very reason that it is a resultant and not an immediate nothing. (2) It follows from this that the "reasonable" result, though it be only a thought and abstract, is still a concrete, being not a plain formal unity, but a unity of distinct propositions. Bare abstractions or formal thoughts are therefore no business of philosophy, which has to deal only with concrete thoughts. (3) The logic of mere Understanding is involved in Speculative logic, and can at will be elicited from it, by the simple process of omitting the dialectical and "reasonable" element. When that is done, it becomes what the common logic is, a descriptive collection of sundry thought-forms and rules which, finite though they are, are taken to be something infinite.

Zusatz. If we consider only what it contains, and not how it contains it, the true reason-world, so far from being the exclusive property of philosophy, is the right of every human being on whatever grade of culture or mental growth he may stand; which would justify man's ancient title of rational being. The general mode by which experience first makes us aware of the reasonable order of things is by accepted and unreasoned belief; and the character of the rational, as already noted (§ 45),* is to be unconditioned, and thus to be self-contained, self-determining. In this sense man above all things becomes aware of the reasonable order, when he knows of God, and knows Him to be the completely self-determined. Similarly, the consciousness a citizen has of his country and its laws is a perception of the reason-world, so long as he looks up to them as unconditioned and likewise universal powers, to which he must subject his individual will. And in the same sense, the knowledge and will of the child is rational, when he knows his parents' will, and wills it.

Now, to turn these rational (of course positively-rational) realities into speculative principles, the only thing needed is that they be *thought*. The expression "Speculation" in common life is often used with a very vague and at the same time secondary sense, as when we speak of a matrimonial or a commercial speculation. By this we only mean two things: first, that what is immediately at hand has to be passed and left behind; and secondly, that the subject-matter of such speculations, though in the first place only subjective, must not remain so, but be realised or translated into objectivity.

What was some time ago remarked respecting the Idea, may be applied to this common usage of the term "speculation": and we may add that people who rank themselves amongst the educated expressly speak of speculation even as if it were something purely subjective. A certain theory of some conditions and circumstances of nature or mind may be, say these people, very fine and correct as a matter of speculation, but it contradicts experience and nothing of the sort is admissible in reality. To this the answer is, that the speculative is in its true signification, neither preliminarily nor even definitively, something merely subjective: that, on the contrary, it expressly rises above such oppositions as that between subjective and objective, which the understanding cannot get over, and absorbing them in itself, evinces its own concrete and all-embracing nature. A one-sided proposition therefore can never even give expression to a speculative truth. If we say, for example, that the absolute is the unity of subjective and objective, we are undoubtedly in the right, but so far one-sided, as we enunciate the unity only and lay the accent upon it,

*See below, pp. 153–154.

forgetting that in reality the subjective and objective are not merely identical but also distinct.

Speculative truth, it may also be noted, means very much the same as what, in special connexion with religious experience and doctrines, used to be called Mysticism. The term Mysticism is at present used, as a rule, to designate what is mysterious and incomprehensible: and in proportion as their general culture and way of thinking vary, the epithet is applied by one class to denote the real and the true, by another to name everything connected with superstition and deception. On which we first of all remark that there is mystery in the mystical, only however for the understanding which is ruled by the principle of abstract identity; whereas the mystical, as synonymous with the speculative, is the concrete unity of those propositions, which understanding only accepts in their separation and opposition. And if those who recognise Mysticism as the highest truth are content to leave it in its original utter mystery, their conduct only proves that for them too, as well as for their antagonists, thinking means abstract identification, and that in their opinion, therefore, truth can only be won by renouncing thought, or as it is frequently expressed, by leading the reason captive. But, as we have seen, the abstract thinking of understanding is so far from being either ultimate or stable, that it shows a perpetual tendency to work its own dissolution and swing round into its opposite. Reasonableness, on the contrary, just consists in embracing within itself these opposites as unsubstantial elements. Thus the reason-world may be equally styled mystical—not however because thought cannot both reach and comprehend it, but merely because it lies beyond the compass of understanding. End *Zusatz.*

83. Logic is subdivided into three parts:

I. The Doctrine of Being
II. The Doctrine of Essence
III. The Doctrine of Notion and Idea

That is, into the Theory of Thought:

I. In its immediacy: the notion implicit and in germ.
II. In its reflection and mediation: the being-for-self and show of the notion.

III. In its return into itself, and its developed abiding by itself: the notion in and for itself.

Zusatz. The division of Logic now given, as well as the whole of the previous discussion on the nature of thought, is anticipatory: and the justification, or proof of it, can only result from the detailed treatment of thought itself. For in philosophy, to prove means to show how the subject by and from itself makes itself what it is. The relation in which these three leading grades of thought, or of the logical Idea, stand to each other must be conceived as follows. Truth comes only with the notion: or, more precisely, the notion is the truth of being and essence, both of which, when separately maintained in their isolation, cannot but be untrue, the former because it is exclusively immediate, and the latter because it is exclusively mediate. Why then, it may be asked, begin with the false and not at once with the true? To which we answer that truth, to deserve the name, must authenticate its own truth: which authentication, here within the sphere of logic, is given, when the notion demonstrates itself to be what is mediated by and with itself, and thus at the same time to be truly immediate. This relation between the three stages of the logical Idea appears in a real and concrete shape thus: God, who is the truth, is known by us in His truth, that is, as absolute spirit, only in so far as we at the same time recognise that the world which He created, nature and the finite spirit, are, in their difference from God, untrue. End *Zusatz.*

WITH WHAT MUST THE SCIENCE BEGIN?

It is only in recent times that thinkers have become aware of the difficulty of finding a beginning in philosophy, and the reason for this difficulty and also the possibility of resolving it has been much discussed. What philosophy begins with must be either *mediated* or *immediate*, and it is easy to show that it can be neither the one nor the other; thus either way of beginning is refuted.

The *principle* of a philosophy does, of course, also express a beginning, but not so much a subjective as an *objective* one, the beginning of *everything*. The principle is a particular determinate *content*—water, the one, *nous*, idea, substance, monad, etc. Or, if it refers to the nature

SOURCE: *Logic*, Miller, pp. 67–78. Reprinted by permission of Humanities Press, New York, and George Allen & Unwin Ltd., London.

of cognition and consequently is supposed to be only a criterion rather than an objective determination—thought, intuition, sensation, ego, subjectivity itself—then here too it is the nature of the content which is the point of interest. The beginning as such, on the other hand, as something subjective in the sense of being a particular, inessential way of introducing the discourse, remains unconsidered, a matter of indifference, and so too the need to find an answer to the question, With what should the beginning be made?, remains of no importance in face of the need for a principle in which alone the interest of the matter in hand seems to lie, the interest as to what is the *truth*, the *absolute ground.*

But the modern perplexity about a beginning proceeds from a further requirement of which those who are concerned with the dogmatic demonstration of a principle or who are sceptical about finding a subjective criterion against dogmatic philosophizing, are not yet aware, and which is completely denied by those who begin, like a shot from a pistol, from their inner revelation, from faith, intellectual intuition, etc., and who would be exempt from *method* and logic. If earlier abstract thought was interested in the principle only as content, but in the course of philosophical development has been impelled to pay attention to the other side, to the behaviour of the cognitive process, this implies that the *subjective* act has also been grasped as an *essential* moment of objective truth, and this brings with it the need to unite the method with the content, the form with the principle. Thus the principle ought also to be the beginning, and what is the first for thought ought also to be the first in the *process* of thinking.

Here we have only to consider how the *logical* beginning appears; the two sides from which it can be taken have already been named, to wit, either as a mediated result or as a beginning proper, as an immediacy. This is not the place to deal with the question apparently so important in present-day thought, whether the knowledge of truth is an immediate knowledge having a pure beginning, a faith, or whether it is a mediated knowledge. In so far as this can be dealt with *preliminarily* it has been done elsewhere.* Here we need only quote from it this, that there is nothing, nothing in heaven or in nature or in mind or anywhere else which does not equally contain both immediacy and mediation, so that these two determinations reveal

---

*In my *Encyclop. of the Phil. Sciences*, 3rd edition, *Preliminary Notion*. Section 61 et seq.

themselves to be *unseparated* and inseparable and the opposition between them to be a nullity. But as regards the philosophical discussion of this, it is to be found in every logical proposition in which
occur the determinations of immediacy and mediation and consequently also the discussion of their opposition and their truth. Inasmuch as this opposition, as related to thinking, to knowing, to cognition, acquires the more concrete form of immediate or mediated
knowledge, it is the nature of cognition simply as such which is considered within the science of logic, while the more concrete form of
cognition falls to be considered in the philosophy of spirit and in the
phenomenology of spirit. But to want the nature of cognition clarified
prior to the science is to demand that it be considered *outside* the
science; *outside* the science this cannot be accomplished, at least not
in a scientific manner and such a manner is alone here in place.

The beginning is *logical* in that it is to be made in the element of
thought that is free and for itself, in *pure knowing*. It is *mediated* because
pure knowing is the ultimate, absolute truth of *consciousness*. In the
Introduction it was remarked that the phenomenology of spirit is the
science of consciousness, the exposition of it, and that consciousness
has for result the *Notion* of science, i.e., pure knowing. Logic, then,
has for its presupposition the science of manifested spirit, which
contains and demonstrates the necessity, and so the truth, of the
standpoint occupied by pure knowing and of its mediation. In this
science of manifested spirit the beginning is made from empirical,
sensuous consciousness and this is *immediate* knowledge in the strict
sense of the word; in that work there is discussed the significance of
this immediate knowledge. Other forms of consciousness such as
belief in divine truths, inner experience, knowledge through inner
revelation, etc., are very ill-fitted to be quoted as examples of immediate knowledge as a little reflection will show. In the work just mentioned immediate consciousness is also the first and that which is
immediate in the science itself, and therefore the presupposition; but
in logic, the presupposition is that which has proved itself to be the
result of that phenomenological consideration—the Idea as pure
knowledge. *Logic is pure science*, that is, pure knowledge in the entire
range of its development. But in the said result, this Idea has determined itself to be the certainty which has become truth, the certainty
which, on the one hand, no longer has the object over against it but
has internalized it, knows it as its own self—and, on the other hand,
has given up the knowledge of itself as of something confronting the
object of which it is only the annihilation, has divested itself of this
subjectivity and is at one with its self-alienation.

Now starting from this determination of pure knowledge, all that is needed to ensure that the beginning remains immanent in its scientific development is to consider, or rather, ridding oneself of all other reflections and opinions whatever, simply to take up, *what is there before us.*

Pure knowing as concentrated into this unity has sublated all reference to an other and to mediation; it is without any distinction and as thus distinctionless, ceases itself to be knowledge; what is present is only *simple immediacy.*

Simple immediacy is itself an expression of reflection and contains a reference to its distinction from what is mediated. This simple immediacy, therefore, in its true expression is *pure being.* Just as *pure* knowing is to mean knowing as such, quite abstractly, so too pure being is to mean nothing but *being* in general: being, and nothing else, without any further specification and filling.

Here the beginning is made with being which is represented as having come to be through mediation, a mediation which is also a sublating of itself; and there is presupposed pure knowing as the outcome of finite knowing, of consciousness. But if no presupposition is to be made and the beginning itself is taken *immediately,* then its only determination is that it is to be the beginning of logic, of thought as such. All that is present is simply the resolve, which can also be regarded as arbitrary, that we propose to consider thought as such. Thus the beginning must be an *absolute,* or what is synonymous here, an *abstract* beginning; and so it *may not presuppose anything,* must not be mediated by anything nor have a ground; rather it is to be itself the ground of the entire science. Consequently, it must be purely and simply *an* immediacy, or rather merely *immediacy* itself. Just as it cannot possess any determination relative to anything else, so too it cannot contain within itself any determination, any content; for any such would be a distinguishing and an interrelationship of distinct moments, and consequently a mediation. The beginning therefore is *pure being.*

To this simple exposition of what is only directly involved in the simplest of all things, the logical beginning, we may add the following further reflections; yet these cannot be meant to serve as elucidations and confirmations of that exposition—this is complete in itself—since they are occasioned by preconceived ideas and reflections and these, like all other preliminary prejudices, must be disposed of within the science itself where their treatment should be awaited with patience.

The insight that absolute truth must be a result, and conversely, that a result presupposes a prior truth which, however, because it is a first, objectively considered is unnecessary and from the subjective side is not known—this insight has recently given rise to the thought that philosophy can only begin with a *hypothetical* and *problematical* truth and therefore philosophizing can at first be only a quest. This view was much stressed by Reinhold in his later philosophical work and one must give it credit for the genuine interest on which it is based, an interest which concerns the speculative nature of the philosophical *beginning*. The detailed discussion of this view is at the same time an occasion for introducing a preliminary understanding of the meaning of progress in logic generally; for that view has a direct bearing on the advance; this it conceives to be such that progress in philosophy is rather a retrogression and a grounding or establishing by means of which we first obtain the result that what we began with is not something merely arbitrarily assumed but is in fact the *truth*, and also the *primary truth*.

It must be admitted that it is an important consideration—one which will be found in more detail in the logic itself—that the advance is a *retreat into the ground*, to what is *primary* and *true*, on which depends and, in fact, from which originates, that with which the beginning is made. Thus consciousness on its onward path from the immediacy with which it began is led back to absolute knowledge as its innermost *truth*. This last, the ground, is then also that from which the first proceeds, that which at first appeared as an immediacy. This is true in still greater measure of absolute spirit which reveals itself as the concrete and final supreme truth of all being, and which at the *end* of the development is known as freely externalizing itself, abandoning itself to the shape of an *immediate being*—opening or unfolding itself [*sich entschliessend*] into the creation of a world which contains all that fell into the development which preceded that result and which through this reversal of its position relatively to its beginning is transformed into something dependent on the result as principle. The essential requirement for the science of logic is not so much that the beginning be a pure immediacy, but rather that the whole of the science be within itself a circle in which the first is also the last and the last is also the first.

We see therefore that, on the other hand, it is equally necessary to consider as *result* that into which the movement returns as into its *ground*. In this respect the first is equally the ground, and the last a derivative; since the movement starts from the first and by correct inferences arrives at the last as the ground, this latter is a result. Further, the *progress* from that which forms the beginning is to be regarded as only a further determination of it, hence that which forms the starting point of the development remains at the base of all that follows and does not vanish from it. The progress does not consist merely in the derivation of an other, or in the effected transition into a genuine other; and in so far as this transition does occur it is equally sublated again. Thus the beginning of philosophy is the foundation which is present and preserved throughout the entire subsequent development, remaining completely immanent in its further determinations.

Through this progress, then, the beginning loses the one-sidedness which attaches to it as something simply immediate and abstract; it becomes something mediated, and hence the line of the scientific advance becomes a *circle*. It also follows that because that which forms the beginning is still undeveloped, devoid of content, it is not truly known in the beginning; it is the science of logic in its whole compass which first constitutes the completed knowledge of it with its developed content and first truly grounds that knowledge.

But because it is the *result* which appears as the absolute ground, this progress in knowing is not something provisional, or problematical and hypothetical; it must be determined by the nature of the subject matter itself and its content. The said beginning is neither an arbitrary and merely provisional assumption, nor is it something which appears to be arbitrarily and tentatively presupposed, but which is subsequently shown to have been properly made the beginning; not as is the case with the constructions one is directed to make in connection with the proof of a theorem in geometry, where it becomes apparent only afterwards in the proof that one took the right course in drawing just those lines and then, in the proof itself, in beginning with the comparison of those lines or angles; drawing such lines and comparing them are not an essential part of the proof itself.

Thus the *ground*, the *reason*, why the beginning is made with pure being in the pure science [of logic] is directly given in the science itself. This pure being is the unity into which pure knowing withdraws, or, if this itself is still to be distinguished as form from its unity, then being is also the content of pure knowing. It is when taken in this way that this *pure being*, this absolute immediacy has equally the character of something absolutely mediated. But it is equally essential that it be taken only in the one-sided character in which it is pure immediacy, *precisely because* here it is the beginning. If it were not this pure indeterminateness, if it were determinate, it would have been taken as something mediated, something already carried a stage further: what is determinate implies an other to a first. Therefore, it lies in the *very nature of a beginning* that it must be being and nothing else. To enter into philosophy, therefore, calls for no other preparations, no further reflections or points of connection.

We cannot really extract any further determination or *positive* content for the beginning from the fact that it is the beginning of philosophy. For here at the start, where the subject matter itself is not yet to hand, philosophy is an empty word or some assumed, unjustified conception. Pure knowing yields only this negative determination, that the beginning is to be *abstract*. If pure being is taken as the *content* of pure knowing, then the latter must stand back from its content, allowing it to have free play and not determining it further. Or again, if pure being is to be considered as the unity into which knowing has collapsed at the extreme point of its union with the object, then knowing itself has vanished in that unity, leaving behind no difference from the unity and hence nothing by which the latter could be determined. Nor is there anything else present, any content which could be used to make the beginning more determinate.

But the determination of *being* so far adopted for the beginning could also be omitted, so that the only demand would be that a pure beginning be made. In that case, we have nothing but the *beginning* itself, and it remains to be seen what this is. This position could also be suggested for the benefit of those who, on the one hand, are dissatisfied for one reason or another with the beginning with being and still more so with the resulting transition of being into nothing, and, on the other hand, simply know no other way of beginning a science than by *presupposing some general idea*, which is then *analysed*, the result of such analysis yielding the first specific concept in the science. If we too were to observe this method, then we should be without a particular object, because the beginning, as the beginning of *thought*, is supposed to be quite abstract, quite general, wholly form without any content; thus we should have nothing at all beyond the general idea of a mere beginning as such. We have therefore only to see what is contained in such an idea.

As yet there is nothing and there is to become something. The beginning is not pure nothing, but a nothing from which something is to proceed; therefore being, too, is already contained in the beginning. The beginning, therefore, contains both, being and nothing, is the unity of being and nothing; or is non-being which is at the same time being, and being which is at the same time non-being.

Further, in the beginning, being and nothing are present as *distin-*

guished from each other; for the beginning points to something else
—it is a non-being which carries a reference to being as to an other;
that which begins, as yet *is* not, it is only on the way to being. The
being contained in the beginning is, therefore, a being which removes
itself from non-being or sublates it as something opposed to it.

But again, that which begins already *is,* but equally, too, *is not* as
yet. The opposites, being and non-being are therefore directly united
in it, or, otherwise expressed, it is their *undifferentiated unity.*

The analysis of the beginning would thus yield the notion of the
unity of being and nothing—or, in a more reflected form, the unity
of differentiatedness and non-differentiatedness, or the identity of
identity and non-identity. This concept could be regarded as the first,
purest, that is, most abstract definition of the absolute—as it would
in fact be if we were at all concerned with the form of definitions and
with the name of the absolute. In this sense, that abstract concept
would be the first definition of this absolute and all further determinations and developments only more specific and richer definitions
of it. But let those who are dissatisfied with *being* as a beginning
because it passes over into nothing and so gives rise to the unity of
being and nothing, let them see whether they find this beginning
which begins with the general idea of a *beginning* and with its analysis
(which, though of course correct, likewise leads to the unity of being
and nothing), more satisfactory than the beginning with being.

But there is a still further observation to be made about this procedure. The said analysis presupposes as familiar the idea of a beginning, thus following the example of other sciences. These presuppose their subject-matter and take it for granted that everyone has
roughly the same general idea of it and can find in it the same determinations as those indicated by the sciences which have obtained
them in one way or another through analysis, comparison and other
kinds of reasoning. But that which forms the absolute beginning must
likewise be something otherwise known; now if it is something concrete and hence is variously determined within itself, then this *internal
relation* is presupposed as something known; it is thus put forward as
an *immediacy* which, however, it is not; for it is a relation only as a
relation of distinct moments, and it therefore contains *mediation*
within itself. Further, with a concrete object, the analysis and the ways
in which it is determined are affected by contingency and arbitrariness. Which determinations are brought out depends on what each
person just *finds* in his own immediate, contingent idea. The relation
contained in something concrete, in a synthetic unity, is *necessary* only

in so far as it is not just given but is produced by the spontaneous return of the moments back into this unity—a movement which is the opposite of the analytical procedure, which is an activity belonging to the subject-thinker and external to the subject matter itself.

The foregoing shows quite clearly the reason why the beginning cannot be made with anything concrete, anything containing a relation *within itself*. For such presupposes an internal process of mediation and transition of which the concrete, now become simple, would be the result. But the beginning ought not itself to be already a first *and* an other; for anything which is in its own self a first *and* an other implies that an advance has already been made. Consequently, that which constitutes the beginning, the beginning itself, is to be taken as something unanalysable, taken in its simple, unfilled immediacy, and therefore *as being*, as the completely empty being.

If impatience with the consideration of the abstract beginning should provoke anyone to say that the beginning should be made not with the beginning, but straightway with the subject matter itself, well then, this subject matter is nothing else but the said empty being; for what this subject matter is, that will be explicated only in the development of the science and cannot be presupposed by it as known beforehand.

Whatever other form the beginning takes in the attempt to begin with something other than empty being, it will suffer from the defects already specified. Let those who are still dissatisfied with this beginning tackle the problem of avoiding these defects by beginning in some other way.

But we cannot leave entirely unmentioned an original beginning of philosophy which has recently become famous, the beginning with the *ego*. It came partly from the reflection that from the first truth the entire sequel must be derived, and partly from the requirement that the *first* truth must be something with which we are acquainted, and still more, something of which we are *immediately certain*. This beginning is, in general, not a contingent idea which can be differently constituted in different subjects. For the ego, this immediate consciousness of self, at first appears to be itself both an immediacy and also something much more familiar to us than any other idea; anything else known belongs to the ego, it is true, but is still a content distinguished from it and therefore contingent; the ego, on the contrary, is the simple certainty of its own self. But the ego as such is *at the same time* also concrete, or rather, the ego is the most concrete of all things—the consciousness of itself as an infinitely manifold world. Before the ego, this concrete Being, can be made the beginning and ground of philosophy, it must be disrupted—this is the absolute act through which the ego purges itself of its content and becomes aware of itself as an abstract ego. Only this pure ego now is *not* immediate, is not the familiar, ordinary ego of our consciousness to which the science of logic could be directly linked for everyone. That act, strictly speaking, would be nothing else but the elevation to the standpoint of pure knowing where the distinction of subject and object has vanished. But as thus *immediately* demanded, this elevation is a subjective postulate; to prove itself a genuine demand, the progression of the concrete ego from immediate consciousness to pure knowing must have been indicated and exhibited through the necessity of the ego itself. Without this objective movement pure knowing, even in the shape of intellectual intuition, appears as an arbitrary standpoint, or even as one of the empirical *states* of consciousness with respect to which everything turns on whether or not it is found or can be produced in each and every individual. But inasmuch as this pure ego must be essential, pure knowing, and pure knowing is not *immediately* present in the individual consciousness but only as posited through the absolute act of the ego in raising itself to that standpoint, we lose the very advantage which is supposed to come from this beginning of philosophy, namely that it is something thoroughly familiar, something everyone finds in himself which can form the starting point for further reflection; that pure ego, on the contrary, in its abstract, essential nature, is something unknown to the ordinary consciousness, something it does not find therein. Instead, such a beginning brings with it the disadvantage of the illusion that whereas the thing under discussion is supposed to be something familiar, the ego of empirical self-consciousness, it is in fact something far removed from it. When pure knowing is characterized as ego, it acts as a perpetual reminder of the subjective ego whose limitations should be forgotten, and it fosters the idea that the propositions and relations resulting from the further development of the ego are present and can already be found in the ordinary consciousness—for in fact it is this of which they are asserted. This confusion, far from clarifying the problem of a beginning, only adds to the difficulties involved and tends completely to mislead; among the uninitiated it has given rise to the crudest misunderstandings.

Further, as regards the *subjective* determinateness of the ego in general, it is true that pure knowing frees the ego from the restricted meaning imposed on it by the insuperable opposition of its object;

but for this reason it would be *superfluous* at least to retain this subjective attitude and the determination of pure knowing as ego. This determination, however, not only introduces the disturbing ambiguity mentioned, but closely examined it also remains a subjective *ego*. The actual development of the science which starts from the ego shows that in that development the object has and retains the perennial character of an other for the ego, and that the ego which formed the starting-point is, therefore, still entangled in the world of appearance and is not the pure knowing which has in truth overcome the opposition of consciousness.

In this connection a further essential observation must be made, namely that although the ego could *in itself* or *in principle* [*an sich*] be characterized as pure knowing or as intellectual intuition and asserted as the beginning, we are not concerned in the science of logic with what is present only in *principle* or as something *inner*, but rather with the determinate reality *in thought* of what is inner and with the *determinateness* possessed by such an inner in this reality. But what, at the *beginning* of the science, is *actually present* of intellectual intuition —or of the eternal, the divine, the absolute, if its object be so named —cannot be anything else than a first, immediate, simple determination. Whatever richer name be given to it than is expressed by mere *being*, the consideration of such absolute must be restricted solely to the way in which it enters into our knowing as *thought* and is enunciated as such. True, intellectual intuition is the forcible rejection of mediation and the ratiocinative, external reflection; but what it enunciates above and beyond simple immediacy is something concrete, something which contains within itself diverse determinations. However, as we have remarked, the enunciation and exposition of such concrete beginning is a process of mediation which starts from *one* of the determinations and advances to the other, even though the latter returns to the first; it is a movement which at the same time may not be arbitrary or assertoric. Consequently, it is not the concrete something itself with which that exposition begins but only the simple immediacy from which the movement starts. And further, if something concrete is taken as the beginning, the conjunction of the determinations contained in it demand proof, and this is lacking.

If, therefore, in the expression of the absolute, or eternal, or God (and *God* has the absolutely undisputed right that the beginning be made with him)—if in the intuition or thought of these there is *implied more* than pure being—then this *more* must make its *appearance* in our knowing only as something *thought*, not as something imagined or figurately conceived; let what is present in intuition or figurate conception be as rich as it may, the determination which *first* emerges in knowing is simple, for only in what is simple is there nothing more than the pure beginning; only the immediate is simple, for only in the immediate has no advance yet been made from a *one* to an *other*. Consequently, whatever is intended to be expressed or implied beyond *being*, in the richer forms of representing the absolute or God, this is in the beginning only an empty word and only being; this simple determination which has no other meaning of any kind, this emptiness, is therefore simply as such the beginning of philosophy.

This insight is itself so simple that this beginning as such requires no preparation or further introduction; and, indeed, these preliminary, external reflections about it were not so much intended to lead up to it as rather to eliminate all preliminaries.

FIRST SUBDIVISION OF *LOGIC*: THE "DOCTRINE OF BEING"

84. Being is the notion implicit only: its special forms have the predicate "is"; when they are distinguished they are each of them an "other," and the shape which dialectic takes in them, *i.e.*, their further specialisation, is a passing over into another. This further determination, or specialisation, is at once a forth-putting and in that way a disengaging of the notion implicit in being; and at the same time the withdrawing of being inwards, its sinking deeper into itself. Thus the explication of the notion in the sphere of being does two things: it brings out the totality of being, and it abolishes the immediacy of being, or the form of being as such.

85. Being itself and the special sub-categories of it which follow, as well as those of logic in general, may be looked upon as definitions of the Absolute, or metaphysical definitions of God: at least the first and third category in every triad may—the first, where the thought-form of the triad is formulated in its simplicity, and the third, being the return from differentiation to a simple self-reference. For a metaphysical definition of God is the expression of His nature in thoughts as such; and logic embraces all thoughts so long as they continue in the thought-form. The second sub-category in each triad, where the grade of thought is in its differentiation, gives, on the other hand, a definition of the finite. The objection to the form of definition is that it implies a something in the mind's eye on which these predicates may fasten. Thus even the Absolute (though it purports to express

SOURCE: *Logic*, Wallace, pp. 156–169.

God in the style and character of thought) in comparison with its predicate (which really and distinctly expresses in thought what the subject does not), is as yet only an inchoate pretended thought—the indeterminate subject of predicates yet to come. The thought, which is here the matter of sole importance, is contained only in the predicate; and hence the propositional form, like the said subject, viz., the Absolute, is a mere superfluity (cf. § 31).*

Zusatz. Each of the three spheres of the logical idea proves to be a systematic whole of thought-terms, and a phase of the Absolute. This is the case with Being, containing the three grades of quality, quantity, and measure. Quality is, in the first place, the character identical with being: so identical, that a thing ceases to be what it is, if it loses its quality. Quantity, on the contrary, is the character external to being, and does not affect the being at all. Thus, *e.g.*, a house remains what it is, whether it be greater or smaller; and red remains red, whether it be brighter or darker. Measure, the third grade of being, which is the unity of the first two, is a qualitative quantity. All things have their measure: *i.e.*, the quantitative terms of their existence, their being so or so great, does not matter within certain limits; but when these limits are exceeded by an additional more or less, the things cease to be what they were. From measure follows the advance to the second sub-division of the idea, Essence.

The three forms of being here mentioned, just because they are the first, are also the poorest, *i.e.*, the most abstract. Immediate (sensible) consciousness, in so far as it simultaneously includes an intellectual element, is especially restricted to the abstract categories of quality and quantity. The sensuous consciousness is in ordinary estimation the most concrete and thus also the richest; but that is only true as regards materials, whereas, in reference to the thought it contains, it is really the poorest and most abstract. End *Zusatz.*

A. Quality

(a) Being.

86. Pure Being makes the beginning: because it is on one hand pure thought, and on the other immediacy itself, simple and indeterminate; and the first beginning cannot be mediated by anything, or be further determined.

*See below, pp. 132–133.

All doubts and admonitions, which might be brought against beginning the science with abstract empty being, will disappear, if we only perceive what a beginning naturally implies. It is possible to define being as "I=I," as "Absolute Indifference" or Identity, and so on. Where it is felt necessary to begin either with what is absolutely certain, *i.e.*, the certainty of oneself, or with a definition or intuition of the absolute truth, these and other forms of the kind may be looked on as if they must be the first. But each of these forms contains a mediation, and hence cannot be the real first: for all mediation implies advance made from a first on to a second, and proceeding from something different. If I=I, or even the intellectual intuition, are really taken to mean no more than the first, they are in this mere immediacy identical with being: while conversely, pure being, if abstract no longer, but including in it mediation, is pure thought or intuition.

If we enunciate Being as a predicate of the Absolute, we get the first definition of the latter. The Absolute is Being. This is (in thought) the absolutely initial definition, the most abstract and stinted. It is the definition given by the Eleatics, but at the same time is also the well-known definition of God as the sum of all realities. It means, in short, that we are to set aside that limitation which is in every reality, so that God shall be only the real in all reality, the superlatively real. Or, if we reject reality, as implying a reflection, we get a more immediate or unreflected statement of the same thing, when Jacobi says that the God of Spinoza is the *principium* of being in all existence.

Zusatz. (1) When thinking is to begin, we have nothing but thought in its merest indeterminateness: for we cannot determine unless there is both one and another; and in the beginning there is yet no other. The indeterminate, as we here have it, is the blank we begin with, not a featurelessness reached by abstraction, not the elimination of all character, but the original featurelessness which precedes all definite character and is the very first of all. And this we call Being. It is not to be felt, or perceived by sense, or pictured in imagination: it is only and merely thought, and as such it forms the beginning. Essence also is indeterminate, but in another sense: it has traversed the process of mediation and contains implicit the determination it has absorbed.

(2) In the history of philosophy the different stages of the logical Idea assume the shape of successive systems, each based on a particular definition of the Absolute. As the logical Idea is seen to unfold

itself in a process from the abstract to the concrete, so in the history of philosophy the earliest systems are the most abstract, and thus at the same time the poorest. The relation too of the earlier to the later systems of philosophy is much like the relation of the corresponding stages of the logical Idea: in other words, the earlier are preserved in the later; but subordinated and submerged. This is the true meaning of a much misunderstood phenomenon in the history of philosophy—the refutation of one system by another, of an earlier by a later. Most commonly the refutation is taken in a purely negative sense to mean that the system refuted has ceased to count for anything, has been set aside and done for. Were it so, the history of philosophy would be of all studies most saddening, displaying, as it does, the refutation of every system which time has brought forth. Now, although it may be admitted that every philosophy has been refuted, it must be in an equal degree maintained, that no philosophy has been refuted, nay, or can be refuted. And that in two ways. For first, every philosophy that deserves the name always embodies the Idea: and secondly, every system represents one particular factor or particular stage in the evolution of the Idea. The refutation of a philosophy, therefore, only means that its barriers are crossed, and its special principle reduced to a factor in the completer principle that follows. Thus the history of philosophy, in its true meaning, deals not with a past, but with an eternal and veritable present; and, in its results, resembles not a museum of the aberrations of the human intellect, but a Pantheon of Godlike figures. These figures of Gods are the various stages of the Idea, as they come forward one after another in dialectical development. To the historian of philosophy it belongs to point out more precisely, how far the gradual evolution of his theme coincides with, or swerves from, the dialectical unfolding of the pure logical Idea. It is sufficient to mention here, that logic begins where the proper history of philosophy begins. Philosophy began in the Eleatic school, especially with Parmenides. Parmenides, who conceives the absolute as Being, says that "Being alone is and Nothing is not." Such was the true starting-point of philosophy, which is always knowledge by thought; and here for the first time we find pure thought seized and made an object to itself.

Men indeed thought from the beginning (for thus only were they distinguished from the animals). But thousands of years had to elapse before they came to apprehend thought in its purity, and to see in it the truly objective. The Eleatics are celebrated as daring thinkers. But this nominal admiration is often accompanied by the remark that they went too far, when they made Being alone true, and denied the truth of every other object of consciousness. We must go further than mere Being, it is true; and yet it is absurd to speak of the other contents of our consciousness as somewhat as it were outside and beside Being, or to say that there are other things, as well as Being. The true state of the case is rather as follows. Being, as Being, is nothing fixed or ultimate: it yields to dialectic and sinks into its opposite, which, also taken immediately, is Nothing. After all, the point is, that Being is the first pure Thought; whatever else you may begin with (the I = I, the absolute indifference, or God Himself), you begin with a figure of materialised conception, not a product of thought; and that, so far as its thought-content is concerned, such beginning is merely Being. End *Zusatz.*

87. But this mere Being, as it is mere abstraction, is therefore the absolutely negative: which, in a similarly immediate aspect, is just Nothing.

(1) Hence was derived the second definition of the Absolute; the Absolute is the Nought. In fact this definition is implied in saying that the thing-in-itself is the indeterminate, utterly without form and so without content—or in saying that God is only the supreme Being and nothing more; for this is really declaring Him to be the same negativity as above. The Nothing which the Buddhists make the universal principle, as well as the final aim and goal of everything, is the same abstraction.

(2) If the opposition in thought is stated in this immediacy as Being and Nothing, the shock of its nullity is too great not to stimulate the attempt to fix Being and secure it against the transition into Nothing. With this intent, reflection has recourse to the plan of discovering some fixed predicate for Being, to mark it off from Nothing. Thus we find Being identified with what persists amid all change, with *matter*, susceptible of innumerable determinations—or even, unreflectingly, with a single existence, any chance object of the senses or of the mind. But every additional and more concrete characterisation causes Being to lose that integrity and simplicity it has in the beginning. Only in, and by virtue of, this mere generality is it Nothing, something inexpressible, whereof the distinction from Nothing is a mere intention or *meaning*.

All that is wanted is to realise that these beginnings are nothing but these empty abstractions, one as empty as the other. The instinct that induces us to attach a settled import to Being, or to both, is the very necessity which leads to the onward movement of Being and Nothing, and gives them a true or concrete significance. This advance is the logical deduction and the movement of thought exhibited in the sequel. The reflection which finds a profounder connotation for Being and Nothing is nothing but logical thought, through which such connotation is evolved, not, however, in an accidental, but a necessary way. Every signification, therefore, in which they afterwards appear, is only a more precise specification and truer definition of the Absolute. And when that is done, the mere abstract Being and Nothing are replaced by a concrete in which both these elements form an organic part. The supreme form of Nought as a separate principle would be Freedom: but Freedom is negativity in that stage, when it sinks self-absorbed to supreme intensity, and is itself an affirmation, and even absolute affirmation.

Zusatz. The distinction between Being and Nought is, in the first place, only implicit, and not yet actually made: they only *ought* to be distinguished. A distinction of course implies two things, and that one of them possesses an attribute which is not found in the other. Being however is an absolute absence of attributes, and so is Nought. Hence the distinction between the two is only meant to be; it is a quite nominal distinction, which is at the same time no distinction. In all other cases of difference there is some common point which comprehends both things. Suppose, *e.g.*, we speak of two different species; the genus forms a common ground for both. But in the case of mere Being and Nothing, distinction is without a bottom to stand upon: hence there can be no distinction, both determinations being the same bottomlessness. If it be replied that Being and Nothing are both of them thoughts, so that thought may be reckoned common ground, the objector forgets that Being is not a particular or definite thought, and hence, being quite indeterminate, is a thought not to be distinguished from Nothing. It is natural too for us to represent Being as absolute riches, and Nothing as absolute poverty. But if when we view the whole world we can only say that everything *is*, and nothing more, we are neglecting all speciality and, instead of absolute plenitude, we have absolute emptiness. The same stricture is applicable to those who define God to be mere Being; a definition not a whit better than that of the Buddhists, who make God to be Nought, and who from that principle draw the further conclusion that self-annihilation is the means by which man becomes God. End *Zusatz.*

88. Nothing, if it be thus immediate and equal to itself, is also conversely the same as Being is. The truth of Being and of Nothing is accordingly the unity of the two: and this unity is Becoming.

(1) The proposition that Being and Nothing is the same seems so paradoxical to the imagination or understanding, that it is perhaps taken for a joke. And indeed it is one of the hardest things thought expects itself to do: for Being and Nothing exhibit the fundamental contrast in all its immediacy, that is, without the one term being invested with any attribute which would involve its connexion with the other. This attribute however, as the above paragraph points out, is implicit in them—the attribute which is just the same in both. So far the deduction of their unity is completely analytical: indeed the whole progress of philosophising in every case, if it be a methodical, that is to say a necessary, progress, merely renders explicit what is implicit in a notion. It is as correct however to say that Being and Nothing are altogether different, as to assert their unity. The one is *not* what the other is. But since the distinction has not at this point assumed definite shape (Being and Nothing are still the immediate), it is, in the way that they have it, something unutterable, which we merely *mean*.

(2) No great expenditure of wit is needed to make fun of the maxim that Being and Nothing are the same, or rather to adduce absurdities which, it is erroneously asserted, are the consequences and illustrations of that maxim.

If Being and Nought are identical, say these objectors, it follows that it makes no difference whether my home, my property, the air I breathe, this city, the sun, the law, mind, God, are or are not. Now in some of these cases, the objectors foist in private aims, the utility a thing has for me, and then ask, whether it be all the same to me if the thing exist and if it do not. For that matter indeed, the teaching of philosophy is precisely what frees man from the endless crowd of finite aims and intentions, by making him so insensible to them, that their existence or non-existence is to him a matter of indifference. But it is never to be forgotten that, once mention something substantial, and you thereby create a connexion with other existences and other purposes which are *ex hypothesi* worth having: and on such hypothesis it comes to depend whether the Being and not-Being of a determinate subject are the same or not. A substantial distinction is in these cases secretly substituted for the empty distinction of Being and Nought. In others of the cases referred to, it is virtually absolute existences and vital ideas and aims, which are placed under the mere category of Being or not-Being. But there is more to be said of these concrete objects, than that they merely are or are not. Barren abstractions, like Being and Nothing—the initial categories which, for that reason, are the scantiest anywhere to be found—are utterly inadequate to the nature of these objects. Substantial truth is something far above these abstractions and their oppositions. And always when a concrete existence is disguised under the name of Being and not-Being, empty-headedness makes its usual mistake of speaking about, and having in the mind an image of, something else than what is in question: and in this place the question is about abstract Being and Nothing.

(3) It may perhaps be said that nobody can form a notion of the unity of Being and Nought. As for that, the notion of the unity is stated in the sections preceding, and that is all: apprehend that, and you have comprehended this unity. What the objector really means by comprehension—by a notion—is more than his language properly implies: he wants a richer and more complex state of mind, a pictorial conception which will propound the notion as a concrete case and one more familiar to the ordinary operations of thought. And so long as incomprehensibility means only the want of habituation for the effort needed to grasp an abstract thought, free from all sensuous admixture, and to seize a speculative truth, the reply to the criticism is, that philosophical knowledge is undoubtedly distinct in kind from the mode of knowledge best known in common life, as well as from that which reigns in the other sciences. But if to have no notion merely means that we cannot represent in imagination the oneness of Being and Nought, the statement is far from being true; for every one has countless ways of envisaging this unity. To say that we have no such conception can only mean, that in none of these images do we recognise the notion in question, and that we are not aware that they exemplify it. The readiest example of it is Becoming. Every one has a mental idea of Becoming, and will even allow that it is *one* idea: he will further allow that, when it is analysed, it involves the attribute of Being, and also what is the very reverse of Being, viz., Nothing: and that these two attributes lie undivided in the one idea: so that Becoming is the unity of Being and Nothing. Another tolerably plain example is a Beginning. In its beginning, the thing is not yet, but it is more than merely nothing, for its Being is already in the beginning. Beginning is itself a case of Becoming; only the former term is employed with an eye to the further advance. If we were to adapt logic to the more usual method of the sciences, we might start with the represen-

tation of a Beginning as abstractly thought, or with Beginning as such, and then analyse this representation; and perhaps people would more readily admit, as a result of this analysis, that Being and Nothing present themselves as undivided in unity.

(4) It remains to note that such phrases as "Being and Nothing are the same," or "The unity of Being and Nothing"—like all other such unities, that of subject and object, and others—give rise to reasonable objection. They misrepresent the facts, by giving an exclusive prominence to the unity, and leaving the difference which undoubtedly exists in it (because it is Being and Nothing, for example, the unity of which is declared) without any express mention or notice. It accordingly seems as if the diversity had been unduly put out of court and neglected. The fact is, no speculative principle can be correctly expressed by any such propositional form, for the unity has to be conceived *in* the diversity, which is all the while present and explicit. "To become" is the true expression for the resultant of "To be" and "Not to be"; it is the unity of the two, but not only is it the unity, it is also inherent unrest—the unity, which is no mere reference-to-self and therefore without movement, but which, through the diversity of Being and Nothing that is in it, is at war within itself. Determinate being, on the other hand, is this unity, or Becoming in this form of unity: hence all that "is there and so," is one-sided and finite. The opposition between the two factors seems to have vanished; it is only implied in the unity, it is not explicitly put in it.

(5) The maxim of Becoming, that Being is the passage into Nought, and Nought the passage into Being, is controverted by the maxim of Pantheism, the doctrine of the eternity of matter, that from nothing comes nothing, and that something can only come out of something. The ancients saw plainly that the maxim, "From nothing comes nothing, from something something," really abolishes Becoming: for what it comes from and what it becomes are one and the same. Thus explained, the proposition is the maxim of abstract identity as upheld by the understanding. It cannot but seem strange, therefore, to hear such maxims as "Out of nothing comes nothing: Out of something comes something," calmly taught in these days, without the teacher being in the least aware that they are the basis of Pantheism, and even without his knowing that the ancients have exhausted all that is to be said about them.

Zusatz. Becoming is the first concrete thought, and therefore the first notion: whereas Being and Nought are empty abstractions. The notion of Being, therefore, of which we sometimes speak, must mean Becoming; not the mere point of Being, which is empty Nothing, any more than Nothing, which is empty Being. In Being then we have Nothing, and in Nothing Being: but this Being which does not lose itself in Nothing is Becoming. Nor must we omit the distinction, while we emphasise the unity of Becoming: without that distinction we should once more return to abstract Being. Becoming is only the explicit statement of what Being is in its truth.

We often hear it maintained that thought is opposed to being. Now in the face of such a statement, our first question ought to be, what is meant by being. If we understand being as it is defined by reflection, all that we can say of it is that it is what is wholly identical and affirmative. And if we then look at thought, it cannot escape us that thought also is at least what is absolutely identical with itself. Both therefore, being as well as thought, have the same attribute. This identity of being and thought is not however to be taken in a concrete sense, as if we could say that a stone, so far as it has being, is the same as a thinking man. A concrete thing is always very different from the abstract category as such. And in the case of being, we are speaking of nothing concrete: for being is the utterly abstract. So far then the question regarding the *being* of God—a being which is in itself concrete above all measure—is of slight importance.

As the first concrete thought-term, Becoming is the first adequate vehicle of truth. In the history of philosophy, this stage of the logical Idea finds its analogue in the system of Heraclitus. When Heraclitus says "All is flowing" (πάντα ῥεί), he enunciates Becoming as the fundamental feature of all existence, whereas the Eleatics, as already remarked, saw the only truth in Being, rigid processless Being. Glancing at the principle of the Eleatics, Heraclitus then goes on to say: Being no more is than not-Being (οὐδέν μᾶλλον τὸ ὂν τοῦ μὴ ὄντος ἐστί): a statement expressing the negativity of abstract Being, and its identity with not-Being, as made explicit in Becoming: both abstractions being alike untenable. This may be looked at as an instance of the real refutation of one system by another. To refute a philosophy is to exhibit the dialectical movement in its principle, and thus reduce it to a constituent member of a higher concrete form of the Idea. Even Becoming however, taken at its best on its own ground, is an extremely poor term: it needs to grow in depth and weight of meaning. Such deepened force we find, *e.g.*, in Life. Life is a Becoming; but that is not enough to exhaust the notion of life. A still higher form is found in Mind. Here too is Becoming, but richer and more intensive than mere logical Becoming. The elements, whose unity constitutes mind, are not the bare abstracts of Being and of Nought, but the system of the logical Idea and of Nature. End *Zusatz.*

IV

Toward a Concrete Metaphysics: Rationalism, Empiricism, Critical Philosophy, and the Idea

In this section we have something of an historical interlude before moving on to the more concrete content of the philosophies of Nature and Spirit. Hegel prefaces the *Encyclopaedia* with an historical *Vorbegriff*, which, lacking space for inclusion of material from his *Lectures on the History of Philosophy*, gives us valuable insight into Hegel's construal of the metaphysics and epistemology of previous philosophy. He groups his discussion under three headings, three "attitudes of thought to objectivity" or ways in which Mind relates to and regards its world. They correspond to (1) the metaphysics of *Verstand*, (2) empiricism and the Critical Philosophy, and (3) the theory of immediate or intuitive knowledge. In what follows, the chapter on immediate knowledge has been deleted in favor of Hegel's section on the Absolute Idea at the close of the *Encyclopaedia Logic*, which sums up the notion of truth inadequately expressed by the three above-mentioned attitudes and opens out into the Philosophy of Nature, our next section.

By "metaphysic of the past" Hegel means a philosophical attitude, the chief characteristic of which is "to make abstract identity its principle" and to try to grasp the truth by "the abstract and finite categories of the understanding [*Verstand*]." This pre-Kantian metaphysic is dogmatic, in the sense that it "maintains half-truths in their isolation," allowing the categories to become permanently fixed and not subject to further negation and development. As a result, these universals become finite by excluding from themselves the particular, which as thus excluded, stand over against this thinking as an antithetical objective, rendering the thought a thought *about* them and merely subjective. Thus in Descartes, for example, the soul becomes a thing; in Locke, the substance of things becomes a "*something, we know not what,*" and in Hume the ultimate irony of the metaphysical method, shared alike by abstractive rationalism and empiricism, emerges in the doctrine that the self which knows is itself unknown. The classical traditions of empiricism and rationalism after Locke and Descartes represent a kind of circus in response to the ill-formed question: "If the 'real' is outside or other than the mind, and the 'known' is inside or one with the mind, how can the *real* be *known?*" The empiricists and Kant turn the world's outside in, so to speak, and the rationalists turn the mind's inside out, but no solution in these terms satisfies, and in Hume, the Cartesian God, self, and world all alike disintegrate in the gap between cause and effect.[1]

Empiricism, which "abandons the search for truth in thought itself and goes to fetch it from experience, the outward and the inward present," shares the same defect as rationalist metaphysics: both locate the guarantee for the correctness of their definitions in "facts which emanate from experience," i.e., *Vorstellungen,* and in their method, both "proceed from data or assumptions which they accept as ultimate." But Hegel goes on to say that metaphysics and empiricism each have their positive side. The former possesses merit in affirming that "to think a thing was the means of finding its very self and nature." This position puts metaphysics on higher ground than the Critical Philosophy, which instead "bade man go and feed on mere husks and chaff [i.e., *phenomena*]." Likewise, empiricism contains "the great principle that whatever is true must be in the actual world and present to sensation." Elsewhere Hegel goes so far as to say that

Everything is in sensation (feeling): if you will, everything that emerges in conscious intelligence and in reason has its source and origin in sensation; for source and origin just means the first immediate manner in which a thing appears.[2]

Hegel elaborates on this in Lasson's third edition of the *Lectures on the Philosophy of History:*

It is true that everything spiritual . . . must also, and originally does, exist in the mode of feeling. But feeling is not the fount from which this content flows to man, but only a primal mode in which it exists in him. It is indeed the worst mode, a mode which he has in common with the animal. . . . If one says: "I feel such and such and so and so," then one has secluded himself in himself. Everybody else has the same right to say: "I don't feel it that way."[3]

We can detect in these words an affinity with Kant's claim in the *Critique of Pure Reason* that while all our knowledge *begins* with sense-experience, it does not follow that it is all reducible to this form.

The selections in this chapter, on the three possible "attitudes of thought to objectivity" of which the third (Idea) is a synthesis of the first and second, give us what amounts to an analytical history of epistemology. Hegel's standpoint throughout is essentially Kantian but also "post-Kantian," forcing the Kantian arguments on the human capacity to know to conclusions Kant declined to draw. Hegel's analysis of Kant's philosophy is pertinent, concise, and clearly written, and we shall not here try to summarize it. With the possible exception of Aristotle, Kant has probably been the most influential force behind Hegel's thinking, which is always cognizant and respectful of its predecessors.

Notes. Toward a Concrete Metaphysics: Rationalism, Empiricism, Critical Philosophy, and the Idea

1. In his brilliant criticism of British empiricism in *Retreat from Truth*, G.R.G. Mure remarks that the "traditional account of empiricism from Locke to Hume always reminds me of the magical vacuum-cleaner. Some years ago, when vacuum-cleaners were a fascinating novelty, *Punch* published a brilliant little story told in pictures which succeeded one another roughly as follows. In the first, the householder, intrigued but sceptical, stands contemplating his newly purchased machine. In the second he has reaped a noble heap of dust. Then, sucking superbly and far beyond its advertised powers, the cleaner absorbs the carpet and various articles of furniture. The delighted owner rushes out into the street and easily collects several vehicles and a troop of cavalry. Finally, his face alight with the eternal curiosity of mankind from Pandora to the sorcerer's apprentice, he peeps over the edge of the funnel and vanishes." *Retreat from Truth* (Oxford: Basil Blackwell, 1958), pp. 55–56.

2. *Philosophy of Mind*, p.73.

3. Trans. Robert S. Hartman in *Reason in History* (Indianapolis: Bobbs-Merrill, 1953), p. 17.

ATTITUDES OF THOUGHT TO OBJECTIVITY

25. The term "Objective Thoughts" indicates the *truth*—the truth which is to be the absolute *object* of philosophy, and not merely the goal at which it aims. But the very expression cannot fail to suggest an opposition, to characterise and appreciate which is the main motive of the philosophical attitude of the present time, and which forms the real problem of the question about truth and our means of ascertaining it. If the thought-forms are vitiated by a fixed antithesis, *i.e.*, if they are only of a finite character, they are unsuitable for the self-centred universe of truth, and truth can find no adequate receptacle in thought. Such thought, which can produce only limited and partial categories and proceed by their means, is what in the stricter sense of the word is termed Understanding. The finitude, further, of these categories lies in two points. Firstly, they are only subjective, and the antithesis of an objective permanently clings to them. Secondly, they are always of restricted content, and so persist in antithesis to one another and still more to the Absolute. In order more fully to explain the position and import here attributed to logic, the attitudes in which thought is supposed to stand to objectivity will next be examined by way of further introduction.

In my *Phenomenology of the Spirit*, which on that account was at its publication described as the first part of the "System of Philosophy," the method adopted was to begin with the first and simplest phase of mind, immediate consciousness, and to show how that stage gradually of necessity worked onward to the philosophical point of view, the necessity of that view being proved by the process. But in these circumstances it was impossible to restrict the quest to the mere form of consciousness. For the stage of philosophical knowledge is the richest in material and organisation, and therefore, as it came before us in the shape of a result, it pre-supposed the existence of the concrete formations of consciousness, such as individual and social morality, art, and religion. In the development of consciousness, which at first sight appears limited to the point of form merely, there is thus at the same time included the development of the matter or of the objects discussed in the special branches of philosophy. But the latter process must, so to speak, go on behind consciousness, since those facts are the essential nucleus which is raised into conscious-

SOURCE: *Logic*, Wallace, pp. 57–75.

ness. The exposition accordingly is rendered more intricate, because so much that properly belongs to the concrete branches is prematurely dragged into the introduction. The survey which follows in the present work has even more the inconvenience of being only historical and inferential in its method. But it tries especially to show how the questions men have proposed, outside the school, on the nature of Knowledge, Faith, and the like—questions which they imagine to have no connexion with abstract thoughts—are really reducible to the simple categories, which first get cleared up in Logic.

FIRST ATTITUDE OF THOUGHT TO OBJECTIVITY

26. The first of these attitudes of thought is seen in the method which has no doubts and no sense of the contradiction in thought, or of the hostility of thought against itself. It entertains an unquestioning belief that reflection is the means of ascertaining the truth, and of bringing the objects before the mind as they really are. And in this belief it advances straight upon its objects, takes the materials furnished by sense and perception, and reproduces them from itself as facts of thought; and then, believing this result to be the truth, the method is content. Philosophy in its earliest stages, all the sciences, and even the daily action and movement of consciousness live in this faith.

27. This method of thought has never become aware of the antithesis of subjective and objective; and to that extent there is nothing to prevent its statements from possessing a genuinely philosophical and speculative character, though it is just as possible that they may never get beyond finite categories, or the stage where the antithesis is still unresolved. In the present introduction the main question for us is to observe this attitude of thought in its extreme form; and we shall accordingly first of all examine its second and inferior aspect as a philosophic system. One of the clearest instances of it, and one lying nearest to ourselves, may be found in the Metaphysic of the Past as it subsisted among us previous to the philosophy of Kant. It is however only in reference to the history of philosophy that this Metaphysic can be said to belong to the past: the thing is always and at all places to be found, as the view which the abstract understanding takes of the objects of reason. And it is in this point that the real and immediate good lies of a closer examination of its main scope and its *modus operandi.*

28. This metaphysical system took the laws and forms of thought to be the fundamental laws and forms of things. It assumed that to

think a thing was the means of finding its very self and nature: and to that extent it occupied higher ground than the Critical Philosophy which succeeded it. But in the first instance (1) *these terms of thought were cut off from their connexion*, their solidarity; each was believed valid by itself and capable of serving as a predicate of the truth. It was the general assumption of this metaphysic that a knowledge of the Absolute was gained by assigning predicates to it. It neither inquired what the terms of the understanding specially meant or what they were worth, nor did it test the method which characterises the Absolute by the assignment of predicates.

As an example of such predicates may be taken, Existence, in the proposition, "God has existence": Finitude or Infinity, as in the question; "Is the world finite or infinite?": Simple and Complex, in the proposition, "The soul is simple"—or again, "The thing is a unity, a whole," &c. Nobody asked whether such predicates had any intrinsic and independent truth, or if the propositional form could be a form of truth.

Zusatz. The Metaphysic of the past assumed, as unsophisticated belief always does that thought apprehends the very self of things, and that things, to become what they truly are, require to be thought. For Nature and the human soul are a very Proteus in their perpetual transformations; and it soon occurs to the observer that the first crude impression of things is not their essential being. This is a point of view the very reverse of the result arrived at by the Critical Philosophy; a result, of which it may be said, that it bade man go and feed on mere husks and chaff.

We must look more closely into the procedure of that old metaphysic. In the first place it never went beyond the province of the analytic understanding. Without preliminary inquiry it adopted the abstract categories of thought and let them rank as predicates of truth. But in using the term thought we must not forget the difference between finite or discursive thinking and the thinking which is infinite and rational. The categories, as they meet us *primâ facie* and in isolation, are finite forms. But truth is always infinite, and cannot be expressed or presented to consciousness in finite terms. The phrase *infinite thought* may excite surprise, if we adhere to the modern conception that thought is always limited. But it is, speaking rightly, the very essence of thought to be infinite. The nominal explanation of calling a thing finite is that it has an end, that it exists up to a certain

point only, where it comes into contact with, and is limited by, its
other. The finite therefore subsists in reference to its other, which is
its negation and presents itself as its limit. Now thought is always in
its own sphere; its relations are with itself, and it is its own object. In
having a thought for object, I am at home with myself. The thinking
power, the "I," is therefore infinite, because, when it thinks, it is in
relation to an object which is itself. Generally speaking, an object
means a something else, a negative confronting me. But in the case
where thought thinks itself, it has an object which is at the same time
no object: in other words, its objectivity is suppressed and transformed into an idea. Thought, as thought, therefore in its unmixed
nature involves no limits; it is finite only when it keeps to limited
categories, which it believes to be ultimate. Infinite or speculative
thought, on the contrary, while it no less defines, does in the very act
of limiting and defining make that defect vanish. And so infinity is not,
as most frequently happens, to be conceived as an abstract away and
away for ever and ever, but in the simple manner previously indicated.

The thinking of the old metaphysical system was finite. Its whole
mode of action was regulated by categories, the limits of which it
believed to be permanently fixed and not subject to any further negation. Thus, one of its questions was: Has God existence? The question supposes that existence is an altogether positive term, a sort of
ne plus ultra. We shall see however at a later point that existence is by
no means a merely positive term, but one which is too low for the
Absolute Idea, and unworthy of God. A second question in these
metaphysical systems was: Is the world finite or infinite? The very
terms of the question assume that the finite is a permanent contradictory to the infinite: and one can easily see that, when they are so
opposed, the infinite, which of course ought to be the whole, only
appears as a single aspect and suffers restriction from the finite. But
a restricted infinity is itself only a finite. In the same way it was asked
whether the soul was simple or composite. Simpleness was, in other
words, taken to be an ultimate characteristic, giving expression to a
whole truth. Far from being so, simpleness is the expression of a
half-truth, as one-sided and abstract as existence: a term of thought,
which, as we shall hereafter see, is itself untrue and hence unable to
hold truth. If the soul be viewed as merely and abstractly simple, it
is characterised in an inadequate and finite way.

It was therefore the main question of the pre-Kantian metaphysic
to discover whether predicates of the kind mentioned were to be

ascribed to its objects. Now these predicates are after all only limited formulae of the understanding which, instead of expressing the truth, merely impose a limit. More than this, it should be noted that the chief feature of the method lay in "assigning" or "attributing" predicates to the object that was to be cognised, for example, to God. But attribution is no more than an external reflection about the object: the predicates by which the object is to be determined are supplied from the resources of picture-thought, and are applied in a mechanical way. Whereas, if we are to have genuine cognition, the object must characterise its own self and not derive its predicates from without. Even supposing we follow the method of predicating, the mind cannot help feeling that predicates of this sort fail to exhaust the object. From the same point of view the Orientals are quite correct in calling God the many-named or the myriad-named One. One after another of these finite categories leaves the soul unsatisfied, and the Oriental sage is compelled unceasingly to seek for more and more of such predicates. In finite things it is no doubt the case that they have to be characterised through finite predicates: and with these things the understanding finds proper scope for its special action. Itself finite, it knows only the nature of the finite. Thus, when I call some action a theft, I have characterised the action in its essential facts; and such a knowledge is sufficient for the judge. Similarly, finite things stand to each other as cause and effect, force and exercise, and when they are apprehended in these categories, they are known in their finitude. But the objects of reason cannot be defined by these finite predicates. To try to do so was the defect of the old metaphysic. End *Zusatz.*

29. Predicates of this kind, taken individually, have but a limited range of meaning, and no one can fail to perceive how inadequate they are, and how far they fall below the fullness of detail which our imaginative thought gives, in the case, for example, of God, Mind, or Nature. Besides, though the fact of their being all predicates of one subject supplies them with a certain connexion, their several meanings keep them apart; and consequently each is brought in as a stranger in relation to the others.

The first of these defects the Orientals sought to remedy, when, for example, they defined God by attributing to Him many names; but still they felt that the number of names would have had to be infinite.

30. (2) In the second place, *the metaphysical systems adopted a wrong criterion.* Their objects were no doubt totalities which in their own

proper selves belong to reason—that is, to the organised and systematically developed universe of thought. But these totalities—God,
the Soul, the World—were taken by the metaphysician as subjects
made and ready, to form the basis for an application of the categories
of the understanding. They were assumed from popular conception.
Accordingly popular conception was the only canon for settling
whether or not the predicates were suitable and sufficient.

31. The common conceptions of God, the Soul, the World may be
supposed to afford thought a firm and fast footing. They do not really
do so. Besides having a particular and subjective character clinging
to them, and thus leaving room for great variety of interpretation,
they themselves first of all require a firm and fast definition by
thought. This may be seen in any of these propositions where the
predicate, or in philosophy the category, is needed to indicate what
the subject, or the conception we start with, is.

In such a sentence as "God is eternal," we begin with the conception of God, not knowing as yet what he is: to tell us that, is the
business of the predicate. In the principles of logic, accordingly,
where the terms formulating the subject-matter are those of thought
only, it is not merely superfluous to make these categories predicates
to propositions in which God, or, still vaguer, the Absolute, is the
subject, but it would also have the disadvantage of suggesting another canon than the nature of thought. Besides, the propositional
form (and for proposition, it would be more correct to substitute
judgment) is not suited to express the concrete—and the true is
always concrete—or the speculative. Every judgment is by its form
one-sided and, to that extent, false.

Zusatz. This metaphysic was not free or objective thinking. Instead
of letting the object freely and spontaneously expound its own characteristics, metaphysic pre-supposed it ready-made. If any one wishes
to know what free thought means, he must go to Greek philosophy:
for Scholasticism, like these metaphysical systems, accepted its facts,
and accepted them as a dogma from the authority of the Church. We
moderns, too, by our whole up-bringing, have been initiated into
ideas which it is extremely difficult to overstep, on account of their
far-reaching significance. But the ancient philosophers were in a different position. They were men who lived wholly in the perceptions
of the senses, and who, after their rejection of mythology and its
fancies, pre-supposed nothing but the heaven above and the earth
around. In these material, non-metaphysical surroundings, thought

is free and enjoys its own privacy—cleared of everything material, and thoroughly at home. This feeling that we are all our own is character-istic of free thought—of that voyage into the open, where nothing is below us or above us, and we stand in solitude with ourselves alone. End *Zusatz*.

32. (3) In the third place, *this system of metaphysic turned into Dogma-tism*. When our thought never ranges beyond narrow and rigid terms, we are forced to assume that of two opposite assertions, such as were the above propositions, the one must be true and the other false.

Zusatz. Dogmatism may be most simply described as the contrary of Scepticism. The ancient Sceptics gave the name of Dogmatism to every philosophy whatever holding a system of definite doctrine. In this large sense Scepticism may apply the name even to philosophy which is properly Speculative. But in the narrower sense, Dogmatism consists in the tenacity which draws a hard and fast line between certain terms and others opposite to them. We may see this clearly in the strict "Either-or." For instance, The world is either finite or infinite; but one of these two it must be. The contrary of this rigidity is the characteristic of all Speculative truth. There no such inadequate formulae are allowed, nor can they possibly exhaust it. These for-mulae Speculative truth holds in union as a totality, whereas Dogma-tism invests them in their isolation with a title to fixity and truth.

It often happens in philosophy that the half-truth takes its place beside the whole truth and assumes on its own account the position of something permanent. But the fact is that the half-truth, instead of being a fixed or self-subsistent principle, is a mere element ab-solved and included in the whole. The metaphysic of understanding is dogmatic, because it maintains half-truths in their isolation: whereas the idealism of speculative philosophy carries out the princi-ple of totality and shows that it can reach beyond the inadequate formularies of abstract thought. Thus idealism would say: The soul is neither finite only, nor infinite only; it is really the one just as much as the other, and in that way neither the one nor the other. In other words, such formularies in their isolation are inadmissible, and only come into account as formative elements in a larger notion. Such idealism we see even in the ordinary phases of consciousness. Thus we say of sensible things, that they are changeable: that is, they *are*, but it is equally true that they are *not*. We show more obstinacy in dealing with the categories of the understanding. These are terms which we believe to be somewhat firmer—or even absolutely firm and fast. We look upon them as separated from each other by an infinite chasm, so that opposite categories can never get at each other. The battle of reason is the struggle to break up the rigidity to which the understanding has reduced everything. End *Zusatz.*

33. The *first* part of this metaphysic in its systematic form is Ontology, or the doctrine of the abstract characteristics of Being. The multitude of these characteristics, and the limits set to their applicability, are not founded upon any principle. They have in consequence to be enumerated as experience and circumstances direct, and the import ascribed to them is founded only upon common sensualised conceptions, upon assertions that particular words are used in a particular sense, and even perhaps upon etymology. If experience pronounces the list to be complete, and if the usage of language, by its agreement, shows the analysis to be correct, the metaphysician is satisfied; and the intrinsic and independent truth and necessity of such characteristics is never made a matter of investigation at all.

To ask if being, existence, finitude, simplicity, complexity, &c., are notions intrinsically and independently true, must surprise those who believe that a question about truth can only concern propositions (as to whether a notion is or is not with truth to be attributed, as the phrase is, to a subject), and that falsehood lies in the contradiction existing between the subject in our ideas, and the notion to be predicated of it. Now as the notion is concrete, it and every character of it in general is essentially a self-contained unity of distinct characteristics. If truth then were nothing more than the absence of contradiction, it would be first of all necessary in the case of every notion to examine whether it, taken individually, did not contain this sort of intrinsic contradiction.

34. The *second* branch of the metaphysical system was Rational Psychology or Pneumatology. It dealt with the metaphysical nature of the Soul—that is, of the Mind regarded as a thing. It expected to find immortality in a sphere dominated by the laws of composition, time, qualitative change, and quantitative increase or decrease.

Zusatz. The name "rational," given to this species of psychology, served to contrast it with empirical modes of observing the phenomena of the soul. Rational psychology viewed the soul in its metaphysical nature, and through the categories supplied by abstract thought. The rationalists endeavoured to ascertain the inner nature of the soul as it is in itself and as it is for thought. In philosophy at present we hear little of the soul: the favourite term now is mind (spirit). The two are distinct, soul being as it were the middle term between body and spirit, or the bond between the two. The mind, as soul, is immersed in corporeity, and the soul is the animating principle of the body.

The pre-Kantian metaphysic, we say, viewed the soul as a thing. "Thing" is a very ambiguous word. By a thing, we mean, firstly, an immediate existence, something we represent in sensuous form; and in this meaning the term has been applied to the soul. Hence the question regarding the seat of the soul. Of course, if the soul has a seat, it is in space and sensuously envisaged. So, too, if the soul be viewed as a thing, we can ask whether the soul is simple or composite. The question is important as bearing on the immortality of the soul, which is supposed to depend on the absence of composition. But the fact is, that in abstract simplicity we have a category, which as little corresponds to the nature of the soul, as that of compositeness.

One word on the relation of rational to empirical psychology. The former, because it sets itself to apply thought to cognise mind and even to demonstrate the result of such thinking, is the higher; whereas empirical psychology starts from perception, and only recounts and describes what perception supplies. But if we propose to think the mind, we must not be quite so shy of its special phenomena. Mind is essentially active in the same sense as the Schoolmen said that God is "absolute actuosity." But if the mind is active it must as it were utter itself. It is wrong therefore to take the mind for a processless *ens*, as did the old metaphysic which divided the processless inward life of the mind from its outward life. The mind, of all things, must be looked at in its concrete actuality, in its energy; and in such a way that its manifestations are seen to be determined by its inward force. End *Zusatz*.

35. The *third* branch of metaphysics was Cosmology. The topics it embraced were the world, its contingency, necessity, eternity, limitation in time and space; the laws (only formal) of its changes; the freedom of man and the origin of evil.

To these topics it applied what were believed to be thorough-going contrasts: such as contingency and necessity; external and internal necessity; efficient and final cause, or causality in general and design; essence or substance and phenomenon; form and matter; freedom and necessity; happiness and pain; good and evil.

Zusatz. The object of Cosmology comprised not merely Nature, but Mind too, in its external complication in its phenomenon, in fact, existence in general, or the sum of finite things. This object however it viewed not as a concrete whole, but only under certain abstract points of view. Thus the questions Cosmology attempted to solve were such as these: Is accident or necessity dominant in the world? Is the world eternal or created? It was therefore a chief concern of this study to lay down what were called general Cosmological laws: for instance, that Nature does not act by fits and starts. And by fits and starts (*saltus*) they meant a qualitative difference or qualitative alteration showing itself without any antecedent determining mean: whereas, on the contrary, a gradual change (of quantity) is obviously not without intermediation.

In regard to Mind as it makes itself felt in the world, the questions which Cosmology chiefly discussed turned upon the freedom of man and the origin of evil. Nobody can deny that these are questions of the highest importance. But to give them a satisfactory answer, it is above all things necessary not to claim finality for the abstract formulae of understanding, or to suppose that each of the two terms in an antithesis has an independent subsistence or can be treated in its isolation as a complete and self-centred truth. This however is the general position taken by the metaphysicians before Kant, and appears in their cosmological discussions, which for that reason were incapable of compassing their purpose, to understand the phenomena of the world. Observe how they proceed with the distinction between freedom and necessity, in their application of these categories to Nature and Mind. Nature they regard as subject in its workings to necessity; Mind they hold to be free. No doubt there is a real foundation for this distinction in the very core of the Mind itself: but freedom and necessity, when thus abstractly opposed, are terms applicable only in the finite world to which, as such, they belong. A freedom involving no necessity, and mere necessity without freedom, are abstract and in this way untrue formulae of thought. Freedom is no blank indeterminateness: essentially concrete, and unvaryingly self-determinate, it is so far at the same time necessary.

Necessity, again, in the ordinary acceptation of the term in popular philosophy, means determination from without only, as in finite mechanics, where a body moves only when it is struck by another body, and moves in the direction communicated to it by the impact. This however is a merely external necessity, not the real inward necessity which is identical with freedom.

The case is similar with the contrast of Good and Evil—the favourite contrast of the introspective modern world. If we regard Evil as possessing a fixity of its own, apart and distinct from Good, we are to a certain extent right: there is an opposition between them: nor do those who maintain the apparent and relative character of the opposition mean that Evil and Good in the Absolute are one, or, in accordance with the modern phrase, that a thing first becomes evil from our way of looking at it. The error arises when we take Evil as a permanent positive, instead of—what it really is—a negative which, though it would fain assert itself, has no real persistence, and is, in fact, only the absolute sham-existence of negativity in itself. End *Zusatz.*

36. The *fourth* branch of metaphysics is Natural or Rational Theology. The notion of God, or God as a possible being, the proofs of his existence, and his properties, formed the study of this branch.

(*a*) When understanding thus discusses the Deity, its main purpose is to find what predicates correspond or not to the fact we have in our imagination as God. And in so doing it assumes the contrast between positive and negative to be absolute; and hence, in the long run, nothing is left for the notion as understanding takes it, but the empty abstraction of indeterminate Being, of mere reality or positivity, the lifeless product of modern "Deism."

(*b*) The method of demonstration employed in finite knowledge must always lead to an inversion of the true order. For it requires the statement of some objective ground for God's being, which thus acquires the appearance of being derived from something else. This mode of proof, guided as it is by the canon of mere analytical identity, is embarrassed by the difficulty of passing from the finite to the infinite. Either the finitude of the existing world, which is left as much a fact as it was before, clings to the notion of Deity, and God has to be defined as the immediate substance of that world—which is Pantheism: or He remains an object set over against the subject, and in this way, finite—which is Dualism.

(*c*) The attributes of God which ought to be various and precise, had, properly speaking, sunk and disappeared in the abstract notion of pure reality, of indeterminate Being. Yet in our material thought, the finite world continues, meanwhile, to have a real being, with God as a sort of antithesis: and thus arises the further picture of different relations of God to the world. These, formulated as properties, must, on the one hand, as relations to finite circumstances, themselves possess a finite character (giving us such properties as just, gracious, mighty, wise, &c.); on the other hand they must be infinite. Now on this level of thought the only means, and a hazy one, of reconciling these opposing requirements was quantitative exaltation of the properties, forcing them into indeterminateness—into the *sensus eminentior*. But it was an expedient which really destroyed the property and left a mere name.

Zusatz. The object of the old metaphysical theology was to see how far unassisted reason could go in the knowledge of God. Certainly a reason-derived knowledge of God is the highest problem of philosophy. The earliest teachings of religion are figurate conceptions of God. These conceptions, as the Creed arranges them, are imparted to us in youth. They are the doctrines of our religion, and in so far as the individual rests his faith on these doctrines and feels them to be the truth, he has all he needs as a Christian. Such is faith: and the science of this faith is Theology. But until Theology is something more than a bare enumeration and compilation of these doctrines *ab extra*, it has no right to the title of science. Even the method so much in vogue at present—the purely historical mode of treatment—which for example reports what has been said by this or the other Father of the Church—does not invest theology with a scientific character. To get that, we must go on to comprehend the facts by thought—which is the business of philosophy. Genuine theology is thus at the same time a real philosophy of religion, as it was, we may add, in the Middle Ages.

And now let us examine this rational theology more narrowly. It was a science which approached God not by reason but by understanding, and, in its mode of thought, employed the terms without any sense of their mutual limitations and connexions. The notion of God formed the subject of discussion; and yet the criterion of our knowledge was derived from such an extraneous source as the materialised conception of God. Now thought must be free in its movements. It is no doubt to be remembered, that the result of independent thought harmonises with the import of the Christian religion:

for the Christian religion is a revelation of reason. But such a harmony surpassed the efforts of rational theology. It proposed to define the figurate conception of God in terms of thought; but it resulted in a notion of God which was what we may call the abstract of positivity or reality, to the exclusion of all negation. God was accordingly defined to be the most real of all beings. Any one can see however that this most real of beings, in which negation forms no part, is the very opposite of what it ought to be and of what understanding supposes it to be. Instead of being rich and full above all measure, it is so narrowly conceived that it is, on the contrary, extremely poor and altogether empty. It is with reason that the heart craves a concrete body of truth; but without definite feature, that is, without negation, contained in the notion, there can only be an abstraction. When the notion of God is apprehended only as that of the abstract or most real being, God is, as it were, relegated to another world beyond: and to speak of a knowledge of him would be meaningless. Where there is no definite quality, knowledge is impossible. Mere light is mere darkness.

The second problem of rational theology was to prove the existence of God. Now, in this matter, the main point to be noted is that demonstration, as the understanding employs it, means the dependence of one truth on another. In such proofs we have a pre-supposition—something firm and fast, from which something else follows; we exhibit the dependence of some truth from an assumed starting-point. Hence, if this mode of demonstration is applied to the existence of God, it can only mean that the being of God is to depend on other terms, which will then constitute the ground of his being. It is at once evident that this will lead to some mistake: for God must be simply and solely the ground of everything, and in so far not dependent upon anything else. And a perception of this danger has in modern times led some to say that God's existence is not capable of proof, but must be immediately or intuitively apprehended. Reason, however, and even sound common sense give demonstration a meaning quite different from that of the understanding. The demonstration of reason no doubt starts from something which is not God. But, as it advances, it does not leave the starting-point a mere unexplained fact, which is what it was. On the contrary it exhibits that point as derivative and called into being, and then God is seen to be primary, truly immediate and self-subsisting, with the means of derivation wrapt up and absorbed in himself. Those who say: "Consider Nature, and Nature will lead you to God; you will find an absolute final cause:" do not mean that God is something derivative: they mean that it is we who proceed to God himself from another; and in this way God, though the consequence, is also the absolute ground of the initial step. The relation of the two things is reversed; and what came as a consequence, being shown to be an antecedent, the original antecedent is reduced to a consequence. This is always the way, moreover, whenever reason demonstrates.

If in the light of the present discussion we cast one glance more on the metaphysical method as a whole, we find its main characteristic was to make abstract identity its principle and to try to apprehend the objects of reason by the abstract and finite categories of the understanding. But this infinite of the understanding, this pure essence, is still finite: it has excluded all the variety of particular things, which thus limit and deny it. Instead of winning a concrete, this metaphysic stuck fast on an abstract, identity. Its good point was the perception that thought alone constitutes the essence of all that is. It derived its materials from earlier philosophers, particularly the Schoolmen. In speculative philosophy the understanding undoubtedly forms a stage, but not a stage at which we should keep for ever standing. Plato is no metaphysician of this imperfect type, still less Aristotle, although the contrary is generally believed. End *Zusatz*.

SECOND ATTITUDE

I. Empiricism.

37. Under these circumstances a double want began to be felt. Partly it was the need of a concrete subject-matter, as a counterpoise to the abstract theories of the understanding, which is unable to advance unaided from its generalities to specialisation and determination. Partly, too, it was the demand for something fixed and secure, so as to exclude the possibility of proving anything and everything in the sphere, and according to the method, of the finite formulae of thought. Such was the genesis of Empirical philosophy, which abandons the search for truth in thought itself, and goes to fetch it from Experience, the outward and the inward present.

Zusatz. The rise of Empiricism is due to the need thus stated of concrete contents, and a firm footing—needs which the abstract metaphysic of the understanding failed to satisfy. Now by concrete-

SOURCE: *Logic*, Wallace, pp. 76–110, 115–120.

ness of contents it is meant that we must know the objects of consciousness as intrinsically determinate and as the unity of distinct characteristics. But, as we have already seen, this is by no means the case with the metaphysic of understanding, if it conform to its principle. With the mere understanding, thinking is limited to the form of an abstract universal, and can never advance to the particularisation of this universal. Thus we find the metaphysicians engaged in an attempt to elicit by the instrumentality of thought, what was the essence or fundamental attribute of the Soul. The Soul, they said, is simple. The simplicity thus ascribed to the Soul meant a mere and utter simplicity, from which difference is excluded: difference, or in other words composition, being made the fundamental attribute of body, or of matter in general. Clearly, in simplicity of this narrow type we have a very shallow category, quite incapable of embracing the wealth of the soul or of the mind. When it thus appeared that abstract metaphysical thinking was inadequate, it was felt that resource must be had to empirical psychology. The same happened in the case of Rational Physics. The current phrases there were, for instance, that space is infinite, that Nature makes no leap, &c. Evidently this phraseology was wholly unsatisfactory in presence of the plenitude and life of nature. End *Zusatz.*

38. To some extent this source from which Empiricism draws is common to it with metaphysic. It is in our materialised conceptions, *i.e.*, in facts which emanate, in the first instance, from experience, that metaphysic also finds the guarantee for the correctness of its definitions (including both its initial assumptions and its more detailed body of doctrine). But, on the other hand, it must be noted that the single sensation is not the same thing as experience, and that the Empirical School elevates the facts included under sensation, feeling, and perception into the form of general ideas, propositions or laws. This, however, it does with the reservation that these general principles (such as force), are to have no further import or validity of their own beyond that taken from the sense-impression, and that no connexion shall be deemed legitimate except what can be shown to exist in phenomena. And on the subjective side Empirical cognition has its stable footing in the fact that in a sensation consciousness is directly present and certain of itself.

In Empiricism lies the great principle that whatever is true must be in the actual world and present to sensation. This principle contradicts that "ought to be" on the strength of which "reflection" is vain enough to treat the actual present with scorn and to point to a scene beyond—a scene which is assumed to have place and being only in the understanding of those who talk of it. No less than Empiricism, philosophy (§7)* recognises only what is, and has nothing to do with what merely ought to be and what is thus confessed not to exist. On the subjective side, too, it is right to notice the valuable principle of freedom involved in Empiricism. For the main lesson of Empiricism is that man must see for himself and feel that he is present in every fact of knowledge which he has to accept.

When it is carried out to its legitimate consequences, Empiricism —being in its facts limited to the finite sphere—denies the super-sensible in general, or at least any knowledge of it which would define its nature; it leaves thought no powers except abstraction and formal universality and identity. But there is a fundamental delusion in all scientific empiricism. It employs the metaphysical categories of matter, force, those of one, many, generality, infinity, &c.; following the clue given by these categories it proceeds to draw conclusions, and in so doing pre-supposes and applies the syllogistic form. And all the while it is unaware that it contains metaphysics—in wielding which, it makes use of those categories and their combinations in a style utterly thoughtless and uncritical.

Zusatz. From Empiricism came the cry: "Stop roaming in empty abstractions, keep your eyes open, lay hold on man and nature as they are here before you, enjoy the present moment." Nobody can deny that there is a good deal of truth in these words. The every-day world, what is here and now, was a good exchange for the futile other-world —for the mirages and the chimeras of the abstract understanding. And thus was acquired an infinite principle—that solid footing so much missed in the old metaphysic. Finite principles are the most that the understanding can pick out—and these being essentially unstable and tottering, the structure they supported must collapse with a crash. Always the instinct of reason was to find an infinite principle. As yet, the time had not come for finding it in thought. Hence, this instinct seized upon the present, the Here, the This—where doubtless there is implicit infinite form, but not in the genuine existence of that form. The external world is the truth, if it could but know it: for the truth is actual and must exist. The infinite principle, the self-centred truth, therefore, is in the world for reason to discover: though it exists in an individual and sensible shape, and not in its truth.

*See above, pp. 25–26.

Besides, this school makes sense-perception the form in which fact is to be apprehended: and in this consists the defect of Empiricism. Sense-perception as such is always individual, always transient: not indeed that the process of knowledge stops short at sensation: on the contrary, it proceeds to find out the universal and permanent element in the individual apprehended by sense. This is the process leading from simple perception to experience.

In order to form experiences, Empiricism makes especial use of the form of Analysis. In the impression of sense we have a concrete of many elements, the several attributes of which we are expected to peel off one by one, like the coats of an onion. In thus dismembering the thing, it is understood that we disintegrate and take to pieces these attributes which have coalesced, and add nothing but our own act of disintegration. Yet analysis is the process from the immediacy of sensation to thought: those attributes, which the object analysed contains in union, acquire the form of universality by being separated. Empiricism therefore labours under a delusion, if it supposes that, while analysing the objects, it leaves them as they were: it really transforms the concrete into an abstract. And as a consequence of this change the living thing is killed: life can exist only in the concrete and one. Not that we can do without this division, if it be our intention to comprehend. Mind itself is an inherent division. The error lies in forgetting that this is only one-half of the process, and that the main point is the re-union of what has been parted. And it is where analysis never gets beyond the stage of partition that the words of the poet are true:

> If you want to describe life and gather its meaning,
> To drive out its spirit must be your beginning,
> Then though fast in your hand lie the parts one by one
> The spirit that linked them, alas is gone
> And "Nature's Laboratory" is only a name
> That the chemist bestows on't to hide his own shame.[*]

Analysis starts from the concrete; and the possession of this material gives it a considerable advantage over the abstract thinking of the old metaphysics. It establishes the differences in things: and this is very important: but these very differences are nothing after all

---

[*] *Faust,* part I, sc. 4. (Wallace's rendering, but see his note on p. 398 of his translation of the *Encyclopaedia Logic.* Only the last four lines are quoted, though in a different order, by Hegel, and a prose version of them would run: "Nature's laboratory" the chemist calls it, mocking himself and confessing his ignorance. The parts, certainly, he holds in his hand, but alas the spiritual link is missing.)

but abstract attributes, *i.e.* thoughts. These thoughts, it is assumed, contain the real essence of the objects; and thus once more we see the axiom of bygone metaphysics reappear, that the truth of things lies in thought.

Let us next compare the empirical theory with that of metaphysics in the matter of their respective contents. We find the latter, as already stated, taking for its theme the universal objects of the reason, viz., God, the Soul, and the World: and these themes, accepted from popular conception, it was the problem of philosophy to reduce into the form of thoughts. Another specimen of the same method was the Scholastic philosophy, the theme pre-supposed by which was formed by the dogmas of the Christian Church: and it aimed at fixing their meaning and giving them a systematic arrangement through thought. The facts on which Empiricism is based are of entirely different kind. They are the sensible facts of nature and the facts of the finite mind. In other words, Empiricism deals with a finite material—and the old metaphysicians had an infinite—though, let us add, they made this infinite content finite by the finite form of the understanding. The same finitude of form reappears in Empiricism—but here the facts are finite also. To this extent, then, both modes of philosophising have the same method; both proceed from data or assumptions, which they accept as ultimate. Generally speaking, Empiricism finds the truth in the outward world; and even if it allow a super-sensible world, it holds knowledge of that world to be impossible, and would restrict us to the province of sense-perception. This doctrine when systematically carried out produces what has been latterly termed Materialism. Materialism of this stamp looks upon matter, *quâ* matter, as the genuine objective world. But with matter we are at once introduced to an abstraction, which as such cannot be perceived: and it may be maintained that there is no matter, because, as it exists, it is always something definite and concrete. Yet the abstraction we term matter is supposed to lie at the basis of the whole world of sense, and expresses the sense-world in its simplest terms as out-and-out individualisation, and hence a congeries of points in mutual exclusion. So long then as this sensible sphere is and continues to be for Empiricism a mere datum, we have a doctrine of bondage: for we become free, when we are confronted by no absolutely alien world, but depend upon a fact which we ourselves are. Consistently with the empirical point of view, besides, reason and unreason can only be subjective: in other words, we must take what is given just as it is, and we have no right to ask whether and to what extent it is rational in its own nature. End *Zusatz*.

39. Touching this principle it has been justly observed that in what we call Experience, as distinct from mere single perception of single facts, there are two elements. The one is the matter, infinite in its multiplicity, and as it stands a mere set of singulars: the other is the form, the characteristics of universality and necessity. Mere experience no doubt offers many, perhaps innumerable cases of similar perceptions: but, after all, no multitude, however great, can be the same thing as universality. Similarly, mere experience affords perceptions of changes succeeding each other and of objects in juxtaposition; but it presents no necessary connexion. If perception, therefore, is to maintain its claim to be the sole basis of what men hold for truth, universality and necessity appear something illegitimate: they become an accident of our minds, a mere custom, the content of which might be otherwise constituted than it is.

It is an important corollary of this theory, that on this empirical mode of treatment legal and ethical principles and laws, as well as the truths of religion, are exhibited as the work of chance, and stripped of their objective character and inner truth.

The scepticism of Hume, to which this conclusion was chiefly due, should be clearly marked off from Greek scepticism. Hume assumes the truth of the empirical element, feeling and sensation, and proceeds to challenge universal principles and laws, because they have no warranty from sense-perception. So far was ancient scepticism from making feeling and sensation the canon of truth, that it turned against the deliverances of sense first of all. (On Modern Scepticism as compared with Ancient, see Schelling and Hegel's *Critical Journal of Philosophy*: 1802, vol. I. i.)

II. The Critical Philosophy

40. In common with Empiricism the Critical philosophy assumes that experience affords the one sole foundation for cognitions; which however it does not allow to rank as truths, but only as knowledge of phenomena.

The Critical theory starts originally from the distinction of elements presented in the analysis of experience, viz. the matter of sense, and its universal relations. Taking into account Hume's criticism on this distinction as given in the preceding section, viz. that sensation does not explicitly apprehend more than an individual or more than a mere event, it insists at the same time on the *fact* that universality and necessity are seen to perform a function equally essential in constituting what is called experience. This element, not being derived from the empirical facts as such, must belong to the spontaneity of thought; in other words, it is *a priori*. The Categories or Notions of the Understanding constitute the *objectivity* of experiential cognitions. In every case they involve a connective reference, and hence through their means are formed synthetic judgments *a priori*, that is, primary and underivative connexions of opposites.

Even Hume's scepticism does not deny that the characteristics of universality and necessity are found in cognition. And even in Kant this fact remains a presupposition after all; it may be said, to use the ordinary phraseology of the sciences, that Kant did no more than offer another *explanation* of the fact.

41. The Critical Philosophy proceeds to test the value of the categories employed in metaphysic, as well as in other sciences and in ordinary conception. This scrutiny however is not directed to the content of these categories, nor does it inquire into the exact relation they bear to one another: but simply considers them as affected by the contrast between subjective and objective. The contrast, as we are to understand it here, bears upon the distinction (see preceding §) of the two elements in experience. The name of objectivity is here given to the element of universality and necessity, *i.e.* to the categories themselves, or what is called the *a priori* constituent. The Critical Philosophy however widened the contrast in such a way, that the subjectivity comes to embrace the *ensemble* of experience, including both of the aforesaid elements; and nothing remains on the other side but the "thing-in-itself."

The special forms of the *a priori* element, in other words, of thought, which in spite of its objectivity is looked upon as a purely subjective act, present themselves as follows in a systematic order which, it may be remarked, is solely based upon psychological and historical grounds.

Zusatz. (1) A very important step was undoubtedly made, when the terms of the old metaphysic were subjected to scrutiny. The plain thinker pursued his unsuspecting way in those categories which had offered themselves naturally. It never occurred to him to ask to what extent these categories had a value and authority of their own. If, as has been said, it is characteristic of free thought to allow no assumptions to pass unquestioned, the old metaphysicians were not free thinkers. They accepted their categories as they were, without further trouble, as an *a priori* datum, not yet tested by reflection. The Critical philosophy reversed this. Kant undertook to examine how far the forms of thought were capable of leading to the knowledge of truth. In particular he demanded a criticism of the faculty of cognition as preliminary to its exercise. That is a fair demand, if it mean that even the forms of thought must be made an object of investigation. Unfortunately there soon creeps in the misconception of already knowing before you know—the error of refusing to enter the water until you have learnt to swim. True, indeed, the forms of thought should be subjected to a scrutiny before they are used: yet what is this scrutiny but *ipso facto* a cognition? So that what we want is to combine in our process of inquiry the action of the forms of thought with a criticism of them. The forms of thought must be studied in their essential nature and complete development: they are at once the object of research and the action of that object. Hence they examine themselves: in their own action they must determine their limits, and point out their defects. This is that action of thought, which will hereafter be specially considered under the name of Dialectic, and regarding which we need only at the outset observe that, instead of being brought to bear upon the categories from without, it is immanent in their own action.

We may therefore state the first point in Kant's philosophy as follows: Thought must itself investigate its own capacity of knowledge. People in the present day have got over Kant and his philosophy: everybody wants to get further. But there are two ways of going further—a backward and a forward. The light of criticism soon shows that many of our modern essays in philosophy are mere repetitions of the old metaphysical method, an endless and uncritical thinking in a groove determined by the natural bent of each man's mind.

(2) Kant's examination of the categories suffers from the grave defect of viewing them, not absolutely and for their own sake, but in order to see whether they are *subjective* or *objective.* In the language of common life we mean by objective what exists outside of us and reaches us from without by means of sensation. What Kant did, was to deny that the categories, such as cause and effect, were, in this sense of the word, objective, or given in sensation, and to maintain on the contrary that they belonged to our own thought itself, to the spontaneity of thought. To that extent therefore, they were subjective. And yet in spite of this, Kant gives the name objective to what is thought, to the universal and necessary, while he describes as subjective whatever is merely felt. This arrangement apparently reverses the first-mentioned use of the word, and has caused Kant to

be charged with confusing language. But the charge is unfair if we more narrowly consider the facts of the case. The vulgar believe that the objects of perception which confront them, such as an individual animal, or a single star, are independent and permanent existences, compared with which, thoughts are unsubstantial and dependent on something else. In fact however the perceptions of sense are the properly dependent and secondary feature, while the thoughts are really independent and primary. This being so, Kant gave the title objective to the intellectual factor, to the universal and necessary; and he was quite justified in so doing. Our sensations on the other hand are subjective; for sensations lack stability in their own nature, and are no less fleeting and evanescent than thought is permanent and self-subsisting. At the present day, the special line of distinction established by Kant between the subjective and objective is adopted by the phraseology of the educated world. Thus the criticism of a work of art ought, it is said, to be not subjective, but objective; in other words, instead of springing from the particular and accidental feeling or temper of the moment, it should keep its eye on those general points of view which the laws of art establish. In the same acceptation we can distinguish in any scientific pursuit the objective and the subjective interest of the investigation.

But after all, objectivity of thought, in Kant's sense, is again to a certain extent subjective. Thoughts, according to Kant, although universal and necessary categories, are *only our* thoughts—separated by an impassable gulf from the thing, as it exists apart from our knowledge. But the true objectivity of thinking means that the thoughts, far from being merely ours, must at the same time be the real essence of the things, and of whatever is an object to us.

Objective and subjective are convenient expressions in current use, the employment of which may easily lead to confusion. Up to this point, the discussion has shown three meanings of objectivity. First, it means what has external existence, in distinction from which the subjective is what is only supposed, dreamed, &c. Secondly, it has the meaning, attached to it by Kant, of the universal and necessary, as distinguished from the particular, subjective and occasional element which belongs to our sensations. Thirdly, as has been just explained, it means the thought-apprehended essence of the existing thing, in contradistinction from what is merely *our* thought, and what consequently is still separated from the thing itself, as it exists in independent essence. End *Zusatz.*

42. (a) The Theoretical Faculty—Cognition *quâ* cognition. The specific ground of the categories is declared by the Critical system to lie in the primary identity of the "I" in thought—what Kant calls the "transcendental unity of self-consciousness." The impressions from feeling and perception are, if we look to their contents, a multiplicity or miscellany of elements; and the multiplicity is equally conspicuous in their form. For sense is marked by a mutual exclusion of members; and that under two aspects, namely space and time, which, being the forms, that is to say, the universal type of perception, are themselves *a priori*. This congeries, afforded by sensation and perception, must however be reduced to an identity or primary synthesis. To accomplish this the "I" brings it in relation to itself and unites it there in *one* consciousness which Kant calls "pure apperception." The specific modes in which the Ego refers to itself the multiplicity of sense are the pure concepts of the understanding, the Categories.

Kant, it is well known, did not put himself to much trouble in discovering the categories. "I," the unity of self-consciousness, being quite abstract and completely indeterminate, the question arises, how are we to get at the specialised forms of the "I," the categories? Fortunately, the common logic offers to our hand an empirical classification of the kinds of *judgment*. Now, to judge is the same as to *think* of a determinate object. Hence the various modes of judgment, as enumerated to our hand, provide us with the several categories of thought. To the philosophy of Fichte belongs the great merit of having called attention to the need of exhibiting the *necessity* of these categories and giving a genuine *deduction* of them. Fichte ought to have produced at least one effect on the method of logic. One might have expected that the general laws of thought, the usual stock-in-trade of logicians, or the classification of notions, judgments, and syllogisms, would be no longer taken merely from observation and so only empirically treated, but be deduced from thought itself. If thought is to be capable of proving anything at all, if logic must insist upon the necessity of proofs, and if it proposes to teach the theory of demonstration, its first care should be to give a reason for its own subject-matter, and to see that it is necessary.

Zusatz. (1) Kant therefore holds that the categories have their source in the "Ego," and that the "Ego" consequently supplies the characteristics of universality and necessity. If we observe what we have before us primarily, we may describe it as a congeries or diversity; and in the categories we find the simple points or units, to which this congeries is made to converge. The world of sense is a scene of mutual exclusion: its being is outside itself. That is the fundamental feature of the sensible. "Now" has no meaning except in reference to a before and a hereafter. Red, in the same way, only subsists by being opposed to yellow and blue. Now this other thing is outside the sensible; which latter is, only in so far as it is not the other, and only in so far as that other is. But thought, or the "Ego," occupies a position the very reverse of the sensible, with its mutual exclusions, and its being outside itself. The "I" is the primary identity—at one with itself and all at home in itself. The word "I" expresses the mere act of bringing-to-bear-upon-self; and whatever is placed in this unit or focus, is affected by it and transformed into it. The "I" is as it were the crucible and the fire, which consumes the loose plurality of sense and reduces it to unity. This is the process which Kant calls pure apperception in distinction from the common apperception, to which the plurality it receives is a plurality still; whereas pure apperception is rather an act by which the "I" makes the materials "mine."

This view has at least the merit of giving a correct expression to the nature of all consciousness. The tendency of all man's endeavours is to understand the world, to appropriate and subdue it to himself: and to this end the positive reality of the world must be as it were crushed and pounded, in other words, idealised. At the same time we must note that it is not the mere act of *our* personal self-consciousness, which introduces an absolute unity into the variety of sense. Rather, this identity is itself the absolute. The absolute is, as it were, so kind as to leave individual things to their own enjoyment, and it again drives them back to the absolute unity.

(2) Expressions like "transcendental unity of self-consciousnes" have an ugly look about them, and suggest a monster in the background; but their meaning is not so abstruse as it looks. Kant's meaning of transcendental may be gathered by the way he distinguishes it from transcendent. The *transcendent* may be said to be what steps out beyond the categories of the understanding: a sense in which the term is first employed in mathematics. Thus in geometry you are told to conceive the circumference of a circle as formed of an infinite number of infinitely small straight lines. In other words, characteristics which the understanding holds to be totally different, the straight line and the curve, are expressly invested with identity. Another transcendent of the same kind is the self-consciousness which is identical with itself

and infinite in itself, as distinguished from the ordinary consciousness which derives its form and tone from finite materials. That unity of self-consciousness, however, Kant called *transcendental* only; and he meant thereby that the unity was only in our minds and did not attach to the objects apart from our knowledge of them.

(3) To regard the categories as subjective only, *i.e.*, as a part of ourselves, must seem very odd to the natural mind; and no doubt there is something queer about it. It is quite true however that the categories are not contained in the sensation as it is given us. When, for instance, we look at a piece of sugar, we find it is hard, white, sweet, &c. All these properties we say are united in one object. Now it is this unity that is not found in the sensation. The same thing happens if we conceive two events to stand in the relation of cause and effect. The senses only inform us of the two several occurrences which follow each other in time. But that the one is cause, the other effect—in other words, the causal nexus between the two—is not perceived by sense; it is only evident to thought. Still, though the categories, such as unity, or cause and effect, are strictly the property of thought, it by no means follows that they must be ours merely and not also characteristics of the objects. Kant however confines them to the subject-mind, and his philosophy may be styled subjective idealism; for he holds that both the form and the matter of knowledge are supplied by the Ego—or knowing subject—the form by our intellectual, the matter by our sentient ego.

So far as regards the content of this subjective idealism, not a word need be wasted. It might perhaps at first sight be imagined, that objects would lose their reality when their unity was transferred to the subject. But neither we nor the objects would have anything to gain by the mere fact that they possessed being. The main point is not *that* they are, but *what* they are, and whether or not their content is true. It does no good to the things to say merely that they have being. What has being, will also cease to be when time creeps over it. It might also be alleged that subjective idealism tended to promote self-conceit. But surely if a man's world be the sum of his sensible perceptions, he has no reason to be vain of such a world. Laying aside therefore as unimportant this distinction between subjective and objective, we are chiefly interested in knowing what a thing is: *i.e.*, its content, which is no more objective than it is subjective. If mere existence be enough to make objectivity, even a crime is objective: but it is an existence which is nullity at the core, as is definitely made apparent when the day of punishment comes. End *Zusatz.*

43. The Categories may be viewed in two aspects. On the one hand it is by their instrumentality that the mere perception of sense rises to objectivity and experience. On the other hand these notions are unities in our consciousness merely: they are consequently conditioned by the material given to them, and having nothing of their own they can be applied to use only within the range of experience. But the other constituent of experience, the impressions of feeling and perception, is not one whit less subjective than the categories.

Zusatz. To assert that the categories taken by themselves are empty can scarcely be right, seeing that they have a content, at all events, in the special stamp and significance which they possess. Of course the content of the categories is not perceptible to the senses, nor is it in time and space; but that is rather a merit than a defect. A glimpse of this meaning of *content* may be observed to affect our ordinary thinking. A book or a speech for example is said to have a great deal in it, to be full of content, in proportion to the greater number of thoughts and general results to be found in it; whilst, on the contrary, we should never say that any book, *e.g.*, a novel, had much in it, because it included a great number of single incidents, situations, and the like. Even the popular voice thus recognises that something more than the facts of sense is needed to make a work pregnant with matter. And what is this additional desideratum but thoughts, or in the first instance the categories? And yet it is not altogether wrong, it should be added, to call the categories of themselves empty, if it be meant that they and the logical Idea, of which they are the members, do not constitute the whole of philosophy, but necessarily lead onwards in due progress to the real departments of Nature and Mind. Only let the progress not be misunderstood. The logical Idea does not thereby come into possession of a content originally foreign to it: but by its own native action is specialised and developed to Nature and Mind. End *Zusatz.*

44. It follows that the categories are no fit terms to express the Absolute—the Absolute not being given in perception; and Understanding, or knowledge by means of the categories, is consequently incapable of knowing the Things-in-themselves.

The Thing-in-itself (and under "thing" is embraced even Mind and God) expresses the object when we leave out of sight all that consciousness makes of it, all its emotional aspects, and all specific thoughts of it. It is easy to see what is left—utter abstraction, total emptiness, only described still as an "other-world"—the negative of every image, feeling, and definite thought. Nor does it require much penetration to see that this *caput mortuum* is still only a product of thought, such as accrues when thought is carried on to abstraction unalloyed: that it is the work of the empty "Ego," which makes an object out of this empty self-identity of its own. The *negative* characteristic which this abstract identity receives as an *object*, is also enumerated among the categories of Kant, and is no less familiar than the empty identity aforesaid. Hence one can only read with surprise the perpetual remark that we do not know the Thing-in-itself. On the contrary there is nothing we can know so easily.

45. It is Reason, the faculty of the Unconditioned, which discovers the conditioned nature of the knowledge comprised in experience. What is thus called the object of Reason, the Infinite or Unconditioned, is nothing but self-sameness, or the primary identity of the "Ego" in thought (mentioned in § 42). Reason itself is the name given to the abstract "Ego" or thought, which makes this pure identity its aim or object (cf., note to the preceding §). Now this identity, having no definite attribute at all, can receive no illumination from the truths of experience, for the reason that these refer always to definite facts. Such is the sort of Unconditioned that is supposed to be the absolute truth of Reason—what is termed the *Idea;* whilst the cognitions of experience are reduced to the level of untruth and declared to be appearances.

Zusatz. Kant was the first definitely to signalise the distinction between Reason and Understanding. The object of the former, as he applied the term, was the infinite and unconditioned, of the latter the finite and conditioned. Kant did valuable service when he enforced the finite character of the cognitions of the understanding founded merely upon experience, and stamped their contents with the name of appearance. But his mistake was to stop at the purely negative point of view, and to limit the unconditionality of Reason to an abstract self-sameness without any shade of distinction. It degrades Reason to a finite and conditioned thing, to identify it with a mere stepping beyond the finite and conditioned range of understanding.

The real infinite, far from being a mere transcendence of the finite, always involves the absorption of the finite into its own fuller nature. In the same way Kant restored the Idea to its proper dignity: vindicating it for Reason, as a thing distinct from abstract analytic determinations or from the merely sensible conceptions which usually appropriate to themselves the name of ideas. But as respects the Idea also, he never got beyond its negative aspect, as what ought to be but is not.

The view that the objects of immediate consciousness, which constitute the body of experience, are mere appearances (phenomena), was another important result of the Kantian philosophy. Common Sense, that mixture of sense and understanding, believes the objects of which it has knowledge to be severally independent and self-supporting; and when it becomes evident that they tend towards and limit one another, the interdependence of one upon another is reckoned something foreign to them and to their true nature. The very opposite is the truth. The things immediately known are mere appearances—in other words, the ground of their being is not in themselves but in something else. But then comes the important step of defining what this something else is. According to Kant, the things that we know about are *to us* appearances only, and we can never know their essential nature, which belongs to another world we cannot approach. Plain minds have not unreasonably taken exception to this subjective idealism, with its reduction of the facts of consciousness to a purely personal world, created by ourselves alone. For the true statement of the case is rather as follows. The things of which we have direct consciousness are mere phenomena, not for us only, but in their own nature; and the true and proper case of these things, finite as they are, is to have their existence founded not in themselves but in the universal divine Idea. This view of things, it is true, is as idealist as Kant's; but in contradistinction to the subjective idealism of the Critical philosophy should be termed absolute idealism. Absolute idealism, however, though it is far in advance of vulgar realism, is by no means merely restricted to philosophy. It lies at the root of all religion; for religion too believes the actual world we see, the sum total of existence, to be created and governed by God. End *Zusatz.*

46. But it is not enough simply to indicate the existence of the object of Reason. Curiosity impels us to seek for knowledge of this identity, this empty thing-in-itself. Now *knowledge* means such an ac-

quaintance with the object as apprehends its distinct and special subject-matter. But such subject-matter involves a complex inter-connexion in the object itself, and supplies a ground of connexion with many other objects. In the present case, to express the nature of the features of the Infinite or Thing-in-itself, Reason would have nothing except the categories: and in any endeavour so to employ them Reason becomes over-soaring or "transcendent."

Here begins the second stage of the Criticism of Reason—which, as an independent piece of work, is more valuable than the first. The first part, as has been explained above, teaches that the categories originate in the unity of self-consciousness; that any knowledge which is gained by their means has nothing objective in it, and that the very objectivity claimed for them is only subjective. So far as this goes, the Kantian Criticism presents that "common" type of idealism known as Subjective Idealism. It asks no questions about the meaning or scope of the categories, but simply considers the abstract form of subjec-tivity and objectivity, and that even in such a partial way, that the former aspect, that of subjectivity, is retained as a final and purely affirmative term of thought. In the second part, however, when Kant examines the *application*, as it is called, which Reason makes of the categories in order to know its objects, the content of the categories, at least in some points of view, comes in for discussion: or, at any rate, an opportunity presented itself for a discussion of the question. It is worth while to see what decision Kant arrives at on the subject of metaphysic, as this application of the categories to the unconditioned is called. His method of procedure we shall here briefly state and criticise.

47. (α) The first of the unconditioned entities which Kant exam-ines, is the Soul (see above, § 34). "In my consciousness," he says, "I always find that I (1) am the determining subject; (2) am singular, or abstractly simple; (3) am identical, or one and the same, in all the variety of what I am conscious of; (4) distinguish myself as thinking from all the things outside me."

Now the method of the old metaphysic, as Kant correctly states it, consisted in substituting for these statements of experience the corre-sponding categories or metaphysical terms. Thus arise these four new propositions: (a) the Soul is a substance: (b) it is a simple sub-stance: (c) it is numerically identical at the various periods of exis-tence: (d) it stands in relation to space.

Kant discusses this translation, and draws attention to the Paralo-gism or mistake of confounding one kind of truth with another. He points out that empirical attributes have here been replaced by categories; and shows that we are not entitled to argue from the former to the latter, or to put the latter in place of the former.

This criticism obviously but repeats the observation of Hume (§39) that the categories as a whole—ideas of universality and necessity—are entirely absent from sensation; and that the empirical fact both in form and contents differs from its intellectual formulation.

If the purely empirical fact were held to constitute the credentials of the thought, then no doubt it would be indispensable to be able precisely to identify the "idea" in the "impression."

And in order to make out, in his criticism of the metaphysical psychology, that the soul cannot be described as substantial, simple, self-same, and as maintaining its independence in intercourse with the material world, Kant argues from the single ground, that the several attributes of the soul, which consciousness lets us feel in *experience*, are not exactly the same attributes as result from the action of *thought* thereon. But we have seen above, that according to Kant all knowledge, even experience, consists in thinking our impressions —in other words, in transforming into intellectual categories the attributes primarily belonging to sensation.

Unquestionably one good result of the Kantian criticism was that it emancipated mental philosophy from the "soul-thing," from the categories, and, consequently, from questions about the simplicity, complexity, materiality, &c., of the soul. But even for the common sense of ordinary men, the true point of view, from which the inadmissibility of these forms best appears, will be, not that they are thoughts, but that thoughts of such a stamp neither can nor do contain truth.

If thought and phenomenon do not perfectly correspond to one another, we are free at least to choose which of the two shall be held the defaulter. The Kantian idealism, where it touches on the world of Reason, throws the blame on the thoughts; saying that the thoughts are defective, as not being exactly fitted to the sensations and to a mode of mind wholly restricted within the range of sensation, in which as such there are no traces of the presence of these thoughts. But as to the actual content of the thought, no question is raised.

Zusatz. Paralogisms are a species of unsound syllogism, the especial vice of which consists in employing one and the same word in the two premisses with a different meaning. According to Kant the method adopted by the rational psychology of the old metaphysicians, when they assumed that the qualities of the phenomenal soul, as given in experience, formed part of its own real essence, was based upon such a Paralogism. Nor can it be denied that predicates like simplicity, permanence, &c., are inapplicable to the soul. But their unfitness is not due to the ground assigned by Kant, that Reason, by applying them, would exceed its appointed bounds. The true ground is that this s···le of abstract terms is not good enough for the soul, which is very much more than a mere simple or unchangeable sort of thing. And thus, for example, while the soul may be admitted to be simple self-sameness, it is at the same time active and institutes distinctions in its own nature. But whatever is merely or abstractly simple is as such also a mere dead thing. By his polemic against the metaphysic of the past Kant discarded those predicates from the soul or mind. He did well; but when he came to state his reasons, his failure is apparent. End *Zusatz.*

48. *(β)* The second unconditioned object is the World (§35). In the attempt which reason makes to comprehend the unconditioned nature of the World, it falls into what are called Antinomies. In other words it maintains two opposite propositions about the same object, and in such a way that each of them has to be maintained with equal necessity. From this it follows that the body of cosmical fact, the specific statements descriptive of which run into contradiction, cannot be a self-subsistent reality, but only an appearance. The explanation offered by Kant alleges that the contradiction does not affect the object in its own proper essence, but attaches only to the Reason which seeks to comprehend it.

In this way the suggestion was broached that the contradiction is occasioned by the subject-matter itself, or by the intrinsic quality of the categories. And to offer the idea that the contradiction introduced into the world of Reason by the categories of Understanding is inevitable and essential, was to make one of the most important steps in the progress of Modern Philosophy. But the more important the issue thus raised the more trivial was the solution. Its only motive was an excess of tenderness for the things of the world. The blemish of contradiction, it seems, could not be allowed to mar the essence of the world; but there could be no objection to attach it to the thinking Reason, to the essence of mind. Probably nobody will feel disposed to deny that the phenomenal world presents contradictions to the observing mind; meaning by "phenomenal" the world as it presents itself to the senses and understanding, to the subjective mind. But if a comparison is instituted between the essence of the world and the essence of the mind, it does seem strange to hear how calmly and confidently the modest dogma has been advanced by one, and repeated by others, that thought or Reason, and not the World, is the seat of contradiction. It is no escape to turn round and explain that Reason falls into contradiction only by applying the categories. For this application of the categories is maintained to be necessary, and Reason is not supposed to be equipped with any other forms but the categories for the purpose of cognition. But cognition is determining and determinate thinking: so that, if Reason be mere empty indeterminate thinking, it thinks nothing. And if in the end Reason be reduced to mere identity without diversity (see next §), it will in the end also win a happy release from contradiction at the slight sacrifice of all its facts and contents.

It may also be noted that his failure to make a more thorough study of Antinomy was one of the reasons why Kant enumerated only *four* Antinomies. These four attracted his notice, because, as may be seen in his discussion of the so-called Paralogisms of Reason, he assumed the list of the categories as a basis of his argument. Employing what has subsequently become a favourite fashion, he simply put the object under a rubric otherwise ready to hand, instead of deducing its characteristics from its notion. Further deficiencies in the treatment of the Antinomies I have pointed out, as occasion offered, in my "Science of Logic." Here it will be sufficient to say that the Antinomies are not confined to the four special objects taken from Cosmology: they appear in all objects of every kind, in all conceptions, notions, and Ideas. To be aware of this and to know objects in this property of theirs, makes a vital part in a philosophical theory. For the property thus indicated is what we shall afterwards describe as the Dialectical influence in logic.

Zusatz. The principles of the metaphysical philosophy gave rise to the belief that, when cognition lapsed into contradictions, it was a mere accidental aberration, due to some subjective mistake in argument and inference. According to Kant, however, thought has a natural tendency to issue in contradictions or antinomies, whenever it seeks to apprehend the infinite. We have in the latter part of the above paragraph referred to the philosophical importance of the

antinomies of reason, and shown how the recognition of their existence helped largely to get rid of the rigid dogmatism of the metaphysic of understanding, and to direct attention to the Dialectical
movement of thought. But here too Kant, as we must add, never got
beyond the negative result that the thing-in-itself is unknowable, and
never penetrated to the discovery of what the antinomies really and
positively mean. That true and positive meaning of the antinomies is
this: that every actual thing involves a coexistence of opposed elements. Consequently to know, or, in other words, to comprehend an
object is equivalent to being conscious of it as a concrete unity of
opposed determinations. The old metaphysic, as we have already
seen, when it studied the objects of which it sought a metaphysical
knowledge, went to work by applying categories abstractly and to the
exclusion of their opposites. Kant, on the other hand, tried to prove
that the statements, issuing through this method, could be met by
other statements of contrary import with equal warrant and equal
necessity. In the enumeration of these antinomies he narrowed his
ground to the cosmology of the old metaphysical system, and in his
discussion made out four antinomies, a number which rests upon the
list of the categories. The first antinomy is on the question: Whether
we are or are not to think the world limited in space and time. In the
second antinomy we have a discussion of the dilemma: Matter must
be conceived either as endlessly divisible, or as consisting of atoms.
The third antinomy bears upon the antithesis of freedom and necessity, to such extent as it is embraced in the question, Whether everything in the world must be supposed subject to the condition of
causality, or if we can also assume free beings, in other words, absolute initial points of action, in the world. Finally, the fourth antinomy
is the dilemma: Either the world as a whole has a cause or it is
uncaused.

The method which Kant follows in discussing these antinomies is
as follows. He puts the two propositions implied in the dilemma over
against each other as thesis and antithesis, and seeks to prove both:
that is to say he tries to exhibit them as inevitably issuing from
reflection on the question. He particularly protests against the charge
of being a special pleader and of grounding his reasoning on illu-
sions. Speaking honestly, however, the arguments which Kant offers
for his thesis and antithesis are mere shams of demonstration. The
thing to be proved is invariably implied in the assumption he starts
from, and the speciousness of his proofs is only due to his prolix and
apagogic mode of procedure. Yet it was, and still is, a great achieve-

ment for the Critical philosophy, when it exhibited these antinomies: for in this way it gave some expression (at first certainly subjective and unexplained) to the actual unity of those categories which are kept persistently separate by the understanding. The first of the cosmological antinomies, for example, implies a recognition of the doctrine that space and time present a discrete as well as a continuous aspect: whereas the old metaphysic, laying exclusive emphasis on the continuity, had been led to treat the world as unlimited in space and time. It is quite correct to say that we can go beyond every *definite* space and beyond every *definite* time: but it is no less correct that space and time are real and actual only when they are defined or specialised into "here" and "now"—a specialisation which is involved in the very notion of them. The same observations apply to the rest of the antinomies. Take, for example, the antinomy of freedom and necessity. The main gist of it is that freedom and necessity as understood by abstract thinkers are not independently real, as these thinkers suppose, but merely ideal factors (moments) of the true freedom and the true necessity, and that to abstract and isolate either conception is to make it false. End *Zusatz.*

49. (γ) The third object of the Reason is God (§36): He also must be known and defined in terms of thought. But in comparison with an unalloyed identity, every defining term as such seems to the understanding to be only a limit and a negation: every reality accordingly must be taken as limitless, *i.e.*, undefined. Accordingly God, when He is defined to be the sum of all realities, the most real of beings, turns into a *mere abstract.* And the only term under which that most real of real things can be defined is that of Being—itself the height of abstraction. These are the two elements, abstract identity, on one hand, which is spoken of in this place as the notion; and Being on the other —which Reason seeks to unify. And their union is the *Ideal* of Reason.

50. To carry out this unification two ways or two forms are admissible. Either we may begin with Being and proceed to the *abstractum* of Thought: or the movement may begin with the abstraction and end in Being.

We shall, in the first place, start from Being. But Being, in its natural aspect, presents itself to view as a Being of infinite variety, a World in all its plenitude. And this world may be regarded in two ways: first, as a collection of innumerable unconnected facts; and second, as a collection of innumerable facts in mutual relation, giving evidence of design. The first aspect is emphasised in the Cosmological proof: the latter in the proofs of Natural Theology. Suppose now that this fulness of being passes under the agency of thought. Then it is stripped of its isolation and unconnectedness, and viewed as a universal and absolutely necessary being which determines itself and acts by general purposes or laws. And this necessary and self-determined being, different from the being at the commencement, is God.

The main force of Kant's criticism on this process attacks it for being a syllogising, *i.e.*, a transition. Perceptions, and that aggregate of perceptions we call the world, exhibit as they stand no traces of that universality which they afterwards receive from the purifying act of thought. The empirical conception of the world therefore gives no warrant for the idea of universality. And so any attempt on the part of thought to ascend from the empirical conception of the world to God is checked by the argument of Hume (as in the paralogisms, §47), according to which we have no right to think sensations, that is, to elicit universality and necessity from them.

Man is essentially a thinker; and therefore sound Common Sense, as well as Philosophy, will not yield up their right of rising to God from and out of the empirical view of the world. The only basis on which this rise is possible is the thinking study of the world, not the bare sensuous, animal, intuition of it. Thought and thought alone has eyes for the essence, substance, universal power, and ultimate design of the world. And what men call the proofs of God's existence are, rightly understood, ways of describing and analysing the native course of the mind, the course of *thought* thinking the *data* of the senses. The rise of thought beyond the world of sense, its passage from the finite to the infinite, the leap into the super-sensible which it takes when it snaps asunder the chain of sense, all this transition is thought and nothing but thought. Say there must be no such passage, and you say there is to be no thinking. And in sooth, animals make no such transition. They never get further than sensation and the perception of the senses, and in consequence they have no religion.

Both on general grounds, and in the particular case, there are two remarks to be made upon the criticism of this exaltation in thought. The first remark deals with the question of form. When the exaltation is exhibited in a syllogistic process, in the shape of what we call *proofs* of the being of God, these reasonings cannot but start from some sort of theory of the world, which makes it an aggregate either of contingent facts or of final causes and relations involving design. The merely syllogistic thinker may deem this starting-point a solid basis and suppose that it remains throughout in the same empirical light, left at last as it was at the first. In this case, the bearing of the beginning upon the conclusion to which it leads has a purely affirmative aspect, as if we were only reasoning from one thing which *is* and continues to *be*, to another thing which in like manner is. But the great error is to restrict our notions of the nature of thought to its form in understanding alone. To think the phenomenal world rather means to re-cast its form, and transmute it into a universal. And thus the action of thought has also a *negative* effect upon its basis; and the matter of sensation, when it receives the stamp of universality, at once loses its first and phenomenal shape. By the removal and negation of the shell, the kernel within the sense-percept is brought to the light(§13).*And it is because they do not, with sufficient prominence, express the negative features implied in the exaltation of the mind from the world to God, that the metaphysical proofs of the being of a God are defective interpretations and descriptions of the process. If the world is only a sum of incidents, it follows that it is also deciduous and phenomenal, in *esse* and *posse* null. That upward spring of the mind signifies, that the being which the world has is only a semblance, no real being, no absolute truth; it signifies that, beyond and above that appearance, truth abides in God, so that true being is another name for God. The process of exaltation might thus appear to be transition and to involve a means, but it is not a whit less true, that every trace of transition and means is absorbed; since the world, which might have seemed to be the means of reaching God, is explained to be a nullity. Unless the being of the world is nullified, the *point d'appui* for the exaltation is lost. In this way the apparent means vanishes, and the process of derivation is cancelled in the very act by which it proceeds. It is the affirmative aspect of this relation, as supposed to subsist between two things, either of which *is* as much as the other, which Jacobi mainly has in his eye when he attacks the demonstrations of the understanding. Justly censuring them for seeking conditions (*i.e.*, the world) for the unconditioned, he remarks that the Infinite or God must on such a method be presented as dependent and derivative. But that elevation, as it takes place in the mind, serves to correct this semblance; in fact, it has no other meaning than to correct that semblance. Jacobi, however, failed to recognise the genuine nature of essential thought—by which it cancels the media-

*See above, pp. 32–33.

tion in the very act of mediating; and consequently, his objection, though it tells against the merely "reflective" understanding, is false when applied to thought as a whole, and in particular to reasonable thought.

To explain what we mean by the neglect of the negative factor in thought, we may refer by way of illustration to the charges of Pantheism and Atheism brought against the doctrines of Spinoza. The absolute Substance of Spinoza certainly falls short of absolute spirit, and it is a right and proper requirement that God should be defined as absolute spirit. But when the definition in Spinoza is said to identify the world with God, and to confound God with nature and the finite world, it is implied that the finite world possesses a genuine actuality and affirmative reality. If this assumption be admitted, of course a union of God with the world renders God completely finite, and degrades Him to the bare finite and adventitious congeries of existence. But there are two objections to be noted. In the first place Spinoza does not define God as the unity of God with the world, but as the union of thought with extension, that is, with the material world. And secondly, even if we accept this awkward popular statement as to this unity, it would still be true that the system of Spinoza was not Atheism but Acosmism, defining the world to be an appearance lacking in true reality. A philosophy, which affirms that God and God alone is, should not be stigmatised as atheistic, when even those nations which worship the ape, the cow, or images of stone and brass, are credited with some religion. But as things stand the imagination of ordinary men feels a vehement reluctance to surrender its dearest conviction, that this aggregate of finitude, which it calls a world, has actual reality; and to hold that there is no world is a way of thinking they are fain to believe impossible, or at least much less possible than to entertain the idea that there is no God. Human nature, not much to its credit, is more ready to believe that a system denies God, than that it denies the world. A denial of God seems so much more intelligible than a denial of the world.

The second remark bears on the criticism of the material propositions to which that elevation in thought in the first instance leads. If these propositions have for their predicate such terms as substance of the world, its necessary essence, cause which regulates and directs it according to design, they are certainly inadequate to express what is or ought to be understood by God. Yet apart from the trick of adopting a preliminary popular conception of God, and criticising a result by this assumed standard, it is certain that these characteristics have great value, and are necessary factors in the idea of God. But if we wish in this way to bring before thought the genuine idea of God, and give its true value and expression to the central truth, we must be careful not to start from a subordinate level of facts. To speak of the "merely contingent" things of the world is a very inadequate description of the premisses. The organic structures, and the evidence they afford of mutual adaptation, belong to a higher province, the province of animated nature. But even without taking into consideration the possible blemish which the study of animated nature and of the other teleological aspects of existing things may contract from the pettiness of the final causes, and from puerile instances of them and their bearings, merely animated nature is, at the best, incapable of supplying the material for a truthful expression to the idea of God. God is more than life: He is Spirit. And therefore if the thought of the Absolute takes a starting-point for its rise, and desires to take the nearest, the most true and adequate starting-point will be found in the nature of spirit alone.

51. The other way of unification by which to realise the Ideal of Reason is to set out from the *abstractum* of Thought and seek to characterise it: for which purpose Being is the only available term. This is the method of the Ontological proof. The opposition, here presented from a merely subjective point of view, lies between Thought and Being; whereas in the first way of junction, being is common to the two sides of the antithesis, and the contrast lies only between its individualisation and universality. Understanding meets this second way with what is implicitly the same objection, as it made to the first. It denied that the empirical involves the universal: so it denies that the universal involves the specialisation, which specialisation in this instance is being. In other words it says: Being cannot be deduced from the notion by any analysis.

The uniformly favourable reception and acceptance which attended Kant's criticism of the Ontological proof was undoubtedly due to the illustration which he made use of. To explain the difference between thought and being, he took the instance of a hundred sovereigns, which, for anything it matters to the notion, are the same hundred whether they are real or only possible, though the difference of the two cases is very perceptible in their effect on a man's purse. Nothing can be more obvious than that anything we only think or conceive is not on that account actual: that mental representation, and even notional comprehension, always falls short of being. Still it may not unfairly be styled a barbarism in language, when the name of notion is given to things like a hundred sovereigns. And, putting that mistake aside, those who perpetually urge against the philosophic Idea the difference between Being and Thought, might have admitted that philosophers were not wholly ignorant of the fact. Can there be any proposition more trite than this? But after all, it is well to remember, when we speak of God, that we have an object of another kind than any hundred sovereigns, and unlike any one particular notion, representation, or however else it may be styled. It is in fact this and this alone which marks everything finite: its being in time and space is discrepant from its notion. God, on the contrary, expressly has to be what can only be "thought as existing"; His notion involves being. It is this unity of the notion and being that constitutes the notion of God.

If this were all, we should have only a formal expression of the divine nature which would not really go beyond a statement of the nature of the notion itself. And that the notion, in its most abstract terms, involves being is plain. For the notion, whatever other determination it may receive, is at least reference back on itself, which results by abolishing the intermediation, and thus is immediate. And what is that reference to self, but being? Certainly it would be strange if the notion, the very inmost of mind, if even the "Ego," or above all, the concrete totality we call God, were not rich enough to include so poor a category as being, the very poorest and most abstract of all. For, if we look at the thought it holds, nothing can be more insignificant than being. And yet there may be something still more insignificant than being—that which at first sight is perhaps supposed to *be*, an external and sensible existence, like that of the paper lying before me. However, in this matter, nobody proposes to speak of the sensible existence of a limited and perishable thing. Besides, the petty stricture of the *Kritik* that "thought and being are different" can at most molest the path of the human mind from the thought of God to the certainty that He *is*: it cannot take it away. It is this process of transition, depending on the absolute inseparability of the *thought* of God from His being, for which its proper authority has been revindicated in the theory of faith or immediate knowledge—whereof hereafter.

52. In this way thought, at its highest pitch, has to go outside for any determinateness; and although it is continually termed Reason, is out-and-out abstract thinking. And the result of all is that Reason supplies nothing beyond the formal unity required to simplify and systematise experiences; it is a *canon*, not an *organon* of truth, and can

furnish only a *criticism* of knowledge, not a *doctrine* of the infinite. In its final analysis this criticism is summed up in the assertion that in strictness thought is only the indeterminate unity and the action of this indeterminate unity.

Zusatz. Kant undoubtedly held reason to be the faculty of the un-conditioned; but if reason be reduced to abstract identity only, it by implication renounces its unconditionality and is in reality no better than empty understanding. For reason is unconditioned, only in so far as its character and quality are not due to an extraneous and foreign content, only in so far as it is self-characterising, and thus, in point of content, is its own master. Kant, however, expressly explains that the action of reason consists solely in applying the categories to systematise the matter given by perception, *i.e.*, to place it in an outside order, under the guidance of the principle of non-contradiction. . . . End *Zusatz.*

A general remark may still be offered on the result to which the Critical philosophy led as to the nature of knowledge; a result which has grown one of the current "idols" or axiomatic beliefs of the day. In every dualistic system, and especially in that of Kant, the funda-mental defect makes itself visible in the inconsistency of unifying at one moment, what a moment before had been explained to be inde-pendent and therefore incapable of unification. And then, at the very moment after unification has been alleged to be the truth, we sud-denly come upon the doctrine that the two elements, which, in their true status of unification, had been refused all independent subsist-ence, are only true and actual in their state of separation. Philosophis-ing of this kind wants the little penetration needed to discover, that this shuffling only evidences how unsatisfactory each one of the two terms is. And it fails simply because it is incapable of bringing two thoughts together. (And in point of form there are never more than two.) It argues an utter want of consistency to say, on the one hand, that the understanding only knows phenomena, and, on the other, assert the absolute character of this knowledge, by such statements as "Cognition can go no further"; "Here is the *natural* and absolute limit of human knowledge." But "natural" is the wrong word here. The things of nature are limited and are natural things only to such extent as they are not aware of their universal limit, or to such extent as their mode or quality is a limit from our point of view, and not from their own. No one knows, or even feels, that anything is a limit or defect, until he is at the same time above and beyond it. Living beings, for example, possess the privilege of pain which is denied to the inanimate; even with living beings, a single mode or quality passes into the feeling of a negative. For living beings as such possess within them a universal vitality, which overpasses and includes the single mode; and thus, as they maintain themselves in the negative of themselves, they feel the contradiction to *exist* within them. But the contradiction is within them, only in so far as one and the same subject includes both the universality of their sense of life, and the individual mode which is in negation with it. This illustration will show how a limit or imperfection in knowledge comes to be termed a limit or imperfection, only when it is compared with the actually-present Idea of the universal, of a total and perfect. A very little consideration might show, that to call a thing finite or limited proves by implication the very presence of the infinite and unlimited, and that our knowledge of a limit can only be when the unlimited is *on this side* in consciousness.

The result however of Kant's view of cognition suggests a second remark. The philosophy of Kant could have no influence on the method of the sciences. It leaves the categories and method of ordinary knowledge quite unmolested. Occasionally, it may be, in the first sections of a scientific work of that period, we find propositions borrowed from the Kantian philosophy; but the course of the treatise renders it apparent that these propositions were superfluous decoration, and that the few first pages might have been omitted without producing the least change in the empirical contents.*

We may next institute a comparison of Kant with the metaphysics of the empirical school. Natural plain Empiricism, though it unquestionably insists most upon sensuous perception, still allows a super-sensible world or spiritual reality, whatever may be its structure and constitution, and whether derived from intellect, or from imagination, &c. So far as form goes, the facts of this super-sensible world rest on the authority of mind, in the same way as the other facts,

---

*Even Hermann's "Handbook of Prosody" begins with paragraphs of Kantian philosophy. In § 8 it is argued that a law of rhythm must be (1) objective, (2) formal, and (3) determined *à priori*. With these requirements and with the principles of Causality and Reciprocity which follow later, it were well to compare the treatment of the various measures, upon which those formal principles do not exercise the slightest influence.

embraced in empirical knowledge, rest on the authority of external perception. But when Empiricism becomes reflective and logically consistent, it turns its arms against this dualism in the ultimate and highest species of fact; it denies the independence of the thinking principle and of a spiritual world which develops itself in thought. Materialism or Naturalism, therefore, is the consistent and thorough-going system of Empiricism. In direct opposition to such an Empiricism, Kant asserts the principle of thought and freedom, and attaches himself to the first-mentioned form of empirical doctrine, the general principles of which he never departed from. There is a dualism in his philosophy also. On one side stands the world of sensation, and of the understanding which reflects upon it. This world, it is true, he alleges to be a world of appearances. But that is only a title or formal description; for the source, the facts, and the modes of observation continue quite the same as in Empiricism. On the other side and independent stands a self-apprehending thought, the principle of freedom, which Kant has in common with ordinary and bygone meta-physic, but emptied of all that it held, and without his being able to infuse into it anything new. For, in the Critical doctrine, thought, or, as it is there called, Reason, is divested of every specific form, and thus bereft of all authority. The main effect of the Kantian philosophy has been to revive the consciousness of Reason, or the absolute inwardness of thought. Its abstractness indeed prevented that in-wardness from developing into anything, or from originating any special forms, whether cognitive principles or moral laws; but never-theless it absolutely refused to accept or indulge anything possessing the character of an externality. Henceforth the principle of the inde-pendence of Reason, or of its absolute self-subsistence, is made a general principle of philosophy, as well as a foregone conclusion of the time.

Zusatz. (1) The Critical philosophy has one great negative merit. It has brought home the conviction that the categories of understand-ing are finite in their range, and that any cognitive process confined within their pale falls short of the truth. But Kant had only a sight of half the truth. He explained the finite nature of the categories to mean that they were subjective only, valid only for our thought, from which the thing-in-itself was divided by an impassable gulf. In fact, however, it is not because they are subjective, that the categories are finite: they are finite by their very nature, and it is on their own selves that it is requisite to exhibit their finitude. Kant however holds that what we think is false, because it is we who think it. A further deficiency in the system is that it gives only an historical description of thought, and a mere enumeration of the factors of consciousness. The enumeration is in the main correct; but not a word touches upon the necessity of what is thus empirically colligated. The observations, made on the various stages of consciousness, culminate in the summary statement, that the content of all we are acquainted with is only an appearance. And as it is true at least that all finite thinking is concerned with appearances, so far the conclusion is justified. This stage of "appearance" however—the phenomenal world—is not the terminus of thought: there is another and a higher region. But that region was to the Kantian philosophy an inaccessible "other world."

(2) After all it was only formally, that the Kantian system established the principle that thought is spontaneous and self-determining. Into details of the manner and the extent of this self-determination of thought, Kant never went. It was Fichte who first noticed the omission; and who, after he had called attention to the want of a deduction for the categories, endeavoured really to supply something of the kind. With Fichte, the "Ego" is the starting-point in the philosophical development; and the outcome of its action is supposed to be visible in the categories. But in Fichte the Ego is not really presented as a free, spontaneous energy; it is supposed to receive its first excitation by a shock or impulse from without. Against this shock the "Ego" will, it is assumed, react, and only through this reaction does it first become conscious of itself. Meanwhile, the nature of the impulse remains a stranger beyond our pale; and the "Ego," with something else always confronting it, is weighted with a condition. Fichte, in consequence, never advanced beyond Kant's conclusion, that the finite only is knowable, while the infinite transcends the range of thought. What Kant calls the thing-by-itself, Fichte calls the impulse from without—that abstraction of something else than "I," not otherwise describable or definable than as the negative or non-Ego in general. The "I" is thus looked at as standing in essential relation with the not-I, through which its act of self-determination is first awakened. And in this manner the "I" is but the continuous act of self-liberation from this impulse, never gaining a real freedom, because with the surcease of the impulse the "I," whose being is its action, would also cease to be. Nor is the content produced by the action of the "I" at all different from the ordinary content of experience, except by the supplementary remark, that this content is mere appearance. End *Zusatz*.

THE IDEA

213. The Idea is truth in itself and for itself—the absolute unity of the notion and objectivity. Its "ideal" content is nothing but the notion in its detailed terms; its "real" content is only the exhibition which the notion gives itself in the form of external existence, whilst yet, by enclosing this shape in its ideality, it keeps it in its power, and so keeps itself in it.

The definition, which declares the Absolute to be the Idea, is itself absolute. All former definitions come back to this. The Idea is the Truth: for Truth is the correspondence of objectivity with the notion —not of course the correspondence of external things with my conceptions—for these are only *correct* conceptions held by *me*, the individual person. In the idea we have nothing to do with the individual, nor with figurate conceptions, nor with external things. And yet, again, everything actual, in so far as it is true, is the Idea, and has its truth by and in virtue of the Idea alone. Every individual being is some one aspect of the Idea; for which, therefore, yet other actualities are needed, which in their turn appear to have a self-subsistence of their own. It is only in them altogether and in their relation that the notion is realised. The individual by itself does not correspond to its notion. It is this limitation of its existence which constitutes the finitude and the ruin of the individual.

The Idea itself is not to be taken as an idea of something or other, any more than the notion is to be taken as merely a specific notion. The Absolute is the universal and one idea, which, by an act of "judgment," particularises itself to the system of specific ideas; which after all are constrained by their nature to come back to the one idea where their truth lies. As issued out of this "judgment" the Idea is *in the first place* only the one universal *substance;* but its developed and genuine actuality is to be as a *subject* and in that way as mind.

Because it has no *existence* for starting-point and *point d'appui*, the Idea is frequently treated as a mere logical form. Such a view must be abandoned to those theories, which ascribe so-called reality and genuine actuality to the existent thing and all the other categories which have not yet penetrated as far as the Idea. It is no less false to imagine the Idea to be mere abstraction. It is abstract certainly, in so far as everything untrue is consumed in it; but in its own self it is essentially concrete, because it is the free notion giving character to

SOURCE: *Logic*, Wallace, pp. 352–375, 378–379.

itself, and that character, reality. It would be an abstract form, only if the notion, which is its principle, were taken as an abstract unity, and not as the negative return of it into self and as the subjectivity which it really is.

Zusatz. Truth is at first taken to mean that I *know* how something *is.* This is truth, however, only in reference to consciousness; it is formal truth, bare correctness. Truth in the deeper sense consists in the identity between objectivity and the notion. It is in this deeper sense of truth that we speak of a true state, or of a true work of art. These objects are true, if they are as they ought to be, *i.e.*, if their reality corresponds to their notion. When thus viewed, to be untrue means much the same as to be bad. A bad man is an untrue man, a man who does not behave as his notion or his vocation requires. Nothing however can subsist, if it be *wholly* devoid of identity between the notion and reality. Even bad and untrue things have being, in so far as their reality still, somehow, conforms to their notion. Whatever is thoroughly bad or contrary to the notion, is for that very reason on the way to ruin. It is by the notion alone that the things in the world have their subsistence; or, as it is expressed in the language of religious conception, things are what they are, only in virtue of the divine and thereby creative thought which dwells within them.

When we hear the Idea spoken of, we need not imagine something far away beyond this mortal sphere. The idea is rather what is completely present; and it is found, however confused and degenerated, in every consciousness. We conceive the world to ourselves as a great totality which is created by God, and so created that in it God has manifested Himself to us. We regard the world also as ruled by Divine Providence: implying that the scattered and divided parts of the world are continually brought back, and made conformable, to the unity from which they have issued. The purpose of philosophy has always been the intellectual ascertainment of the Idea; and everything deserving the name of philosophy has constantly been based on the consciousness of an absolute unity where the understanding sees and accepts only separation. It is too late now to ask for proof that the Idea is the truth. The proof of that is contained in the whole deduction and development of thought up to this point. The idea is the result of this course of dialectic. Not that it is to be supposed that the idea is mediate only, *i.e.*, mediated through something else than itself.

It is rather its own result, and being so, is no less immediate than mediate. The stages hitherto considered, viz., those of Being and Essence, as well as those of Notion and of Objectivity, are not, when so distinguished, something permanent, resting upon themselves. They have proved to be dialectical; and their only truth is that they are dynamic elements of the idea. End *Zusatz*.

214. The Idea may be described in many ways. It may be called reason (and this is the proper philosophical signification of reason); subject-object; the unity of the ideal and the real, of the finite and the infinite, of soul and body; the possibility which has its actuality in its own self; that of which the nature can be thought only as existent, &c. All these descriptions apply, because the Idea contains all the relations of understanding, but contains them in their infinite self-return and self-identity.

It is easy work for the understanding to show that everything said of the Idea is self-contradictory. But that can quite as well be retaliated, or rather in the Idea the retaliation is actually made. And this work, which is the work of reason, is certainly not so easy as that of the understanding. Understanding may demonstrate that the Idea is self-contradictory: because the subjective is subjective only and is always confronted by the objective; because being is different from notion and therefore cannot be picked out of it; because the finite is finite only, the exact antithesis of the infinite, and therefore not identical with it; and so on with every term of the description. The reverse of all this, however, is the doctrine of Logic. Logic shows that the subjective which is to be subjective only, the finite which would be finite only, the infinite which would be infinite only, and so on, have no truth, but contradict themselves, and pass over into their opposites. Hence this transition, and the unity in which the extremes are merged and become factors, each with a merely reflected existence, reveals itself as their truth.

The understanding, which addresses itself to deal with the Idea, commits a double misunderstanding. It takes *first* the extremes of the Idea (be they expressed as they will, so long as they are in their unity), not as they are understood when stamped with this concrete unity, but as if they remained abstractions outside of it. It no less mistakes the relation between them, even when it has been expressly stated. Thus, for example it overlooks even the nature of the copula in the judgment, which affirms that the individual, or subject, is after all not individual, but universal. But, in the *second* place, the understanding believes *its* "reflection"—that the self-identical Idea contains its own negative, or contains contradiction—to be an external reflection which does not lie within the Idea itself. But the reflection is really no peculiar cleverness of the understanding. The Idea itself is the dialectic which forever divides and distinguishes the self-identical from the differentiated, the subjective from the objective, the finite from the infinite, soul from body. Only on these terms is it an eternal creation, eternal vitality, and eternal spirit. But while it thus passes or rather translates itself into the abstract understanding, it forever remains reason. The Idea is the dialectic which again makes this mass of understanding and diversity understand its finite nature and the pseudo-independence in its productions, and which brings the diversity back to unity. Since this double movement is not separate or distinct in time, nor indeed in any other way—otherwise it would be only a repetition of the abstract understanding—the Idea is the eternal vision of itself in the other—notion which in its objectivity *has* carried out *itself*—object which is inward design, essential subjectivity.

The different modes of apprehending the Idea as unity of ideal and real, of finite and infinite, of identity and difference, &c., are more or less formal. They designate some one stage of the *specific* notion. Only the notion itself, however, is free and the genuine universal: in the Idea, therefore, the specific character of the notion is only the notion itself—an objectivity, viz., into which it, being the universal, continues itself, and in which it has only its own character, the total character. The Idea is the infinite judgment, of which the terms are severally the independent totality; and in which, as each grows to the fulness of its own nature, it has thereby at the same time passed into the other. None of the other specific notions exhibits this totality complete on both its sides as the notion itself and objectivity.

215. The Idea is essentially a process, because its identity is the absolute and free identity of the notion, only in so far as it is absolute negativity and for that reason dialectical. It is the round of movement, in which the notion, in the capacity of universality which is individuality, gives itself the character of objectivity and of the antithesis thereto; and this externality which has the notion for its substance, finds its way back to subjectivity through its immanent dialectic.

As the idea is *(a)* a process, it follows that such an expression for the Absolute as *unity* of thought and being, of finite and infinite, &c., is false; for unity expresses an abstract and merely quiescent identity.

As the Idea is *(b)* subjectivity, it follows that the expression is equally false on another account. That unity of which it speaks expresses a merely virtual or underlying presence of the genuine unity. The infinite would thus seem to be merely *neutralised* by the finite, the subjective by the objective, thought by being. But in the negative unity of the Idea, the infinite overlaps and includes the finite, thought overlaps being, subjectivity overlaps objectivity. The unity of the Idea is thought, infinity, and subjectivity, and is in consequence to be essentially distinguished from the Idea as *substance*, just as this overlapping subjectivity, thought, or infinity is to be distinguished from the one-sided subjectivity, one-sided thought, one-sided infinity to which it descends in judging and defining.

Zusatz. The idea as a process runs through three stages in its development. The first form of the idea is Life: that is, the idea in the form of immediacy. The second form is that of mediation or differentiation; and this is the idea in the form of Knowledge, which appears under the double aspect of the Theoretical and Practical idea. The process of knowledge eventuates in the restoration of the unity enriched by difference. This gives the third form of the idea, the Absolute Idea: which last stage of the logical idea evinces itself to be at the same time the true first, and to have a being due to itself alone. End *Zusatz.*

(a) Life.

216. The *immediate* idea is Life. As *soul*, the notion is realised in a body of whose externality the soul is the immediate self-relating universality. But the soul is also its particularisation, so that the body expresses no other distinctions than follow from the characterisations of its notion. And finally it is the Individuality of the body as infinite negativity—the dialectic of that bodily objectivity, with its parts lying out of one another, conveying them away from the semblance of independent subsistence back into subjectivity, so that all the members are reciprocally momentary means as well as momentary ends. Thus as life is the initial particularisation, so it results in the negative self-asserting unity: in the dialectic of its corporeity it only coalesces with itself. In this way life is essentially something alive, and in point of its immediacy this individual living thing. It is characteristic of finitude in this sphere that, by reason of the immediacy of the idea, body and soul are separable. This constitutes the mortality of the

living being. It is only, however, when the living being is dead, that these two sides of the idea are different *ingredients*.

Zusatz. The single members of the body are what they are only by and in relation to their unity. A hand, *e.g.*, when hewn off from the body is, as Aristotle has observed, a hand in name only, not in fact. From the point of view of understanding, life is usually spoken of as a mystery, and in general as incomprehensible. By giving it such a name, however, the Understanding only confesses its own finitude and nullity. So far is life from being incomprehensible, that in it the very notion is presented to us, or rather the immediate idea existing as a notion. And having said this, we have indicated the defect of life. Its notion and reality do not thoroughly correspond to each other. The notion of life is the soul, and this notion has the body for its reality. The soul is, as it were, infused into its corporeity; and in that way it is at first sentient only, and not yet freely self-conscious. The process of life consists in getting the better of the immediacy with which it is still beset; and this process, which is itself threefold, results in the idea under the form of judgment, *i.e.*, the idea as Cognition. End *Zusatz.*

217. A living being is a syllogism, of which the very elements are in themselves systems and syllogisms. They are however active syllogisms or processes; and in the subjective unity of the vital agent make only one process. Thus the living being is the process of its coalescence with itself, which runs on through three processes.

218. (1) The first is the process of the living being inside itself. In that process it makes a split on its own self, and reduces its corporeity to its object or its inorganic nature. This corporeity, as an aggregate of correlations, enters in its very nature into difference and opposition of its elements, which mutually become each other's prey, and assimilate one another, and are retained by producing themselves. Yet this action of the several members (organs) is only the living subject's one act to which their productions revert; so that in these productions nothing is produced except the subject; in other words, the subject only reproduces itself.

Zusatz. The process of the vital subject within its own limits has in Nature the threefold form of Sensibility, Irritability, and Reproduction. As Sensibility, the living being is immediately simple self-relation—it is the soul omnipresent in its body, the outsideness of each member of which to others has for it no truth. As Irritability, the living being appears split up in itself; and as Reproduction, it is perpetually restoring itself from the inner distinction of its members and organs. A vital agent only exists as this continually self-renewing process within its own limits. End *Zusatz.*

219. (2) But the judgment of the notion proceeds, as free, to discharge the objective or bodily nature as an independent totality from itself; and the negative relation of the living thing to itself makes, as immediate individuality, the pre-supposition of an inorganic nature confronting it. As this negative of the animate is no less a function in the notion of the animate itself, it exists consequently in the latter (which is at the same time a concrete universal) in the shape of a defect or want. The dialectic by which the object, being implicitly null, is merged, is the action of the self-assured living thing, which in this process against an inorganic nature thus retains, develops, and objectifies itself.

Zusatz. The living being stands face to face with an inorganic nature, to which it comports itself as a master and which it assimilates to itself. The result of the assimilation is not, as in the chemical process, a neutral product in which the independence of the two confronting sides is merged; but the living being shows itself as large enough to embrace its other which cannot withstand its power. The inorganic nature which is subdued by the vital agent suffers this fate, because it is *virtually* the same as what life is *actually.* Thus in the other the living being only coalesces with itself. But when the soul has fled from the body, the elementary powers of objectivity begin their play. These powers are, as it were, continually on the spring, ready to begin their process in the organic body; and life is the constant battle against them. End *Zusatz.*

220. (3) The living individual, which in its first process comports itself as intrinsically subject and notion, through its second assimilates its external objectivity and thus puts the character of reality into

itself. It is now therefore implicitly a Kind, with essential universality of nature. The particularising of this Kind is the relation of the living subject to another subject of its Kind; and the judgment is the tie of Kind over these individuals thus appointed for each other. This is the Affinity of the Sexes.

221. The process of Kind brings it to a being of its own. Life being no more than the idea immediate, the product of this process breaks up into two sides. On the one hand, the living individual, which was at first pre-supposed as immediate, is now seen to be mediated and generated. On the other, however, the living individuality, which, on account of its first immediacy, stands in a negative attitude towards universality, sinks in the superior power of the latter.

Zusatz. The living being dies, because it is a contradiction. Implicitly it is the universal or Kind, and yet immediately it exists as an individual only. Death shows the Kind to be the power that rules the immediate individual. For the animal the process of Kind is the highest point of its vitality. But the animal never gets so far in its Kind as to have a being of its own; it succumbs to the power of Kind. In the process of Kind the immediate living being mediates itself with itself, and thus rises above its immediacy, only however to sink back into it again. Life thus runs away, in the first instance, only into the false infinity of the progress *ad infinitum.* The real result, however, of the process of life, in the point of its notion, is to merge and overcome that immediacy with which the idea, in the shape of life, is still beset. End *Zusatz.*

222. In this manner however the idea of life has thrown off not some one particular and immediate "This," but this first immediacy as a whole. It thus comes to itself, to its truth: it enters upon existence as a free Kind self-subsistent. The death of merely immediate and individual vitality is the "procession" of spirit.

(b) Cognition in general.

223. The idea exists free for itself, in so far as it has universality for the medium of its existence—as objectivity itself has notional being —as the idea is its own object. Its subjectivity, thus universalised, is *pure* self-contained distinguishing of the idea—intuition which keeps itself in this identical universality. But, as *specific* distinguishing, it is

the further judgment of repelling itself as a totality from itself, and thus, in the first place, pre-supposing itself as an external universe. There are two judgments, which though implicitly identical are not yet explicitly put as identical.

224. The relation of these two ideas, which implicitly and as life are identical, is thus one of correlation; and it is that correlativity which constitutes the characteristic of finitude in this sphere. It is the relationship of reflection, seeing that the distinguishing of the idea in its own self is only the first judgment—presupposing the other and not yet supposing itself to constitute it. And thus for the subjective idea the objective is the immediate world found ready to hand, or the idea as life is in the phenomenon of individual existence. At the same time, in so far as this judgment is pure distinguishing within its own limits (§223), the idea realises in one both itself and its other. Consequently it is the certitude of the virtual identity between itself and the objective world. Reason comes to the world with an absolute faith in its ability to make the identity actual, and to raise its certitude to truth; and with the instinct of realising explicitly the nullity of that contrast which it sees to be implicitly null.

225. This process is in general terms Cognition. In Cognition in a single act the contrast is virtually superseded, as regards both the one-sidedness of subjectivity and the one-sidedness of objectivity. At first, however, the supersession of the contrast is but implicit. The process as such is in consequence immediately infected with the finitude of this sphere, and splits into the twofold movement of the instinct of reason, presented as two different movements. On the one hand it supersedes the one-sidedness of the Idea's subjectivity by receiving the existing world into itself, into subjective conception and thought; and with this objectivity, which is thus taken to be real and true, for its content it fills up the abstract certitude of itself. On the other hand, it supersedes the one-sidedness of the objective world, which is now, on the contrary, estimated as only a mere semblance, a collection of contingencies and shapes at bottom visionary. It modifies and informs that world by the inward nature of the subjective, which is here taken to be the genuine objective. The former is the instinct of science after Truth, Cognition properly so called: the Theoretical action of the idea. The latter is the instinct of the Good to fulfil the same—the practical activity of the idea or Volition.

(a) Cognition proper.

226. The universal finitude of Cognition, which lies in the one judgment, the pre-supposition of the contrast (§224)—a pre-supposi-

tion in contradiction of which its own act lodges protest, specialises itself more precisely on the face of its own idea. The result of that specialisation is, that its two elements receive the aspect of being diverse from each other, and, as they are at least complete, they take up the relation of "reflection," not of "notion," to one another. The assimilation of the matter, therefore, as a datum, presents itself in the light of a reception of it into categories which at the same time remain external to it, and which meet each other in the same style of diversity. Reason is active here, but it is reason in the shape of understanding. The truth which such Cognition can reach will therefore be only finite: the infinite truth (of the notion) is isolated and made transcendent, an inaccessible goal in a world of its own. Still in its external action cognition stands under the guidance of the notion, and notional principles form the secret clue to its movement.

Zusatz. The finitude of Cognition lies in the pre-supposition of a world already in existence, and in the consequent view of the knowing subject as a *tabula rasa.* The conception is one attributed to Aristotle; but no man is further than Aristotle from such an outside theory of Cognition. Such a style of Cognition does not recognise in itself the activity of the notion—an activity which it is implicitly, but not consciously. In its own estimation its procedure is passive. Really that procedure is active. End *Zusatz.*

227. Finite Cognition, when it pre-supposes what is distinguished from it to be something already existing and confronting it—to be the various facts of external nature or of consciousness—has, in the first place, (1) Formal identity or the abstraction of universality for the form of its action. Its activity therefore consists in analysing the given concrete object, isolating its differences, and giving them the form of abstract universality. Or it leaves the concrete thing as a ground, and by setting aside the unessential-looking particulars, brings into relief a concrete universal, the Genus, or Force and Law. This is the Analytical method.

Zusatz. People generally speak of the analytical and synthetical methods, as if it depended solely on our choice which we pursued. This is far from the case. It depends on the form of the objects of our investigation, which of the two methods, that are derivable from the notion of finite cognition, ought to be applied. In the first place, cognition is analytical. Analytical cognition deals with an object which is presented in detachment, and the aim of its action is to trace back to a universal the individual object before it. Thought in such circumstances means no more than an act of abstraction or of formal identity. That is the sense in which thought is understood by Locke and all empiricists. Cognition, it is often said, can never do more than separate the given concrete objects into their abstract elements, and then consider these elements in their isolation. It is, however, at once apparent that this turns things upside down, and that cognition, if its purpose be to take things as they are, thereby falls into contradiction with itself. Thus the chemist *e.g.* places a piece of flesh in his retort, tortures it in many ways, and then informs us that it consists of nitrogen, carbon, hydrogen, &c. True, but these abstract matters have ceased to be flesh. The same defect occurs in the reasoning of an empirical psychologist when he analyses an action into the various aspects which it presents, and then sticks to these aspects in their separation. The object which is subjected to analysis is treated as a sort of onion from which one coat is peeled off after another. End *Zusatz*.

228. This universality is (2) also a specific universality. In this case the line of activity follows the three "moments" of the notion, which (as it has not its infinity in finite cognition) is the specific or definite notion of understanding. The reception of the object into the forms of this notion is the Synthetic Method.

Zusatz. The movement of the Synthetic method is the reverse of the Analytical method. The latter starts from the individual, and proceeds to the universal; in the former the starting-point is given by the universal (as a definition), from which we proceed by particularising (in division) to the individual (the theorem). The Synthetic method thus presents itself as the development of the "moments" of the notion on the object. End *Zusatz*.

229. (a) When the object has been in the first instance brought by cognition into the form of the specific notion in general, so that in this way its genus and its universal character or speciality are explic-

itly stated, we have the Definition. The materials and the proof of Definition are procured by means of the Analytical method (§ 227). The specific character however is expected to be a "mark" only: that is to say it is to be in behoof only of the purely subjective cognition which is external to the object.

Zusatz. Definition involves the three organic elements of the notion: the universal or proximate genus *(genus proximum)*, the particular or specific character of the genus *(qualitas specifica)*, and the individual, or object defined. The first question that definition suggests, is where it comes from. The general answer to this question is to say, that definitions originate by way of analysis. This will explain how it happens that people quarrel about the correctness of proposed definitions; for here everything depends on what perceptions we started from, and what points of view we had before our eyes in so doing. The richer the object to be defined is, that is, the more numerous are the aspects which it offers to our notice, the more various are the definitions we may frame of it. Thus there are quite a host of definitions of life, of the state, &c. Geometry, on the contrary, dealing with a theme so abstract as space, has an easy task in giving definitions. Again, in respect of the matter or contents of the objects defined, there is no constraining necessity present. We are expected to admit that space exists, that there are plants, animals, &c., nor is it the business of geometry, botany, &c., to demonstrate that the objects in question necessarily are. This very circumstance makes the synthetical method of cognition as little suitable for philosophy as the analytical: for philosophy has above all things to leave no doubt of the necessity of its objects. And yet several attempts have been made to introduce the synthetical method into philosophy. Thus Spinoza, in particular, begins with definitions. He says, for instance, that substance is the *causa sui*. His definitions are unquestionably a storehouse of the most speculative truth, but it takes the shape of dogmatic assertions. The same thing is also true of Schelling. End *Zusatz.*

230. (β) The statement of the second element of the notion, *i.e.*, of the specific character of the universal as particularising, is given by Division in accordance with some external consideration.

Zusatz. Division we are told ought to be complete. That requires a principle or ground of division so constituted, that the division based upon it embraces the whole extent of the region designated by the definition in general. But, in division, there is the further requirement that the principle of it must be borrowed from the nature of the object in question. If this condition be satisfied, the division is natural and not merely artificial, that is to say, arbitrary. Thus, in zoology, the ground of division adopted in the classification of the mammalia is mainly afforded by their teeth and claws. That is so far sensible, as the mammals themselves distinguish themselves from one another by these parts of their bodies; back to which therefore the general type of their various classes is to be traced. In every case the genuine division must be controlled by the notion. To that extent a division, in the first instance, has three members: but as particularity exhibits itself as double, the division may go to the extent even of four members. In the sphere of mind trichotomy is predominant, a circumstance which Kant has the credit of bringing into notice. End *Zusatz.*

231. (γ) In the concrete individuality, where the mere unanalysed quality of the definition is regarded as a correlation of elements, the object is a synthetical nexus of distinct characteristics. It is a Theorem. Being different, these characteristics possess but a mediated identity. To supply the materials, which form the middle terms, is the office of Construction: and the process of mediation itself, from which cognition derives the necessity of that nexus, is the Demonstration.

As the difference between the analytical and synthetical methods is commonly stated, it seems entirely optional which of the two we employ. If we assume, to start with, the concrete thing which the synthetic method presents as a result, we can analyse from it as consequences the abstract propositions which formed the pre-suppositions and the material for the proof. Thus, algebraical definitions of curved lines are theorems in the method of geometry. Similarly even the Pythagorean theorem, if made the definition of a right-angled triangle, might yield to analysis those propositions which geometry had already demonstrated on its behoof. The optionalness of either method is due to both alike starting from an external pre-supposition. So far as the nature of the notion is concerned, analysis is prior; since it has to raise the given material with its empirical concreteness into the form of general abstractions, which may then be set in the front of the synthetical method as definitions.

That these methods, however indispensable and brilliantly success-ful in their own province, are unserviceable for philosophical cogni-tion, is self-evident. They have pre-suppositions; and their style of cognition is that of understanding, proceeding under the canon of formal identity. In Spinoza, who was especially addicted to the use of the geometrical method, we are at once struck by its characteristic formalism. Yet his ideas were speculative in spirit; whereas the system of Wolff, who carried the method out to the height of pendantry, was even in subject-matter a metaphysic of the understanding. The abuses which these methods with their formalism once led to in philosophy and science have in modern times been followed by the abuses of what is called "Construction." Kant brought into vogue the phrase that mathematics "construes" its notions. All that was meant by the phrase was that mathematics has not to do with notions, but with abstract qualities of sense-perceptions. The name "Construction (*construing*) of notions" has since been given to a sketch or statement of sensible attributes which were picked up from perception, quite guiltless of any influence of the notion, and to the additional formal-ism of classifying scientific and philosophical objects in a tabular form on some pre-supposed rubric, but in other respects at the fancy and discretion of the observer. In the background of all this, certainly, there is a dim consciousness of the Idea, of the unity of the notion and objectivity—a consciousness, too, that the idea is concrete. But that play of what is styled "construing" is far from presenting this unity adequately—a unity which is none other than the notion prop-erly so called; and the sensuous concreteness of perception is as little the concreteness of reason and the idea.

Another point calls for notice. Geometry works with the sensuous but abstract perception of space; and in space it experiences no difficulty in isolating and defining certain simple analytic modes. To geometry alone therefore belongs in its perfection the synthetical method of finite cognition. In its course, however (and this is the remarkable point), it finally stumbles upon what are termed irrational and incommensurable quantities; and in their case any attempt at further specification drives it beyond the principle of the understand-ing. This is only one of many instances in terminology, where the title rational is perversely applied to the province of understanding, while we stigmatise as irrational that which shows a beginning and a trace of rationality. Other sciences, removed as they are from the simplicity of space or number, often and necessarily reach a point where under-standing permits no further advance; but they get over the difficulty without trouble. They make a break in the strict sequence of their

procedure, and assume whatever they require, though it be the reverse of what preceded, from some external quarter—opinion, perception, conception or any other source. Its inobservancy as to the
nature of its methods and their relativity to the subject-matter prevents this finite cognition from seeing that, when it proceeds by
definitions and divisions, &c., it is really led on by the necessity of the
laws of the notion. For the same reason it cannot see when it has
reached its limit; nor, if it have transgressed that limit, does it perceive that it is in a sphere where the categories of understanding,
which it still continues rudely to apply, have lost all authority.

232. The necessity, which finite cognition produces in the Demonstration, is, in the first place, an external necessity, intended for the
subjective intelligence alone. But in necessity as such, cognition itself
has left behind its presupposition and starting-point, which consisted
in accepting its content as given or found. Necessity *qua* necessity is
implicitly the self-relating notion. The subjective idea has thus implicitly reached an original and objective determinateness—a something
not-given, and for that reason immanent in the subject. It has passed
over into the idea of Will.

Zusatz. The necessity which cognition reaches by means of the
demonstration is the reverse of what formed its starting-point. In its
starting-point cognition had a given and a contingent content; but
now, at the close of its movement, it knows its content to be necessary.
This necessity is reached by means of subjective agency. Similarly,
subjectivity at starting was quite abstract, a bare *tabula rasa.* It now
shows itself as a modifying and determining principle. In this way we
pass from the idea of cognition to that of will. The passage, as will
be apparent on a closer examination, means that the universal, to be
truly apprehended, must be apprehended as subjectivity, as a notion
self-moving, active, and form-imposing. End *Zusatz.*

(β) Volition.

233. The subjective idea as original and objective determinateness,
and as a simple uniform content, is the Good. Its impulse towards
self-realisation is in its behaviour the reverse of the idea of truth, and
rather directed towards moulding the world it finds before it into a
shape conformable to its purposed End. This Volition has, on the one

hand, the certitude of the nothingness of the pre-supposed object; but, on the other, as finite, it at the same time pre-supposes the purposed End of the Good to be a mere subjective idea, and the object to be independent.

234. This action of the Will is finite: and its finitude lies in the contradiction that in the inconsistent terms applied to the objective world the End of the Good is just as much not executed as executed —the end in question put as unessential as much as essential,—as actual and at the same time as merely possible. This contradiction presents itself to imagination as an endless progress in the actualising of the Good; which is therefore set up and fixed as a mere "ought," or goal of perfection. In point of form however this contradiction vanishes when the action supersedes the subjectivity of the purpose, and along with it the objectivity, with the contrast which makes both finite; abolishing subjectivity as a whole and not merely the one-sidedness of this form of it. (For another new subjectivity of the kind, that is, a new generation of the contrast, is not distinct from that which is supposed to be past and gone.) This return into itself is at the same time the content's own "recollection" that it is the Good and the implicit identity of the two sides—it is a "recollection" of the pre-supposition of the theoretical attitude of mind (§ 224) that the objective world is its own truth and substantiality.

Zusatz. While Intelligence merely proposes to take the world as it is, Will takes steps to make the world what it ought to be. Will looks upon the immediate and given present not as solid being, but as mere semblance without reality. It is here that we meet those contradictions which are so bewildering from the standpoint of abstract morality. This position in its "practical" bearings is the one taken by the philosophy of Kant, and even by that of Fichte. The Good, say these writers, has to be realised: we have to work in order to produce it, and Will is only the Good actualising itself. If the world then were as it ought to be, the action of Will would be at an end. The Will itself therefore requires that its End should not be realised. In these words, a correct expression is given to the *finitude* of Will. But finitude was not meant to be the ultimate point: and it is the process of Will itself which abolishes finitude and the contradiction it involves. The recon-ciliation is achieved, when Will in its result returns to the pre-supposi-tion made by cognition. In other words, it consists in the unity of the theoretical and practical idea. Will knows the end to be its own, and

Intelligence apprehends the world as the notion actual. This is the right attitude of rational cognition. Nullity and transitoriness constitute only the superficial features and not the real essence of the world. That essence is the notion in *posse* and in *esse;* and thus the world is itself the idea. All unsatisfied endeavour ceases, when we recognise that the final purpose of the world is accomplished no less than ever accomplishing itself. Generally speaking, this is the man's way of looking; while the young imagine that the world is utterly sunk in wickedness, and that the first thing needful is a thorough transformation. The religious mind, on the contrary, views the world as ruled by Divine Providence, and therefore correspondent with what it ought to be. But this harmony between the "is" and the "ought to be" is not torpid and rigidly stationary. Good, the final end of the world, has being, only while it constantly produces itself. And the world of spirit and the world of nature continue to have this distinction, that the latter moves only in a recurring cycle, while the former certainly also makes progress. End *Zusatz.*

235. Thus the truth of the Good is laid down as the unity of the theoretical and practical idea in the doctrine that the Good is radically and really achieved, that the objective world is in itself and for itself the Idea, just as it at the same time eternally lays itself down as End, and by action brings about its actuality. This life which has returned to itself from the bias and finitude of cognition, and which by the activity of the notion has become identical with it, is the Speculative or Absolute Idea.

(c) The Absolute Idea.

236. The Idea, as unity of the Subjective and Objective Idea, is the notion of the Idea—a notion whose object *(Gegenstand)* is the Idea as such, and for which the objective *(Objekt)* is Idea—an Object which embraces all characteristics in its unity. This unity is consequently the absolute and all truth, the Idea which thinks itself—and here at least as a thinking or Logical Idea.

Zusatz. The Absolute Idea is, in the first place, the unity of the theoretical and practical idea, and thus at the same time the unity of the idea of life with the idea of cognition. In cognition we had the idea in a biassed, one-sided shape. The process of cognition has issued in the overthrow of this bias and the restoration of that unity, which as unity, and in its immediacy, is in the first instance the Idea of Life. The defect of life lies in its being only the idea implicit or natural: whereas cognition is in an equally one-sided way the merely conscious idea, or the idea for itself. The unity and truth of these two is the Absolute Idea, which is both in itself and for itself. Hitherto *we* have had the idea in development through its various grades as *our* object, but now the idea comes to be its *own object*. This is the νόησις νοήσεως which Aristotle long ago termed the supreme form of the idea. End *Zusatz*.

237. Seeing that there is in it no transition, or pre-supposition, and in general no specific character other than what is fluid and transparent, the Absolute Idea is for itself the pure form of the notion, which contemplates its content as its own self. It is its own content, in so far as it ideally distinguishes itself from itself, and the one of the two things distinguished is a self-identity in which however is contained the totality of the form as the system of terms describing its content. This content is the system of Logic. All that is at this stage left as form for the idea is the Method of this content,—the specific consciousness of the value and currency of the "moments" in its development.

Zusatz. To speak of the absolute idea may suggest the conception that we are at length reaching the right thing and the sum of the whole matter. It is certainly possible to indulge in a vast amount of senseless declamation about the idea absolute. But its true content is only the whole system of which we have been hitherto studying the development. It may also be said in this strain that the absolute idea is the universal, but the universal not merely as an abstract form to which the particular content is a stranger, but as the absolute form, into which all the categories, the whole fullness of the content it has given being to, have retired. The absolute idea may in this respect be compared to the old man who utters the same creed as the child, but for whom it is pregnant with the significance of a lifetime. Even if the child understands the truths of religion, he cannot but imagine them to be something outside of which lies the whole of life and the whole of the world. The same may be said to be the case with human life as a whole and the occurrences with which it is fraught. All work is directed only to the aim or end; and when it is attained, people are surprised to find nothing else but just the very thing which they had wished for. The interest lies in the whole movement. When a man traces up the steps of his life, the end may appear to him very restricted: but in it the whole *decursus vitae* is comprehended. So, too, the content of the absolute idea is the whole breadth of ground which has passed under our view up to this point. Last of all comes the discovery that the whole evolution is what constitutes the content and the interest. It is indeed the prerogative of the philosopher to see that everything, which, taken apart, is narrow and restricted, receives its value by its connexion with the whole, and by forming an organic element of the idea. Thus it is that we have had the content already, and what we have now is the knowledge that the content is the living development of the idea. This simple retrospect is contained in the *form* of the idea. Each of the stages hitherto reviewed is an image of the absolute, but at first in a limited mode, and thus it is forced onwards to the whole, the evolution of which is what we termed Method. . . . End *Zusatz*.

243. It thus appears that the method is not an extraneous form, but the soul and notion of the content, from which it is only distinguished, so far as the dynamic elements of the notion even on their own part come in their own specific character to appear as the totality of the notion. This specific character, or the content, leads itself with the form back to the idea; and thus the idea is presented as a systematic totality which is only one idea, of which the several elements are each implicitly the idea, whilst they equally by the dialectic of the notion produce the simple independence of the idea. The science in this manner concludes by apprehending the notion of itself, as of the pure idea for which the idea is.

244. The Idea which is independent or for itself, when viewed on the point of this its unity with itself, is Perception or Intuition, and the percipient Idea is Nature. But as intuition the idea is, through an external "reflection," invested with the one-sided characteristic of immediacy, or of negation. Enjoying however an absolute liberty, the Idea does not merely pass over into life, or as finite cognition allow life to show in it: in its own absolute truth it resolves to let the "moment" of its particularity, or of the first characterisation and other-being, the immediate idea, as its reflected image, go forth freely as Nature.

Zusatz. We have now returned to the notion of the Idea with which we began. This return to the beginning is also an advance. We began with Being, abstract Being; where we now are we also have the Idea as Being; but this Idea which has Being is Nature. End *Zusatz*.

V

Nature and Spirit: Self-Estrangement and Reconciliation

While it is not difficult to set out, in Hegel's words, the place and relation of Nature and Spirit in his scheme of things, getting a firm grasp of the matter in ordinary language is something else. "God," Hegel says in a theological vein, "reveals Himself in two different ways: as Nature and as Spirit. Both manifestations are temples of God, which He fills, and in which He is present. God, as an abstraction [i.e., in the *Logic*], is not the true God, but only as the living process of positing His Other, the world, which, comprehended in its divine form is His Son; and it is only in unity with His Other, in Spirit, that God is Subject."[1] In less theological terms, "Nature is Spirit estranged from itself; in Nature, Spirit lets itself go (*ausgelassen*), a Bacchic god unrestrained and unmindful of itself; in Nature, the unity of the Notion is concealed."[2] And again: "The study of Nature is thus the liberation of Spirit in her; implicitly she is Reason, but it is through Spirit that Reason as such first emerges from Nature into existence."[3]

In Hegel's *Logic*, there are categories of contingency, which accommodate the natural realm—the Idea or Reason in its immediacy—but no contingent categories. There, "the rustle of Nature's life is silenced in the stillness of thought; her abundant life, wearing a thousand wonderful and delightful shapes, shrivels into arid forms and shapeless generalities resembling a murky northern fog."[4] The natural world is one of contingency, a loosely connected, seemingly endless array of particulars yawning in time and space, each more or less unique and opposing every other—the Idea but in the form of otherness or externality, the "bad infinite."[5] It is only in life, Nature's highest form, that we first meet with subjectivity and the "counter" to this externality. The living thing is itself a triumph over its own diversity, an entelechy *(Selbst-zweck)*, and the calling of life as such is to bring everything into the unity which it implicitly is. Nature produces Spirit out of itself as its truth, the negation of its own negativity, but "Spirit, just because it is the goal of Nature, is [logically] prior to it."[6] "Nature is the first in point of time, but the absolute *prius* is the Idea; this absolute *prius* is the last, the true beginning."[7] Time is thus the measure only of motion, the coming-into-being and passing away of the finite, whose time and place begins and ends with it. The Idea of Nature, however, is eternal, not in the sense of an endless temporal process, but rather in the sense that this finitude, this incessant beginning and death, is superceded *(aufgehoben)* in the scientific or philosophical grasp of Nature as the Idea qua other-being or in a state of self-diremption. Nature waits, but in expectation, so to speak, pregnant with the Idea but powerless without Spirit to bring to birth the truth laboring within.

For all its apparent richness and splendor, Nature is, in Hegel's view, only abstract and inward (undeveloped), its materiality or externality being the very antithesis of the order and unity which mind introduces, the mere possibility of that unity. *"Immediately,* therefore, God is *only* Nature. Or, Nature is only the *inner* God. . . ."[8] For Hegel, Nature and Spirit represent the outer and inner being of God, respectively (see below). But as we noted in chapter I, in no case are the two so opposed or self-sufficient as to constitute anything in abstraction from each other. "Neither in heaven nor in earth, neither in the world of Mind nor of Nature, is there anywhere such an abstract 'Either-or' as the understanding [*Verstand*] maintains."[9] In his *Logic* Hegel says "The appearance [the external, Nature] shows nothing that is not in the essence [the internal, Spirit], and in the essence there is nothing but what is manifested."[10] Both have the same content, the Idea, and only the form it takes differentiates them. Hegel has this to say about the apparent paradox of the inner and outer:

The one [the inner] is the abstraction of identity with self; the other [the outward or external], of mere multiplicity or reality. . . . Therefore what is only internal is also only external; and what is only external, is so far only at first internal. . . . In mere sense-perception, the notion is at first only an inward, and for that very reason is something external to Being, a subjective thinking and being, devoid of truth. . . . As for Nature, it certainly is in the gross external. . . . But to call it external "in the gross" is not to imply an abstract externality—for there is no such thing. It means rather that the Idea which forms the common content of Nature and Mind, is found in Nature as outward only, and for that very reason only inward. . . . Any object indeed is faulty and imperfect when it is only inward, and thus at the same time only outward, or (which is the same thing) when it is only an outward and thus only an inward.[11]

The hallmark of anything "natural" is to be, to some degree or other, *other* than mind, which means nothing more than that its existence is, to the same degree, out of joint with its essence or notion. But there is nothing either *so* inward or *so* external that it escapes knowing and being altogether. Thus the truth, when it is only immediate, first, or inner (undeveloped), has the form of otherness, externality, disunity. When it is developed, that outward show is reduced, again in stages, to unity. The natural sciences only reduce the sensuous flux to a formal and abstract identity, necessity, because "their mode of thought, as a merely formal act, derives its content from without."[12] Whatever the explanatory efficiency of their categories, the natural world as such remains, in their view, finite, and the relations within it rigid and deterministic, because they take their world for granted; their laws and determinations, therefore, are explanatory, but not self-explanatory. Necessity, as Plato says, is the mother of invention, but freedom is its father, and the entire nisus toward self-comprehension on the part of science ultimately fails without it.

Hegel's construal of Nature must therefore be understood in terms of the teleological dialectic of *first* and *last*, which characterizes his entire philosophy, and which we outlined in our first chapter. It is not merely evolutionary but developmental.[13] As Hegel's tripartite system is the philosophical expression of the religious mystery of the Trinity, so also the dialectical (which, for Hegel, means "through-itself" or "self-mediating") relation of its major moments serves to interpret the Christian *Vorstellung* of the immaculate conception. "Man," says Hegel, "in so far as he is Spirit is not the creature of Nature."[14] The truth that Spirit liberates from Nature is, as previously noted, the revelation that Nature in itself has no truth. "Spirit is only that into which it makes itself, and it makes itself actually into that which it is in itself (potentially)."[15] And again: "God, who is the truth, is known by us in His truth, that is, as Absolute Spirit, only in so far as we at the same time recognise that the world which He created, Nature and the finite spirit [man], are, in their difference from God, untrue."[16]

Until recently, Hegel's *Philosophy of Nature* has been the most neglected part of his system. But the last few years have witnessed the publication of two translations of the *Naturphilosophie* into English and the conducting of a major symposium in America on "Hegel and the Sciences." "The *Philosophy of Nature,*" remarks Professor Findlay, "is an integral part of Hegel's system . . ."

and one can no more understand that system without taking account of it, than one can understand Aristotelianism while ignoring the *Physics* or the *History of Animals,* or Cartesianism while ignoring the physical portions of the *Principles of Philosophy.* In Hegel's theory of Nature, as in the parallel theories of Aristotle and Descartes, one sees the philosopher's principles at work, casting their slant upon our talk and thought about the world around us. The complete misunderstanding of Hegel's idealism by British philosophers, and its reduction to a refined form of subjectivism, are probably due to their ignoring of the *Naturphilosophie.*[17]

No previous philosopher, with the possible exceptions of Aristotle and Kant, brought to the study of Nature the wealth of knowledge of natural science and mathematics that Hegel did, and his text literally bristles with detailed illustrations of the experimental science of his day. Our selection of the Introduction to this text provides a synopsis of the philosophical standpoint from which Hegel approaches this material.

The *Philosophy of Mind* (or Spirit) is the richest part of Hegel's system, and the lion's share of his work is devoted to its exposition. With the exception of the section on Subjective Mind with its wealth of *Zusätze* on Anthropology, Phenomenology, and Psychology, the relatively brief treatment of *Geistesphilosophie* in the third part of the *Encyclopaedia* is only the bare outline of the life of Mind come into its own, which Hegel fully and brilliantly develops in his *Philosophy of Right* and *Lectures on the Philosophy of History, Philosophy of Fine Art, Philosophy of Religion,* and *History of Philosophy,* which together constitute twelve large volumes in their English translations. By "philosophy of mind" Hegel means a *moral* philosophy or philosophy of man, in the broad sense of this term, which has today been obscured if not lost by our compartmentalized approach to human experience.

Its subject is the moral as opposed to the physical aspect of reality: the inner and ideal life as opposed to the merely external and real materials of it: the world of intelligence and of humanity. It displays Man in the several stages of that process by which he expresses the full meaning of nature, or discharges the burden of that task which is implicit in him from the first. It traces the steps of that growth by which what was no better than a fragment of nature—an intelligence located (as it seemed) in one piece of matter—comes to realise the truth of it and of himself. . . . Thus the philosophy of mind, beginning with man as a sentient organism, the focus in which the universe gets its first dim confused expression through mere feeling, shows how he "erects himself above himself" and realises what ancient thinkers called his kindred with the divine.[18]

We have already brought the function of Spirit generally into focus in its relation to Nature. While the realm of Nature is that of external-ity to self (*Aussersichseyn*), the sphere of Mind or Spirit is one of return and reconciliation, its distinctive characteristic being ideality, infini-tude, freedom: the triumph over externality. In Hegel's dialectical scheme of things, this return or reflection-into-self is not a regression but an advance, and it is, furthermore, no tranquil one, for family quarrels are the fiercest, and in the domain of Spirit proper, the "development, which in Nature is [largely] a quiet unfolding, is in Spirit a hard, infinite struggle against itself."[19] Many aspects of this conflict have already been set out in our selections from Hegel's *Phenomenology*, and more will follow below in those from Hegel's doctrine of Objective Spirit and especially his teaching on World History, in which "the pages on happiness are all blank."

The first two moments of Mind emergent from Nature—Subjective and Objective Spirit—are still finite, the one struggling to overcome the vestiges of a natural heritage everywhere in the bonds of individu-alism, the other battling to construct and maintain about itself a world of objective institutions—the family, civil society, and the state—which will provide the ground upon which it can stand to get its first unobstructed view of itself as Absolute Spirit. In these pages Hegel brings home the insight of St. Augustine's Christian pessimism, that for all the tears, sweat, and blood of human moral, social, and politi-cal existence, it is not the will of men but that of God that is accom-plished in history.

Notes. Nature and Spirit:
Self-Estrangement and Reconciliation

1. *Philosophy of Nature*, p. 13.
2. Ibid., p. 14.

3. Ibid., p. 13.

4. Ibid., p. 7.

5. *Logic*, Wallace, p. 196. Hegel quotes the poet Haller, whose lines contrast the false infinity of quantitative *progressus in infinitum* with God's infinity:

> I heap up monstrous numbers,
> Mountains of millions,
> I pile time upon time
> And world on the top of world,
> And when from the awful height
> I cast a dizzy look toward Thee:
> All the power of number
> Multiplied a thousand times,
> Is not yet one part of Thee.
> These I remove and Thou liest all before me.

6. *Philosophy of Nature*, p. 444.

7. Ibid., p. 19.

8. *Logic*, Miller, p. 527.

9. *Logic*, Wallace, p. 223.

10. Ibid., p. 252.

11. Ibid., pp. 252–254.

12. Ibid., p. 243.

13. Hegel finds apt and beautiful poetical expression for this teleological and developmental view of Nature in the lines of the Mohammedan poet, especially stanzas 5 and 9, which he quotes in the section on Philosophy at the close of *Philosophy of Mind;* see below, pp. 332–333.

14. *Logic*, Wallace, p. 57.

15. Robert S. Hartman, *Reason in History* (Indianapolis: Bobbs-Merrill, 1953), p. 69.

16. *Logic*, Wallace, p. 155.

17. J. N. Findlay, *Hegel: A Re-examination* (New York: Humanities Press, 1958), p. 269.

18. *Philosophy of Mind*, p. 14.

19. Hartman, *Reason in History*, p. 69.

PHILOSOPHY OF NATURE

Introduction

Zusatz. It can be said perhaps that in our time, philosophy does not enjoy any special favour and liking. At least, it is no longer recognized, as it was formerly, that the study of philosophy must constitute the indispensable introduction and foundation for all further scientific education and professional study. But this much may be assumed *without hesitation* as correct, that the *Philosophy of Nature* in particular is in considerable disfavour. I do not intend to deal at length with the extent to which this prejudice against the Philosophy of Nature in particular, is justified; and yet I cannot altogether pass it over. What is seldom absent from a period of great intellectual ferment has, of course, happened in connection with the *idea of the Philosophy of Nature* as recently expounded. It can be said that in the first satisfaction afforded by its discovery, this idea met with crude treatment at unskilled hands, instead of being cultivated by thinking Reason; and it has been brought low not so much by its opponents as by its friends. It has in many respects, in fact for the most part, been transformed into an external formalism and perverted into a thoughtless instrument for superficial thinking and fanciful imagination. I do not want to characterize in any further detail the eccentricities for which the Idea, or rather its lifeless forms, have been used. I said more about this some while ago in the preface to the *Phenomenology of Spirit.* It is, then, not to be wondered at that a more thoughtful examination of Nature, as well as crude empiricism, a knowing led by the Idea, as well as the external, abstract Understanding, alike turned their backs on a procedure which was as fantastic as it was pretentious, which itself made a chaotic mixture of crude empiricism and uncomprehended thoughts, of a purely capricious exercise of the imagination and the most commonplace way of reasoning by superficial analogy, and which passed off such a hotchpotch as the Idea, Reason, philosophical science, divine knowledge, and pretended that the complete lack of method and scientific procedure was the acme of scientific procedure. It is on account of such charlatanism that the Philosophy of Nature, especially Schelling's has become discredited.

It is quite another thing, however, to reject the Philosophy of

SOURCE: *Philosophy of Nature,* pp. 1–27. Reprinted by permission of the Clarendon Press, Oxford.

Nature itself because of such aberration and misunderstanding of the Idea. It not infrequently happens that those who are obsessed by a hatred of philosophy, welcome abuses and perversions of it, because they use the perversion to disparage the science itself and they hope to make their reasoned rejection of the perversion a justification in some vague way for their claim to have hit philosophy itself.

It might seem appropriate first of all, in view of the existing misunderstandings and prejudices in regard to the Philosophy of Nature, to set forth the *true* Notion of this science. But this opposition which we encounter at the outset, is to be regarded as something contingent and external, and all such opposition we can straightway leave on one side. Such a treatment of the subject tends to become polemical and is not a procedure in which one can take any pleasure. What might be instructive in it falls partly within the science itself, but it would not be so instructive as to justify reducing still further the available space which is already restricted enough for the wealth of material contained in an *Encyclopaedia*. We shall therefore content ourselves with the observation made above; it can serve as a kind of protest against that style of philosophizing about Nature, as an assurance that such a style is not to be expected in this exposition. That style, it is true, often appears brilliant and entertaining, arousing astonishment at least; but it can only satisfy those who openly confess to seeing in the Philosophy of Nature simply a brilliant display of fireworks, thus sparing themselves the effort of thought. What we are engaged on here, is not an affair of imagination and fancy, but of the Notion, of Reason.

In keeping with this standpoint, we do not propose to discuss here the Notion, the task, the manner and method, of the Philosophy of Nature; but it is quite in place to preface a scientific work with a statement of the specific character of its subject-matter and purpose, and what is to be considered in it, and how it is to be considered. The opposition between the Philosophy of Nature and a perverted form of it, disappears of its own accord when we determine its Notion more precisely. The science of philosophy is a circle in which each member has an antecedent and a successor, but in the philosophical encyclopaedia, the Philosophy of Nature appears as only one circle in the whole, and therefore the procession of Nature from the eternal Idea, its creation, the proof that there necessarily is a Nature, lies in the preceding exposition (§ 244); here we have to presuppose it as known. If we do want to determine what the Philosophy of Nature is, our best method is to separate it off from the subject-matter with which it is contrasted; for all determining requires two terms. In the first place, we find the Philosophy of Nature in a peculiar relationship to natural science in general, to physics, natural history, and physiology; it is itself physics, but *rational physics*. It is at this point that we have to grasp what the Philosophy of Nature is and, in particular, to determine its relationship to physics. In so doing, one may imagine that this contrast between natural science and the Philosophy of Nature is something new. The Philosophy of Nature may perhaps be regarded prima facie as a new science: this is certainly correct in one sense, but in another sense it is not. For it is ancient, as ancient as any study of Nature at all; it is not distinct from the latter and it is, in fact, older than physics; Aristotelian physics, for example, is far more a Philosophy of Nature than it is physics. It is only in modern times that the two have been separated. We already see this separation in the science which, as cosmology, was distinguished in Wolff's philosophy from physics, and though supposed to be a metaphysics of the world or of Nature was confined to the wholly abstract categories of the Understanding. This metaphysics was, of course, further removed from physics than is the Philosophy of Nature as we now understand it. In connection with this distinction between physics and the Philosophy of Nature, and of the specific character of each as contrasted with the other, it must be noted, right from the start, that the two do not lie so far apart as is at first assumed. Physics and natural history are called empirical sciences *par excellence*, and they profess to belong entirely to the sphere of perception and experience, and in this way to be opposed to the Philosophy of Nature, i.e., to a knowledge of Nature from thought. The fact is, however, that the principal charge to be brought against physics is that it contains much more thought than it admits and is aware of, and that it is better than it supposes itself to be; or if, perhaps, all thought in physics is to be counted a defect, then it is worse than it supposes itself to be. Physics and the Philosophy of Nature, therefore, are not distinguished from each other as perception and thought, but only by *the kind and manner of their thought;* they are both a thinking apprehension of Nature.

It is this which we shall consider *first,* i.e., how thought is present in physics; then, *secondly,* we have to consider what Nature is: and, *thirdly,* to give the divisions of the philosophy of Nature.

A. *Ways of considering Nature.*

In order to find the *Notion of the Philosophy of Nature,* we must *first* of all indicate the Notion of the knowledge of Nature in general, and *secondly,* develop the *distinction between physics and the Philosophy of Nature.*

What is Nature? We propose to answer this general question by reference to the knowledge of Nature and the Philosophy of Nature. Nature confronts us as a riddle and a problem, whose solution both attracts and repels us: attracts us, because Spirit is presaged in Nature; repels us, because Nature seems an alien existence, in which Spirit does not find itself. That is why Aristotle said that philosophy started from wonder. We start to perceive, we collect facts about the manifold formations and laws of Nature; this procedure, on its own account, runs on into endless detail in all directions, and just because no end can be perceived in it, this method does not satisfy us. And in all this wealth of knowledge the question can again arise, or perhaps come to us for the first time: What is Nature? It remains a problem. When we see Nature's processes and transformations we want to grasp its simple essence, to compel this Proteus to cease its transformations and show itself to us and declare itself to us; so that it may not present us with a variety of ever new forms, but in simpler fashion bring to our consciousness in language what it *is.* This inquiry after the *being* of something has a number of meanings, and can often refer simply to its name, as in the question: What kind of a plant *is* this? or it can refer to perception if the name is given; if I do not know what a compass is, I get someone to show me the instrument, and I say, now I know what a compass is. 'Is' can also refer to status, as for example when we ask: What is this man? But this is not what we mean when we ask: What is Nature? It is the meaning to be attached to this question that we propose to examine here, remembering that we want to acquire a knowledge of the Philosophy of Nature.

We could straightway resort to the philosophical Idea and say that the Philosophy of Nature ought to give us the Idea of Nature. But to begin thus might be confusing. For we must grasp the Idea itself as concrete and thus apprehend its various specifications and then bring them together. In order therefore to possess the Idea, we must traverse a series of specifications through which it is first there for us. If we now take these up in forms which are familiar to us, and say that we want to approach Nature as thinkers, there are, in the first place, other ways of approaching Nature which I will mention, not for the sake of completeness, but because we shall find in them the elements or moments which are requisite for a knowledge of the Idea and which individually reach our consciousness earlier in other *ways of considering Nature.* In so doing, we shall come to the point where the characteristic feature of our inquiry becomes prominent. Our approach to Nature is partly practical and partly theoretical. An examination of the theoretical approach will reveal a contradiction which, thirdly, will lead us to our standpoint; to resolve the contradiction we must incorporate what is peculiar to the practical approach, and by this means practical and theoretical will be united and integrated into a totality. End *Zusatz.*

245

In man's *practical* approach to Nature, the latter is, for him, something immediate and external; and he himself is an external and therefore sensuous individual, although in relation to natural objects, he correctly regards himself as *end.* A consideration of Nature according to this relationship yields the standpoint of *finite* teleology. In this, we find the correct presupposition that Nature does not itself contain the absolute, final end. But if this way of considering the matter starts from particular, *finite* ends, on the one hand it makes them into presuppositions whose contingent content may in itself be even insignificant and trivial. On the other hand, the end-relationship demands for itself a deeper mode of treatment than that appropriate to external and finite relationships, namely, the mode of treatment of the Notion, which in its own general nature is immanent and therefore is immanent in Nature as such.

Zusatz. The practical approach to Nature is, in general, determined by appetite, which is self-seeking; need impels us to use Nature for our own advantage, to wear her out, to wear her down, in short, to annihilate her. And here, two characteristics at once stand out. (α) The practical approach is concerned only with individual products of Nature, or with individual aspects of those products. The necessities and the wit of man have found an endless variety of ways of using and mastering Nature. Sophocles says:

οὐδὲν ἀνθρώπου δεινότερον πέλει,—
ἄπορος ἐπ' οὐδὲν ἔρχεται.

Whatever forces Nature develops and lets loose against man—cold, wild beasts, water, fire—he knows means to counter them; indeed, he takes these means from Nature and uses them against herself. The cunning of his reason enables him to preserve and maintain himself in face of the forces of Nature, by sheltering behind other products of Nature, and letting these suffer her destructive attacks. Nature herself, however, in her universal aspect, he cannot overcome in this way, nor can he turn her to his own purposes. (β) The other characteristic of the practical approach is that, since it is *our* end which is paramount, not natural things themselves, we convert the latter into means, the destiny of which is determined by us, not by the things themselves; an example of this is the conversion of food into blood. (γ) What is achieved is our satisfaction, our self-feeling, which had been disturbed by a lack of some kind or another. The negation of myself which I suffer within me in hunger, is at the same time present as an other than myself, as something to be consumed; my act is to annul this contradiction by making this other identical with myself or by restoring my self-unity through sacrificing the thing.

The teleological standpoint which was formerly so popular, was based, it is true, on a reference to Spirit, but it was confined to external purposiveness only, and took Spirit in the sense of finite Spirit caught up in natural ends; but because the finite ends which natural objects were shown to subserve were so trivial, teleology has become discredited as an argument for the wisdom of God. The notion of end, however, is not merely external to Nature, as it is, for example, when I say that the wool of the sheep is there only to provide me with clothes; for this often results in trivial reflections, as in the *Xenia*,* where God's wisdom is admired in that He has provided cork-trees for bottle-stoppers, or herbs for curing disordered stomachs, and cinnabar for cosmetics. The notion of end as immanent in natural objects is their simple determinateness, e.g., the seed of a plant, which contains the real possibility of all that is to exist in the tree, and thus, as a purposive activity, is directed solely to self-preservation. This notion of end was already recognized by Aristotle, too, and he called this activity the *nature of a thing;* the true teleological method—and this is the highest—consists, therefore, in the method of regarding Nature as free in her own peculiar vital activity. End *Zusatz.*

246

What is now called *physics* was formerly called *natural philosophy*, and it is also a *theoretical*, and indeed a *thinking* consideration of Nature; but, on the one hand, it does not start from determinations which are external to Nature, like those ends already mentioned; and secondly,

*Goethe-Schiller, *Xenien* (1796), No. 286.

it is directed to a knowledge of the *universal* aspect of Nature, a universal which is also *determined* within itself—directed to a knowledge of forces, laws and genera, whose content must not be a simple aggregate, but arranged in orders and classes, must present itself as an organism. As the Philosophy of Nature is a *comprehending (begreifend)* treatment, it has as its object the same *universal*, but *explicitly*, and it considers this universal in its *own immanent necessity* in accordance with the self-determination of the Notion.

Remark.

The relation of philosophy to the empirical sciences was discussed in the general introduction [to the *Encyclopaedia*]. Not only must philosophy be in agreement with our empirical knowledge of Nature, but the *origin* and *formation* of the Philosophy of Nature presupposes and is conditioned by empirical physics. However, the course of a science's origin and the preliminaries of its construction are one thing, while the science itself is another. In the latter, the former can no longer appear as the foundation of the science; here, the foundation must be the necessity of the Notion.

It has already been mentioned that, in the progress of philosophical knowledge, we must not only give an account of the object *as determined by its Notion*, but we must also name the *empirical* appearance corresponding to it, and we must show that the appearance does, in fact, correspond to its Notion. However, this is not an appeal to experience in regard to the necessity of the content. Even less admissible is an appeal to what is called *intuition (Anschauung)*, which is usually nothing but a fanciful and sometimes fantastic exercise of the imagination on the lines of *analogies*, which may be more or less significant, and which impress determinations and schemata on objects only *externally*.

Zusatz. In the theoretical approach to Nature (α) the first point is that we stand back from natural objects, leaving them as they are and adjusting ourselves to them. Here, we start from our sense-knowledge of Nature. However, if physics were based solely on perceptions, and perceptions were nothing more than the evidence of the senses, then the physical act would consist only in seeing, hearing, smelling, etc., and animals, too, would in this way be physicists. But what sees, hears, etc., is a spirit, a thinker. Now if we said that, in our theoretical approach to Nature, we left things free, this applied only partly to the outer senses, for these are themselves partly theoretical and partly practical; it is only our ideational faculty (*Vorstellen*), our intelligence, that has this free relationship to things. We can, of course, consider things practically, as means; but then knowing is itself only a means, not an end in itself. (β) The second bearing of things on us is that things acquire the character of universality for us or that we transform them into universals. The more thought enters into our representation of things, the less do they retain their naturalness, their singularity and immediacy. The wealth of natural forms, in all their infinitely manifold configuration, is impoverished by the all-pervading power of thought, their vernal life and glowing colours die and fade away. The rustle of Nature's life is silenced in the stillness of thought; her abundant life, wearing a thousand wonderful and delightful shapes, shrivels into arid forms and shapeless generalities resembling a murky northern fog. (γ) These two characteristics are not only opposed to the two practical ones, but we also find that the theoretical approach is self-contradictory, for it seems to bring about the direct opposite of what it intends; for we want to know the Nature that really is, not something that is not. But instead of leaving Nature as she is, and taking her as she is in truth, instead of simply perceiving her, we make her into something quite different. In thinking things, we transform them into something universal; but things are singular and the Lion as Such does not exist. We give them the form of something subjective, of something produced by us and belonging to us, and belonging to us in our specifically human character; for natural objects do not think, and are not presentations or thoughts. But according to the second characteristic of the theoretical approach referred to above, it is precisely this inversion which does take place; in fact, it might seem that what we are beginning is made impossible for us at the outset. The theoretical approach begins with the arrest of appetite, is disinterested, lets things exist and go on just as they are; with this attitude to Nature, we have straightway established a duality of object and subject and their separation, something here and something yonder. Our intention, however, is rather to grasp, to comprehend Nature, to make her ours, so that she is not something alien and yonder. Here, then, comes the difficulty: How do we, as subjects, come into contact with objects? If we venture to bridge this gulf and mislead ourselves along that line and so think this Nature, we make Nature, which is an Other than we are, into an Other than she is. Both theoretical approaches are also directly opposed to each other: we transform things into universals, or make them our own, and yet as natural objects they are supposed to have a free, self-subsistent being. This, therefore, is the point with which we are concerned in regard to the nature of cognition—this is the interest of philosophy.

But the Philosophy of Nature is in the unfavourable position of having to demonstrate its existence, and, in order to justify it, we must trace it back to something familiar. Mention must be made here of a special solution of the contradiction between subjectivity and objectivity, a solution which has been made familiar both by science and religion—in the latter case in the past—and which makes short shrift of the whole difficulty. The union of the two determinations is, namely, what is called the *primal state of innocence*, where Spirit is identical with Nature, and the spiritual eye is placed directly in the centre of Nature; whereas the standpoint of the divided consciousness is the fall of man from the eternal, divine unity. This unity is represented as a primal intuition *(Anschauung)*, a Reason, which is at the same time one with fantasy, i.e., it forms sensuous shapes, and in so doing gives them a rational significance. This intuitive Reason is the divine Reason; for God, we are entitled to say, is that Being in whom Spirit and Nature are united, in whom intelligence at the same time also has being and shape. The eccentricities of the Philosophy of Nature originate partly in such an idea, namely in the idea that, although nowadays we no longer dwell in this paradisal state, there still are favoured ones, seers to whom God imparts true knowledge and wisdom in sleep; or that man, even without being so favoured, can at least by faith in it, transport himself into a state where the inner side of Nature is immediately revealed to him, and where he need only let fancies occur to him, i.e., give free play to his fancy, in order to declare prophetically what is true. This visionary state, about the source of which nothing further can be said, has, in general, been regarded as the consummation of the scientific faculty; and it is, perhaps, added that such a state of perfect knowledge preceded the present history of the world, and that, since man's fall from his unity with Nature, there has remained for us in myths, traditions or in other vestiges, still some fragments and faint echoes of that spiritual, illuminated state. These fragments have formed the basis for the further religious education of humanity, and are the source of all scientific knowledge. If it had not been made so difficult to know the truth, but one needed only to sit on the tripod and utter oracles, then, of course, the labour of thought would not be needed.

In order to state briefly what is the defect of this conception, we must at once admit that there is something lofty in it which at first glance makes a strong appeal. But this unity of intelligence and intuition, of the inwardness of Spirit and its relation to externality, must be, not the beginning, but the goal, not an immediate, but a resultant unity. A natural unity of thought and intuition is that of the child and the animal, and this can at the most be called feeling, not spirituality. But man must have eaten of the tree of the knowledge of good and evil and must have gone through the labour and activity of thought in order to become what he is, having overcome this separation between himself and Nature. The immediate unity is thus only an abstract, implicit truth, not the actual truth; for not only must the content be true, but the form also. The healing of this breach must be in the form of the knowing Idea, and the moments of the solution must be sought in consciousness itself. It is not a question of betaking oneself to abstraction and vacuity, of taking refuge in the negation of knowing; on the contrary, consciousness must preserve itself in that we must use the ordinary consciousness itself to refute the assumptions which have given rise to the contradiction.

The difficulty arising from the one-sided assumption of the theoretical consciousness, that natural objects confront us as permanent and impenetrable objects, is directly negatived by the practical approach which acts on the absolutely idealistic belief that individual things are nothing in themselves. The defect of appetite, from the side of its relationship to things, is not that it is realistic towards them, but that it is all too idealistic. Philosophical, true idealism consists in nothing else but laying down that the truth about things is that as such immediately single, i.e., sensuous things, they are only a show, an appearance *(Schein)*. Of a metaphysics prevalent today which maintains that we cannot know things because they are absolutely shut to us, it might be said that not even the animals are so stupid as these metaphysicians; for they go after things, seize and consume them. The same thing is laid down in the second aspect of the theoretical approach referred to above, namely, that we think natural objects. Intelligence familiarizes itself with things, not of course in their sensuous existence, but by thinking them and positing their content in itself; and in, so to speak, adding form, universality, to the practical ideality which, by itself, is only negativity, it gives an affirmative character to the negativity of the singular. This universal aspect of things is not something subjective, something belonging to us: rather is it, in contrast to the transient phenomenon, the noumenon, the true, objective, actual nature of things themselves, like the Platonic Ideas, which are not somewhere afar off in the beyond, but exist in individual things as their substantial genera. Not until one does violence to Proteus—that is not until one turns one's back on the sensuous appearance of Nature—is he compelled to speak the truth. The inscription on the veil of Isis, "I am that which was, is, and will be, and my veil no mortal hath lifted," melts away before thought. "Nature," Hamann therefore rightly says, "is a Hebrew word written only with consonants and the understanding must point it."

Now although the empirical treatment of Nature has this category of universality in common with the Philosophy of Nature, the empiricists are sometimes uncertain whether this universal is subjective or objective; one can often hear it said that these classes and orders are only made as aids to cognition. This uncertainty is still more apparent in the search for distinguishing marks, not in the belief that they are essential, objective characteristics of things, but that they only serve our convenience to help us to distinguish things. If nothing more than that were involved, we might, e.g., take the lobe of the ear as the sign of man, for no animal has it; but we feel at once that such a characteristic is not sufficient for a knowledge of the essential nature of man. When, however, the universal is characterized as law, force, matter, then we cannot allow that it counts only as an external form and a subjective addition; on the contrary, objective reality is attributed to laws, forces are immanent, and matter is the true nature of the thing itself. Something similar may be conceded in regard to genera too, namely that they are not just a grouping of similarities, an abstraction made by us, that they not only have common features but that they are the objects' own inner essence; the orders not only serve to give us a general view, but form a graduated scale of Nature itself. The distinguishing marks, too, should be the universal, substantial element of the genus. Physics looks on these universals as its triumph: one can say even that, unfortunately, it goes too far in its generalizations. Present-day philosophy is called the philosophy of identity: this name can be much more appropriately given to that physics which simply ignores specific differences (*Bestimmtheiten*), as occurs, for example, in the current theory of electro-chemistry in which magnetism, electricity, and chemistry are regarded as one and the same. It is the weakness of physics that it is too much dominated by the category of identity; for identity is the fundamental category of the Understanding.

The Philosophy of Nature takes up the material which physics has prepared for it empirically, at the point to which physics has brought it, and reconstitutes it, so that experience is not its final warrant and base. Physics must therefore work into the hands of philosophy, in order that the latter may translate into the Notion the abstract universal transmitted to it, by showing how this universal, as an intrinsically necessary whole, proceeds from the Notion. The philosophical way of putting the facts is no mere whim, once in a way to walk on one's head for a change, after having walked for a long while on one's legs, or once in a way to see our everyday face bedaubed with paint: no, it is because the method of physics does not satisfy the Notion, that we have to go further.

What distinguishes the Philosophy of Nature from physics is, more precisely, the kind of metaphysics used by them both; for metaphysics is nothing else but the entire range of the universal determinations of thought, as it were, the diamond net into which everything is brought and thereby first made intelligible. Every educated consciousness has its metaphysics, an instinctive way of thinking, the absolute power within us of which we become master only when we make it in turn the object of our knowledge. Philosophy in general has, as philosophy, other categories than those of the ordinary consciousness: all education *(Bildung)* reduces to the distinction of categories. All revolutions, in the sciences no less than in world history, originate solely from the fact that Spirit, in order to understand and comprehend itself with a view to possessing itself, has changed its categories, comprehending itself more truly, more deeply, more intimately, and more in unity with itself. Now the inadequacy of the thought-determinations used in physics can be traced to two points which are closely bound up with each other. (α) The universal of physics is abstract or only formal; its determination is not immanent in it and it does not pass over into particularity. (β) The determinate content falls for that very reason outside the universal; and so is split into fragments, into parts which are isolated and detached from each other, devoid of any necessary connection, and it is just this which stamps it as only finite. If we examine a flower, for example, our understanding notes its particular qualities; chemistry dismembers and analyses it. In this way, we separate colour, shape of the leaves, citric acid, etheric oil, carbon, hydrogen, etc.; and now we say that the plant consists of all these parts.

> If you want to describe life and gather its meaning,
> To drive out its spirit must be your beginning,
> Then though fast in your hand lie the parts one by one

> The spirit that linked them, alas is gone
> And "Nature's Laboratory" is only a name
> That the chemist bestows on't to hide his own shame.*

as Goethe says. Spirit cannot remain at this stage of thinking in terms of detached, unrelated concepts (*Verstandesreflexion*) and there are two ways in which it can advance beyond it. (α) The naïve mind (*der unbefangene Geist*), when it vividly contemplates Nature, as in the suggestive examples we often come across in Goethe, feels the life and the universal relationship in Nature; it divines that the universe is an organic whole and a totality pervaded by Reason, and it also feels in single forms of life an intimate oneness with itself; but even if we put together all those ingredients of the flower the result is still not a flower. And so, in the Philosophy of Nature, people have fallen back on intuition (*Anschauung*) and set it above reflective thought; but this is a mistake, for one cannot philosophize out of intuition. (β) What is intuited must also be thought, the isolated parts must be brought back by thought to simple universality; this thought unity is the Notion, which contains the specific differences, but as an immanent self-moving unity. The determinations of philosophical universality are not indifferent; it is the universality which fulfils itself, and which, in its diamantine identity, also contains difference.

The true infinite is the unity of itself and the finite; and this, now, is the category of philosophy and so, too, of the Philosophy of Nature. If genera and forces are the inner side of Nature, the universal, in face of which the outer and individual is only transient, then still a third stage is demanded, namely, the inner side of the inner side, and this, according to what has been said, would be the unity of the universal and the particular.

> To Nature's heart there penetrates no mere created mind:
> Too happy if she but display the outside of her rind.

> I swear—of course but to myself—as rings within my ears
> That same old warning o'er and o'er again for sixty years,
> And thus a thousand times I answer in my mind:—
> With gladsome and ungrudging hand metes Nature from her store:

Faust, part I, sc. 4. (Wallace's rendering, but see his note on p. 398 of his translation of the *Encyclopaedia Logic*. Only the last four lines are quoted, though in a different order, by Hegel, and a prose version of them would run: "Nature's laboratory" the chemist calls it, mocking himself and confessing his ignorance. The parts, certainly, he holds in his hand, but alas the spiritual link is missing.)

She keeps not back the core,
Nor separates the rind,
But all in each both rind and core has evermore combined.*

In grasping this inner side, the one-sidedness of the theoretical and
practical approaches is transcended, and at the same time each side
receives its due. The former contains a universal without determinateness, the latter an individuality without a universal; the cognition
which comprehends *(begreifendes Erkennen)* is the middle term in which
universality does not remain on *this* side, in *me*, over against the
individuality of the objects; on the contrary, while it stands in a
negative relation to things and assimilates them to itself, it equally
finds individuality in them and does not encroach upon their independence, or interfere with their free self-determination. The cognition which comprehends is thus the unity of the theoretical and practical approaches: the negation of individuality is, as negation of the
negative, the affirmative universality which gives permanence to its
determinations; for the true individuality is at the same time within
itself a universality.

As regards the objections which can be raised against this standpoint, the first question which can be asked is: How does the universal
determine itself? How does the infinite become finite? A more concrete form of the question is: How has God come to create the world?
God is, of course, conceived to be a subject, a self-subsistent actuality
far removed from the world; but such an abstract infinity, such a
universality which had the particular outside it, would itself be only
one side of the relation, and therefore itself only a particular and
finite: it is characteristic of the Understanding that it unwittingly
nullifies the very determination it posits, and thus does the very
opposite of what it intends. The particular is supposed to be separate
from the universal, but this very separateness, this independence,
makes it a universal, and so what is present is only the unity of the
universal and the particular. God reveals Himself in two different
ways: as Nature and as Spirit. Both manifestations are temples of God
which He fills, and in which He is present. God, as an abstraction, is
not the true God, but only as the living process of positing His Other,
the world, which, comprehended in its divine form is His Son; and
it is only in unity with His Other, in Spirit, that God is Subject. This,
now, is the specific character and the goal of the Philosophy of Na-

*Goethe, *Zur Morphologie*, vol. i, part 3, 1820. (Wallace's rendering in the
Encyclopaedia Logic, pp. 421-2.)

ture, that Spirit finds in Nature its own essence, i.e., the Notion, finds its counterpart in her. The study of Nature is thus the liberation of Spirit in her, for Spirit is present in her in so far as it is in relation, not with an Other, but with itself. This is also the liberation of Nature; implicitly she is Reason, but it is through Spirit that Reason as such first emerges from Nature into existence. Spirit has the certainty which Adam had when he looked on Eve: "This is flesh of my flesh, and bone of my bone." Thus Nature is the bride which Spirit weds. But is this certainty also truth? Since the inner being of Nature is none other than the universal, then in our thoughts of this inner being we are at home with ourselves. Truth in its subjective meaning is the agreement of thought with the object: in its objective meaning, truth is the agreement of the object with its own self, the correspondence of its reality with its Notion. The Ego in its essence is the Notion, which is equal to itself and pervades all things, and which, because it retains the mastery over the particular differences, is the universal which returns into itself. This Notion is directly the true Idea, the divine Idea of the universe which alone is the Actual. Thus God alone is the Truth, in Plato's words, the immortal Being whose body and soul are joined in a single nature. The first question here is: Why has God willed to create Nature? End *Zusatz.*

B. The Notion of Nature.

247

Nature has presented itself as the Idea in the form of *otherness.* Since therefore the Idea is the negative of itself, or is *external to itself,* Nature is not merely external in relation to this Idea (and to its subjective existence Spirit); the truth is rather that *externality* constitutes the specific character in which Nature, as Nature, exists.

Zusatz. If God is all-sufficient and lacks nothing, why does He disclose Himself in a sheer Other of Himself? The divine Idea is just this: to disclose itself, to posit this Other outside itself and to take it back again into itself, in order to be subjectivity and Spirit. The Philosophy of Nature itself belongs to this path of return; for it is that which overcomes the division between Nature and Spirit and assures to Spirit the knowledge of its essence in Nature. This, now, is the place of Nature in the whole; its determinateness is this, that the Idea determines itself, posits difference within itself, an Other, but in such a way that in its indivisible nature it is infinite goodness, imparting to its otherness and sharing with it its entire fullness of content. God, therefore, in determining Himself, remains equal to Himself; each of these moments is itself the whole Idea and must be posited as the divine totality. The different moments can be grasped under three different forms: the universal, the particular, and the individual. First, the different moments remain preserved in the eternal unity of the Idea; this is the Logos, the eternal Son of God as Philo conceived it. The other to this extreme is individuality, the form of finite Spirit. As a return into itself individuality is, indeed, Spirit; but, as otherness with exclusion of all others, it is finite or human Spirit; for finite spirits other than human beings do not concern us here. The individual man grasped as also in unity with the divine essence is the object of the Christian religion; and this is the most tremendous demand that can be made on him. The third form which concerns us here, the Idea in the mode of particularity, is Nature, which lies between the two extremes. This form presents the least difficulty for the Understanding; Spirit is posited as the contradiction existing explicitly, for the Idea in its infinite freedom, and again in the form of individuality, are in objective contradiction; but in Nature, the contradiction is only implicit or for us, the otherness appearing in the Idea as a quiescent form. In Christ, the contradiction is posited and overcome, as His life, passion, and resurrection: Nature is the son of God, but not as the Son, but as abiding in otherness—the divine Idea as held fast for a moment outside the divine love. Nature is Spirit estranged from itself; in Nature, Spirit lets itself go *(ausgelassen)*, a Bacchic god unrestrained and unmindful of itself; in Nature, the unity of the Notion is concealed.

A rational consideration of Nature must consider how Nature is in its own self this process of becoming Spirit, of sublating its otherness —and how the Idea is present in each grade or level of Nature itself; estranged from the Idea, Nature is only the corpse of the Understanding. Nature is, however, only implicitly the Idea, and Schelling therefore called her a petrified intelligence, others even a frozen intelligence; but God does not remain petrified and dead; the very stones cry out and raise themselves to Spirit. God is subjectivity, activity, infinite actuosity, in which otherness has only a transient being, remaining implicit within the unity of the Idea, because it is itself this totality of the Idea. Since Nature is the Idea in the form of otherness, the Idea, comformable to its Notion, is not present in Nature as it is in and for itself, although nevertheless, Nature is one of the ways in which the Idea manifests itself, and is a necessary mode of the Idea. However, the fact that this mode of the Idea is Nature, is the second question to be discussed and demonstrated; to this end we must compare our definition with the ordinary idea of Nature and see whether the two correspond; this will occur in the sequel. In other respects, however, philosophy need not trouble itself about ordinary ideas, nor is it bound to realize in every respect what such ideas demand, for ideas are arbitrary; but still, generally speaking, the two must agree.

In connection with this fundamental determination of Nature, attention must be drawn to the metaphysical aspect which has been dealt with in the form of the question of the *eternity of the world.* It might be thought that we need pay no attention to metaphysics here; but this is the very place to bring it to notice, and we need not hesitate to do so, for it does not lead to prolixity and is readily dealt with. Now the metaphysics of Nature, i.e., Nature's essential and distinctive characteristic, is to be the Idea in the form of otherness, and this implies that the being of Nature is essentially ideality, or that, as only relative, Nature is essentially related to a First. The question of the eternity of the world (this is confused with Nature, since it is a collection of both spiritual and natural objects) has, in the first place, the meaning of the conception of time, of an eternity as it is called, of an infinitely long time, so that the world had no beginning in time; secondly, the question implies that Nature is conceived as uncreated, eternal, as existing independently of God. As regards this second meaning, it is completely set aside and eliminated by the distinctive character of Nature to be the Idea in its otherness. As regards the first meaning, after removing the sense of the absoluteness of the world, we are left only with eternity in connection with the conception of time.

About this, the following is to be said: (α) eternity is not before or after time, not before the creation of the world, nor when it perishes; rather is eternity the absolute present, the Now, without before and after. The world is created, is now being created, and has eternally been created; this presents itself in the form of the preservation of the world. Creating is the activity of the absolute Idea; the Idea of Nature, like the Idea as such, is eternal. (β) In the question whether the world or Nature, in its finitude, has a beginning in time or not, one thinks of the world or Nature as such, i.e., as the universal; and the true universal is the Idea, which we have already said is eternal. The finite, however, is temporal, it has a before and an after; and when the finite is our object we are in time. It has a beginning but not an absolute one; its time begins with it, and time belongs only to the sphere of finitude. Philosophy is timeless comprehension, of time too and of all things generally in their eternal mode. Having rid oneself of the conception of the absolute beginning of time, one assumes the opposite conception of an infinite time; but infinite time, when it is still conceived as time, not as sublated time, is also to be distinguished from eternity. It is not this time but another time, and again another time, and so on, if thought cannot resolve the finite into the eternal. Thus matter is infinitely divisible; that is, its nature is such that what is posited as a Whole, as a One, is completely self-external and within itself a Many. But matter is not in fact so divided, as if it consisted of atoms; on the contrary, this infinite divisibility of matter is a possibility and only a possibility: that is, this division *ad infinitum* is not something positive and actual, but is only a subjective idea. Similarly, infinite time is only an idea, a going into the beyond, which remains infected with the negative; a necessary idea so long as one is confined to a consideration of the finite as finite. However, if I pass on to the universal, to the non-finite, I leave behind the standpoint where singularity and its alternate variations have their place. In our ordinary way of thinking, the world is only an aggregate of finite existences, but when it is grasped as a universal, as a totality, the question of a beginning at once disappears. Where to make the beginning is therefore undetermined; a beginning is to be made, but it is only a relative one. We pass beyond it, but not to infinity, but only to another beginning which, of course, is also only a conditioned one; in short, it is only the nature of the relative which is expressed, because we are in the sphere of finitude.

This is the metaphysics which passes hither and thither from one abstract determination to another, taking them for absolute. A plain, positive answer cannot be given to the question whether the world has, or has not, a beginning in time. A plain answer is supposed to state that *either* the one *or* the other is true. But the plain answer is, rather, that the question itself, this "either-or," is badly posed. If we are talking of the finite, then we have both a beginning and a non-beginning; these opposed determinations in their unresolved and unreconciled conflict with each other, belong to the finite: and so the finite, because it is this contradiction, perishes. The finite is preceded by an Other, and in tracing out the context of the finite, its antecedents must be sought, e.g., in the history of the earth or of man. There is no end to such an inquiry, even though we reach an end of each finite thing; time has its power over the manifoldness of the finite. The finite has a beginning, but this beginning is not the First; the finite has an independent existence, but its immediacy is also limited. When ordinary thinking forsakes this determinate finite, which is preceded and followed by other finites, and goes on to the empty thought of time as such, or the world as such, it flounders about in empty ideas, i.e., merely abstract thoughts. End *Zusatz.*

248

In this externality, the determinations of the Notion have the show of an *indifferent subsistence* and *isolation (Vereinzelung)* in regard to each other, and the Notion, therefore, is present only as something inward. Consequently, Nature exhibits no freedom in its existence, but only *necessity* and *contingency.*

Remark.

For this reason, Nature in the determinate existence which makes it Nature, is not to be deified; nor are sun, moon, animals, plants, etc., to be regarded and cited as more excellent, as works of God, than human actions and events. *In itself,* in the Idea, Nature is divine: but as it *is,* the being of Nature does not accord with its Notion; rather is Nature the *unresolved contradiction.* Its characteristic is *positedness,* the negative, in the same way that the ancients grasped matter in general as the *non-ens.* Thus Nature has also been spoken of as the *self-degradation of the Idea,* in that the Idea, in this form of externality, is in a disparity with its own self. It is only to the external and immediate stage of consciousness, that is, to *sensuous* consciousness, that Nature appears as the First, the immediate, as mere being *(das Seiende).* But because, even in this element of externality, Nature is a representation of the *Idea,* one may, and indeed ought, to admire in it the wisdom of God. Vanini said that a stalk of straw suffices to demonstrate God's being: but every mental image, the slightest fancy of mind, the play of its most capricious whims, every word, affords a superior ground for a knowledge of God's being than any single object of Nature. In Nature, not only is the play of forms a prey to boundless and unchecked contingency, but each separate entity is without the Notion of itself. The highest level to which Nature attains is life; but this, as only a natural mode of the Idea, is at the mercy of the unreason of externality, and the living creature is throughout its whole life entangled with other alien existences, whereas in every expression of Spirit there is contained the moment of free, universal self-relation. It is equally an error to regard the products of mind as inferior to natural objects, and to regard the latter as superior to *human works of art*, on the ground that these must take their material from outside, and that they are not alive. As if the spiritual form did not contain a higher kind of life, and were not more worthy of the Spirit, than the natural form, and as though form generally were not superior to matter, and throughout the ethical sphere even what can be called matter did not belong to Spirit alone: as if in Nature the higher form, the living creature, did not also receive its matter from outside. It is put forward as a further superiority of Nature that throughout all the contingency of its manifold existence it remains obedient to eternal laws. But surely this is also true of the realm of self-consciousness, a fact which finds recognition in the belief that human affairs are governed by Providence; or are the laws of this Providence in the field of human affairs supposed to be only contingent and irrational? But if the contingency of Spirit, the free will (*Willkür*) does *evil*, this is still infinitely superior to the regular motions of the celestial bodies, or to the innocence of plant life; for what thus errs is still Spirit.

Zusatz. The infinite divisibility of matter simply means that matter is external to itself. The immeasurableness of Nature, which at first excites our wonder, is precisely this same externality. Because each material point seems to be entirely independent of all the others, a failure to hold fast to the Notion prevails in Nature which is unable to bring together its determinations. The sun, planets, comets, the Elements, plants, animals, exist separately by themselves. The sun is an individual other than the earth, connected with the planets only by gravity. It is only in *life* that we meet with subjectivity and the counter to externality. The heart, liver, eye, are not self-subsistent individualities on their own account, and the hand, when separated from the body, putrefies. The organic body is still a whole composed of many members external to each other; but each individual member exists only in the subject, and the Notion exists as the power over these members. Thus it is that the Notion, which at the stage of Notionlessness (*Begrifflosigkeit*) is only something inward, first comes into existence in life, as soul. The spatiality of the organism has no truth whatever for the soul; otherwise there would be as many souls as material points, for the soul feels in each point of the organism. One must not be deceived by the show of mutual externality, but must comprehend that mutually external points form only one unity. The celestial bodies only *appear* to be independent of each other, they are the guardians of *one* field. But because the unity in Nature is a relation between things which are apparently self-subsistent, Nature is not free, but is only necessary and contingent. For necessity is the inseparability of different terms which yet appear as indifferent towards each other; but because this abstract state of externality also receives its due, there is contingency in Nature, i.e., external necessity, not the inner necessity of the Notion. There has been a lot of talk in physics about polarity. This concept is a great advance in the metaphysics of the science; for the concept of polarity is simply nothing else but the specific relation of necessity between two different terms which are one, in that when one is given, the other is also given. But this polarity is restricted to the opposition. However, through the opposition there is also given the return of the opposition into unity, and this is the third term which the necessity of the Notion has over and above polarity. In Nature, as the otherness [of the Idea], there also occur the square or the tetrad, for example, the four Elements, the four colours, etc., and even the pentad, e.g., the fingers and the senses. In Spirit, the fundamental form of necessity is the triad. The totality of the disjunction of the Notion exists in Nature as a tetrad because the first term is the universal as such, and the second, or the difference, appears itself as a duality—in Nature, the Other must exist explicitly as Other; with the result that the subjective unity of the universal and the particular is the fourth term which then has a separate existence in face of the other three terms. Further, as the monad and the dyad themselves constitute the entire particularity, the totality of the Notion can go as far as the pentad.

Nature is the negative because it is the negative of the Idea. Jacob Boehme says that God's first-born is Lucifer; and this son of Light centred his imagination on himself and became evil: that is the moment of difference, of otherness held fast against the Son, who is otherness within the divine love. The ground and significance of such conceptions which occur wildly in an oriental style, is to be found in the negative nature of Nature. The other form of otherness is immediacy, which consists in the moment of difference existing abstractly on its own. This existence, however, is only momentary, not a true existence; the Idea alone exists eternally, because it is being in and for itself, i.e., being which has returned into itself. Nature is the first in point of time, but the absolute *prius* is the Idea; this absolute *prius* is the last, the true beginning, Alpha is Omega. What is unmediated is often held to be superior, the mediated being thought of as dependent. The Notion, however, has both aspects: it is mediation through the sublation of mediation, and so is immediacy. People speak, for example, of an immediate belief in God; but this is the inferior mode of being, not the higher; the primitive religions were religions of nature-worship. The affirmative element in Nature is the manifestation of the Notion in it; the nearest instance of the power of the Notion is the perishableness of this outer existence; all natural existences form but a single body in which dwells the soul [the Notion]. The Notion manifests itself in these giant members, but not *qua* Notion; this occurs only in Spirit where the Notion exists as it is. End *Zusatz.*

249

Nature is to be regarded as a *system of stages*, one arising necessarily from the other and being the proximate truth of the stage from which it results; but it is not generated *naturally* out of the other but only in the inner Idea which constitutes the ground of Nature. *Metamorphosis* pertains only to the Notion as such, since only *its* alteration is development. But in Nature, the Notion is partly only something inward, partly existent only as a living individual; *existent* metamorphosis, therefore, is limited to this individual alone.

Remark.

It has been an inept conception of ancient and also recent Philosophy of Nature to regard the progression and transition of one natural form and sphere into a higher as an outwardly-actual production which, however, to be made *clearer*, is relegated to the *obscurity* of the past. It is precisely externality which is characteristic of Nature, that is, differences are allowed to fall apart and to appear as indifferent to each other: the dialectical Notion which leads forward the *stages*, is the inner side of them. A thinking consideration must reject such nebulous, at bottom, sensuous ideas, as in particular the so-called *origination*, for example, of plants and animals from water, and then the *origination* of the more highly developed animal organisms from the lower, and so on.

Zusatz. The consideration of the utility of natural objects contains this truth, that they are not an absolute end in and for themselves. This negative aspect, however, is not external to them but is the immanent moment of their Idea, which effects their perishability and transition into another existence, but at the same time into a higher Notion. The Notion timelessly and in a universal manner posits all particularity in existence. It is a completely empty thought to represent species as developing successively, one after the other, in time. Chronological difference has no interest whatever for thought. If it is only a question of enumerating the series of living species in order to show the mind how they are divided into classes, either by starting from the poorest and simplest terms, and rising to the more developed and richer in determinations and content, or by proceeding in the reverse fashion, this operation will always have a general interest. It will be a way of arranging things as in the division of Nature into three kingdoms; this is preferable to jumbling them together, a procedure which would be somewhat repellent to an intelligence which had an inkling of the Notion. But it must not be imagined that such a dry series is made dynamic or philosophical, or more intelligible, or whatever you like to say, by representing the terms as producing each other. Animal nature is the truth of vegetable nature, vegetable of mineral; the earth is the truth of the solar system. In a system, it is the most abstract term which is the first, and the truth of each sphere is the last; but this again is only the first of a higher sphere. It is the necessity of the Idea which causes each sphere to complete itself by passing into another higher one, and the variety of forms must be considered as necessary and determinate. The land animal did not develop *naturally* out of the aquatic animal, nor did it fly into the air on leaving the water, nor did perhaps the bird again fall back to earth. If we want to compare the different stages of Nature, it is quite proper to note that, for example, a certain animal has one ventricle and another has two; but we must not then talk of the fact as if we were dealing with parts which had been put together. Still less must the category of earlier spheres be used to explain others; for this is a formal error, as when it is said that the plant is a carbon pole and the animal a nitrogen pole.

The two forms under which the serial progression of Nature is conceived are *evolution* and *emanation*. The way of evolution, which starts from the imperfect and formless, is as follows: at first there was the liquid element and aqueous forms of life, and from the water there evolved plants, polyps, molluscs, and finally fishes; then from the fishes were evolved the land animals, and finally from the land animals came man. This gradual alteration is called an explanation and understanding; it is a conception which comes from the Philosophy of Nature, and it still flourishes. But though this quantitative difference is of all theories the easiest to understand, it does not really explain anything at all. The way of emanation is peculiar to the oriental world. It involves a series of degradations of being, starting from the perfect being, the absolute totality, God. God has created, and from Him have proceeded splendours, lightnings and likenesses in such fashion that the first likeness is that which most resembles God. This first likeness in its turn, is supposed to have generated another but less perfect one, and so on, so that each created being has become, in its turn, a creative being, down to the negative being, matter, the extreme of evil. Emanation thus ends with the absence of all form. Both ways are one-sided and superficial, and postulate an indeterminate goal. That which proceeds from the perfect to the imperfect has this advantage, that then we have before us the type of the complete organism; and this is the type which picture-thinking must have before it in order to understand the imperfect organisms. What appear in the latter as subordinate, for example, organs which have no functions, is first understood through the more developed organisms which enable one to see the place the organ fills. The perfect, if it is to have the advantage over the imperfect, must exist not only in picture-thinking but also in reality.

The basis of the idea of metamorphosis is also a single Idea which persists in the various genera and even in each particular organ, so that these genera and organs are only the diverse forms of a single, self-same type. Similarly, one speaks of the metamorphosis of an insect, in that the caterpillar, the pupa and the butterfly, are one and the same individual. In the case of individuals, the development certainly takes place in time, but it is otherwise with the genus. With the existence of the genus in a particular form, the other modes of its existence are necessarily postulated. Water being given, then air, fire, etc., too, are necessarily postulated. It is important to hold fast to identity; but to hold fast to difference is no less important, and this gets pushed into the background when a change is conceived only quantitatively. This makes the mere idea of metamorphosis inadequate.

Under the same heading, too, comes the idea of the *series* formed by things, and especially living things. The desire to know the necessity of this development leads to the search for a law of the series, a basic determination which, while positing difference, repeats itself in such difference and in so doing also produces a fresh difference. But to enlarge a series merely by the successive addition of elements similarly determined, and to see only the same relationship between all the members of the series, is not the way in which the Notion generates its determinations. It is this very fact of imagining a *series* of stages and the like, which has been such a hindrance to any progress in understanding the necessity of the various forms of Nature. To seek to arrange in serial form the planets, the metals or chemical substances in general, plants and animals, and then to ascertain the law of the series, is a fruitless task, because Nature does not arrange its forms in such articulate series: the Notion differentiates things according to their own specific qualitative character, and to that extent advances by leaps. The old saying, or so-called law, *non datur saltus in natura*, is altogether inadequate to the diremption of the Notion. The continuity of the Notion with itself is of an entirely different character. End *Zusatz*.

250

The *contradiction* of the Idea, arising from the fact that, as Nature, it is external to itself, is more precisely this: that on the one hand there is the *necessity* of its forms which is generated by the Notion, and their rational determination in the organic totality; while on the other hand, there is their indifferent *contingency* and indeterminable irregularity. In the sphere of Nature contingency and determination from without has its right, and this contingency is at its greatest in the realm of concrete individual forms, which however, as products of Nature, are concrete only in an *immediate* manner. The *immediately* concrete thing is a group of properties, external to one another and more or less indifferently related to each other; and for that very reason, the simple subjectivity which exists for itself is also indifferent and abandons them to contingent and external determination. This is the *impotence* of Nature, that it preserves the determinations of the Notion only *abstractly*, and leaves their detailed specification to external determination.

Remark.

The infinite wealth and variety of forms and, what is most irrational, the contingency which enters into the external arrangement of natural things, have been extolled as the sublime freedom of Nature, even as the divinity *of* Nature, or at least the divinity present *in* it. This confusion of contingency, caprice, and disorder, with freedom and rationality is characteristic of sensuous and unphilosophical thinking. This impotence of Nature sets limits to philosophy and it is quite improper to expect the Notion to comprehend—or as it is said, con strue or deduce—these contingent products of Nature. It is even imagined that the more trivial and isolated the object, the easier is the task of deducing it.* Undoubtedly, traces of determination by the Notion are to be found even in the most particularized object, although these traces do not exhaust its nature. Traces of this influence of the Notion and of this inner coherence of natural objects will often surprise the investigator, but especially will they seem startling, or rather incredible, to those who are accustomed to see only contingency in natural, as in human, history. One must, however, be careful to avoid taking such trace of the Notion for the total determination of the object, for that is the route to the analogies previously mentioned.

In the impotence of Nature to adhere strictly to the Notion in its realization, lies the difficulty and, in many cases, the impossibility of finding fixed distinctions for classes and orders from an empirical consideration of Nature. Nature everywhere blurs the essential limits of species and genera by intermediate and defective forms, which continually furnish counter examples to every fixed distinction; this even occurs within a specific genus, that of man, for example, where monstrous births, on the one hand, must be considered as belonging to the genus, while on the other hand, they lack certain essential determinations characteristic of the genus. In order to be able to consider such forms as defective, imperfect and deformed, one must presuppose a fixed, invariable type. This type, however, cannot be furnished by experience, for it is experience which also presents these so-called monstrosities, deformities, intermediate products, etc. The fixed type rather presupposes the self-subsistence and dignity of the determination stemming from the Notion.

251

Nature is, in itself, a living Whole. The movement through its stages is more precisely this: that the Idea *posits* itself as that which it is *in itself*; or what is the same thing, that it returns *into itself* out of its immediacy and externality which is *death*, in order to be, first a *living creature*, but further, to sublate this determinateness also in

---

*It was in this—and other respects too—quite naïve sense that Herr Krug once challenged the Philosophy of Nature to perform the feat of deducing *only* his pen. One could perhaps give him hope that *his* pen would have the glory of being deduced, if ever philosophy should advance so far and have such a clear insight into every great theme in heaven and on earth, past and present, that there was nothing more important to comprehend.

which it is only Life, and to give itself an existence as Spirit, which is the truth and the final goal of Nature and the genuine actuality of the Idea.

Zusatz. The development of the Notion towards its destination, its end or, if you like, its purpose, is to be grasped as a positing of what it is in itself, so that these determinations of its content come into existence, are manifested, but at the same time not as independent and self-subsistent, but as moments which remain in the unity of the Notion, as ideal, i.e., posited moments. This positing can therefore be grasped as an utterance or expression, a coming forth, a setting forth, a coming-out-of-self, in so far as the subjectivity of the Notion is lost in the mutual outsideness of its determinations. But it pre-serves itself in them, as their unity and ideality; and this going out of the centre from itself to the periphery is therefore, looked at from the opposite side, equally a taking up again of this outer into the inner, an inwardizing or remembering *(Erinnern)* that it is it, the Notion, that exists in this externality. Starting therefore from the externality in which the Notion at first exists, its progress is a movement into itself, into the centre, i.e., a bringing of immediate and external existence which is inadequate to itself, to subjective unity, to being-within-self: not in such a way that the Notion withdraws itself from this external-ity, leaving it behind like a dead shell, but rather that existence as such is within self or conforms to the Notion, that the being-within-self itself exists, which is Life. The Notion strives to burst the shell of outer existence and to become for itself. Life is the Notion which has attained to the manifestation of itself, which has explicated, set forth, what it is in itself; but the Understanding finds this the most difficult of things to grasp because what it finds easiest to grasp is the most simple of things, i.e. the abstract and the dead. End *Zusatz.*

C. Division

252

The Idea as Nature is:

I. In the determination of asunderness or mutual outsideness, of infinite separatedness, the unity of form being outside it; this unity, as *ideal*, is only *in itself* and is consequently a unity which is only *sought.* This is *matter* and its ideal system—Mechanics;

II. In the determination of *particularity*, so that reality is posited with an immanent determinateness of form and with an existent difference in it. This is a relationship of Reflection (*Reflexionsverhältnis*) whose being-within-self is natural *individuality*—Physics;

III. In the determination of *subjectivity*, in which the real differences of form are also brought back to the *ideal* unity which has found itself and is for itself—Organics.

Zusatz. The division is made from the standpoint of the Notion grasped in its totality, and it indicates the diremption of the Notion into its determinations; and since in this diremption the Notion explicates its determinations and gives them a self-subsistence, though only as moments, the process is one of self-realization in which the Notion posits itself as Idea. But the Notion not only sets forth its moments, and not only articulates itself in its differences, but it also brings these apparently self-subsequent stages back to their ideality and unity, to itself; and only then, in fact, has it made itself the concrete Notion, the Idea, and the Truth. It seems, therefore, that there are two ways of presenting both the Division and the scientific exposition: one way would start from the concrete Notion, and in Nature this is Life, which would be considered on its own account. It would then be led to consider the externalized forms of the Notion, the forms being thrown out by the Notion to exist separately as spheres of Nature, the Notion being related to them as to other— consequently more abstract—modes of its existence; this way would close with the complete extinction of life. The other way is the reverse of this. It starts with the, at first, only immediate mode of the Notion's existence, with its uttermost self-externality, and it closes with the true existence of the Notion, with the truth of the whole course of its exposition. The first way can be compared to the process implied in the conception of emanation, the second, to the process implied in the conception of evolution (§ 249, *Zusatz*). Each of these forms taken separately is one-sided, but they exist together; the eternal divine process is a flowing in two opposite directions which meet and permeate each other in what is simply and solely *one*. The First, let it be called by the loftiest name, is only an immediate, even though we mean by it something concrete. Matter, for example, negates itself as an untrue existence and from this negation emerges a higher existence. From one aspect, it is by an evolution that the earlier stages are cancelled, but from another aspect matter remains in the background and is produced anew by emanation. Evolution is thus also an involution, in that matter interiorizes itself to become life. In virtue of the urge of the Idea to become objective to itself, the self-subsistent becomes a moment: the senses of the animal, for example, made objective and external, are the Sun and the lunar and cometary bodies. Even in the sphere of Physics these bodies lose their independence although they still retain the same form with some modifications; they are the Elements [air, fire, and water]. The subjective sense of sight existing outwardly is the Sun, taste is water, and smell is the air. But as our task here is to posit the determinations of the Notion, we must not start from the most concrete, the true sphere, but from the most abstract.

Matter is the form in which the self-externality of Nature achieves its first being-within-self, an abstract being-for-self which is exclusive and therefore a plurality, which has its unity, as what brings the independent many into a universal being-for-self, at once within and outside itself: gravity. In the sphere of Mechanics, being-for-self is not yet an individual, stable unity having the power to subordinate plurality to itself. Heavy matter does not yet possess the individuality which preserves its determinations; and since in matter the determinations of the Notion are still external to each other, its differences are not qualitative but indifferent or purely quantitative, and matter, merely as mass, has no form. Form is acquired by individual bodies in Physics, and with this we have at once gravity revealed for the first time as the mastery of being-for-self over multiplicity, a being-for-self which is no longer merely a striving but which has come to rest, although at first only in the mode of appearance (*nur auf erscheinende Weise*). Each atom of gold, for example, contains all the determinations or properties of the whole lump of gold, and matter is immanently specified and particularized. The second determination is that here, still, particularity as qualitative determinateness, and being-for-self as the point of individuality, fall together in unity, and therefore body is finitely determined; individuality is still bound to definite exclusive specific properties, does not yet exist as totality. If such a body enters into a process in which it loses such properties, then it ceases to be what it is; the qualitative determinateness is therefore affirmatively posited, but not at the same time also negatively. The organic being is totality as found in Nature, an individuality which is for itself and which internally develops into its differences: but in such a way that first, these determinations are not only specific properties but also concrete totalities; secondly, they remain also qualitatively determined against each other, and, as thus finite, are posited as ideal moments by Life, which preserves itself in the process of these members. Thus we have a number of beings-for-self which, however, are brought back to the being-for-self which is for itself and which, as its own end *(Selbstzweck)*, subdues the members and reduces them to means: this is the unity of qualitatively determined being and gravity, which finds itself in Life.

Each stage is a specific realm of Nature and all appear to have independent existence. But the last is the concrete unity of all the preceding ones, just as, in general, each successive stage embodies the lower stages, but equally posits these, as its non-organic nature, over against itself. One stage is the power of the other, and this relation is reciprocal. Here can be seen the true meaning of *powers* *(Potenzen)*. The non-organic Elements are powers opposed to what is individual, subjective—the non-organic destroys the organic. But equally the organism, in its turn, is the power which subdues its universal powers, air, water; these are perpetually liberated and also perpetually subdued and assimilated. The eternal life of Nature consists in this: first, that the Idea displays itself in each sphere so far as it can within the finitude of that sphere, just as each drop of water provides an image of the sun, and secondly, that the Notion, through its dialectic, breaks through the limitation of this sphere, since it cannot rest content with an inadequate element, and necessarily passes over into a higher stage. End *Zusatz.*

PHILOSOPHY OF SPIRIT

Introduction

377

The knowledge of Mind is the highest and hardest, just because it is the most "concrete" of sciences. The significance of that "absolute" commandment, *Know thyself*—whether we look at it in itself or under the historical circumstances of its first utterance—is not to promote mere self-knowledge in respect of the *particular* capacities, character, propensities, and foibles of the single self. The knowledge it commands means that of man's genuine reality—of what is essentially and ultimately true and real—of mind as the true and essential being. Equally little is it the purport of mental philosophy to teach

SOURCE: *Philosophy of Mind,* pp. 1–24. Reprinted by permission of the Clarendon Press, Oxford.

what is called *knowledge of men*—the knowledge whose aim is to detect the *peculiarities*, passions, and foibles of other men, and lay bare what are called the recesses of the human heart. Information of this kind is, for one thing, meaningless, unless on the assumption that we know the *universal*—man as man, and, that always must be, as mind. And for another, being only engaged with casual, insignificant, and *untrue* aspects of mental life, it fails to reach the underlying essence of them all—the mind itself.

Zusatz. The difficulty of the philosophical cognition of mind consists in the fact that in this we are no longer dealing with the comparatively abstract, simple logical Idea, but with the most concrete, most developed form achieved by the Idea in its self-actualization. Even finite or subjective mind, not only absolute mind, must be grasped as an actualization of the Idea. The treatment of mind is only truly philosophical when it cognizes the Notion of mind in its living development and actualization, which simply means, when it comprehends mind as a type of the absolute Idea. But it belongs to the nature of mind to cognize its Notion. Consequently, the summons to the Greeks of the Delphic Apollo, *Know thyself*, does not have the meaning of a law externally imposed on the human mind by an alien power; on the contrary, the god who impels to self-knowledge is none other than the absolute law of mind itself. Mind is, therefore, in its every act only apprehending itself, and the aim of all genuine science is just this, that mind shall recognize itself in everything in heaven and on earth. An out-and-out Other simply does not exist for mind. Even the Oriental does not wholly lose himself in the object of his worship; but the Greeks were the first to grasp expressly as mind what they opposed to themselves as the Divine, although even they did not attain, either in philosophy or in religion, to a knowledge of the absolute infinitude of mind; therefore with the Greeks the relation of the human mind to the Divine is still not one of absolute freedom. It was Christianity, by its doctrine of the Incarnation and of the presence of the Holy Spirit in the community of believers, that first gave to human consciousness a perfectly free relationship to the infinite and thereby made possible the comprehensive knowledge of mind in its absolute infinitude.

Henceforth, such a knowledge alone merits the name of a philosophical treatment. Self-knowledge in the usual trivial meaning of an inquiry into the foibles and faults of the single self has interest and importance only for the individual, not for philosophy; but even in relation to the individual, the more the focus of interest is shifted from the general intellectual and moral nature of man, and the more the inquiry, disregarding duties and the genuine content of the will, degenerates into a self-complacent absorption of the individual in the idiosyncrasies so dear to him, the less is the value of that self-knowledge. The same is true of the so-called knowledge of *human nature*, which likewise is directed to the peculiarities of individual minds. This knowledge is, of course, useful and necessary in the conduct of life, especially in bad political conditions where right and morality have given place to the self-will, whims and caprice of individuals, in the field of intrigues where characters do not rely on the nature of the matter in hand but hold their own by cunningly exploiting the peculiarities of others and seeking by this means to attain their arbitrary ends. For philosophy, however, this knowledge of human nature is devoid of interest in so far as it is incapable of rising above the consideration of contingent particularities to the understanding of the characters of great men, by which alone the true nature of man in its serene purity is brought to view. But this knowledge of human nature can even be harmful for philosophy if, as happens in the so-called pragmatic treatment of history, through failure to appreciate the substantial character of world-historical individuals and to see that great deeds can only be carried out by great characters, the supposedly clever attempt is made to trace back the greatest events in history to the accidental idiosyncrasies of those heroes, to their presumed petty aims, propensities, and passions. In such a procedure history, which is ruled by divine Providence, is reduced to a play of meaningless activity and contingent happenings. End *Zusatz.*

378

Pneumatology, or, as it was also called, Rational Psychology, has been already alluded to in the Introduction to the Logic as an *abstract* and generalizing metaphysic of the subject. *Empirical* (or inductive) psychology, on the other hand, deals with the "concrete" mind; and, after the revival of the sciences, when observation and experience had been made the distinctive methods for the study of concrete reality, such psychology was worked on the same lines as other sciences. In this way it came about that the metaphysical theory was kept outside the inductive science, and so prevented from getting any concrete embodiment or detail; whilst at the same time the inductive science clung to the conventional common-sense metaphysic, with its analysis into forces, various activities, etc., and rejected any attempt at a "speculative" treatment.

The books of Aristotle on the Soul, along with his discussions on its special aspects and states, are for this reason still by far the most admirable, perhaps even the sole, work of philosophical value on this topic. The main aim of a philosophy of mind can only be to reintroduce unity of idea and principle into the theory of mind, and so reinterpret the lesson of those Aristotelian books.

Zusatz. Genuinely speculative philosophy, which excludes the mode of treatment discussed in the previous Paragraph which is directed to the unessential, isolated, empirical phenomena of mind, also excludes the precisely opposite mode of so-called Rational Psychology or Pneumatology, which is concerned only with abstractly universal determinations, with the supposedly unmanifested essence, the "in-itself" of mind. For speculative philosophy may not take its subject-matter from picture thinking as a *datum,* nor may it determine such given material merely by categories of the abstractive intellect *(Verstand)* as the said psychology did when it posed the question whether mind or soul is simple and immaterial, whether it is substance. In these questions mind was treated as a thing; for these categories were regarded, in the general manner of the abstractive intellect, as inert, fixed; as such, they are incapable of expressing the nature of mind. Mind is not an inert being but, on the contrary, absolutely restless being, pure activity, the negating or ideality of every fixed category of the abstractive intellect; not abstractly simple but, in its simplicity, at the same time a distinguishing of itself from itself; not an essence that is already finished and complete before its manifestation, keeping itself aloof behind its host of appearances, but an essence which is truly actual only through the specific forms of its necessary self-manifestation; and it is not, as that psychology supposed, a soul-thing only externally connected with the body, but is inwardly bound to the latter by the unity of the Notion.

In the middle, between observation which is directed to the contingent particularity of mind and pneumatology which concerns itself only with the unmanifested essence, stands empirical psychology which has as its starting-point the observation and description of the particular faculties of mind. But neither does this lead to the veritable union of the individual and the universal, to the knowledge of the concretely universal nature or Notion of mind, and therefore it, too, has no claim to the name of genuinely speculative philosophy. It is not only mind as such which empirical psychology takes as a *datum* from picture-thinking, but also the special faculties into which it analyses mind without deriving these particularities from the Notion of mind and so demonstrating that in mind there are necessarily just these faculties and no others.

With this defect of the form there is necessarily linked the despiritualization of the content. When in the two modes of treatment already described, empirical psychology takes the individual on the one hand, and the universal on the other, each as a fixed, independent category, it also holds the particular forms into which it analyses mind to be fixed in their limitation; so that mind is converted into a mere aggregate of independent forces, each of which stands only in reciprocal relation with the others, hence is only externally connected with them. For though this psychology also demands that the various spiritual forces shall be harmoniously integrated—a favourite and oft-recurring catch-phrase on this topic, but one which is just as indefinite as "perfection" used to be—this gives expression to a unity of mind which only *ought* to be, not to the original unity, and still less does it recognize as necessary and rational the particularization to which the Notion of mind, its intrinsic unity, progresses. This harmonious integration remains, therefore, a vacuous idea which expresses itself in high-sounding but empty phrases but remains ineffective in face of the spiritual forces presupposed as independent. End *Zusatz.*

379

Even our own sense of the mind's *living* unity naturally protests against any attempt to break it up into different faculties, forces, or, what comes to the same thing, activities, conceived as independent of each other. But the craving for a *comprehension* of the unity is still further stimulated, as we soon come across distinctions between mental freedom and mental determinism, antitheses between free *psychic* agency and the corporeity that lies external to it, whilst we equally note the intimate interdependence of the one upon the other. In modern times especially the phenomena of *animal magnetism* have given, even in experience, a lively and visible confirmation of the underlying unity of soul, and of the power of its "ideality." Before these facts, the rigid distinctions of practical common sense are struck with confusion; and the necessity of a "speculative" examination with a view to the removal of difficulties is more directly forced upon the student.

Zusatz. All those finite interpretations of mind depicted in the two previous Paragraphs have been ousted, partly by the vast transformation undergone by philosophy in recent years, and partly, from the empirical side itself, by the phenomena of animal magnetism which are a stumbling-block to finite thought. As regards the former, philosophy has risen above the finite mode of treatment based on merely reflective thought which, since Wolff, had become universal, and also above Fichte's so-called "facts of consciousness," to a comprehension of mind as the self-knowing, actual Idea, to the Notion of living mind which, in a necessary manner, immanently differentiates itself and returns out of its differences into unity with itself. But in doing so, it has not only overcome the abstractions prevalent in those finite interpretations of mind, the merely individual, merely particular, and merely universal, reducing them to moments of the Notion which is their truth; but also, instead of externally describing a material already to hand, it has vindicated as the only scientific method the rigorous form of the necessary self-development of the content. In contrast to the empirical sciences, where the material as given by experience is taken up from outside and is ordered and brought into context in accordance with an already established general rule, speculative thinking has to demonstrate each of its objects and the explication of them, in their absolute necessity. This is effected by deriving each particular Notion from the self-originating and self-actualizing universal Notion, or the logical Idea. Philosophy must therefore comprehend mind as a necessary development of the eternal Idea and must let the science of mind, as constituted by its particular parts, unfold itself entirely from its Notion. Just as in the living organism generally, everything is already contained, in an ideal manner, in the germ and is brought forth by the germ itself, not by an alien power, so too must all the particular forms of living mind grow out of its Notion as from their germ. In so doing, our thinking, which is actuated by the Notion, remains for the object, which likewise is actuated by the Notion, absolutely immanent; we merely look on, as it were, at the object's own development, not altering it by importing into it our own subjective ideas and fancies. The Notion does not require any external stimulus for its actualization; it embraces the contradiction of simplicity and difference, and therefore its own restless nature impels it to actualize itself, to unfold into actuality the difference which, in the Notion itself, is present only in an ideal manner, that is to say, in the contradictory form of differencelessness, and by this removal of its simplicity as of a defect, a one-sidedness, to make itself actually that whole, of which to begin with it contained only the possibility.

But the Notion is no less independent of our caprice in the conclusion of its development than it is in the beginning and in the course of it. In a merely ratiocinative mode of treatment the conclusion, to be sure, appears more or less arbitrary; in philosophical science, on the contrary, the Notion itself sets a limit to its self-development by giving itself an actuality that is perfectly adequate to it. Already in the living being we see this self-limitation of the Notion. The germ of the plant, this sensuously present Notion, closes its development with an actuality like itself, with the production of the seed. The same is true of mind; its development, too, has achieved its goal when the Notion of mind has completely actualized itself or, what is the same thing, when mind has attained to complete consciousness of its Notion. But this contraction of beginning and end into one, this coming of the Notion to its own self in its actualization, appears in mind in a yet more complete form than in the merely living being; for whereas in the latter, the seed produced is not identical with the seed from which it came, in self-knowing mind the product is one and the same as that which produces it.

Only when we contemplate mind in this process of the self-actualization of its Notion, do we know it in its truth (for truth means precisely agreement of the Notion with its actuality). In its immediacy, mind is not yet true, has not yet made its Notion objective to it, has not yet transformed what confronts it in immediate guise, into something which it has posited, has not yet transformed its actuality into one which is adequate to its Notion. The entire development of mind is nothing else but the raising of itself to its truth, and the so-called psychic forces have no other meaning than to be the stages of this ascent. By this self-differentiation, this self-transformation, and the bringing back of its differences to the unity of its Notion, mind as a true being is also a living, organic, systematic being; and only by knowing this its nature is the science of mind likewise true, living, organic, systematic; predicates bestowable neither on rational nor empirical psychology, for the former makes mind into a dead essence divorced from its actualization, while the latter kills the living mind by tearing it asunder into a manifold of independent forces which neither derive from the Notion nor are held together by it.

We have already remarked that animal magnetism has played a part in ousting the untrue, finite interpretation of mind from the standpoint of the merely abstractive intellect. This has been brought about by those marvellous phenomena especially in connection with the treatment of mind on its natural side. Though the other kinds of conditions and natural determinations of mind and also its conscious activities can be grasped, at least externally, by the abstractive intellect which is able to grasp the external connection of cause and effect obtaining alike in the intellect and in finite things, the so-called natural course of things; yet, on the other hand, intellect shows itself incapable of belief in the phenomena of animal magnetism, because in these the bondage of mind to place and time—which in the opinion of the abstractive intellect is absolutely fixed—and to the finite category of causality, loses its meaning, and the elevation of mind over the externality of spatial and temporal relationships, which to intellect remains an incredible miracle, is manifest in sensuous existence itself. Now although it would be very foolish to see in the phenomena of animal magnetism an elevation of mind above even Reason with its ability to comprehend, and to expect from this state a higher knowledge of the eternal than that imparted by philosophy, and although the fact is that the magnetic state must be declared pathological and a degradation of mind below the level even of ordinary consciousness in so far as in that state mind surrenders its thinking as an activity creative of specific distinctions, as an activity contradistinguished from Nature; yet, on the other hand, in the visible liberation of mind in those magnetic phenomena from the limitations of space and time and from all finite associations, there is something akin to philosophy, something which, as brute fact, defies the scepticism of the abstractive intellect and so necessitates the advance from ordinary psychology to the comprehension afforded by speculative philosophy for which alone animal magnetism is not an incomprehensible miracle. End *Zusatz*.

380

The "concrete" nature of mind involves for the observer the peculiar difficulty that the several grades and special types which develop its intelligible unity in detail are not left standing as so many separate existences confronting its more advanced aspects. It is otherwise in external nature. There, matter and movement, for example, have a manifestation all their own—it is the solar system; and similarly the *differentiae* of sense-perception have a sort of earlier existence in the properties of *bodies*, and still more independently in the four elements. The species and grades of mental evolution, on the contrary, lose their separate existence and become factors, states, and features in the higher grades of development. As a consequence of this, a lower and more abstract aspect of mind betrays the presence in it, even to experience, of a higher grade. Under the guise of sensation, for example, we may find the very highest mental life as its modification or its embodiment. And so sensation, which is but a mere form and vehicle, may to the superficial glance seem to be the proper seat and, as it were, the source of those moral and religious principles with which it is charged; and the moral and religious principles thus modified may seem to call for treatment as species of sensation. But at the same time, when lower grades of mental life are under examination, it becomes necessary, if we desire to point to actual cases of them in experience, to direct attention to more advanced grades for which they are mere forms. In this way subjects will be treated of by anticipation which properly belong to later stages of development (e.g., in dealing with natural awaking from sleep we speak by anticipation of consciousness, or in dealing with mental derangement we must speak of intellect).

What Mind (or Spirit) is.

381

From our point of view mind has for its *presupposition* Nature, of which it is the truth, and for that reason its *absolute prius.* In this its truth Nature is vanished, and mind has resulted as the "Idea" entered on possession of itself. Here the subject and object of the Idea are one—either is the intelligent unity, the notion. This identity is *absolute negativity*—for whereas in Nature the intelligent unity has its objectivity perfect but externalized, this self-externalization has been nullified and the unity in that way been made one and the same with itself. Thus at the same time it *is* this identity only so far as it is a return out of nature.

Zusatz. We have already stated, in the *Zusatz* to § 379, that the Notion of mind is the self-knowing, actual Idea. Philosophy has to demonstrate the necessity of this Notion, as of all its other Notions, which means that philosophy must cognize it as the result of the development of the universal Notion or of the logical Idea. But in this development, mind is preceded not only by the logical Idea but also by external Nature. For the cognition already contained in the simple *logical* Idea is only the Notion of cognition thought *by us*, not cognition existing on its own account, not actual mind but merely its possibility. Actual mind which, in the science of mind, is alone our subject-matter, has external Nature for its proximate, and the logical Idea for its first, presupposition. The Philosophy of Nature, and indirectly Logic, must have, therefore, as its final outcome the proof of the necessity of the Notion of mind. The science of mind, on its part, has to authenticate this Notion by its development and actualization. Accordingly, what we say here assertorically about mind at the beginning of our treatment of it, can only be scientifically proved by philosophy in its entirety. All we can do at the outset is to elucidate the Notion of mind for ordinary thinking.

In order to establish what this Notion is, we must indicate the determinateness by which the Idea has being as mind. But every determinateness is a determinateness only counter to another determinateness; to that of mind in general is opposed, in the first instance, that of Nature: the former can, therefore, only be grasped simultaneously with the latter. We must designate as the distinctive determinateness of the Notion of mind, *ideality*, that is, the reduction of the Idea's otherness to a *moment*, the process of returning—and the accomplished return—into itself of the Idea from its Other; whereas the distinctive feature of the logical Idea is immediate, simple being-within-self, but for Nature it is the self-externality of the Idea. A more detailed development of what was said in passing in the *Zusatz* to § 379 about the logical Idea, would involve too wide a digression here; more necessary at this point is an elucidation of what has been assigned as characteristic of external Nature, for it is to the latter, as we have already remarked, that mind is proximately related.

External Nature, too, like mind, is rational, divine, a representation of the Idea. But in Nature, the Idea appears in the element of asunderness, is external not only to mind but also to itself, precisely because it is external to that actual, self-existent inwardness which constitutes the essential nature of mind. This Notion of Nature which was already enunciated by the Greeks and quite familiar to them, is in complete agreement with our ordinary idea of Nature. We know that natural things are spatial and temporal, that in Nature one thing exists alongside another, that one thing follows another, in brief, that in Nature all things are mutually external, *ad infinitum;* further, that matter, this universal basis of every existent form in Nature, not merely offers resistance to *us,* exists apart from our mind, but holds itself asunder against its own self, divides itself into concrete points, into material atoms, of which it is composed. The differences into which the Notion of Nature unfolds itself are more or less mutually independent existences; true, through their original unity they stand in mutual connection, so that none can be comprehended without the others; but this connection is in a greater or less degree external to them. We rightly say, therefore, that not freedom but necessity reigns in Nature; for this latter in its strictest meaning is precisely the merely internal, and for that reason also merely external, connection of mutually independent existences. Thus, for example, light and the [four] elements appear as mutually independent; similarly the planets, though attracted by the sun and despite this relation to their centre, appear to be independent of it and of one another, this contradiction being represented by the motion of the planet round the sun.

In the living being, of course, a higher necessity is dominant than in the inorganic sphere. Even in the plant, we see a centre which has overflowed into the periphery, a concentration of the differences, a self-development from within outwards, a unity which differentiates itself and from its differentiation produces itself in the bud, something, therefore, to which we attribute an urge (*Trieb*); but this unity remains incomplete because the plant's process of articulating itself is a coming-forth-from-self of the vegetable subject, each part is the whole plant, a repetition of it, and consequently the organs are not held in complete subjection to the unity of the subject.

An even more complete triumph over externality is exhibited in the animal organism; in this not only does each member generate the other, is its cause and effect, its means and end, so that it is at the same time itself and its Other, but the whole is so pervaded by its unity that nothing in it appears as independent, every determinateness is at once ideal, the animal remaining in every determinateness the same one universal, so that in the animal body the complete untruth of asunderness is revealed. Through this being-with-itself in the determinateness, through this immediate reflectedness-into-self in and out of its externality, the animal is self-existent subjectivity and has feeling; feeling is just this omnipresence of the unity of the animal in all its members which immediately communicate every impression to the one whole which, in the animal, is an incipient being-for-self. It follows from this subjective inwardness, that the animal is self-determined, from within outwards, not merely from outside, that is to say, it has an urge and instinct. The subjectivity of the animal contains a contradiction and the urge to preserve itself by resolving this contradiction; this self-preservation is the privilege of the living being and, in a still higher degree, of mind. The sentient being is determinate, has a content, and thus a difference within itself; this difference is in the first place still wholly ideal, simple, resolved in the unity of feeling; the resolved difference subsisting in the unity is a contradiction which is resolved by the difference positing itself *as* difference. The animal is, therefore, forced out of its simple self-relation into opposition to external Nature. By this opposition the animal falls into a fresh contradiction, for the difference is now posited in a mode which contradicts the unity of the Notion; accordingly it, too, must be resolved like the undifferentiated unity in the first instance. This resolution of the difference is effected by the animal consuming what is destined for it in external Nature and preserving itself by what it consumes. Thus by the annihilation of the Other confronting the animal, the original, simple self-relation and the contradiction contained in it is posited afresh. What is needed for a veritable resolution of this contradiction is that the Other with which the animal enters into relation, itself be similar to the latter. This occurs in the sexual relation; here, each sex feels in the other not an alien externality but its own self, or the genus common to both. The sexual relation is, therefore, the highest point of animate Nature; on this level, Nature is freed in the fullest measure from external necessity, since the distinct existences in their mutual relationship are no longer external to each other but have the feeling of their unity. Yet the animal soul is still not free; for it is always manifest as a *one* determined as feeling or excitation, as tied to one determinateness; it is only in the form of individuality that the genus is *for* the animal; the latter merely feels the genus, but does not know it; in the animal, the soul is not yet *for* the soul, the universal as such is not *for* the universal. By the removal of the particularity of the sexes which occurs in the genus-process, the animal does not attain to a production of the genus; what is produced by this process is again only a single individual. And thus Nature, even at the highest point of its elevation over finitude, always falls back into it again and in this way exhibits a perpetual cycle. Death, too, which necessarily results from the contradiction between the individual and the genus, since it is not the affirmative supersession of individuality but only the empty, destructive negation of it, even appearing in the form of immediate individuality, likewise does not bring forth the universality that is in and for itself, or the individuality that is in and for itself universal, the subjectivity that has itself for object. Therefore, even in the most perfect form to which Nature raises itself, in animal life, the Notion does not attain to an actuality resembling its soul-like nature, to complete victory over the externality and finitude of its existence. This is first achieved in mind which, just by winning this victory, *distinguishes itself* from Nature, so that this distinguishing is not merely the act of an *external* reflection about the nature of mind.

This triumph over externality which belongs to the Notion of mind, is what we have called the ideality of mind. Every activity of mind is nothing but a distinct mode of reducing what is external to the inwardness which mind itself is, and it is only by this reduction, by this idealization or assimilation, of what is external that it becomes and is mind.

If we consider mind more closely, we find that its primary and simplest determination is the "I." The "I" is something perfectly simple, universal. When we say "I," we mean, to be sure, an individual; but since everyone is "I," when we say "I," we only say something quite universal. The universality of the "I" enables it to abstract from everything, even from its life. But mind is not merely this abstractly simple being equivalent to light, which was how it was considered when the simplicity of the soul in contrast to the composite nature of the body was under discussion; on the contrary, mind in spite of its simplicity is distinguished within itself; for the "I" sets itself over against itself, makes itself its own object and returns from this difference, which is, of course, only abstract, not yet concrete, into unity with itself. This being-with-itself of the "I" in its difference from itself is the "I"'s infinitude or ideality. But this ideality is first authenticated in the relation of the "I" to the infinitely manifold material confronting it. This material, in being seized by the "I," is at the same time poisoned and transfigured by the latter's universality; it loses its isolated, independent existence and receives a spiritual one. So far, therefore, is mind from being forced out of its simplicity, its being-with-itself, by the endless multiplicity of its images and ideas, into a spatial asunderness, that, on the contrary, its simple self, in undimmed clarity, pervades this multiplicity through and through and does not let it reach an independent existence.

But mind is not satisfied, as *finite* mind, with transposing things by its own ideational activity into its own interior space and thus stripping them of their externality in a manner which is still external; on the contrary, as *religious* consciousness, it pierces through the seemingly absolute independence of things to the one, infinite power of God operative in them and holding all together; and as *philosophical* thinking, it consummates this idealization of things by discerning the specific mode in which the eternal Idea forming their common principle is represented in them. By this cognition, the idealistic nature of mind which is already operative in finite mind, attains its completed, concretest shape, and becomes the actual Idea which perfectly apprehends itself and hence becomes absolute mind. Already in finite mind, ideality has the meaning of a movement returning into its beginning, by which mind, moving onward from its undifferentiated stage, its first position, to an Other, to the negation of that position, and by means of the negation of this negation returning to itself, demonstrates itself to be absolute negativity, infinite self-affirmation; and we have to consider finite mind, conformably to this its nature, first, in its immediate unity with Nature, then in its opposition to it, and lastly, in a unity which contains that opposition as overcome and is mediated by it. Grasped in this manner, finite mind is known as totality, as Idea, and moreover as the Idea which is for itself, which returns to itself out of that opposition and is actual. But in finite mind there is only the beginning of this return which is consummated only in absolute mind; for only in this does the Idea apprehend itself in a form which is neither merely the one-sided form of Notion or subjectivity, nor merely the equally one-sided form of objectivity or actuality, but is the perfect unity of these its distinct moments, that is, in its absolute truth.

What we have said above about the nature of mind is something which philosophy alone can and does demonstrate; it does not need to be confirmed by our ordinary consciousness. But in so far as our non-philosophical thinking, on its part, needs an understandable account of the developed Notion of mind or spirit, it may be reminded that Christian theology, too, conceives of God, that is, of Truth, as spirit and contemplates this, not as something quiescent, something abiding in empty identicalness but as something which necessarily enters into the process of distinguishing itself from itself, of positing its Other, and which comes to itself only through this Other, and by positively overcoming it—not by abandoning it. Theology, as we

know, expresses this process in picture-thinking by saying that God
the Father (this simple universal or being-within-self), putting aside
his solitariness creates Nature (the being that is external to itself,
outside of itself), begets a Son (his other "I"), but in the power of his
love beholds in this Other himself, recognizes his likeness therein and
in it returns to unity with himself; but this unity is no longer abstract
and immediate, but a concrete unity mediated by the moment of
difference; it is the Holy Spirit which proceeds from the Father and
the Son, reaching its perfect actuality and truth in the community of
Christians; and it is as this that God must be known if he is to be
grasped in his absolute truth, as the actual Idea in and for itself, and
not merely in the form of the pure Notion, of abstract being-within-
self, or in the equally untrue form of a detached actuality not corresponding to the universality of his Notion, but in the full agreement
of his Notion and his actuality.

So much for the distinctive determinatenesses of external Nature
and Mind as such. The explicated difference at the same time provides an indication of the relation in which Nature and mind stand to
each other. Since this relation is often misunderstood, this is the
appropriate place in which to elucidate it. We have said that mind
negates the externality of Nature, assimilates Nature to itself and
thereby idealizes it. In finite mind which places Nature outside of it,
this idealization has a one-sided shape; here the activity of our willing,
as of our thinking, is confronted by an external material which is
indifferent to the alteration which we impose on it and suffers quite
passively the idealization which thus falls to its lot.

But a different relationship obtains with the mind or spirit that
makes world-history. In this case, there no longer stands, on the one
side, an activity external to the object, and on the other side, a merely
passive object; but the spiritual activity is directed to an object which
is active in itself, an object which has spontaneously worked itself up
into the result to be brought about by that activity, so that in the
activity and in the object, one and the same content is present. Thus,
for example, the people and the time which were moulded by the
activity of Alexander and Caesar as *their* object, on their own part,
qualified themselves for the deeds to be performed by these individuals; it is no less true that the time created these men as that it was
created by them; they were as much the instruments of the mind or
spirit of their time and their people, as conversely, their people
served these heroes as an instrument for the accomplishment of their
deeds.

Similar to the relationship just delineated is the manner in which the philosophizing mind relates itself to external Nature. That is to say, philosophical thinking knows that Nature is idealized not merely by us, that Nature's asunderness is not an absolutely insuperable barrier for Nature itself, for its Notion; but that the external Idea immanent in Nature or, what is the same thing, the essence of mind itself at work within Nature brings about the idealization, the triumph over the asunderness, because this form of mind's existence conflicts with the inwardness of its essence. Therefore philosophy has, as it were, only to watch how Nature itself overcomes its externality, how it takes back what is self-external into the centre of the Idea, or causes this centre to show forth in the external, how it liberates the Notion concealed in Nature from the covering of externality and thereby overcomes external necessity. This transition from necessity to freedom is not a simple transition but a progression through many stages, whose exposition constitutes the Philosophy of Nature. At the highest stage of this triumph over asunderness, in feeling, the essence of mind which is held captive in Nature attains to an incipient being-for-self and begins to be free. By this being-for-self which is itself still burdened with the form of individuality and externality, consequently also with unfreedom, Nature is driven onwards beyond itself to mind as such, that is, to mind which, by thinking, is in the form of universality, of self-existent, actually free mind.

But it is already evident from our preceding exposition that the procession of mind or spirit from Nature must not be understood as if Nature were the absolutely immediate and the *prius*, and the original positing agent, mind, on the contrary, were only something posited by Nature; rather it is Nature which is posited by mind, and the latter is the absolute *prius*. Mind which exists in and for itself is not the mere result of Nature, but is in truth its own result; it brings forth itself from the presuppositions which it makes for itself, from the logical Idea and external Nature, and is as much the truth of the one as of the other, i.e., is the true form of the mind which is only internal, and of the mind which is only external, to itself. The illusory appearance which makes mind seem to be mediated by an Other is removed by mind itself, since this has, so to speak, the sovereign ingratitude of ridding itself of, of mediatizing, that by which it appears to be mediated, of reducing it to something dependent solely on mind and in this way making itself completely self-subsistent.

From what has been said, it already follows that the transition from Nature to mind is not a transition to an out-and-out Other, but is only a coming-to-itself of mind out of its self-externality in Nature. But equally, the differentia of Nature and mind is not abolished by this transition, for mind does not proceed in a natural manner from Nature. When it was said in § 222 that the death of the merely immediate, individual form of life is the procession of mind or spirit, this procession is not "according to the flesh" but spiritual, is not to be understood as a natural procession but as a development of the Notion; for in the Notion, the one-sidedness of the genus which fails properly to actualize itself, proving itself in death to be rather the negative power opposed to that actuality, and also the opposite one-sidedness of the animal existence which is tied to individuality, these are both overcome in the individuality which is in and for itself universal or, what is the same thing, in the universal which exists for itself in a universal mode, which universal is mind.

Nature as such in its inwardizing of itself does not attain to this being-for-self, to the consciousness of itself; the animal, the most perfect form of this inwardization, represents only the non-spiritual dialectic of transition from one single sensation filling its whole soul to another single sensation which equally exclusively dominates it; it is man who first raises himself above the singleness of sensation to the universality of thought, to self-knowledge, to the grasp of his subjectivity, of his "I" in a word, it is only man who is thinking mind and by this, and by this alone, is essentially distinguished from Nature. What belongs to Nature as such lies at the back of mind; it is true that mind has within itself the entire filling of Nature, but in mind the determinations of Nature exist in a radically different manner from their existence in external Nature. End *Zusatz*.

382

For this reason the essential, but formally essential, feature of mind is Liberty: i.e., it is the notion's absolute negativity or self-identity. Considered as this formal aspect, it *may* withdraw itself from everything external and from its own externality, its very existence; it can thus submit to infinite *pain*, the negation of its individual immediacy: in other words, it can keep itself affirmative in this negativity and possess its own identity. All this is possible so long as it is considered in its abstract self-contained universality.

Zusatz. The substance of mind is freedom, i.e., the absence of dependence on an Other, the relating of self to self. Mind is the actualized Notion which is for itself and has itself for object. Its truth and its freedom alike consist in this unity of Notion and objectivity present in it. The truth, as Christ said, makes spirit free; freedom makes it true. But the freedom of mind or spirit is not merely an absence of dependence on an Other won outside of the Other, but won in it; it attains actuality not by fleeing from the Other but by overcoming it. Mind can step out of its abstract, self-existent universality, out of its simple self-relation, can posit within itself a determinate, actual difference, something other than the simple "I," and hence a negative; and this relation to the Other is, for mind, not merely possible but necessary, because it is through the Other and by the triumph over it, that mind comes to authenticate itself and to be in fact what it ought to be according to its Notion, namely, the ideality of the external, the Idea which returns to itself out of its otherness; or, expressed more abstractly, the self-differentiating universal which in its difference is at home with itself and for itself. The Other, the negative, contradiction, disunity, therefore also belongs to the nature of mind. In this disunity lies the possibility of *pain*. Pain has therefore not reached mind from the outside as is supposed when it is asked in what manner pain entered into the world. Nor does evil, the negative of absolutely self-existent infinite mind, any more than pain, reach mind from the outside; on the contrary, evil is nothing else than mind which puts its separate individuality before all else. Therefore, even in this its extreme disunity, in this violent detachment of itself from the root of its intrinsically ethical nature, in this complete self-contradiction, mind yet remains identical with itself and therefore free. What belongs to external Nature is destroyed by contradiction; if, for example, gold were given a different specific gravity from what it has, it would cease to be gold. But mind has power to preserve itself in contradiction, and, therefore, in pain; power over evil, as well as over misfortune. Ordinary logic is, therefore, in error in supposing that mind completely excludes contradiction from itself. On the contrary, all consciousness contains a unity and a dividedness, hence a contradiction. Thus, for example, the idea of "house" is completely contradictory to my "I" and yet the latter endures it. But mind endures contradiction because it knows that it contains no determination that it has not posited itself, and consequently that it cannot in turn get rid of. This power over every content present in it forms the basis of the freedom of mind. But in its immediacy, mind is free only implicitly, in principle or potentially, not yet in actuality; actual freedom does not therefore belong to mind in its immediacy but has to be brought into being by mind's own activity. It is thus as the creator of its freedom that we have to consider mind in philosophy. The entire development of the Notion of mind represents only mind's freeing of itself from all its existential forms which do not accord with its Notion: a liberation which is brought about by the transformation of these forms into an actuality perfectly adequate to the Notion of mind. End *Zusatz*.

383

This universality is also its determinate sphere of being. Having a being of its own, the universal is self-particularizing, whilst it still remains self-identical. Hence the special mode of mental being is *"manifestation."* The spirit is not some one mode or meaning which finds utterance or externality only in a form distinct from itself: it does not manifest or reveal *something*, but its very mode and meaning is this revelation. And thus in its mere possibility mind is at the same moment an infinite, "absolute," *actuality*.

Zusatz. Earlier on, we placed the differentia of mind in *ideality*, in the abolition of the otherness of the Idea. If, now, in § 383 above, "manifestation" is assigned as the determinateness of mind, this is not a new, not a second, determination of mind, but only a development of the determination discussed earlier. For by getting rid of its otherness, the logical Idea, or mind which is only in itself, becomes for itself, in other words, becomes manifest to itself. Mind which is for itself, or mind as such—in distinction from mind which does not know itself and is manifest only to us, which is poured out into the asunderness of Nature and only ideally present therein—is, therefore, that which manifests itself not merely to an Other but to itself; or, what amounts to the same thing, is that which accomplishes its manifestation in its own element, not in an alien material. This determination belongs to mind as such; it holds true therefore of mind not only in so far as this relates itself simply to itself and is an "I" having itself for object, but also in so far as mind steps out of its abstract, self-existent universality, posits within itself a specific distinction, something other than itself; for mind does not lose itself in this Other, but, on the contrary, preserves and actualizes itself therein, impresses it with mind's own inner nature, converts the Other into an existence corresponding to it, and therefore by this triumph over the Other, over the specific, actual difference, attains to concrete being-for-self, becomes definitely manifest to itself. In the Other, therefore, mind manifests only itself, its own nature; but this consists in self-manifestation. The manifestation of itself to itself is therefore itself the content of mind and not, as it were, only a form externally added to the content; consequently mind, by its manifestation, does not manifest a content different from its form, but manifests its form which expresses the entire content of mind, namely, its self-manifestation. In mind, therefore, form and content are identical with each other. Admittedly, manifestation is usually thought of as an empty form to which must still be added a content from elsewhere; and by content is understood a being-within-self which remains within itself, and by form, on the other hand, the external mode of the relation of the content to something else. But in speculative logic it is demonstrated that, in truth, the content is not merely something which is and remains within itself, but something which spontaneously enters into relation with something else; just as, conversely, in truth, the form must be grasped not merely as something dependent on and external to the content, but rather as that which makes the content into a content, into a being-within-self, into something distinct from something else. The true content contains, therefore, form within itself, and the true form is its own content. But we have to know mind as this true content and as this true form.

In order to elucidate for ordinary thinking this unity of form and content present in mind, the unity of manifestation and what is manifested, we can refer to the teaching of the Christian religion. Christianity says: God has revealed himself through Christ, his only-begotten Son. Ordinary thinking straightway interprets this statement to mean that Christ is only the organ of this revelation, as if what is revealed in this manner were something other than the source of the revelation. But, in truth, this statement properly means that God has revealed that his nature consists in having a Son, i.e., in making a distinction within himself, making himself finite, but in his difference remaining in communion with himself, beholding and revealing himself in the Son, and that by this unity with the Son, by this being-for-himself in the Other, he is absolute mind or spirit; so that the Son is not the mere organ of the revelation but is himself the content of the revelation.

Just as mind represents the unity of form and content, so too is it the unity of possibility and actuality. We understand by the possible as such, that which is still inward, that which has not yet come to utterance, to manifestation. But now we have seen that mind as such only is, in so far as it manifests itself to itself. Actuality, which consists just in mind's manifestation, belongs therefore to its Notion. In finite mind the Notion of mind does not, of course, reach its absolute actualization; but absolute mind is the absolute unity of actuality and the Notion or possibility of mind. End *Zusatz.*

384

Revelation, taken to mean the revelation of the *abstract* Idea, is an unmediated transition to Nature which *comes* to be. As mind is free, its manifestation is to *set forth* Nature as *its* world; but because it is reflection, it, in thus setting forth its world, at the same time *presupposes* the world as a nature independently existing. In the intellectual sphere to reveal is thus to create a world as its being—a being in which the mind procures the *affirmation* and *truth* of its freedom.

The Absolute is Mind (Spirit)—this is the supreme definition of the Absolute. To find this definition and to grasp its meaning and burden was, we may say, the ultimate purpose of all education and all philosophy: it was the point to which turned the impulse of all religion and science; and it is this impulse that must explain the history of the world. The word "Mind" (Spirit)—and some glimpse of its meaning —was found at an early period: and the spirituality of God is the lesson of Christianity. It remains for philosophy in its own element of intelligible unity to get hold of what was thus given as a mental image, and what implicitly is the ultimate reality; and that problem is not genuinely, and by rational methods, solved so long as liberty and intelligible unity is not the theme and the soul of philosophy.

Zusatz. Self-manifestation is a determination belonging to mind as such; but it has three distinct forms. The first mode in which mind, as [only] in itself or as the logical Idea, manifests itself, consists in the direct release (*Umschlagen*) of the Idea into the immediacy of external and particularized existence. This release is the coming-to-be of Nature. Nature, too, is a posited existence; but its positedness has the form of immediacy, of a being outside of the Idea. This form contradicts the inwardness of the self-positing Idea which brings forth itself from its presuppositions. The Idea, or mind implicit, slumbering in Nature, overcomes, therefore, the externality, separateness, and immediacy, creates for itself an existence conformable to its inwardness and universality and thereby becomes mind which is reflected into itself and is for itself, self-conscious and awakened mind or mind as such.

This gives the second form of mind's manifestation. On this level, mind which is no longer poured out into the asunderness of Nature but exists for itself and is manifest to itself, opposes itself to unconscious Nature which just as much conceals mind as manifests it. Mind converts Nature into an object confronting it, reflects on it, takes back the externality of Nature into its own inwardness, idealizes Nature and thus in its object becomes for itself. But this first being-for-self of mind is itself still immediate, abstract, not absolute; the self-externality of mind is not absolutely overcome by it. The awakening mind does not yet discern here its unity with the mind concealed and implicit in Nature, to which it stands, therefore, in an external relation, does not appear as all in all, but only as one side of the relation; it is true that in its relation to the Other it is also reflected into itself and so is self-consciousness, but yet it lets this unity of consciousness and self-consciousness, still exist as a unity that remains so external, empty and superficial that in it self-consciousness and consciousness still fall asunder; and mind, despite its self-communion is at the same time in communion not with itself but with an Other, and its unity with the mind implicitly present and active in the Other does not as yet become *for* mind. Here, mind posits Nature as a reflectedness-into-self, as *its* world, strips Nature of its form of otherness and converts the Other confronting it into something it has itself posited; but, at the same time, this Other still remains independent of mind, something immediately given, not posited but only presupposed by mind, as something, therefore, the positing of which is antecedent to reflective thought. Hence from this standpoint the positedness of Nature by mind is not yet absolute but is effected only in the reflective consciousness; Nature is, therefore, not yet comprehended as existing only through infinite mind, as its creation. Here, consequently, mind still has in Nature a limitation and just by this limitation is finite mind.

Now this limitation is removed by absolute knowledge, which is the third and supreme manifestation of mind. On this level there vanishes, on the one hand, the dualism of a self-subsistent Nature or of mind poured out into asunderness, and, on the other hand, the merely incipient self-awareness of mind which, however, does not yet comprehend its unity with the former. Absolute mind knows that it posits being itself, that it is itself the creator of its Other, of Nature and finite mind, so that this Other loses all semblance of independence in face of mind, ceases altogether to be a limitation for mind and appears only as a means whereby mind attains to absolute being-for-self, to the absolute unity of what it is in itself and what it is for itself, of its Notion and its actuality.

The highest definition of the Absolute is that it is not merely mind in general but that it is mind which is absolutely manifest to itself, self-conscious, infinitely creative mind, which we have just characterized as the third form of its manifestation. Just as in philosophy we progress from the imperfect forms of mind's manifestation delineated above to the highest form of its manifestation, so, too, world-history exhibits a series of conceptions of the Eternal, the last of which first shows forth the Notion of absolute mind. The oriental religions, and the Hebrew, too, stop short at the still abstract concept of God and of spirit (as is done even by the Enlightenment, which wants to know only of God the Father); for God the Father, by himself, is the God who is shut up within himself, the abstract god, therefore not yet the spiritual, not yet the true God. In the Greek religion God did, indeed, begin to be manifest in a definite manner. The representation of the Greek gods had beauty for its law, Nature raised to the level of mind. The Beautiful does not remain something abstractly ideal, but in its ideality is at once perfectly determinate, individualized. The Greek gods are, however, at first only representations for sensuous intuition or for picture-thinking, they are not yet grasped in thought. But the medium of sense can only exhibit the totality of mind as an asunderness, as a circle of independent, mental or spiritual shapes; the unity embracing all these shapes remains, therefore, a wholly indeterminate, alien power over against the gods. It is in the Christian religion that the immanently differentiated *one* nature of God, the totality of the divine mind in the form of unity, has first been manifested. This content, presented in the guise of picture-thinking, has to be raised by philosophy into the form of the Notion or of absolute knowledge which, as we have said, is the highest manifestation of that content. End *Zusatz*.

Subdivision

385

The development of Mind (Spirit) is in three stages:

(1) In the form of self-relation: within it it has the *ideal* totality of the Idea, i.e., it has before it all that its notion contains—its being is to be self-contained and free. This is *Mind Subjective*.

(2) In the form of *reality:* realized, i.e., in a *world* produced and to

be produced by it—in this world freedom presents itself under the shape of necessity. This is *Mind Objective.*

(3) In that unity of mind as objectivity and of mind as ideality and concept, which essentially and actually is and forever produces itself, mind in its absolute truth. This is *Mind Absolute.*

Zusatz. Mind is always Idea; but to begin with it is only the Notion of the Idea, or the Idea in its indeterminateness, in the most abstract mode of reality, in other words, in the mode of being. In the beginning we have only the quite universal, undeveloped determination of mind, not yet mind in its particular aspect; this we obtain only when we pass from one thing to something else: for the particular contains a One and an Other; but it is just at the beginning that we have not yet made this transition. The reality of mind is, therefore, to begin with still a quite universal, not particularized reality; the development of this reality will be completed only by the entire Philosophy of Mind. The still quite abstract, immediate reality is, however, the natural, the unspiritual. This is the reason why the child is still in the grip of natural life, has only natural impulses, is not actually but only potentially or notionally a rational being. Accordingly, we must characterize the first reality of mind as the most inappropriate for mind, simply because it is still an abstract, immediate reality in the natural sphere; but the true reality must be defined as the totality of the developed moments of the Notion which remains the soul, the unity of these moments. In this development of its reality, the Notion's progress is prescribed by necessity, for the form of immediacy, of indeterminateness, which its reality has at first is in contradiction with it; that which in mind appears to be immediately present is not truly immediate, but is intrinsically something posited, mediated. Mind is impelled by this contradiction to rid itself of its own presupposition in the guise of immediacy, of otherness. It is by doing this that it first comes to itself, first emerges *as* mind. Consequently, we cannot begin with mind as such, but must start from its most inappropriate reality. Mind, it is true, is already mind at the outset, but it does not yet know that it is. It is not mind itself that, at the outset, has already grasped its Notion; it is only we who contemplate it who know its Notion. That mind comes to a knowledge of what it is, this constitutes its realization. Mind is essentially only what it knows itself to be. At first, it is only potentially mind; its becoming-for-itself makes it an actuality. But it becomes for itself only by particularizing, determining itself, making itself into its own presupposition, into the Other of itself, first relating itself to this Other as to its immediacy, but making itself free of this Other *qua* Other. As long as mind stands related to itself as to an Other, it is only *subjective* mind, originating in Nature and at first itself natural mind. But the entire activity of subjective mind is directed to grasping itself as its own self, proving itself to be the ideality of its immediate reality. When it has attained to a being-for-self, then it is no longer merely subjective, but *objective* mind. Whereas subjective mind on account of its connection with an Other is still unfree or, what is the same thing, is free only in principle, in objective mind there comes into existence freedom, mind's knowledge of itself as free. Mind that is objective is a person, and as such has a reality of its freedom in property; for in property, the thing is posited as what it is, namely, something lacking a subsistence of its own, something which essentially has the significance of being only the reality of the free will of a person, and for that reason, of being for any other person inviolable. Here we see a subjective mind that knows itself to be free, and, at the same time, an external reality of this freedom; here, therefore, mind attains to a being-for-self, the objectivity of mind receives its due. Thus mind has emerged from the form of mere subjectivity. But the full realization of that freedom which in property is still incomplete, still [only] formal, the consummation of the realization of the Notion of objective mind, is achieved only in the State, in which mind develops its freedom into a world posited by mind itself, into the ethical world. Yet mind must pass beyond this level too. The defect of this objectivity of mind consists in its being only posited. Mind must again freely let go the world, what mind has posited must at the same time be grasped as having an immediate being. This happens on the third level of mind, the standpoint of absolute mind, i.e., of art, religion, and philosophy. End *Zusatz*.

386

The two first parts of the doctrine of Mind embrace the finite mind. Mind is the infinite Idea, and finitude here means the disproportion between the concept and the reality—but with the qualification that it is a shadow cast by the mind's own light—a show or illusion which the mind implicitly imposes as a barrier to itself, in order, by its removal, actually to realize and become conscious of freedom as *its* very being, i.e., to be fully *manifested*. The several steps of this activity, on each of which, with their semblance of being, it is the function of the finite mind to linger, and through which it has to pass, are steps

in its liberation. In the full truth of that liberation is given the identification of the three stages—finding a world presupposed before us,
generating a world as our own creation, and gaining freedom from
it and in it. To the infinite form of this truth the show purifies itself
till it becomes a consciousness of it.

A rigid application of the category of finitude by the abstract logi-
cian is chiefly seen in dealing with Mind and reason; it is held not a
mere matter of strict logic, but treated also as a moral and religious
concern, to adhere to the point of view of finitude, and the wish to
go further is reckoned a mark of audacity, if not of insanity, of
thought. Whereas in fact such a *modesty* of thought, as treats the finite
as something altogether fixed and *absolute*, is the worst of virtues; and
to stick to a post which has no sound ground in itself is the most
unsound sort of theory. The category of finitude was at a much earlier
period elucidated and explained at its place in the Logic: an elucidation which, as in logic for the more specific though still simple
thought-forms of finitude, so in the rest of philosophy for the concrete forms, has merely to show that the finite *is not*, i.e., is not the
truth, but merely a transition and an emergence to something higher.
This finitude of the spheres so far examined is the dialectic that makes
a thing have its cessation by another and in another; but Spirit, the
intelligent unity and the *implicit* Eternal, is itself just the consummation of that internal act by which nullity is nullified and vanity is made
vain. And so, the modesty alluded to is a retention of this vanity—the
finite—in opposition to the true: it is itself therefore vanity. In the
course of the mind's development we shall see this vanity appear as
wickedness at that turning-point at which mind has reached its extreme
immersion in its subjectivity and its most central contradiction.

Zusatz. Subjective and objective mind are still finite. But it is necessary
to know what we mean by the finitude of mind. This is usually thought
of as an absolute limitation, as a fixed quality, the removal of which
would result in mind ceasing to be mind; just as the essence of natural
things is tied to a specific quality, as, for example, gold cannot be
separated from its specific gravity, this or that animal cannot be
without claws, incisors, etc. But in truth, the finitude of mind must be
regarded not as a fixed determination, but must be recognized as a
mere moment; for as we have already said, mind is essentially the Idea
in the form of ideality, in other words, in the form of the negatedness
of the finite. In mind, therefore, the finite has only the significance

of a being which is not simply affirmative but has been reduced to a moment. Accordingly, the peculiar quality of mind is rather to be the true infinite, that is, the infinite which does not one-sidedly stand over against the finite but contains the finite within itself as a moment. It is, therefore, meaningless to say: There are finite minds. Mind *qua* mind *is* not finite, it *has* finitude within itself, but only as a finitude which is to be, and has been, reduced to a moment. The genuine definition of finitude here—this is not the place for a detailed discussion of it—must be that the finite is a reality that is not adequate to its Notion. Thus the sun is a finite entity, for it cannot be thought without other entities, since the reality of its Notion comprises not merely the sun itself but the entire solar system. Indeed, the whole solar system is a finite entity, because every heavenly body in it exhibits an illusory independence of the others; consequently this collective reality does not as yet correspond to its Notion, does not as yet represent the same ideality which the nature of the Notion is. It is only the reality of mind that is itself ideality, and it is therefore only in mind that we find absolute unity of Notion and reality, and hence true infinitude. The very fact that we know a limitation is evidence that we are beyond it, evidence of our freedom from limitation. Natural objects are finite simply because their limitation does not exist for the objects themselves, but only for us who compare them with one another. We make ourselves finite by receiving an Other into our consciousness; but in the very fact of our knowing this Other we have transcended this limitation. Only he who does not know is limited, for he does not know his limitation; whereas he who knows the limitation knows it, not as a limitation of his knowing, but as something known, as something belonging to his knowledge; only the unknown would be a limitation of knowledge, whereas the known limitation, on the contrary, is not; therefore to know one's limitation means to know of one's unlimitedness. But when we pronounce mind to be unlimited, truly infinite, this does not mean that mind is free from any limitation whatsoever; on the contrary, we must recognize that mind must determine itself and so make itself finite, limit itself. But the abstractive intellect *(Verstand)* is wrong in treating this finitude as something inflexible, in holding the difference between the limitation and infinitude to be absolutely fixed, and accordingly maintaining that mind is *either* limited *or* unlimited. Finitude, truly comprehended, is as we have said, contained in infinitude, limitation in the unlimited. Mind is, therefore, *as well* infinite *as* finite, and *neither* merely the one *nor* merely the other; in making itself finite it remains infinite, for it reduces the finitude within it to a mere moment; nothing in it is fixed, simply affirmatively present but, on the contrary, everything is only an ideal moment, only an appearance. So must God, because he is mind or spirit, determine himself, posit finitude in himself (else he would be only a dead, empty abstraction); but since the reality he gives himself by his self-determining is perfectly conformable to him, God is not thereby made finite. Therefore, limitation is not in God and in mind: it is only posited by mind in order to be reduced to a moment. Only momentarily can mind seem to be fixed in a finite content; by its ideality it is raised above it and it knows that the limitation is not a permanent one. It therefore transcends it, frees itself from it; and this liberation is not, as the abstractive intellect supposes, something never completed, a liberation only striven for endlessly; on the contrary, mind wrests itself out of this progress to infinity, frees itself absolutely from the limitation, from its Other, and so attains to absolute being-for-self, makes itself truly infinite. End *Zusatz*.

VI

Objective Spirit: Human Conduct and Philosophic Truth

The philosophical sciences of Objective Spirit are outlined in the *Encyclopaedia* under the headings Law (or abstract right), Morality (or personal ethics), and Ethical Associations (or the interrelations of family life, civil society, politics, and history). The *Encyclopaedia* outline on these subjects is elaborated in two major Hegelian works that have had a tremendous impact on world affairs: The *Philosophy of Right* and the *Lectures on the Philosophy of History.*

These sciences are objective in the strict sense. Like the natural sciences of mechanics, physics, and organics, they study the phenomena of an objective world, empirically given. But it is not a world that could conceivably exist without human activity. Rather, it is the world that willful human intelligence makes for itself once it has overcome the subjectivity of the stages of mental development described in the preceding sciences of anthropology, phenomenology, and psychology—the sciences that make up the sphere of Subjective Spirit.

The *Philosophy of Right* is Hegel's equivalent of both the *Ethics* and *Politics* of Aristotle. Man's essential right as man, according to Hegel, is to be free. But freedom has a variety of meanings—subjective and objective, individual and social, theoretical and practical—all of which Hegel takes into account and links together philosophically in a vast dialectical progression. He starts on an abstract level with the claims to freedom of the individual as a *person*, having legally definable rights, which are exercisable objectively in the I-It relations of property and the I-Thou relations of contract, pledge, wrong, revenge, and punishment. Then he takes up man's rights of conscience

253

as a moral *subject*, determined to judge his own acts according to his intentions, regardless of how they may be judged externally by others. Lastly, and at greatest length, Hegel takes up the social actuality of freedom in our shared experiences as family *members*, as competing *burghers* in civil society, and as *citizens* in the nonbiological brotherhood of political community.

From Marx and Engels to Marcuse and Angela Davis, communist philosophers and activists have repeatedly "plunged" for inspiration, as Marx phrased it, into the "ocean" of Hegelian dialectical thought on the conflicting rights of persons, the frustrations of alienated moral subjects, and the group and class conflicts that make up the web of civil society. Marx himself acknowledged that his life-long revolutionary critique of political economy—which is the science of civil society—was a painstakingly detailed and passionate elaboration of what Hegel summed up in two terse pages (paragraphs 243–248) of the *Philosophy of Right.* Hegel there shows how, in an advanced economy, governmental *laissez-faire* leads inevitably to concentration of productive capital in the hands of a few, while the many, demoralized by division of labor and cycles of unemployment, are depressed to the status of an unproductive rabble.

According to Marx, the necessary consequence of such polarization of rich and poor is a class revolution, leading to total liquidation of the old possessing classes under a dictatorship of the proletariat (the coercive powers of which will in turn "wither away" as the danger of counter-revolutionary opposition fades). Hegel concludes, on the contrary, that the most likely result of mounting class tensions and conflicts in an advanced society will be a universalized longing for political solutions accompanied by an outward thrust of the society—a prosperous outpouring of goods and people—into other lands. This part of Hegel's work most impressed Lenin who, following the lead of J. A. Hobson, traced its consequences from a revolutionary perspective in his doctrine of capitalist imperialism.

The last third of the *Philosophy of Right* gives us Hegel's theory of the rationally constituted state with its separation of functions and integration of powers. Though less publicized than his analysis of civil society, it has really had a far greater influence both theoretically and practically. Hegel wrote no manual of statecraft. Yet it is a fact that the builders of the Soviet Union and Red China, of the fascist regimes of Germany, Italy, and Japan, of the Keynesian and Deweyan "welfare states" of England and America, have all made constructive use, in diverse ways, of the Hegelian political doctrine.

Hegel was no idolator of statehood or the historical process, despite the charges that are often made to the contrary. For him, as for Aristotle, the state is a means not an end. To read him as if he taught otherwise, gives rise immediately, as Carl J. Friedrich of Harvard has correctly observed, to "authoritarian, not to say totalitarian implications, which are far removed from the essential liberalism of Hegel's conceptions."

When we turn to the *Lectures on the Philosophy of History*, we see at once that, in Hegel's view, the passage of time must sooner or later overwhelm all states. That does not mean, however, that the course of history is blind or meaningless. Though individuals and nations fail, mankind as a whole is moved forward, in a continuous dialectical progression (Marx held to this part of the Hegelian doctrine all his life), toward actualization of all its potentialities for freedom. For long ages, says Hegel, there have been societies in which only one person, the absolute ruler, was free (the ancient East); then came the classical civilization of the Mediterranean world in which some, an aristocratic governing few, were free; now, with the world-wide spread of Western civilization, we are at a time when all adult human beings must be recognized, and therefore held accountable for their deeds, as free persons.

Yet, from a moral standpoint, Hegel is essentially a pessimist about the motive force of history. Passion, greed, ambition dominate its course. Viewed objectively, it is a pageant of horrors that makes us suffer "mental torture," unless we are able to discern beneath its surface confusion a pattern of rational necessity. The ancient pagans called it Fate; Jewish and Christian historians called it Divine Providence; Hegel uses both those terms, but speaks of it also as the cunning of reason in history; for Marx it is the historical dialectic.

Who can work out the truth of history's rational pattern? Hegel held that only men of high artistic, religious, or philosophical inspiration—freed from the activist passions of economics and statecraft—could grasp the meaning of history. Marx, on the contrary, contended passionately that knowledge of the rational necessity of history was reserved exclusively for revolutionary activists like himself, who yearned not merely to understand the world, but to change it.

FROM THE PREFACE AND INTRODUCTION TO THE
PHILOSOPHY OF RIGHT

Preface

. . . the truth about Right, Ethics, and the state is as old as its public recognition and formulation in the law of the land, in the morality of everyday life, and in religion. What more does this truth require—since the thinking mind is not content to possess it in this ready fashion? It requires to be grasped in thought as well; the content which is already rational in principle must win the *form* of rationality and so appear well-founded to untrammelled thinking. Such thinking does not remain stationary at the given, whether the given be upheld by the external positive authority of the state or the *consensus hominum*, or by the authority of inward feeling and emotion and by the "witness of the spirit" which directly concurs with it. On the contrary, thought which is free starts out from itself and thereupon claims to know itself as united in its innermost being with the truth.

The unsophisticated heart takes the simple line of adhering with trustful conviction to what is publicly accepted as true and then building on this firm foundation its conduct and its set position in life. Against this simple line of conduct there may at once be raised the alleged difficulty of how it is possible, in an infinite variety of opinions, to distinguish and discover what is universally recognized and valid. This perplexity may at first sight be taken for a right and really serious attitude to the thing, but in fact those who boast of this perplexity are in the position of not being able to see the wood for the trees; the only perplexity and difficulty they are in is one of their own making. Indeed, this perplexity and difficulty of theirs is proof rather that they want as the substance of the right and the ethical not what is universally recognized and valid, but something else. If they had been serious with what is universally accepted instead of busying themselves with the vanity and particularity of opinions and things, they would have clung to what is substantively right, namely to the commands of the ethical order and the state, and would have regulated their lives in accordance with these.

A more serious difficulty arises, however, from the fact that man thinks and tries to find in thinking both his freedom and the basis of ethical life. But however lofty, however divine, the right of thought

SOURCE: *Philosophy of Right,* pp. 3–13, 14–20. Reprinted by permission of the Clarendon Press, Oxford.

may be, it is perverted into wrong if it is only this [opining] which passes for thinking and if thinking knows itself to be free only when it diverges from what is *universally* recognized and valid and when it has discovered how to invent for itself some *particular* character.

At the present time, the idea that freedom of thought, and of mind generally, evinces itself only in divergence from, indeed in hostility to, what is publicly recognized, might seem to be most firmly rooted in connexion with the state, and it is chiefly for this reason that a philosophy of the state might seem essentially to have the task of discovering and promulgating still another theory, and a special and original one at that. In examining this idea and the activity in conformity with it, we might suppose that no state or constitution had ever existed in the world at all or was even in being at the present time, but that nowadays—and this "nowadays" lasts for ever—we had to start all over again from the beginning, and that the ethical world had just been waiting for such present-day projects, proofs, and investigations. So far as nature is concerned, people grant that it is nature as it is which philosophy has to bring within its ken, that the philosopher's stone lies concealed somewhere, somewhere within nature itself, that nature is inherently rational, and that what knowledge has to investigate and grasp in concepts is this actual reason present in it; not the formations and accidents evident to the superficial observer, but nature's eternal harmony, its harmony, however, in the sense of the law and essence immanent within it. The ethical world, on the other hand, the state (i.e., reason as it actualizes itself in the element of self-consciousness), is not allowed to enjoy the good fortune which springs from the fact that it is reason which has achieved power and mastery within that element and which maintains itself and has its home there. The universe of mind is supposed rather to be left to the mercy of chance and caprice, to be God-forsaken, and the result is that if the ethical world is Godless, truth lies outside it, and at the same time, since even so reason is supposed to be in it as well, truth becomes nothing but a problem. But it is this also that is to authorize, nay to oblige, every thinker to take his own road, though not in search of the philosopher's stone, for he is saved this search by the philosophizing of our contemporaries, and everyone nowadays is assured that he has this stone in his grasp as his birthright. Now admittedly it is the case that those who live their lives in the state as it actually exists here and now and find satisfaction there for their knowledge and volition (and of these there are many, more in fact than think or know it, because ultimately this is the position of everybody), or those at any rate who *consciously* find their satisfaction in the state, laugh at these operations and affirmations and regard them as an empty game, sometimes rather funny, sometimes rather serious, now amusing, now dangerous. Thus this restless activity of empty reflection, together with its popularity and the welcome it has received, would be a thing on its own, developing in privacy in its own way, were it not that it is philosophy itself which has earned all kinds of scorn and discredit by its indulgence in this occupation. The worst of these kinds of scorn is this, that, as I said just now, everyone is convinced that his mere birthright puts him in a position to pass judgment on philosophy in general and to condemn it. No other art or science is subjected to this last degree of scorn, to the supposition that we are masters of it without ado.

In fact, what we have seen recent philosophical publications proclaiming with the maximum of pretension about the state has really justified anybody who cared to busy himself with the subject in this conviction that he could manufacture a philosophy of this kind himself without ado and so give himself proof of his possession of philosophy. Besides, this self-styled "philosophy" has expressly stated that "truth itself cannot be known," that that only is true which each individual allows to rise out of his heart, emotion, and inspiration about ethical institutions, especially about the state, the government, and the constitution. In this connexion what a lot of flattery has been talked, especially to the young! Certainly the young have listened to it willingly enough. "He giveth to his own in sleep" has been applied to science and hence every sleeper has numbered himself among the elect, but the concepts he has acquired in sleep are themselves of course only the wares of sleep.

A ringleader of these hosts of superficiality, of these self-styled "philosophers," Herr Fries, did not blush, on the occasion of a public festival which has become notorious, to express the following ideas in a speech on "The state and the constitution": "In the people ruled by a genuine communal spirit, life for the discharge of all public business would come from below, from the people itself; living associations, indissolubly united by the holy chain of friendship, would be dedicated to every single project of popular education and popular service," and so on. This is the quintessence of shallow thinking, to base philosophic science not on the development of thought and the concept but on immediate sense-perception and the play of fancy; to take the rich inward articulation of ethical life, i.e., the state, the architectonic of that life's rationality—which sets determinate limits to the different circles of public life and their rights, uses the strict accuracy of measurement which holds together every pillar, arch, and buttress and thereby produces the strength of the whole out of the harmony of the parts—to take this structure and confound the completed fabric in the broth of "heart, friendship, and inspiration." According to a view of this kind, the world of ethics (Epicurus, holding a similar view, would have said the "world in general") should be given over—as in fact of course it is not—to the subjective accident of opinion and caprice. By the simple family remedy of ascribing to feeling the labour, the more than millenary labour, of reason and its intellect, all the trouble of rational insight and knowledge directed by speculative thinking is of course saved. On this point, Goethe's Mephistopheles, a good authority!, says something like this, a quotation I have used elsewhere already: "Do but despise intellect and knowledge, the highest of all man's gifts, and thou hast surrendered thyself to the devil and to perdition art doomed." The next thing is that such sentiments assume even the guise of piety, for this bustling activity has used any and every expedient in its endeavour to give itself authority. With godliness and the Bible, however, it has arrogated to itself the highest of justifications for despising the ethical order and the objectivity of law, since it is piety too which envelops in the simpler intuition of feeling the truth which is articulated in the world into an organic realm. But if it is piety of the right sort, it sheds the form of this emotional region so soon as it leaves the inner life, enters upon the daylight of the Idea's development and revealed riches, and brings with it, out of its inner worship of God, reverence for law and for an absolute truth exalted above the subjective form of feeling.

The particular form of guilty conscience revealed by the type of eloquence in which such superficiality flaunts itself may be brought to your attention here and above all if you notice that when it is furthest from mind, superficiality speaks most of mind, when its talk is the most tedious dead-and-alive stuff, its favourite words are "life" and "vitalize," and when it gives evidence of the pure selfishness of baseless pride, the word most on its lips is "people." But the special mark which it carries on its brow is the hatred of law. Right and ethics, and the actual world of justice and ethical life, are understood through thoughts; through thoughts they are invested with a rational form, i.e., with universality and determinacy. This form is law; and this it is which the feeling that stipulates for its own whim, the conscience that places right in subjective conviction, has reason to regard as its chief foe. The formal character of the right as a duty and a law it feels as the letter, cold and dead, as a shackle; for it does not recognize itself in the law and so does not recognize itself as free there, because law is the reason of the thing, and reason refuses to allow feeling to warm itself at its own private hearth. Hence law, as I have remarked somewhere in the course of this text-book, is *par excellence* the shibboleth which marks out these false friends and comrades of what they call the "people."

At the present time, the pettifoggery of caprice has usurped the name of philosophy and succeeded in giving a wide public the opinion that such triflings are philosophy. The result of this is that it has now become almost a disgrace to go on speaking in philosophical terms about the nature of the state, and law-abiding men cannot be blamed if they become impatient so soon as they hear mention of a philosophical science of the state. Still less is it a matter for surprise that governments have at last directed their attention to this kind of philosophy, since, apart from anything else, philosophy with us is not, as it was with the Greeks for instance, pursued in private like an art, but has an existence in the open, in contact with the public, and especially, or even only, in the service of the state. Governments have proved their trust in their scholars who have made philosophy their chosen field by leaving entirely to them the construction and contents of philosophy—though here and there, if you like, it may not have been so much confidence that has been shown as indifference to learning itself, and professorial chairs of philosophy have been retained only as a tradition (in France, for instance, to the best of my knowledge, chairs of metaphysics at least have been allowed to lapse). Their confidence, however, has very often been ill repaid, or alternatively, if you preferred to see indifference, you would have to regard the result, the decay of thorough knowledge, as the penalty of this indifference. *Prima facie,* superficiality seems to be extremely accommodating, one might say, at least in relation to public peace and order, because it fails to touch or even to guess at the substance of the things; no action, or at least no police action, would thus have been taken against it in the first instance, had it not been that there still existed in the state a need for a deeper education and insight, a need which the state required philosophical science to satisfy. On the other hand, superficial thinking about the ethical order, about right and duty in general, starts automatically from the maxims which constitute superficiality in this sphere, i.e., from the principles of the Sophists which are so clearly outlined for our information in Plato. What is right these principles locate in subjective aims and opinions, in subjective feeling and particular conviction, and from them there follows the ruin of the inner ethical life and a good conscience, of love and right dealing between private persons, no less than the ruin of public order and the law of the land. The significance which such phenomena must acquire for governments is not likely to suffer any diminution as a result of the pretentiousness which has used that very grant of confidence and the authority of a professorial chair to support the demand that the state should uphold and give scope to what corrupts the ultimate source of achievement, namely universal principles, and so even to the defiance of the state as if such defiance were what it deserved. "If God gives a man an office, he also gives him brains" is an old joke which in these days surely no one will take wholly in earnest.

In the fresh importance which circumstances have led governments to attach to the character of philosophical·work, there is one element which we cannot fail to notice; this is the protection and support which the study of philosophy now seems to have come to need in several other directions. Think of the numerous publications in the field of the positive sciences, as well as edifying religious works and vague literature of other kinds, which reveal to their readers the contempt for philosophy I have already mentioned, in that, although the thought in them is immature to the last degree and philosophy is entirely alien to them, they treat it as something over and done with. More than this, they expressly rail against it and pronounce its content, namely the speculative knowledge of God, nature, and mind, the knowledge of truth, to be a foolish and even sinful presumptuousness, while reason, and again reason, and reason repeated *ad infinitum* is arraigned, disparaged, and condemned. At the very least such writings reveal to us that, to a majority of those engaged in activities supposedly scientific, the claims of the concept are an embarrassment which none the less they cannot escape. I venture to say that anyone with such phenomena before him may very well begin to think that, if they alone are considered, tradition is now neither worthy of respect nor sufficient to secure for the study of philosophy either tolerance or existence as a public institution. The arrogant declamations current in our time against philosophy present the singular spectacle, on the one hand of deriving their justification from the superficiality to which that study has been degraded, and, on the other, of being themselves rooted in this element against which they turn so ungratefully. For by pronouncing the knowledge of truth a wild-goose chase, this self-styled philosophizing has reduced all thoughts and all topics to the same level, just as the despotism of the Roman Empire abolished the distinction between free men and slaves, virtue and vice, honour and dishonour, learning and ignorance. The result of this levelling process is that the concepts of what is true, the laws of ethics, likewise become nothing more than opinions and subjective convictions. The maxims of the worst of criminals, since they too are convictions, are put on the same level of value as those laws; and at the same time any object, however sorry, however accidental, any material however insipid, is put on the same level of value as what constitutes the interest of all thinking men and the bonds of the ethical world.

It is therefore to be taken as a piece of *luck* for philosophic science —though in actual fact, as I have said, it is the *necessity* of the thing —that this philosophizing which like an exercise in scholasticism might have continued to spin its web in seclusion, has now been put into closer touch and so into open variance with actuality, in which the principles of rights and duties are a serious matter, and which lives in the light of its consciousness of these.

It is just this placing of philosophy in the actual world which meets with misunderstandings, and so I revert to what I have said before, namely that, since philosophy is the exploration of the rational, it is for that very reason the apprehension of the present and the actual, not the erection of a beyond, supposed to exist, God knows where, or rather which exists, and we can perfectly well say where, namely in the error of a one-sided, empty, ratiocination. In the course of this book, I have remarked that even Plato's *Republic*, which passes proverbially as an empty ideal, is in essence nothing but an interpretation of the nature of Greek ethical life. Plato was conscious that there was breaking into that life in his own time a deeper principle which could appear in it directly only as a longing still unsatisfied, and so only as something corruptive. To combat it, he needs must have sought aid from that very longing itself. But this aid had to come from on High and all that Plato could do was to seek it in the first place in a particular external form of that same Greek ethical life. By that means he thought to master this corruptive invader, and thereby he did fatal injury to the deeper impulse which underlay it, namely free infinite personality. Still, his genius is proved by the fact that the principle on which the distinctive character of his Idea of the state turns is precisely the pivot on which the impending world revolution turned at that time.

What is rational is actual and what is actual is rational. On this conviction the plain man like the philosopher takes his stand, and from it philosophy starts in its study of the universe of mind as well as the universe of nature. If reflection, feeling, or whatever form subjective consciousness may take, looks upon the present as something vacuous and looks beyond it with the eyes of superior wisdom, it finds itself in a vacuum, and because it is actual only in the present, it is itself mere vacuity. If on the other hand the Idea passes for "only an Idea," for something represented in an opinion, philosophy rejects such a view and shows that nothing is actual except the Idea. Once that is granted, the great thing is to apprehend in the show of the temporal and transient the substance which is immanent and the eternal which is present. For since rationality (which is synonymous with the Idea) enters upon external existence simultaneously with its actualization, it emerges with an infinite wealth of forms, shapes, and appearances. Around its heart it throws a motley covering with which consciousness is at home to begin with, a covering which the concept has first to penetrate before it can find the inward pulse and feel it still beating in the outward appearances. But the infinite variety of circumstance which is developed in this externality by the light of the essence glinting in it—this endless material and its organization—this is not the subject matter of philosophy. To touch this at all would be to meddle with things to which philosophy is unsuited; on such topics it may save itself the trouble of giving good advice. Plato might have omitted his recommendation to nurses to keep on the move with infants and to rock them continually in their arms. And Fichte too need not have carried what has been called the "construction" of his passport regulations to such a pitch of perfection as to require suspects not merely to sign their passports but to have their likenesses painted on them. Along such tracks all trace of philosophy is lost, and such super-erudition it can the more readily disclaim since its attitude to this infinite multitude of topics should of course be most liberal. In adopting this attitude, philosophic science shows itself to be poles apart from the hatred with which the folly of superior wisdom regards a vast number of affairs and institutions, a hatred in which pettiness takes the greatest delight because only by venting it does it attain a feeling of its self-hood.

This book, then, containing as it does the science of the state, is to be nothing other than the endeavour to apprehend and portray the state as something inherently rational. As a work of philosophy, it must be poles apart from an attempt to construct a state as it ought to be. The instruction which it may contain cannot consist in teaching the state what it ought to be; it can only show how the state, the ethical universe, is to be understood.

Ἰλοῦ 'Ρόλος ἰλοῦ καὶ τὸ πηλημα
Hic Rhodus, *hic* saltus.

To comprehend what is, this is the task of philosophy, because what is, is reason. Whatever happens, every individual is a child of his time; so philosophy too is its own time apprehended in thoughts. It is just as absurd to fancy that a philosophy can transcend its contemporary world as it is to fancy that an individual can overleap his own age, jump over Rhodes. If his theory really goes beyond the world as it is and builds an ideal one as it ought to be, that world exists indeed, but only in his opinions, an unsubstantial element where anything you please may, in fancy, be built.

With hardly an alteration, the proverb just quoted would run:

Here is the rose, dance thou here.

What lies between reason as self-conscious mind and reason as an actual world before our eyes, what separates the former from the latter and prevents it from finding satisfaction in the latter, is the fetter of some abstraction or other which has not been liberated [and so transformed] into the concept. To recognize reason as the rose in the cross of the present and thereby to enjoy the present, this is the rational insight which reconciles us to the actual, the reconciliation which philosophy affords to those in whom there has once arisen an inner voice bidding them to comprehend, not only to dwell in what is substantive while still retaining subjective freedom, but also to possess subjective freedom while standing not in anything particular and accidental but in what exists absolutely.

It is this too which constitutes the more concrete meaning of what was described above rather abstractly as the unity of form and content; for form in its most concrete signification is reason as speculative knowing, and content is reason as the substantial essence of actuality, whether ethical or natural. The known identity of these two is the philosophical Idea. It is a sheer obstinacy, the obstinacy which does honour to mankind, to refuse to recognize in conviction anything not ratified by thought. This obstinacy is the characteristic of our epoch, besides being the principle peculiar to Protestantism. What Luther initiated as faith in feeling and in the witness of the spirit, is precisely what spirit, since become more mature, has striven to apprehend in the concept in order to free and so to find itself in the world as it exists to-day. The saying has become famous that "a half-philosophy leads away from God"—and it is the same half-philosophy that locates knowledge in an "approximation" to truth—"while true philosophy leads to God"; and the same is true of philosophy and the state. Just as reason is not content with an approximation which, as something "neither cold nor hot," it will "spue out of its mouth," so it is just as little content with the cold despair which submits to the view that in this earthly life things are truly bad or at best only tolerable, though here they cannot be improved and that this is the only reflection which can keep us at peace with the world: There is less chill in the peace with the world which knowledge supplies.

One word more about giving instruction as to what the world ought to be. Philosophy in any case always comes on the scene too late to give it. As the thought of the world, it appears only when actuality is already there cut and dried after its process of formation has been completed. The teaching of the concept, which is also history's inescapable lesson, is that it is only when actuality is mature that the ideal first appears over against the real and that the ideal apprehends this same real world in its substance and builds it up for itself into the shape of an intellectual realm. When philosophy paints its grey in grey, then has a shape of life grown old. By philosophy's grey in grey it cannot be rejuvenated but only understood. The owl of Minerva spreads its wings only with the falling of the dusk.

Introduction

Concept of the Philosophy of Right, of the Will, Freedom, and Right

1. The subject-matter of the philosophical science of right is the Idea of right, i.e., the concept of right together with the actualization of that concept.

2. The science of right is a section of philosophy. Consequently, its task is to develop the Idea—the Idea being the rational factor in any object of study—out of the concept, or, what is the same thing, to look on at the proper immanent development of the thing itself. As a section, it has a definite starting-point, i.e., the result and the truth of what has preceded, and it is what has preceded which constitutes the so-called "proof" of the starting-point. Hence the concept of right, so far as its coming to be is concerned, falls outside the science of right; it is to be taken up here as given and its deduction is presupposed.

3. Right is positive in general (a) when it has the *form* of being valid in a particular state, and this legal authority is the guiding principle

for the knowledge of right in this positive form, i.e., for the science of positive law. *(b)* Right in this positive form acquires a positive element in its *content*

(α) through the particular national character of a people, its stage of historical development, and the whole complex of relations connected with the necessities of nature;

(β) because a system of positive law must necessarily involve the application of the universal concept to particular, externally given, characteristics of objects and cases. This application lies outside speculative thought and the development of the concept, and is the subsumption by the Understanding [of the particular under the universal];

(γ) through the finally detailed provisions requisite for actually pronouncing judgement in court.

4. The basis of right is, in general, mind; its precise place and point of origin is the will. The will is free, so that freedom is both the substance of right and its goal, while the system of right is the realm of freedom made actual, the world of mind brought forth out of itself like a second nature.

FREE WILL, ABSTRACT RIGHT, AND MORALITY

34. The absolutely free will, at the stage when its concept is abstract, has the determinate character of immediacy. Accordingly this stage is its negative actuality, an actuality contrasted with the real world, only an abstractly self-related actuality—the inherently single will of a subject. Pursuant to the moment of the particularity of the will, it has in addition a content consisting of determinate aims and, as exclusive individuality, it has this content at the same time as an external world directly confronting it.

35. The universality of this consciously free will is abstract universality, the self-conscious but otherwise contentless and simple relation of itself to itself in its individuality, and from this point of view the subject is a person. Personality implies that as *this* person: (i) I am completely determined on every side (in my inner caprice, impulse, and desire, as well as by immediate external facts) and so finite, yet (ii) nonetheless I am simply and solely self-relation, and therefore in finitude I know myself as something infinite, universal, and free.

SOURCE: *Philosophy of Right*, pp. 37–39, 73–74. Reprinted by permission of the Clarendon Press, Oxford.

Zusatz. Personality begins not with the subject's mere general consciousness of himself as an ego concretely determined in some way or other, but rather with his consciousness of himself as a completely abstract ego in which every concrete restriction and value is negated and without validity. In personality, therefore, knowledge is knowledge of oneself as an object, but an object raised by thinking to the level of simple infinity and so an object purely self-identical. Individuals and nations have no personality until they have achieved this pure thought and knowledge of themselves. Mind fully explicit differs from the phenomenal mind in this, that at the same level at which the latter is only self-consciousness—a consciousness of self but only one pursuant to the natural will and its still external oppositions—the former has itself, as the abstract and free ego, for its object and aim, and so is personality. End *Zusatz.*

36. (1) Personality essentially involves the capacity for rights and constitutes the concept and the basis (itself abstract) of the system of abstract and therefore formal right. Hence the imperative of right is: "Be a person and respect others as persons."

37. (2) The particularity of the will is a moment in the consciousness of the will as a whole (see Paragraph 34), but it is not yet contained in abstract personality as such. Therefore, it is present at this point, but as still sundered from personality, from the character of freedom, present as desire, need, impulse, casual whim, and so forth. In formal right, therefore, there is no question of particular interests, of my advantage or my welfare, any more than there is of the particular motive behind my volition, of insight and intention.

38. In relation to action in the concrete and to moral and ethical ties, abstract right is, in contrast with the further content which these involve, only a possibility, and to have a right is therefore to have only a permission or a warrant. The unconditional commands of abstract right are restricted, once again because of its abstractness, to the negative: "Do not infringe personality and what personality entails." The result is that there are only prohibitions in the sphere of right, and the positive form of any command in this sphere is based in the last resort, if we examine its ultimate content, on prohibition.

39. (3) As *immediate* individuality, a person in making decisions is related to a world of nature directly confronting him, and thus the personality of the will stands over against this world as something subjective. For personality, however, as inherently infinite and uni-

versal, the restriction of being only subjective is a contradiction and a nullity. Personality is that which struggles to lift itself above this restriction and to give itself reality, or in other words to claim that external world as its own.

40. Right is in the first place the immediate embodiment which freedom gives itself in an immediate way, i.e., *(a)* possession, which is *property*-ownership. Freedom is here the freedom of the abstract will in general or, *eo ipso,* the freedom of a single person related only to himself. *(b)* A person by distinguishing himself from himself relates himself to another person, and it is only as owners that these two persons really exist for each other. Their implicit identity is realized through the transference of property from one to the other in conformity with a common will and without detriment to the rights of either. This is *contract. (c)* The will which is differentiated not in the sense of *(b)* as being contrasted with another person, but in the sense of *(a)* as related to itself, is as a particular will at variance with and opposed to itself as an absolute will. This opposition is wrongdoing and *crime. . . .*

104. Crime, and justice in the form of revenge, display (i) the shape which the will's development takes when it has passed over into the distinction between the universal implicit will and the single will explicitly in opposition to the universal; and (ii) the fact that the universal will, returning into itself through superseding this opposition, has now itself become actual and explicit. In this way, the right, upheld in face of the explicitly independent single will, is and is recognized as actual on the score of its necessity. At the same time, however, this external formation which the will has here is *eo ipso* a step forward in the inner determination of the will by the concept. The will's immanent actualization in accordance with its concept is the process whereby it supersedes its implicit stage and the form of immediacy in which it begins and which is the shape it assumes in abstract right; this means that it first puts itself in the opposition between the implicit universal will and the single explicitly independent will; and then, through the supersession of this opposition (through the negation of the negation), it determines itself in its *existence* as a will, so that it is a free will not only in itself but for itself also, i.e., it determines itself as self-related negativity. Its personality —and in abstract right the will is personality and no more—it now has for its object; the infinite subjectivity of freedom, a subjectivity become explicit in this way, is the principle of the *moral* standpoint.

Zusatz. Let us look back more closely over the moments through which the concept of freedom develops itself from the will's determinate character as originally abstract to its character as self-related, and so at this point to its self-determination as subjectivity. In property this determinate character is the abstract one, "mine," and is therefore found in an external thing. In contract, "mine" is mediated by the wills of the parties and means only something common. In wrong the will of the sphere of right has its abstract character of implicit being or immediacy posited as contingency through the act of a single will, itself a contingent will. At the moral standpoint, the abstract determinacy of the will in the sphere of right has been so far overcome that this contingency itself is, as reflected in upon itself and self-identical, the inward infinite contingency of the will, i.e., its subjectivity. End *Zusatz.*

The Morality of Conscience*

503

The free individual, who, in mere law, counts only as a *person*, is now characterized as a *subject*—a will reflected into itself so that, be its affection what it may, it is distinguished (as existing in it) as *its own* from the existence of freedom in an external thing. Because the affection of the will is thus inwardized, the will is at the same time made a particular, and there arise further particularizations of it and relations of these to one another. This affection is partly the essential and implicit will, the reason of the will, the essential basis of law and moral life; partly it is the existent volition, which is before us and throws itself into actual deeds, and thus comes into relationship with the former. The subjective will is *morally* free, so far as these features are its inward institution, its own, and willed by it. Its utterance in deed with this freedom is an *action*, in the externality of which it only admits as its own, and allows to be imputed to it, so much as it has consciously willed.

This subjective or "moral" freedom is what a European especially calls freedom. In virtue of the right thereto a man must possess a personal knowledge of the distinction between good and evil in general: ethical and religious principles shall not merely lay their claim

SOURCE: *Philosophy of Mind*, pp. 249–253. Reprinted by permission of the Clarendon Press, Oxford.
Moralität.

on him as external laws and precepts of authority to be obeyed, but have their assent, recognition, or even justification in his heart, sentiment, conscience, intelligence, etc. The subjectivity of the will in itself is its supreme aim and absolutely essential to it.

The "moral" must be taken in the wider sense in which it does not signify the morally good merely. In French *le moral* is opposed to *le physique*, and means the mental or intellectual in general. But here the moral signifies volitional mode, so far as it is in the interior of the will in general; it thus includes purpose and intention—and also moral wickedness.

(a) Purpose. *

504

So far as the action comes into immediate touch with *existence*, *my part* in it is to this extent formal, that external existence is also *independent* of the agent. This externally can pervert his action and bring to light something else than lay in it. Now, though any alteration as such, which is set on foot by the subjects' action, is its *deed*, † still the subject does not for that reason recognize it as its *action*, ‡ but only admits as its own that experience in the deed which lay in its knowledge and will, which was its *purpose*. Only for that does it hold itself *responsible*.

(b) Intention and Welfare. §

505

As regards its empirically concrete *content* (1) the action has a variety of particular aspects and connections. In point of *form*, the agent must have known and willed the action in its essential feature, embracing these individual points. This is the right of *intention*. While *purpose* affects only the immediate fact of existence, *intention* regards the underlying essence and aim thereof. (2) The agent has no less the right to see that the particularity of content in the action, in point of its matter, is not something external to him, but is a particularity of his own—that it contains his needs, interests, and aims. These aims, when similarly comprehended in a single aim, as in happiness, constitute his *well-being*. This is the right to well-being. Happiness (good fortune) is distinguished from well-being only in this, that happiness

* *Der Vorsatz.*
† *That.*
‡ *Handlung.*
§ *Die Absicht und das Wohl.*

implies no more than some sort of immediate existence, whereas well-being is regarded as having a moral justification.

506

But the essentiality of the intention is in the first instance the abstract form of generality. Reflection can put in this form this and that particular aspect in the empirically concrete action, thus making it essential to the intention or restricting the intention to it. In this way the supposed essentiality of the intention and the real essentiality of the action may be brought into the greatest contradiction—e.g., a good intention in case of a crime. Similarly well-being is abstract and may be placed in this or that: as appertaining to this single agent, it is always something particular.

(c) Goodness and Wickedness*

507

The truth of these particularities and the concrete unity of their formalism is the content of the universal, essential and actual, will— the law and underlying essence of every phase of volition, the essential and actual good. It is thus the absolute final aim of the world, and *duty* for the agent who *ought* to have *insight* into the *good*, make it his *intention* and bring it about by his activity.

508

But though the good is the universal of will—a universal determined in itself—and thus including in it particularity—still so far as this particularity is in the first instance still abstract, there is no principle at hand to determine it. Such determination therefore starts up also outside that universal; and as heteronomy or determinance of a will which is free and has rights of its own, there awakes here the deepest contradiction. (α) In consequence of the indeterminate determinism of the good, there are always *several sorts* of good and *many kinds of duties*, the variety of which is a dialectic of one against another and brings them into *collision*. At the same time because good is one, they *ought* to stand in harmony; and yet each of them, though it is a particular duty, is as good and as duty absolute. It falls upon the agent to be the dialectic which, superseding this absolute claim of each, concludes such a combination of them as excludes the rest.

* *Das Gute und das Bose.*

509

(β) To the agent, who in his existent sphere of liberty is essentially as a *particular*, his *interest and welfare* must, on account of that existent sphere of liberty, be essentially an aim and therefore a duty. But at the same time in aiming at the good, which is the not-particular but only universal of the will, the particular interest *ought not* to be a constituent motive. On account of this independency of the two principles of action, it is likewise an accident whether they harmonize. And yet they *ought* to harmonize, because the agent, as individual and universal, is always fundamentally one identity.

(γ) But the agent is not only a mere particular in his existence; it is also a form of his existence to be an abstract self-certainty, an abstract reflection of freedom into himself. He is thus distinct from the reason in the will, and capable of making the universal itself a particular and in that way a semblance. The good is thus reduced to the level of a mere "may happen" for the agent, who can therefore decide on something opposite to the good, can be wicked.

510

(δ) The external objectivity, following the distinction which has arisen in the subjective will (§ 503), constitutes a peculiar world of its own—another extreme which stands in no rapport with the internal will-determination. It is thus a matter of chance whether it harmonizes with the subjective aims, whether the good is realized, and the wicked, an aim essentially and actually null, nullified in it: it is no less matter of chance whether the agent finds in it his well-being, and more precisely whether in the world the good agent is happy and the wicked unhappy. But at the same time the world *ought* to allow the good action, the essential thing, to be carried out in it; it *ought* to grant the good agent the satisfaction of his particular interest, and refuse it to the wicked; just as it *ought* also to make the wicked itself null and void.

511

The all-round contradiction, expressed by this repeated *ought*, with its absoluteness which yet at the same time is *not*—contains the most abstract "analysis" of the mind in itself, its deepest descent into itself. The only relation the self-contradictory principles have to one another is in the abstract certainty of self; and for this infinitude of subjectivity the universal will, good, right, and duty, no more exist than not. The subjectivity alone is aware of itself as choosing and deciding. This pure self-certitude, rising to its pitch, appears in the two directly inter-changing forms—of *Conscience* and *Wickedness*. The former is the will of goodness; but a goodness which to this pure subjectivity is the *non-objective*, non-universal, the unutterable; and over which the agent is conscious that *he* in his *individuality* has the decision. Wickedness is the same awareness that the single self possesses the decision, so far as the single self does not merely remain in this abstraction, but takes up the content of a subjective interest contrary to the good.

512

This supreme pitch of the *"phenomenon"* of will—sublimating itself to this absolute vanity—to a goodness, which has no objectivity, but is only sure of itself, and a self-assurance which involves the nullification of the universal—collapses by its own force. Wickedness, as the most intimate reflection of subjectivity itself, in opposition to the objective and universal (which it treats as mere sham) is the same as the good sentiment of abstract goodness, which reserves to the subjectivity the determination thereof: the utterly abstract semblance, the bare perversion and annihilation of itself. The result, the truth of this semblance, is, on its negative side, the absolute nullity of this volition which would fain hold its own against the good, and of the good, which would only be abstract. On the affirmative side, in the notion, this semblance thus collapsing is the same simple universality of the will, which is the good. The subjectivity, in this its *identity* with the good, is only the infinite form, which actualizes and develops it. In this way the standpoint of bare reciprocity between two independent sides—the standpoint of the *ought*, is abandoned, and we have passed into the field of ethical life.

SOCIAL LIFE: FAMILY AND CIVIL SOCIETY

513

The moral life is the perfection of spirit objective—the truth of the subjective and objective spirit itself. The failure of the latter consists —partly in having its freedom *immediately* in reality, in something external therefore, in a thing—partly in the abstract universality of its goodness. The failure of spirit subjective similarly consists in this,

SOURCE: *Philosophy of Mind*, pp. 253–258. Reprinted by permission of the Clarendon Press, Oxford.

that it is, as against the universal, abstractly self-determinant in its inward individuality. When these two imperfections are suppressed, subjective *freedom* exists as the covertly and overtly *universal* rational will, which is sensible of itself and actively disposed in the consciousness of the individual subject, whilst its practical operation and immediate universal *actuality* at the same time exist as moral usage, manner and custom—where self-conscious *liberty* has become *nature*.

514

The consciously free substance, in which the absolute "ought" is no less an "is," has actuality as the spirit of a nation. The abstract disruption of this spirit singles it out into *persons*, whose independence it, however, controls and entirely dominates from within. But the person, as an intelligent being, feels that underlying essence to be his own very being—ceases when so minded to be a mere accident of it—looks upon it as his absolute final aim. In its actuality he sees not less an achieved present, than somewhat he brings about by his action—yet somewhat which without all question *is*. Thus, without any selective reflection, the person performs his duty as *his own* and as something which *is;* and in this necessity *he* has himself and his actual freedom.

515

Because the substance is the absolute unity of individuality and universality of freedom, it follows that the actuality and action of each individual to keep and to take care of his own being, while it is on one hand conditioned by the pre-supposed total in whose complex alone he exists, is on the other a transition into a universal product. The social disposition of the individuals is their sense of the substance, and of the identity of all their interests with the total; and that the other individuals mutually know each other and are actual only in this identity, is confidence (trust)—the genuine ethical temper.

516

The relations between individuals in the several situations to which the substance is particularized form their *ethical duties*. The ethical personality, i.e., the subjectivity which is permeated by the substantial life, is *virtue*. In relation to the bare facts of external being, to *destiny*, virtue does not treat them as a mere negation, and is thus a quiet repose in itself: in relation to substantial objectivity, to the total of ethical actuality, it exists as confidence, as deliberate work for the community, and the capacity of sacrificing self thereto; whilst in relation to the incidental relations of social circumstance, it is in the first instance justice and then benevolence. In the latter sphere, and in its attitude to its own visible being and corporeity, the individuality expresses its special character, temperament, etc., as personal *virtues*.

517

The ethical substance is:

(*a*) As "immediate" or *natural* mind—the *Family*.

(*b*) The "relative" totality of the "relative" relations of the individuals as independent persons to one another in a formal universality—*Civil Society*.

(*c*) The self-conscious substance, as the mind developed to an organic actuality—the *Political Constitution*.

(a) The Family

518

The ethical spirit, in its *immediacy*, contains the *natural* factor that the individual has its substantial existence in its natural universal, i.e., in its kind. This is the sexual tie, elevated, however, to a spiritual significance—the unanimity of love and the temper of trust. In the shape of the family, mind appears as feeling.

519

(1) The physical difference of sex thus appears at the same time as a difference of intellectual and moral type. With their exclusive individualities these personalities combine to form a *single person*: the subjective union of hearts, becoming a "substantial" unity, makes this union an ethical tie—*Marriage*. The "substantial" union of hearts makes marriage an indivisible personal bond—monogamic marriage: the bodily conjunction is a sequel to the moral attachment. A further sequel is community of personal and private interests.

520

(2) By the community in which the various members constituting the family stand in reference to property, that property of the one person (representing the family) acquires an ethical interest, as do also its industry, labour, and care for the future.

521

The ethical principle which is conjoined with the natural generation of the children, and which was assumed to have primary importance in first forming the marriage union, is actually realized in the second or spiritual birth of the children—in educating them to independent personality.

522

(3) The children, thus invested with independence, leave the concrete life and action of the family to which they primarily belong, acquire an existence of their own, destined, however, to found anew such an actual family. Marriage is of course broken up by the *natural* element contained in it, the death of husband and wife; but even their union of hearts, as it is a mere "substantiality" of feeling, contains the germ of liability to chance and decay. In virtue of such fortuitousness, the members of the family take up to each other the status of persons; and it is thus that the family finds introduced into it for the first time the element, originally foreign to it, of *legal* regulation.

(b) Civil Society*

523

As the substance, being an intelligent substance, particularizes itself abstractly into many persons (the family is only a single person), into families or individuals, who exist independent and free, as private persons, it loses its ethical character: for these persons as such have in their consciousness and as their aim not the absolute unity, but their own petty selves and particular interests. Thus arises the system of *atomistic;* by which the substance is reduced to a general system of adjustments to connect self-subsisting extremes and their particular interests. The developed totality of this connective system is the state as civil society, or *state external.*

(a) The System of Wants†

524

(a) The particularity of the persons includes in the first instance their wants. The possibility of satisfying these wants is here laid on the social fabric, the general stock from which all derive their satisfaction. In the condition of things in which this method of satisfaction by indirect adjustment is realized, immediate seizure of external objects as means thereto exists barely or not at all: the objects are

---

* *Die bürgerliche Gesellschaft.*
† *Das System der Bedürfnisse.*

already property. To acquire them is only possible by the interven-
tion, on one hand, of the possessor's will, which as particular has in
view the satisfaction of their variously defined interests; while, on the
other hand, it is conditioned by the ever-continued production of
fresh means of exchange by the exchangers' *own labour.* This instrument, by which the labour of all facilitates satisfaction of wants, constitutes the general stock.

525

(β) The glimmer of universal principle in this particularity of wants
is found in the way intellect creates differences in them, and thus
causes an indefinite multiplication both of wants and of means for
their different phases. Both are thus rendered more and more abstract. This "morcellement" of their content by abstraction gives rise
to the *division of labour.* The habit of this abstraction in enjoyment,
information, learning, and demeanour constitutes training in this
sphere, or nominal culture in general.

526

The labour which thus becomes more abstract tends on one hand
by its uniformity to make labour easier and to increase production—
on another to limit each person to a single kind of technical skill, and
thus produce more unconditional dependence on the social system.
The skill itself becomes in this way mechanical, and gets the capability
of letting the machine take the place of human labour.

527

(γ) But the concrete division of the general stock—which is also a
general business (of the whole society)—into particular masses determined by the factors of the notion—masses each of which possesses
its own basis of subsistence, and a corresponding mode of labour, of
needs, and of means for satisfying them, also of aims and interests,
as well as of mental culture and habit—constitutes the difference of
Estates (orders or ranks). Individuals apportion themselves to these
according to natural talent, skill, option, and accident. As belonging
to such a definite and stable sphere, they have their actual existence,
which as existence is essentially a particular; and in it they have their
social morality, which is *honesty,* their recognition and their *honour.*
  Where civil society, and with it the State, exists, there arise the
several estates in their difference: for the universal substance, as vital,
exists only so far as it organically *particularizes* itself. The history of

constitutions is the history of the growth of these estates, of the legal relationships of individuals to them, and of these estates to one another and to their centre.

528

To the "substantial," natural estate the fruitful soil and ground supply a natural and stable capital; its action gets direction and content through natural features, and its moral life is founded on faith and trust. The second, the "reflected" estate has as its allotment the social capital, the medium created by the action of middlemen, of mere agents, and an ensemble of contingencies, where the individual has to depend on his subjective skill, talent, intelligence, and industry. The third, "thinking" estate has for its business the general interests; like the second it has a subsistence procured by means of its own skill, and like the first a certain subsistence, certain, however, because guaranteed through the whole society.

THE DIALECTIC OF INDUSTRIALIZED SOCIETY

236. The differing interests of producers and consumers may come into collision with each other; and although a fair balance between them on the whole may be brought about automatically, still their adjustment also requires a control which stands above both and is consciously undertaken. The right to the exercise of such control in a single case (e.g., in the fixing of the prices of the commonest necessaries of life) depends on the fact that, by being publicly exposed for sale, goods in absolutely universal daily demand are offered not so much to an individual as such but rather to a universal purchaser, the public; and thus both the defence of the public's right not to be defrauded, and also the management of goods inspection, may lie, as a common concern, with a public authority. But public care and direction are most of all necessary in the case of the larger branches of industry, because these are dependent on conditions abroad and on combinations of distant circumstances which cannot be grasped as a whole by the individuals tied to these industries for their living.

Zusatz. At the other extreme to freedom of trade and commerce in civil society is public organization to provide for everything and de-

SOURCE: *Philosophy of Right*, pp. 147–152. Reprinted by permission of the Clarendon Press, Oxford.

termine everyone's labour—take for example in ancient times the labour on the pyramids and the other huge monuments in Egypt and Asia which were constructed for public ends, and the worker's task was not mediated through his private choice and particular interest. This interest invokes freedom of trade and commerce against control from above; but the more blindly it sinks into self-seeking aims, the more it requires such control to bring it back to the universal. Control is also necessary to diminish the danger of upheavals arising from clashing interests and to abbreviate the period in which their tension should be eased through the working of a necessity of which they themselves know nothing. End *Zusatz*.

237. Now while the possibility of sharing in the general wealth is open to individuals and is assured to them by the public authority, still it is subject to contingencies on the subjective side (quite apart from the fact that this assurance must remain incomplete), and the more it presupposes skill, health, capital, and so forth as its conditions, the more is it so subject.

238. Originally the family is the substantive whole whose function it is to provide for the individual on his particular side by giving him either the means and the skill necessary to enable him to earn his living out of the resources of society, or else subsistence and maintenance in the event of his suffering a disability. But civil society tears the individual from his family ties, estranges the members of the family from one another, and recognizes them as self-subsistent persons. Further, for the paternal soil and the external inorganic resources of nature from which the individual formerly derived his livelihood, it substitutes its own soil and subjects the permanent existence of even the entire family to dependence on itself and to contingency. Thus the individual becomes a son of civil society which has as many claims upon him as he has rights against it.

239. In its character as a universal family, civil society has the right and duty of superintending and influencing education, inasmuch as education bears upon the child's capacity to become a member of society. Society's right here is paramount over the arbitrary and contingent preferences of parents, particularly in cases where education is to be completed not by the parents but by others. To the same end, society must provide public educational facilities so far as is practicable.

240. Similarly, society has the right and duty of acting as trustee to

those whose extravagance destroys the security of their own subsistence or their families'. It must substitute for extravagance the pursuit of the ends of society and the individuals concerned.

241. Not only caprice, however, but also contingencies, physical conditions, and factors grounded in external circumstances may reduce men to poverty. The poor still have the needs common to civil society, and yet since society has withdrawn from them the natural means of acquisition and broken the bond of the family—in the wider sense of the clan—their poverty leaves them more or less deprived of all the advantages of society, of the opportunity of acquiring skill or education of any kind, as well as of the administration of justice, the public health services, and often even of the consolations of religion, and so forth. The public authority takes the place of the family where the poor are concerned in respect not only of their immediate want but also of laziness of disposition, malignity, and the other vices which arise out of their plight and their sense of wrong.

242. Poverty and, in general, the distress of every kind to which every individual is exposed from the start in the cycle of his natural life has a subjective side which demands similarly subjective aid, arising both from the special circumstances of a particular case and also from love and sympathy. This is the place where morality finds plenty to do despite all public organization. Subjective aid, however, both in itself and in its operation, is dependent on contingency and consequently society struggles to make it less necessary, by discovering the general causes of penury and general means of its relief, and by organizing relief accordingly.

Zusatz. Casual almsgiving and casual endowments, e.g., for the burning of lamps before holy images, &c., are supplemented by public almshouses, hospitals, street-lighting, and so forth. There is still quite enough left over and above these things for charity to do on its own account. A false view is implied both when charity insists on having this poor relief reserved solely to private sympathy and the accidental occurrence of knowledge and a charitable disposition, and also when it feels injured or mortified by universal regulations and ordinances which are *obligatory*. Public social conditions are on the contrary to be regarded as all the more perfect the less (in comparison with what is arranged publicly) is left for an individual to do by himself as his private inclination directs. End *Zusatz*.

243. When civil society is in a state of unimpeded activity, it is engaged in expanding internally in population and industry. The amassing of wealth is intensified by generalizing *(a)* the linkage of men by their needs, and *(b)* the methods of preparing and distributing the means to satisfy these needs, because it is from this double process of generalization that the largest profits are derived. That is one side of the picture. The other side is the subdivision and restriction of particular jobs. This results in the dependence and distress of the class tied to work of that sort, and these again entail inability to feel and enjoy the broader freedoms and especially the intellectual benefits of civil society.

244. When the standard of living of a large mass of people falls below a certain subsistence level—a level regulated automatically as the one necessary for a member of the society—and when there is a consequent loss of the sense of right and wrong, of honesty and the self-respect which makes a man insist on maintaining himself by his own work and effort, the result is the creation of a rabble of paupers. At the same time this brings with it, at the other end of the social scale, conditions which greatly facilitate the concentration of disproportionate wealth in a few hands.

245. When the masses begin to decline into poverty, *(a)* the burden of maintaining them at their ordinary standard of living might be directly laid on the wealthier classes, or they might receive the means of livelihood directly from other public sources of wealth (e.g., from the endowments of rich hospitals, monasteries, and other foundations). In either case, however, the needy would receive subsistence directly, not by means of their work, and this would violate the principle of civil society and the feeling of individual independence and self-respect in its individual members. *(b)* As an alternative, they might be given subsistence indirectly through being given work, i.e., the opportunity to work. In this event the volume of production would be increased, but the evil consists precisely in an excess of production and in the lack of a proportionate number of consumers who are themselves also producers, and thus it is simply intensified by both of the methods *(a)* and *(b)* by which it is sought to alleviate it. It hence becomes apparent that despite an excess of wealth, civil society is not rich enough, i.e., its own resources are insufficient to check excessive poverty and the creation of a penurious rabble.

Zusatz. In the example of England we may study these phenomena on a large scale and also in particular the results of poor-rates, immense foundations, unlimited private beneficence, and above all the abolition of the Guild Corporations. In Britain, particularly in Scotland, the most direct measure against poverty and especially against the loss of shame and self-respect—the subjective bases of society—as well as against laziness and extravagance, &c., the begetters of the rabble, has turned out to be to leave the poor to their fate and instruct them to beg in the streets. End *Zusatz.*

246. This inner dialectic of civil society thus drives it—or at any rate drives a specific civil society—to push beyond its own limits and seek markets, and so its necessary means of subsistence, in other lands which are either deficient in the goods it has overproduced, or else generally backward in industry, &c.

247. The principle of family life is dependence on the soil, on land, *terra firma.* Similarly, the natural element for industry, animating its outward movement, is the sea. Since the passion for gain involves risk, industry though bent on gain yet lifts itself above it; instead of remaining rooted to the soil and the limited circle of civil life with its pleasures and desires, it embraces the element of flux, danger, and destruction. Further, the sea is the greatest means of communication, and trade by sea creates commercial connexions between distant countries and so relations involving contractual rights. At the same time, commerce of this kind is the most potent instrument of culture, and through it trade acquires its significance in the history of the world.

Zusatz. Rivers are not natural boundaries of separation, which is what they have been accounted to be in modern times. On the contrary, it is truer to say that they, and the sea likewise, link men together. Horace is wrong when he says:

> *deus abscidit*
> *prudens Oceano dissociabili*
> *terras.* *

---

* *Odes,* I. iii [ll. 21-3, "God of set purpose has sundered the lands by the estranging sea"].

The proof of this lies not merely in the fact that the basins of rivers are inhabited by a single clan or tribe, but also, for example, in the ancient bonds between Greece, Ionia, and Magna Graecia, between Brittany and Britain, between Denmark and Norway, Sweden, Finland, Livonia, &c., bonds, further, which are especially striking in contrast with the comparatively slight intercourse between the inhabitants of the littoral and those of the hinterland. To realize what an instrument of culture lies in the link with the sea, consider countries where industry flourishes and contrast their relation to the sea with that of countries which have eschewed sea-faring and which, like Egypt and India, have become stagnant and sunk in the most frightful and scandalous superstition. Notice also how all great progressive peoples press onward to the sea. End *Zusatz.*

248. This far-flung connecting link affords the means for the colonizing activity—sporadic or systematic—to which the mature civil society is driven and by which it supplies to a part of its population a return to life on the family basis in a new land and so also supplies itself with a new demand and field for its industry.

249. While the public authority must also undertake the higher directive function of providing for the interests which lead beyond the borders of its society (see Paragraph 246), its primary purpose is to actualize and maintain the universal contained within the particularity of civil society, and its control takes the form of an external system and organization for the protection and security of particular ends and interests *en masse*, inasmuch as these interests subsist only in this universal. This universal is immanent in the interests of particularity itself and, in accordance with the Idea, particularity makes it the end and object of its own willing and activity. In this way ethical principles circle back and appear in civil society as a factor immanent in it . . . .

THE STATE AND WORLD HISTORY

Zusatz. The town is the seat of the civil life of business. There reflection arises, turns in upon itself, and pursues its atomizing task; each man maintains himself in and through his relation to others who,

SOURCES: Parts one and three of this selection taken from *Philosophy of Right*, pp. 154–155, 179–185, 208–223. Part two is taken from *Philosophy of Mind*, pp. 263–270. Reprinted by permission of the Clarendon Press, Oxford.

like himself, are persons possessed of rights. The country, on the other hand, is the seat of an ethical life resting on nature and the family. Town and country thus constitute the two moments, still ideal moments, whose true ground is the state, although it is from them that the state springs.

The philosophic proof of the concept of the state is this development of ethical life from its immediate phase through civil society, the phase of division, to the state, which then reveals itself as the true ground of these phases. A proof in philosophic science can only be a development of this kind.

Since the state appears as a result in the advance of the philosophic concept through displaying itself as the true ground [of the earlier phases], that show of mediation is now cancelled and the state has become directly present before us. Actually, therefore, the state as such is not so much the result as the beginning. It is within the state that the family is first developed into civil society, and it is the Idea of the state itself which disrupts itself into these two moments. Through the development of civil society, the substance of ethical life acquires its infinite form, which contains in itself these two moments: (1) infinite differentiation down to the inward experience of independent self-consciousness, and (2) the form of universality involved in education, the form of thought whereby mind is objective and actual to itself as an organic totality in laws and institutions which are its will in terms of thought. End *Zusatz*.

The State

535

The State is the *self-conscious* ethical substance, the unification of the family principle with that of civil society. The same unity, which is in the family as a feeling of love, is its essence, receiving, however, at the same time through the second principle of conscious and spontaneously active volition the *form* of conscious universality. This universal principle, with all its evolution in detail, is the absolute aim and content of the knowing subject, which thus identifies itself in its volition with the system of reasonableness.

536

The state is (α) its inward structure as a self-relating development —constitutional (inner-state) law; (β) a particular individual, and therefore in connection with other particular individuals—international (outer-state) law; (γ) but these particular minds are only stages in the general development of mind in its actuality: universal history.

(α) *Constitutional Law.**

537

The essence of the state is the universal, self-originated, and self-developed—the reasonable spirit of will; but, as self-knowing and self-actualizing, sheer subjectivity, and—as an actuality—one individual. Its *work* generally—in relation to the extreme of individuality as the multitude of individuals—consists in a double function. First it maintains them as persons, thus making right a necessary actuality, then it promotes their welfare, which each originally takes care of for himself, but which has a thoroughly general side; it protects the family and guides civil society. Secondly, it carries back both, and the whole disposition and action of the individual—whose tendency is to become a centre of his own—into the life of the universal substance; and, in this direction, as a free power it interferes with those subordinate spheres and maintains them in substantial immanence.

538

The laws express the special provisions for objective freedom. First, to the immediate agent, his independent self-will and particular interest, they are restrictions. But, secondly, they are an absolute final end and the universal work; hence they are a product of the "functions" of the various orders which parcel themselves more and more out of the general particularizing, and are a fruit of all the acts and private concerns of individuals. Thirdly, they are the substance of the volition of individuals—which volition is thereby free—and of their disposition: being as such exhibited as current usage.

539

As a living mind, the state only is as an organized whole, differentiated into particular agencies, which, proceeding from the one notion (though not known as notion) of the reasonable will, continually produce it as their result. The *constitution* is this articulation or organization of state-power. It provides for the reasonable will—in so far as it is in the individuals only *implicitly* the universal will—coming to a consciousness and an understanding of itself and being *found;* also for that will being put in actuality, through the action of the government

* *Inneres Staatsrecht.*

and its several branches, and not left to perish, but protected both against *their* casual subjectivity and against that of the individuals. The constitution is existent *justice*—the actuality of liberty in the development of all its reasonable provisions.

Liberty and Equality are the simple rubrics into which is frequently concentrated what should form the fundamental principle, the final aim and result of the constitution. However true this is, the defect of these terms is their utter abstractness: if stuck to in this abstract form, they are principles which either prevent the rise of the concreteness of the state, i.e., its articulation into a constitution and a government in general, or destroy them. With the state there arises inequality, the difference of governing powers and of governed, magistracies, authorities, directories, etc. The principle of equality, logically carried out, rejects all differences, and thus allows no sort of political condition to exist. Liberty and equality are indeed the foundation of the state, but as the most abstract also the most superficial, and for that very reason naturally the most familiar. It is important therefore to study them closer.

As regards, first, Equality, the familiar proposition, All men are by nature equal, blunders by confusing the "natural" with the "notion." It ought rather to read: *By nature* men are only unequal. But the *notion* of liberty, as it exists as such, without further specification and development, is abstract subjectivity, as a person capable of property. This single abstract feature of personality constitutes the actual *equality* of human beings. But that this freedom should exist, that it should be *man* (and not as in Greece, Rome, etc., *some* men) that is recognized and legally regarded as a person, is so little *by nature*, that it is rather only a result and product of the consciousness of the deepest principle of mind, and of the universality and expansion of this consciousness. That the citizens are equal before the law contains a great truth, but which so expressed is a tautology: it only states that the legal status in general exists, that the laws rule. But, as regards the concrete, the citizens—besides their personality—are equal before the law only in these points when they are otherwise equal *outside the law.* Only that equality which (in whatever way it be) they, as it happens, otherwise have in property, age, physical strength, talent, skill, etc.—or even in crime, can and ought to make them deserve equal treatment before the law: only it can make them—as regards taxation, military service, eligibility to office, etc.—punishment, etc.—equal in the concrete. The laws themselves, except in so far as they concern that narrow circle of personality, presuppose unequal conditions, and provide for the unequal legal duties and appurtenances resulting therefrom.

As regards Liberty, it is originally taken partly in a negative sense against arbitrary intolerance and lawless treatment, partly in the affirmative sense of subjective freedom; but this freedom is allowed great latitude both as regards the agent's self-will and action for his particular ends, and as regards his claim to have a personal intelligence and a personal share in general affairs. Formerly the legally defined rights, private as well as public rights of a nation, town, etc., were called its "liberties." Really, every genuine law is a liberty: it contains a reasonable principle of objective mind; in other words, it embodies a liberty. Nothing has become, on the contrary, more familiar than the idea that each must *restrict* his liberty in relation to the liberty of others: that the state is a condition of such reciprocal restriction, and that the laws are restrictions. To such habits of mind liberty is viewed as only casual good-pleasure and self-will. Hence it has also been said that "modern" nations are only susceptible of equality, or of equality more than liberty; and that for no other reason than that, with an assumed definition of liberty (chiefly the participation of all in political affairs and actions), it was impossible to make ends meet in actuality—which is at once more reasonable and more powerful than abstract presuppositions. On the contrary, it should be said that it is just the great development and maturity of form in modern states which produces the supreme concrete inequality of individuals in actuality; while, through the deeper reasonableness of laws and the greater stability of the legal state, it gives rise to greater and more stable liberty, which it can without incompatibility allow. Even the superficial distinction of the words liberty and equality points to the fact that the former tends to inequality: whereas, on the contrary, the current notions of liberty only carry us back to equality. But the more we fortify liberty—as security of property, as possibility for each to develop and make the best of his talents and good qualities, the more it gets taken for granted; and then the sense and appreciation of liberty especially turns in a *subjective* direction. By this is meant the liberty to attempt action on every side, and to throw oneself at pleasure in action for particular and for general intellectual interests, the removal of all checks on the individual particularity, as well as the inward liberty in which the subject has principles, has an insight and conviction of his own, and thus gains moral independence. But this liberty itself on one hand implies that supreme differentiation in which men are unequal and make themselves more unequal by education; and on another it only grows up under conditions of that objective liberty, and is and could grow to such height only in modern states. If, with this development of particularity, there be simultaneous and endless increase of the number of wants, and of the difficulty of satisfying them, of the lust of argument and the fancy of detecting faults, with its insatiate vanity, it is all but part of that indiscriminating relaxation of individuality in this sphere which generates all possible complications, and must deal with them as it can. Such a sphere is of course also the field of restrictions, because liberty is there under the taint of natural self-will and self-pleasing, and has therefore to restrict itself: and that, not merely with regard to the naturalness, self-will and self-conceit, of others, but especially and essentially with regard to reasonable liberty.

The term political liberty, however, is often used to mean formal participation in the public affairs of state by the will and action even of those individuals who otherwise find their chief function in the particular aims and business of civil society. And it has in part become usual to give the title constitution only to the side of the state which concerns such participation of these individuals in general affairs, and to regard a state, in which this is not formally done, as a state without a constitution. On this use of the term the only thing to remark is that by constitution must be understood the determination of rights, i.e., of liberties in general, and the organization of the actualization of them; and that political freedom in the above sense can in any case only constitute a part of it. Of it the following paragraphs will speak.

540

The guarantee of a constitution (i.e., the necessity that the laws be reasonable, and their actualization secured) lies in the collective spirit of the nation—especially in the specific way in which it is itself conscious of its reason. (Religion is that consciousness in its absolute substantiality.) But the guarantee lies also at the same time in the actual organization or development of that principle in suitable institutions. The constitution presupposes that consciousness of the collective spirit, and conversely that spirit presupposes the constitution; for the actual spirit only has a definite consciousness of its principles, in so far as it has them actually existent before it.

The question, To whom (to what authority and how organized) belongs the power to make a constitution? is the same as the question, Who has to make the spirit of a nation? Separate our idea of a constitution from that of the collective spirit, as if the latter exists or has existed without a constitution, and your fancy only proves how superficially you have apprehended the nexus between the spirit in its self-consciousness and in its actuality. What is thus called "making" a "constitution," is—just because of this inseparability—a thing that has never happened in history, just as little as the making of a code of laws. A constitution only develops from the national spirit identically with that spirit's own development, and runs through at the same time with it the grades of formation and the alterations required by its concept. It is the indwelling spirit and the history of the nation (and, be it added, the history is only that spirit's history) by which constitutions have been and are made.

541

The really living totality—that which preserves, in other words continually produces the state in general and its constitution, is the *government*. The organization which natural necessity gives is seen in the rise of the family and of the "estates" of civil society. The government is the *universal* part of the constitution, i.e., the part which intentionally aims at preserving those parts, but at the same time gets hold of and carries out those general aims of the whole, which rise above the function of the family and of civil society. The organization of the government is likewise its differentiation into powers, as their peculiarities have a basis in principle; yet without that difference losing touch with the *actual unity* they have in the notion's subjectivity.

As the most obvious categories of the notion are those of *universality* and *individuality*, and their relationship that of *subsumption* of individual under universal, it has come about that in the state the legislative and executive power have been so distinguished as to make the former *exist* apart as the absolute superior, and to subdivide the latter again into administrative (government) power and judicial power, according as the laws are applied to public or private affairs. The *division* of these powers has been treated as *the* condition of political equilibrium, meaning by division their *independence* one of another in existence—subject always, however, to the above-mentioned subsumption of the powers of the individual under the power of the general. The theory of such "division" unmistakably implies the elements of the notion, but so combined by "understanding" as to result in an absurd collocation, instead of the self-redintegration of the living spirit. The one essential canon to make liberty deep and real is to give every business belonging to the general interests of the state a separate organization wherever they are essentially distinct. Such real division must be; for liberty is only deep when it is differentiated in all its fullness and these differences manifested in existence. But to make the business of legislation an independent power—to make it the first power, with the further proviso that all citizens shall have part therein, and the government be merely executive and dependent, presupposes ignorance that the true idea, and therefore the living and spiritual actuality, is the self-redintegrating notion, in other words, the subjectivity which contains in it universality as only one of its moments. (A mistake still greater, if it goes with the fancy that the constitution and the fundamental laws were still one day to make—in a state of society, which includes an already existing development of differences.) Individuality is the first and supreme principle which makes itself felt through the state's organization. Only through the government, and by its embracing in itself the particular businesses (including the abstract legislative business, which taken apart is also particular), is the state *one*. These, as always, are the terms on which the different elements essentially and alone truly stand towards each other in the logic of "reason," as opposed to the external footing they stand on in "understanding," which never gets beyond subsuming the individual and particular under the universal. What disorganizes the unity of logical reason, equally disorganizes actuality.

542

In the government—regarded as organic totality—the sovereign power (principate) is (a) *subjectivity* as the *infinite* self-unity of the notion in its development—the all-sustaining, all-decreeing will of the state, its highest peak and all-pervasive unity. In the perfect form of the state, in which each and every element of the notion has reached free existence, this subjectivity is not a so-called "moral person," or a decree issuing from a majority (forms in which the unity of the decreeing will has not an *actual* existence), but an actual individual—the will of a decreeing individual—*monarchy*. The monarchical constitution is therefore the constitution of developed reason; all other constitutions belong to lower grades of the development and realization of reason. . . .

276. (1) The fundamental characteristic of the state as a political entity is the substantial unity, i.e., the ideality, of its moments. (a) In this unity, the particular powers and their activities are dissolved and yet retained. They are retained, however, only in the sense that their authority is no independent one but only one of the order and

breadth determined by the Idea of the whole; from its might they originate, and they are its flexible limbs while it is their single self.

277. (β) The particular activities and agencies of the state are its essential moments and therefore are proper to *it*. The individual functionaries and agents are attached to their office not on the strength of their immediate personality, but only on the strength of their universal and objective qualities. Hence it is in an external and contingent way that these offices are linked with particular persons, and therefore the functions and powers of the state cannot be private property.

278. These two points (α) and (β) constitute the sovereignty of the state. That is to say, sovereignty depends on the fact that the particular functions and powers of the state are not self-subsistent or firmly grounded either on their own account or in the particular will of the individual functionaries, but have their roots ultimately in the unity of the state as their single self.

Zusatz. This is the sovereignty of the state at home. Sovereignty has another side, i.e., sovereignty *vis-à-vis* foreign states, on which see below.

In feudal times, the state was certainly sovereign *vis-à-vis* other states; at home however, not only was the monarch not sovereign at all, but the state itself was not sovereign either. For one thing, the particular functions and powers of the state and civil society were arranged into independent Corporations and societies, so that the state as a whole was rather an aggregate than an organism; and, for another thing, office was the private property of individuals, and hence what they were to do in their public capacity was left to their own opinion and caprice.

The idealism which constitutes sovereignty is the same characteristic as that in accordance with which the so-called "parts" of an animal organism are not parts but members, moments in an organic whole, whose isolation and independence spell disease. The principle here is the same as that which came before us in the abstract concept of the will as self-related negativity, and therefore as the universality of the will determining itself to individuality and so cancelling all particularity and determinacy, as the absolute self-determining ground of all volition. To understand this, one must have mastered the whole conception of the substance and genuine subjectivity of the concept.

The fact that the sovereignty of the state is the ideality of all particular authorities within it gives rise to the easy and also very common misunderstanding that this ideality is only might and pure arbitrariness while "sovereignty" is a synonym for "despotism." But despotism means any state of affairs where law has disappeared and where the particular will as such, whether of a monarch or a mob (ochlocracy), counts as law or rather takes the place of law; while it is precisely in legal, constitutional, government that sovereignty is to be found as the moment of ideality—the ideality of the particular spheres and functions. That is to say, sovereignty brings it about that each of these spheres is not something independent, self-subsistent in its aims and modes of working, something immersed solely in itself, but that instead, even in these aims and modes of working, each is determined by and dependent on the aim of the whole (the aim which has been denominated in general terms by the rather vague expression "welfare of the state").

This ideality manifests itself in a twofold way:

(i) In times of peace, the particular spheres and functions pursue the path of satisfying their particular aims and minding their own business, and it is in part only by way of the unconscious necessity of the thing that their self-seeking is turned into a contribution to reciprocal support and to the support of the whole. In part, however, it is by the direct influence of higher authority that they are not only continually brought back to the aims of the whole and restricted accordingly, but are also constrained to perform direct services for the support of the whole.

(ii) In a situation of exigency, however, whether in home or foreign affairs, the organism of which these particular spheres are members fuses into the single concept of sovereignty. The sovereign is entrusted with the salvation of the state at the sacrifice of these particular authorities whose powers are valid at other times, and it is then that that ideality comes into its proper actuality (see Paragraph 321).*
End *Zusatz.*

279. (2) Sovereignty, at first simply the universal *thought* of this ideality, comes into *existence* only as subjectivity sure of itself, as the will's abstract and to that extent ungrounded self-determination in which finality of decision is rooted. This is the strictly individual aspect of the state, and in virtue of this alone is the state *one.* The truth

*See below, p. 297.

of subjectivity, however, is attained only in a subject, and the truth of personality only in a person; and in a constitution which has become mature as a realization of rationality, each of the three moments of the concept has its explicitly actual and separate formation. Hence this absolutely decisive moment of the whole is not individuality in general, but a single individual, the monarch.

Zusatz. The immanent development of a science, the derivation of its entire content from the concept in its simplicity (a science otherwise derived, whatever its merit, does not deserve the name of a philosophical science) exhibits this peculiarity, that one and the same concept—the will in this instance—which begins by being abstract (because it is at the beginning), maintains its identity even while it consolidates its specific determinations, and that too solely by its own activity, and in this way gains a concrete content. Hence it is the basic moment of personality, abstract at the start in immediate rights, which has matured itself through its various forms of subjectivity, and now—at the stage of absolute rights, of the state, of the completely concrete objectivity of the will—has become the personality of the state, its certainty of itself. This last reabsorbs all particularity into its single self, cuts short the weighing of pros and cons between which it lets itself oscillate perpetually now this way and now that, and by saying "I will" makes its decision and so inaugurates all activity and actuality.

Further, however, personality, like subjectivity in general, as infinitely self-related, has its truth (to be precise, its most elementary, immediate, truth) only in a person, in a subject existing "for" himself, and what exists "for" itself is just simply a unit. It is only as a person, the monarch, that the personality of the state is actual. Personality expresses the concept as such; but the person enshrines the actuality of the concept, and only when the concept is determined as person is it the Idea or truth. A so-called "artificial person," be it a society, a community, or a family, however inherently concrete it may be, contains personality only abstractly, as one moment of itself. In an "artificial person," personality has not achieved its true mode of existence. The state, however, is precisely this totality in which the moments of the concept have attained the actuality correspondent to their degree of truth. All these categories, both in themselves and in their external formations, have been discussed in the whole course of this treatise. They are repeated here, however, because while their existence in their particular external formations is readily granted, it does not follow at all that they are recognized and apprehended again when they appear in their true place, not isolated, but in their truth as moments of the Idea.

The conception of the monarch is therefore of all conceptions the hardest for ratiocination, i.e., for the method of reflection employed by the Understanding. This method refuses to move beyond isolated categories and hence here again knows only *raisonnement*, finite points of view, and deductive argumentation. Consequently it exhibits the dignity of the monarch as something deduced, not only in its form, but in its essence. The truth is, however, that to be something not deduced but purely self-originating is precisely the conception of monarchy. Akin, then, to this reasoning is the idea of treating the monarch's right as grounded in the authority of God, since it is in its divinity that its unconditional character is contained. We are familiar, however, with the misunderstandings connected with this idea, and it is precisely this "divine" element which it is the task of a philosophic treatment to comprehend.

We may speak of the "sovereignty of the people" in the sense that any people whatever is self-subsistent *vis-à-vis* other peoples, and constitutes a state of its own, like the British people for instance. But the peoples of England, Scotland, or Ireland, or the peoples of Venice, Genoa, Ceylon, &c., are not sovereign peoples at all, now that they have ceased to have rulers or supreme governments of their own.

We may also speak of sovereignty in home affairs residing in the people, provided that we are speaking generally about the whole state and meaning only what was shown above (see Paragraphs 277, 278), namely that it is to the state that sovereignty belongs.

The usual sense, however, in which men have recently begun to speak of the "sovereignty of the people" is that it is something opposed to the sovereignty existent in the monarch. So opposed to the sovereignty of the monarch, the sovereignty of the people is one of the confused notions based on the wild idea of the "people." Taken without its monarch and the articulation of the whole which is the indispensable and direct concomitant of monarchy, the people is a formless mass and no longer a state. It lacks every one of those determinate characteristics—sovereignty, government, judges, magistrates, class-divisions, &c.—which are to be found only in a whole which is inwardly organized. By the very emergence into a people's life of moments of this kind which have a bearing on an organization, on political life, a people ceases to be that indeterminate abstraction which, when represented in a quite general way, is called the "people."

If by "sovereignty of the people" is understood a republican form of government, or to speak more specifically (since under "republic" are comprised all sorts of other mixed forms of government, which are purely empirical, let alone irrelevant in a philosophical treatise) a democratic form, then all that is needed in reply has been said already; and besides, such a notion cannot be further discussed in face of the Idea of the state in its full development.

If the "people" is represented neither as a patriarchal clan, nor as living under the simple conditions which make democracy or aristocracy possible as forms of government, nor as living under some other unorganized and haphazard conditions, but instead as an inwardly developed, genuinely organic, totality, then sovereignty is there as the personality of the whole, and this personality is there, in the real existence adequate to its concept, as the person of the monarch.

At the stage at which constitutions are divided, as above mentioned, into democracy, aristocracy, and monarchy, the point of view taken is that of a still substantial unity, abiding in itself, without having yet embarked on its infinite differentiation and the plumbing of its own depths. At that stage, the moment of the final, self-determining, decision of the will does not come on the scene explicitly in its own proper actuality as an organic moment immanent in the state. None the less, even in those comparatively immature constitutional forms, there must always be individuals at the head. Leaders must either be available already, as they are in monarchies of that type, or, as happens in aristocracies, but more particularly in democracies, they may rise to the top, as statesmen or generals, by chance and in accordance with the particular needs of the hour. This must happen, since everything done and everything actual is inaugurated and brought to completion by the single decisive act of a leader. But comprised in a union of powers which remains undifferentiated, this subjectivity of decision is inevitably either contingent in its origin and appearance, or else is in one way or another subordinate to something else. Hence in such states, the power of the leaders was conditioned, and only in something beyond them could there be found a pure unambiguous decision, a *fatum*, determining affairs from without. As a moment of the Idea, this decision had to come into existence, though rooted in something outside the circle of human freedom with which the state is concerned. Herein lies the origin of the need for deriving the last word on great events and important affairs of state from oracles, a "divine sign" (in the case of Socrates), the entrails of animals, the feeding and flight of birds, &c. It was when men had not yet plumbed the depths of self-consciousness or risen out of their undifferentiated unity of substance to their independence that they lacked strength to look within their own being for the final word.

In the "divine sign" of Socrates we see the will which formerly had simply transferred itself beyond itself now beginning to apply itself to itself and so to recognize its own inward nature. This is the beginning of a self-knowing and so of a genuine freedom. This realized freedom of the Idea consists precisely in giving to each of the moments of rationality its own self-conscious actuality here and now. Hence it is this freedom which makes the ultimate self-determining certitude—the culmination of the concept of the will—the function of a single consciousness. This ultimate self-determination, however, can fall within the sphere of human freedom only in so far as it has the position of a pinnacle, explicitly distinct from, and raised above, all that is particular and conditional, for only so is it actual in a way adequate to its concept. End *Zusatz*.

280. (3) This ultimate self in which the will of the state is concentrated is, when thus taken in abstraction, a single self and therefore is *immediate* individuality. Hence its "natural" character is implied in its very conception. The monarch, therefore, is essentially characterized as *this* individual, in abstraction from all his other characteristics, and *this* individual is raised to the dignity of monarchy in an immediate, natural, fashion, i.e., through his birth in the course of nature.

Zusatz. This transition of the concept of pure self-determination into the immediacy of being and so into the realm of nature is of a purely speculative character, and apprehension of it therefore belongs to logic. Moreover, this transition is on the whole the same as that familiar to us in the nature of willing, and there the process is to translate something from subjectivity (i.e., some purpose held before the mind) into existence. But the proper form of the Idea and of the transition here under consideration is the immediate conversion of the pure self-determination of the will (i.e., of the simple concept itself) into a single and natural existent without the mediation of a particular content (like a purpose in the case of action).

In the so-called "ontological" proof of the existence of God, we have the same conversion of the absolute concept into existence. This conversion has constituted the depth of the Idea in the modern world, although recently it has been declared inconceivable, with the result that knowledge of truth has been renounced, since truth is simply the unity of concept and existence. Since the Understanding has no inner consciousness of this unity and refuses to move beyond the separation of these two moments of the truth, it may perhaps, so far as God is concerned, still permit a "faith" in this unity. But since the idea of the monarch is regarded as being quite familiar to ordinary consciousness, the Understanding clings here all the more tenaciously to its separatism and the conclusions which its astute ratiocination deduces therefrom. As a result, it denies that the moment of ultimate decision in the state is linked implicitly and actually (i.e., in the rational concept) with the immediate birthright of the monarch. Consequently it infers, first, that this link is a matter of accident, and further—since it has claimed that the absolute diversity of these moments is the rational thing—that such a link is irrational, and then there follow the other deductions disruptive of the Idea of the state. End *Zusatz.*

281. Both moments in their undivided unity—*(a)* the will's ultimate ungrounded self, and *(b)* therefore its similarly ungrounded objective existence (existence being the category which is at home in nature) —constitute the Idea of something against which caprice is powerless, the "majesty" of the monarch. In this unity lies the actual unity of the state, and it is only through this, its inward and outward immediacy, that the unity of the state is saved from the risk of being drawn down into the sphere of particularity and its caprices, ends, and opinions, and saved too from the war of factions round the throne and from the enfeeblement and overthrow of the power of the state.

Sovereignty vis-à-vis Foreign States.

321. Sovereignty at home (see Paragraph 278) is this ideality in the sense that the moments of mind and its actuality, the state, have become developed in their necessity and subsist as the organs of the state. Mind in its freedom is an infinitely negative relation to itself and hence its essential character from its own point of view is its singleness, a singleness which has incorporated these subsistent differences into itself and so is a unit, exclusive of other units. So characterized,

the state has individuality, and individuality is in essence an individual, and in the sovereign an actual, immediate individual (see Paragraph 279).

322. Individuality is awareness of one's existence as a unit in sharp distinction from others. It manifests itself here in the state as a relation to other states, each of which is autonomous *vis-à-vis* the others. This autonomy embodies mind's actual awareness of itself as a unit and hence it is the most fundamental freedom which a people possesses as well as its highest dignity.

Zusatz. Those who talk of the "wishes" of a collection of people constituting a more or less autonomous state with its own centre, of its "wishes" to renounce this centre and its autonomy in order to unite with others to form a new whole, have very little knowledge of the nature of a collection or of the feeling of selfhood which a nation possesses in its independence.

Thus the dominion which a state has at its first entry into history is this bare autonomy, even if it be quite abstract and without further inner development. For this reason, to have an individual at its head —a patriarch, a chieftain, &c.—is appropriate to this original appearance of the state. End *Zusatz.*

323. This negative relation of the state to itself is embodied in the world as the relation of one state to another and as if the negative were something external. In the world of existence, therefore, this negative relation has the shape of a happening and an entanglement with chance events coming from without. But in fact this negative relation is that moment in the state which is most supremely its own, the state's actual infinity as the ideality of everything finite within it. It is the moment wherein the substance of the state—i.e., its absolute power against everything individual and particular, against life, property, and their rights, even against societies and associations—makes the nullity of these finite things an accomplished fact and brings it home to consciousness.

324. This destiny whereby the rights and interests of individuals are established as a passing phase, is at the same time the positive moment, i.e., the positing of their absolute, not their contingent and unstable, individuality. This relation and the recognition of it is therefore the individual's substantive duty, the duty to maintain this sub-

stantive individuality, i.e., the independence and sovereignty of the state, at the risk and the sacrifice of property and life, as well as of opinion and everything else naturally comprised in the compass of life.

Zusatz. An entirely distorted account of the demand for this sacrifice results from regarding the state as a mere civil society and from regarding its final end as only the security of individual life and property. This security cannot possibly be obtained by the sacrifice of what is to be secured—on the contrary.

The ethical moment in war is implied in what has been said in this Paragraph. War is not to be regarded as an absolute evil and as a purely external accident, which itself therefore has some accidental cause, be it injustices, the passions of nations or the holders of power, &c., or in short, something or other which ought not to be. It is to what is by nature accidental that accidents happen, and the fate whereby they happen is thus a necessity. Here as elsewhere, the point of view from which things seem pure accidents vanishes if we look at them in the light of the concept and philosophy, because philosophy knows accident for a show and sees in it its essence, necessity. It is necessary that the finite—property and life—should be definitely established as accidental, because accidentality is the concept of the finite. From one point of view this necessity appears in the form of the power of nature, and everything is mortal and transient. But in the ethical substance, the state, nature is robbed of this power, and the necessity is exalted to be the work of freedom, to be something ethical. The transience of the finite becomes a willed passing away, and the negativity lying at the roots of the finite becomes the substantive individuality proper to the ethical substance.

War is the state of affairs which deals in earnest with the vanity of temporal goods and concerns—a vanity at other times a common theme of edifying sermonizing. This is what makes it the moment in which the ideality of the particular attains its right and is actualized. War has the higher significance that by its agency, as I have remarked elsewhere, "the ethical health of peoples is preserved in their indifference to the stabilization of finite institutions; just as the blowing of the winds preserves the sea from the foulness which would be the result of a prolonged calm, so also corruption in nations would be the product of prolonged, let alone 'perpetual' peace." This, however, is said to be only a philosophic idea, or, to use another common expression, a "justification of Providence," and it is maintained that actual wars require some other justification. On this point, see below.

The ideality which is in evidence in war, i.e., in an accidental relation of a state to a foreign state, is the same as the ideality in accordance with which the domestic powers of the state are organic moments in a whole. This fact appears in history in various forms, e.g., successful wars have checked domestic unrest and consolidated the power of the state at home. Other phenomena illustrate the same point: e.g., people unwilling or afraid to tolerate sovereignty at home have been subjugated from abroad, and they have struggled for their independence with the less glory and success the less they have been able previously to organize the powers of the state in home affairs— their freedom has died from the fear of dying; states whose autonomy has been guaranteed not by their armed forces but in other ways (e.g., by their disproportionate smallness in comparison with their neighbours) have been able to subsist with a constitution of their own which by itself would not have assured peace in either home or foreign affairs. End *Zusatz.*

325. Sacrifice on behalf of the individuality of the state is the substantial tie between the state and all its members and so is a universal duty. Since this tie is a *single* aspect of the ideality, as contrasted with the reality, of subsistent particulars, it becomes at the same time a *particular* tie, and those who are in it form a class of their own with the characteristic of courage.

326. The matter at issue in disputes between states may be only one particular aspect of their relation to each other, and it is for such disputes that the particular class devoted to the state's defence is principally appointed. But if the state as such, if its autonomy, is in jeopardy, all its citizens are in duty bound to answer the summons to its defence. If in such circumstances the entire state is under arms and is torn from its domestic life at home to fight abroad, the war of defence turns into a war of conquest.

Zusatz. The armed force of the state becomes a standing army, while its appointment to the particular task of state defence makes it a class. This happens from the same necessity as compels other particular moments, interests, and activities in the state to crystallize into a given status or class, e.g., into the status of marriage or into the business or civil servant class, or into the Estates of the Realm. Ratiocination, running hither and thither from ground to consequent, launches forth into reflections about the relative advantages and disadvantages of standing armies. Opinion readily decides that the latter preponderate, partly because the concept of a thing is harder to grasp than its single and external aspects, but also because particular interests and ends (the expense of a standing army, and its result, higher taxation, &c.) are rated in the consciousness of civil society more highly than what is necessary in and by itself. In this way the latter comes to count only as a means to particular ends. End *Zusatz*.

327. In itself, courage is a *formal* virtue, because (i) it is a display of freedom by radical abstraction from all particular ends, possessions, pleasure, and life; but (ii) this negation is a negation of externalities, and their alienation, the culmination of courage, is not intrinsically of a spiritual *(geistiger)* character; (iii) the courageous man's inner motive need only be some particular reason or other, and even the actual result of what he does need be present solely to the minds of others and not to his own.

328. The intrinsic worth of courage as a disposition of mind is to be found in the genuine, absolute, final end, the sovereignty of the state. The work of courage is to actualize this final end, and the means to this end is the sacrifice of personal actuality. This form of experience thus contains the harshness of extreme contradictions: a self-sacrifice which yet is the real existence of one's freedom; the maximum self-subsistence of individuality, yet only as a cog playing its part in the mechanism of an external organization; absolute obedience, renunciation of personal opinions and reasonings, in fact complete *absence* of mind, coupled with the most intense and comprehensive *presence* of mind and decision in the moment of acting; the most hostile and so most personal action against individuals, coupled with an attitude of complete indifference or even liking towards them as individuals.

Zusatz. To risk one's life is better than merely fearing death, but is still purely negative and so indeterminate and without value in itself. It is the positive aspect, the end and content, which first gives significance to this spiritedness. Robbers and murderers bent on crime as their end, adventurers pursuing ends planned to suit their own whims, &c., these too have spirit enough to risk their lives. The principle of the modern world—thought and the universal—

has given courage a higher form, because its display now seems to be more mechanical, the act not of this particular person, but of a member of a whole. Moreover, it seems to be turned not against single persons, but against a hostile group, and hence personal bravery appears impersonal. It is for this reason that thought has invented the gun, and the invention of this weapon, which has changed the purely personal form of bravery into a more abstract one, is no accident. End *Zusatz.*

329. The state's tendency to look abroad lies in the fact that it is an individual subject. Its relation to other states therefore falls to the power of the crown. Hence it directly devolves on the monarch, and on him alone, to command the armed forces, to conduct foreign affairs through ambassadors, &c., to make war and peace, and to conclude treaties of all kinds.

International Law.

330. International law springs from the relations between autonomous states. It is for this reason that what is absolute in it retains the form of an ought-to-be, since its actuality depends on different wills each of which is sovereign.

331. The nation state is mind in its substantive rationality and immediate actuality and is therefore the absolute power on earth. It follows that every state is sovereign and autonomous against its neighbours. It is entitled in the first place and without qualification to be sovereign from their point of view, i.e., to be recognized by them as sovereign. At the same time, however, this title is purely formal, and the demand for this recognition of the state, merely on the ground that it is a state, is abstract. Whether a state is in fact something absolute depends on its content, i.e., on its constitution and general situation; and recognition, implying as it does an identity of both form and content, is conditional on the neighbouring state's judgement and will.

Zusatz. A state is as little an actual individual without relations to other states (see Paragraph 322) as an individual is actually a person without *rapport* with other persons. The legitimate authority of a state and, more particularly, so far as its foreign relations are concerned, of its monarch also, is partly a purely domestic matter (one state should not meddle with the domestic affairs of another). On the other hand, however, it is no less essential that this authority should receive its full and final legitimation through its recognition by other states, although this recognition requires to be safeguarded by the proviso that where a state is to be recognized by others, it shall likewise recognize them, i.e., respect their autonomy; and so it comes about that they cannot be indifferent to each other's domestic affairs.

The question arises how far a nomadic people, for instance, or any people on a low level of civilization, can be regarded as a state. As once was the case with the Jews and the Mohammedan peoples, religious views may entail an opposition at a higher level between one people and its neighbours and so preclude the general identity which is requisite for recognition. End *Zusatz*.

332. The immediate actuality which any state possesses from the point of view of other states is particularized into a multiplicity of relations which are determined by the arbitrary will of both autonomous parties and which therefore possess the formal nature of contracts pure and simple. The subject-matter of these contracts, however, is infinitely less varied than it is in civil society, because in civil society individuals are reciprocally interdependent in the most numerous respects, while autonomous states are principally wholes whose needs are met within their own borders.

333. The fundamental proposition of international law (i.e., the universal law which ought to be absolutely valid between states, as distinguished from the particular content of positive treaties) is that treaties, as the ground of obligations between states, ought to be kept. But since the sovereignty of a state is the principle of its relations to others, states are to that extent in a state of nature in relation to each other. Their rights are actualized only in their particular wills and not in a universal will with constitutional powers over them. This universal proviso of international law therefore does not go beyond an ought-to-be, and what really happens is that international relations in accordance with treaty alternate with the severance of these relations.

Zusatz. There is no Praetor to judge between states; at best there may be an arbitrator or a mediator, and even he exercises his functions contingently only, i.e., in dependence on the particular wills of the disputants. Kant had an idea for securing "perpetual peace" by a League of Nations to adjust every dispute. It was to be a power recognized by each individual state, and was to arbitrate in all cases of dissension in order to make it impossible for disputants to resort to war in order to settle them. This idea presupposes an accord between states; this would rest on moral or religious or other grounds and considerations, but in any case would always depend ultimately on a particular sovereign will and for that reason would remain infected with contingency. End *Zusatz.*

334. It follows that if states disagree and their particular wills cannot be harmonized, the matter can only be settled by war. A state through its subjects has widespread connexions and many-sided interests, and these may be readily and considerably injured; but it remains inherently indeterminable which of these injuries is to be regarded as a specific breach of treaty or as an injury to the honour and autonomy of the state. The reason for this is that a state may regard its infinity and honour as at stake in each of its concerns, however minute, and it is all the more inclined to susceptibility to injury the more its strong individuality is impelled as a result of long domestic peace to seek and create a sphere of activity abroad.

335. Apart from this, the state is in essence mind and therefore cannot be prepared to stop at just taking notice of an injury *after* it has actually occurred. On the contrary, there arises in addition as a cause of strife the *idea* of such an injury as the idea of a danger *threatening* from another state, together with calculations of degrees of probability on this side and that, guessing at intentions, &c., &c.

336. Since states are related to one another as autonomous entities and so as particular wills on which the very validity of treaties depends, and since the particular will of the whole is in content a will for its own welfare pure and simple, it follows that welfare is the highest law governing the relation of one state to another. This is all the more the case since the Idea of the state is precisely the supersession of the clash between right (i.e., empty abstract freedom) and welfare (i.e., the particular content which fills that void), and it is when states become *concrete* wholes that they first attain recognition (see Paragraph 331).

337. The substantial welfare of the state is its welfare as a particular state in its specific interest and situation and its no less special foreign affairs, including its particular treaty relations. Its government there-

fore is a matter of particular wisdom, not of universal Providence. Similarly, its aim in relation to other states and its principle for justifying wars and treaties is not a universal thought (the thought of philanthropy) but only its actually injured or threatened welfare as something specific and peculiar to itself.

Zusatz. At one time the opposition between morals and politics, and the demand that the latter should conform to the former, were much canvassed. On this point only a general remark is required here. The welfare of a state has claims to recognition totally different from those of the welfare of the individual. The ethical substance, the state, has its determinate being, i.e., its right, directly embodied in something existent, something not abstract but concrete, and the principle of its conduct and behaviour can only be this concrete existent and not one of the many universal thoughts supposed to be moral commands. When politics is alleged to clash with morals and so to be always wrong, the doctrine propounded rests on superficial ideas about morality, the nature of the state, and the state's relation to the moral point of view. End *Zusatz.*

338. The fact that states reciprocally recognize each other as states remains, even in war—the state of affairs when rights disappear and force and chance hold sway—a bond wherein each counts to the rest as something absolute. Hence in war, war itself is characterized as something which ought to pass away. It implies therefore the proviso of the *jus gentium* that the possibility of peace be retained (and so, for example, that envoys must be respected), and, in general, that war be not waged against domestic institutions, against the peace of family and private life, or against persons in their private capacity.

339. Apart from this, relations between states (e.g., in war-time, reciprocal agreements about taking prisoners; in peace-time, concessions of rights to subjects of other states for the purpose of private trade and intercourse, &c.) depend principally upon the customs of nations, custom being the inner universality of behaviour maintained in all circumstances.

340. It is as particular entities that states enter into relations with one another. Hence their relations are on the largest scale a maelstrom of external contingency and the inner particularity of passions, private interests and selfish ends, abilities and virtues, vices, force,

and wrong. All these whirl together, and in their vortex the ethical whole itself, the autonomy of the state, is exposed to contingency. The principles of the national minds are wholly restricted on account of their particularity, for it is in this particularity that, as existent individuals, they have their objective actuality and their self-consciousness. Their deeds and destinies in their reciprocal relations to one another are the dialectic of the finitude of these minds, and out of it arises the universal mind, the mind of the world, free from all restriction, producing itself as that which exercises its right—and its right is the highest right of all—over these finite minds in the "history of the world which is the world's court of judgement."

World History

341. The element in which the universal mind exists in art is intuition and imagery, in religion feeling and representative thinking, in philosophy pure freedom of thought. In world history this element is the actuality of mind in its whole compass of internality and externality alike. World history is a court of judgement because in its absolute universality, the particular—i.e., the *Penates*, civil society, and the national minds in their variegated actuality—is present as only ideal, and the movement of mind in this element is the exhibition of that fact.

342. Further, world history is not the verdict of mere might, i.e., the abstract and non-rational inevitability of a blind destiny. On the contrary, since mind is implicitly and actually reason, and reason is explicit to itself in mind as knowledge, world history is the necessary development, out of the concept of mind's freedom alone, of the moments of reason and so of the self-consciousness and freedom of mind. This development is the interpretation and actualization of the universal mind.

343. The history of mind is its own act. Mind is only what it does, and its act is to make itself the object of its own consciousness. In history its act is to gain consciousness of itself as mind, to apprehend itself in its interpretation of itself to itself. This apprehension is its being and its principle, and the completion of apprehension at one stage is at the same time the rejection of that stage and its transition to a higher. To use abstract phraseology, the mind apprehending this apprehension anew, or in other words returning to itself again out of its rejection of this lower stage of apprehension, is the mind of the stage higher than that on which it stood in its earlier apprehension.

Zusatz. The question of the perfectibility and *Education of the Human Race* arises here. Those who have maintained this perfectibility have divined something of the nature of mind, something of the fact that it is its nature to have γνῶθι σεαυτόν as the law of its being, and, since it apprehends that which it is, to have a form higher than that which constituted its mere being. But to those who reject this doctrine, mind has remained an empty word, and history a superficial play of casual, so-called "merely human," strivings and passions. Even if, in connexion with history, they speak of Providence and the plan of Providence, and so express a faith in a higher power, their ideas remain empty because they expressly declare that for them the plan of Providence is inscrutable and incomprehensible. End *Zusatz.*

344. In the course of this work of the world mind, states, nations, and individuals arise animated by their particular determinate principle which has its interpretation and actuality in their constitutions and in the whole range of their life and condition. While their consciousness is limited to these and they are absorbed in their mundane interests, they are all the time the unconscious tools and organs of the world mind at work within them. The shapes which they take pass away, while the absolute mind prepares and works out its transition to its next higher stage.

345. Justice and virtue, wrongdoing, power and vice, talents and their achievements, passions strong and weak, guilt and innocence, grandeur in individual and national life, autonomy, fortune and misfortune of states and individuals, all these have their specific significance and worth in the field of known actuality; therein they are judged and therein they have their partial, though only partial justification. World-history, however, is above the point of view from which these things matter. Each of its stages is the presence of a necessary moment in the Idea of the world mind, and that moment attains its absolute right in that stage. The nation whose life embodies this moment secures its good fortune and fame, and its deeds are brought to fruition.

346. History is mind clothing itself with the form of events or the immediate actuality of nature. The stages of its development are therefore presented as immediate natural principles. These, because they are natural, are a plurality external to one another, and they are present therefore in such a way that each of them is assigned to one

nation in the external form of its geographical and anthropological conditions.

347. The nation to which is ascribed a moment of the Idea in the form of a natural principle is entrusted with giving complete effect to it in the advance of the self-developing self-consciousness of the world mind. This nation is dominant in world history during this one epoch, and it is only once (see Paragraph 345) that it can make its hour strike. In contrast with this its absolute right of being the vehicle of this present stage in the world mind's development, the minds of the other nations are without rights, and they, along with those whose hour has struck already, count no longer in world history.

Zusatz. The history of a single world-historical nation contains (*a*) the development of its principle from its latent embryonic stage until it blossoms into the self-conscious freedom of ethical life and presses in upon world history; and (*b*) the period of its decline and fall, since it is its decline and fall that signalizes the emergence in it of a higher principle as the pure negative of its own. When this happens, mind passes over into the new principle and so marks out another nation for world-historical significance. After this period, the declining nation has lost the interest of the absolute; it may indeed absorb the higher principle positively and begin building its life on it, but the principle is only like an adopted child, not like a relative to whom its ties are immanently vital and vigorous. Perhaps it loses its autonomy, or it may still exist, or drag out its existence, as a particular state or a group of states and involve itself without rhyme or reason in manifold enterprises at home and battles abroad. End *Zusatz.*

348. All actions, including world-historical actions, culminate with individuals as subjects giving actuality to the substantial. They are the living instruments of what is in substance the deed of the world mind and they are therefore directly at one with that deed though it is concealed from them and is not their aim and object (see Paragraph 344). For the deeds of the world mind, therefore, they receive no honour or thanks either from their contemporaries (see Paragraph 344) or from public opinion in later ages. All that is vouchsafed to them by such opinion is undying fame in respect of the subjective form of their acts.

349. A nation does not begin by being a state. The transition from

a family, a horde, a clan, a multitude, &c., to political conditions is the realization of the Idea in the form of that nation. Without this form, a nation, as an ethical substance—which is what it is implicitly, lacks the objectivity of possessing in its own eyes and in the eyes of others, a universal and universally valid embodiment in laws, i.e., in determinate thoughts, and as a result it fails to secure recognition from others. So long as it lacks objective law and an explicitly established rational constitution, its autonomy is formal only and is not sovereignty.

Zusatz. It would be contrary even to commonplace ideas to call patriarchal conditions a "constitution" or a people under patriarchal government a "state" or its independence "sovereignty." Hence, before history actually begins, we have on the one hand dull innocence, devoid of interest, and, on the other, the courage of revenge and of the struggle for formal recognition (see Paragraph 331). End *Zusatz.*

350. It is the absolute right of the Idea to step into existence in clear-cut laws and objective institutions, beginning with marriage and agriculture, whether this right be actualized in the form of divine legislation and favour, or in the form of force and wrong. This right is the right of heroes to found states.

351. The same consideration justifies civilized nations in regarding and treating as barbarians those who lag behind them in institutions which are the essential moments of the state. Thus a pastoral people may treat hunters as barbarians, and both of these are barbarians from the point of view of agriculturists, &c. The civilized nation is conscious that the rights of barbarians are unequal to its own and treats their autonomy as only a formality.

Zusatz. When wars and disputes arise in such circumstances, the trait which gives them a significance for world history is the fact that they are struggles for recognition in connexion with something of specific intrinsic worth. End *Zusatz.*

352. The concrete Ideas, the minds of the nations, have their truth and their destiny in the concrete Idea which is absolute universality,

i.e., in the world mind. Around its throne they stand as the executors of its actualization and as signs and ornaments of its grandeur. As mind, it is nothing but its active movement towards absolute knowledge of itself and therefore towards freeing its consciousness from the form of natural immediacy and so coming to itself. Therefore the principles of the formations of this self-consciousness in the course of its liberation—the world-historical realms—are four in number.

353. In its *first* and immediate revelation, mind has as its principle the shape of the substantial mind, i.e., the shape of the identity in which individuality is absorbed in its essence and its claims are not explicitly recognized.

The *second* principle is this substantial mind endowed with knowledge so that mind is both the positive content and filling of mind and also the individual self-awareness which is the living form of mind. This principle is ethical individuality as beauty.

The *third* principle is the inward deepening of this individual self-awareness and knowledge until it reaches abstract universality and therefore infinite opposition to the objective world which in the same process has become mind-forsaken.

The principle of the *fourth* formation is the conversion of this opposition so that mind receives in its inner life its truth and concrete essence, while in objectivity it is at home and reconciled with itself. The mind which has thus reverted to the substantiality with which it began is the mind which has returned out of the infinite opposition, and which consequently engenders and knows this its truth as thought and as a world of actual laws.

354. In accordance with these four principles, the world-historical realms are the following: (1) the Oriental, (2) the Greek, (3) the Roman, (4) the Germanic.

355. (1) The Oriental realm.

The world-view of this first realm is substantial, without inward division, and it arises in natural communities patriarchically governed. According to this view, the mundane form of government is theocratic, the ruler is also a high priest or God himself; constitution and legislation are at the same time religion, while religious and moral commands, or usages rather, are at the same time natural and positive law. In the magnificence of this régime as a whole, individual personality loses its rights and perishes; the external world of nature is either directly divine or else God's ornament, and the history of the actual is poetry. Distinctions are developed in customs, government, and state on their many sides, and in default of laws and amidst the simplicity of manners, they become unwieldy, diffuse, and superstitious ceremonies, the accidents of personal power and arbitrary rule, and class differences become crystallized into hereditary castes. Hence in the Oriental state nothing is fixed, and what is stable is fossilized; it lives therefore only in an outward movement which becomes in the end an elemental fury and desolation. Its inner calm is merely the calm of non-political life and immersion in feebleness and exhaustion.

Zusatz. A still substantial, natural, mentality is a moment in the development of the state, and the point at which any state takes this form is the absolute beginning of its history. This has been emphasized and demonstrated with learning and profound insight in connexion with the history of particular states by Dr. Stuhr in his book *Der Untergang der Naturstaaten*—a work in which he leads the way to a rational treatment of constitutional history and of history generally. The principle of subjectivity and self-conscious freedom is there too shown to be the principle of the Germanic people, but the book goes no further than the decline of natural states, and consequently the principle is only brought to the point where it appears either as a restless mobility, as human caprice and corruption, or in its particular form as emotion, and where it has not yet developed to the objectivity of the self-conscious substantiality or to an organized legal system. End *Zusatz.*

356. (2) The Greek realm.

This realm possesses this substantial unity of finite and infinite, but only as a mysterious background, suppressed in dim recesses of the memory, in caves and traditional imagery. This background, reborn out of the mind which differentiates itself to individual mentality, emerges into the daylight of knowing and is tempered and transfigured into beauty and a free and unruffled ethical life. Hence it is in a world of this character that the principle of personal individuality arises, though it is still not self-enclosed but kept in its ideal unity. The result is that the whole is divided into a group of particular national minds; ultimate decision is ascribed not to the subjectivity of explicitly independent self-consciousness but to a power standing above and outside it; on the other hand, the due satisfaction of particular needs is not yet comprised in the sphere of freedom but is relegated exclusively to a class of slaves.

357. (3) The Roman realm.

In this realm, differentiation is carried to its conclusion, and ethical life is sundered without end into the extremes of the private self-consciousness of persons on the one hand, and abstract universality on the other. This opposition begins in the clash between the substantial intuition of an aristocracy and the principle of free personality in democratic form. As the opposition grows, the first of these opponents develops into superstition and the maintenance of heartless self-seeking power, while the second becomes more and more corrupt until it sinks into a rabble. Finally, the whole is dissolved and the result is universal misfortune and the destruction of ethical life. National heroes die away into the unity of a Pantheon, all individuals are degraded to the level of private persons equal with one another, possessed of formal rights, and the only bond left to hold them together is abstract insatiable self-will.

358. (4) The Germanic realm.

Mind and its world are thus both alike lost and plunged in the infinite grief of that fate for which a people, the Jewish people, was held in readiness. Mind is here pressed back upon itself in the extreme of its absolute negativity. This is the absolute turning point; mind rises out of this situation and grasps the infinite positivity of this its inward character, i.e., it grasps the principle of the unity of the divine nature and the human, the reconciliation of objective truth and freedom as the truth and freedom appearing within self-consciousness and subjectivity, a reconciliation with the fulfilment of which the principle of the north, the principle of the Germanic peoples, has been entrusted.

359. This principle is first of all inward and abstract; it exists in feeling as faith, love, and hope, the reconciliation and resolution of all contradiction. It then discloses its content, raising it to become actuality and self-conscious rationality, to become a mundane realm proceeding from the heart, fidelity, and comradeship of free men, a realm which in this its subjectivity is equally a realm of crude individual caprice and barbarous manners. This realm it sets over against a world of beyond, an intellectual realm, whose content is indeed the truth of its (the principle's) mind, but a truth not yet thought and so still veiled in barbarous imagery. This world of beyond, as the power of mind over the mundane heart, acts against the latter as a compulsive and frightful force.

360. These two realms stand distinguished from one another though at the same time they are rooted in a single unity and Idea. Here their distinction is intensified to absolute opposition and a stern

struggle ensues in the course of which the realm of mind lowers the place of its heaven to an earthly here and now, to a common worldliness of fact and idea. The mundane realm, on the other hand, builds up its abstract independence into thought and the principle of rational being and knowing, i.e., into the rationality of right and law. In this way their opposition implicitly loses its marrow and disappears. The realm of fact has discarded its barbarity and unrighteous caprice, while the realm of truth has abandoned the world of beyond and its arbitrary force, so that the true reconciliation which discloses the state as the image and actuality of reason has become objective. In the state, self-consciousness finds in an organic development the actuality of its substantive knowing and willing; in religion, it finds the feeling and the representation of this its own truth as an ideal essentiality; while in philosophic science, it finds the free comprehension and knowledge of this truth as one and the same in its mutually complementary manifestations, i.e., in the state, in nature, and in the ideal world.

VII

Absolute Spirit

Aristotle has said that if man were the highest of beings, if his characteristic act of thinking did not mirror in itself something that transcended both his being and his thought, then the highest science would be the science of politics, which includes the history of political associations. Hegel agrees with Aristotle.[1] His system of philosophy would end with his *Philosophy of Right* and *Philosophy of History* were it not that, like Plato and Aristotle, Philo and Plotinus, St. Augustine and St. Thomas, Maimonides and Spinoza, Hegel is a "God-intoxicated" philosopher.

The whole world of the *Phenomenology of Spirit*, which is thought through systematically in the *Science of Logic*, the *Philosophy of Nature*, and the first two parts of the *Philosophy of Spirit*—the spheres of subjective and objective mind—is comprehended in its ultimate significance only in the culminating philosophic experiences indicated in the concluding paragraphs of the *Encyclopaedia* on Art, Religion, and Philosophy. All that has come before is preparation. In their instinctive pursuit of happiness and true knowledge men make states, and states, in their development, maturity, and decline, make history. To survey thoughtfully the course of history, tracing the rise and fall in time of one great civilization after another, is certainly awe inspiring. All that man has wrought, all his making, behaving, explaining, is part of that history. But in the range of human experiences defined by Hegel, the historical vision is by no means on the highest level, no matter how rich its content. Time "rules" history, measuring its course as it measures all that moves and changes. Yet man, Hegel reminds us, is capable of experiences that cannot be measured by time, experiences that resist, even arrest its passage. These are the experiences of high art, of revealed religion, and of that transcendent form of philosophy which is the synthesis of art and religion.

All human beings can share in the experiences of art, religion, and philosophy, though it takes exceptionally gifted persons—great artists, prophets, philosophers—to provide the occasions. All three, Hegel says, originate in *wonder*, and manifest themselves as a reaching-out for divinity, to see God in art *(aesthesis)*, to enter God's being in religion *(ecstasis)*, and to link the objective and subjective experiences of God, art and religion, in the consummate experience of high philosophy *(sophia)*.

Art uses human rationality or logic to level a place in nature where the divinity, otherwise hidden in it, may be suggestively revealed. That is architecture's *symbolic* temple. When the place is ready, the divinity occupies it in the human shapes of *classical* sculpture. To reveal the inward life of the sculptured divinity of the temple is the work of the *romantic* arts of painting, music, and poetry. The aesthetic experience steadily dematerializes in passing from three-dimensional architecture and sculpture, through two-dimensional painting, which is all colorful surface, to music which has only a temporal dimension. In poetry, time as well as space are stripped away, but only to return for the mind's eye and ear. Epic, lyric, and dramatic poetry give all that architecture, sculpture, painting, and music can give, and much more—especially in tragedy, which, for the Greeks at least, was the highest religious as well as aesthetic experience.

Religion begins and develops within the range of artistic experience; but its culminating effect is ecstatic rather than aesthetic. The God of religion is seen, but in such a way as to draw the beholder out of himself into the divine. The paragraphs of the *Encyclopaedia* on Art and Religion are cryptic in their brevity. One must turn to the *Lectures on Aesthetics, Philosophy of Religion,* and *History of Philosophy* for guidance, explanation, and illustration. There Hegel's main thoughts are supported by a seemingly endless flow of illustrative material. Page after page is filled with factual accounts of the lives of artists, religious leaders and philosophers, together with detailed descriptions or summaries of the contents of literally thousands of works in these fields. In the *Philosophy of Religion,* for example, Hegel pursues the varieties of quasi-religious and religious experience up from the religion of nature, which includes magic and animism as well as the annihilating experience of the ancient Hindu cults, Buddhism, and Lamaism, and the Near Eastern religions of light and impenetrable mystery;

through the religion of spirituality, which includes the sublime monotheism of the Jews, the Greek cult of beauty, and the Roman utilitarian worship; to absolute religion, which for Hegel, is Judaic Christianity, with its Trinity, its incarnation of the *Logos*, and its absorption of the faithful into the life of God. The pace in these lectures is leisurely, even more than in those on the *Philosophy of History*. "Here," remarks Professor Findlay, "Hegel's empirical spirit seems to range in barefoot delight over the broad fields of beauty, worship, and speculation, quite freed from the pinch and creak of the dialectical boots."[2]

In the few brief pages on Philosophy, which close Hegel's *Encyclopaedia*, we find nothing new, but everything bathed in a new light. Hegel says, in effect, that if, having progressed through all its pages, we do not yet know what a "notion" is, it is too late now to be told. Like Plato's lost and storied lecture on the Good, we should be unlikely to comprehend it if we still need to ask what it had to say. Philosophy has the last word on what is, and though it speaks a different language than art and religion, it relates the same message and describes the same content. That content is Truth, "in that supreme sense in which God and God only is the Truth."[3] And what is this God, this Truth? Ask Thales, but "drink deep, or taste not the Pierian Spring."

Notes. Absolute Spirit

1. Indeed, Hegel begins and ends his *Philosophy of Spirit* with Aristotle in mind. In this volume, see pp. 228 and 337–338.
2. J. N. Findlay, *Hegel: A Re-examination* (New York: Humanities Press, 1958), p. 339.
3. *Logic*, Wallace, p. 3.

ABSOLUTE SPIRIT*

553

The *notion* of mind has its *reality* in the mind. If this reality in identity with that notion is to exist as the consciousness of the absolute Idea, then the necessary aspect is that the *implicitly* free intelligence be in its actuality liberated to its notion, if that actuality is to be a vehicle worthy of it. The subjective and the objective spirit are to be looked on as the road on which this aspect of *reality* or existence rises to maturity.

554

The absolute mind, while it is self-centred *identity*, is always also identity returning and ever returned into itself; if it is the one and universal *substance* it is so as a spirit, discerning itself into a self and a consciousness, for which it is as substance. *Religion*, as this supreme sphere may be in general designated, if it has on one hand to be studied as issuing from the subject and having its home in the subject, must no less be regarded as objectively issuing from the absolute spirit which as spirit is in its community.

That here, as always, belief or faith is not opposite to consciousness or knowledge, but rather to a sort of knowledge, and that belief is only a particular form of the latter, has been remarked already. If nowadays there is so little consciousness of God, and his objective essence is so little dwelt upon, while people speak so much more of the subjective side of religion, i.e., of God's indwelling in us, and if that and not the truth as such is called for—in this there is at least the correct principle that God must be apprehended as spirit in his community.

555

The subjective consciousness of the absolute spirit is essentially and intrinsically a process, the immediate and substantial unity of which is the *Belief* in the witness of the spirit as the *certainty* of objective truth. Belief, at once this immediate unity and containing it as a

SOURCE: *Philosophy of Mind*, pp. 292–315. Reprinted by permission of the Clarendon Press, Oxford.
* *Der absolute Geist.*

reciprocal dependence of these different terms, has in *devotion*—the implicit or more explicit act of worship *(cultus)*—passed over into the process of superseding the contrast till it becomes spiritual liberation, the process of authenticating that first certainty by this intermediation, and of gaining its concrete determination, viz., reconciliation, the actuality of the spirit.

Art

556

As this consciousness of the Absolute first takes shape, its immediacy produces the factor of finitude in Art. On one hand, that is, it breaks up into a work of external common existence, into the subject which produces that work, and the subject which contemplates and worships it. But, on the other hand, it is the concrete *contemplation* and mental picture of implicitly absolute spirit as the *Ideal*. In this ideal, or the concrete shape born of the subjective spirit, its natural immediacy, which is only a *sign* of the Idea, is so transfigured by the informing spirit in order to express the Idea, that the figure shows it and it alone—the shape or form of *Beauty*.

557

The sensuous externality attaching to the beautiful—the *form of immediacy* as such—at the same time *qualifies* what it *embodies;* and the God (of art) has with his spirituality at the same time the stamp upon him of a natural medium or natural phase of existence—He contains the so-called *unity* of nature and spirit—i.e., the immediate unity in sensuously intuitional form—hence not the spiritual unity, in which the natural would be put only as "ideal," as superseded in spirit, and the spiritual content would be only in self-relation. It is not the absolute spirit which enters this consciousness. On the subjective side the community has of course an ethical life, aware, as it is, of the spirituality of its essence; and its self-consciousness and actuality are in it elevated to substantial liberty. But with the stigma of immediacy upon it, the subject's liberty is only a *manner of life*, without the infinite self-reflection and the subjective inwardness of *conscience*. These considerations govern in their further developments the devotion and the worship in the religion of fine art.

558

For the objects of contemplation it has to produce, Art requires not only an external given material—(under which are also included sub-

jective images and ideas), but—for the expression of spiritual truth
—must use the given forms of nature with a significance which art
must divine and possess. Of all such forms the human is the highest
and the true, because only in it can the spirit have its corporeity and
thus its visible expression.

This disposes of the principle of the *imitation of nature* in art: a point
on which it is impossible to come to an understanding while a distinction is left thus abstract—in other words, so long as the natural is only
taken in its externality, not as the "characteristic" meaningful nature-
form which is significant of spirit.

559

In such single shapes the "absolute" mind cannot be made explicit;
in and to art therefore the spirit is a limited natural spirit whose
implicit universality, when steps are taken to specify its fullness in
detail, breaks up into an indeterminate polytheism. With the essential
restrictedness of its content, Beauty in general goes no further than
a penetration of the vision or image by the spiritual principle—something formal, so that the thought embodied, or the idea, can, like the
material which it uses to work in, be of the most diverse and unessential kind, and still the work be something beautiful and a work of art.

560

The one-sidedness of *immediacy* on the part of the Ideal involves the
opposite one-sidedness (§556) that it is something *made* by the artist.
The subject or agent is the mere technical activity; and the work of
art is only then an expression of the God, when there is no sign of
subjective particularity in it, and the net power of the indwelling spirit
is conceived and born into the world, without admixture and unspot-
ted from its contingency. But as liberty only goes as far as there is
thought, the action inspired with the fullness of this indwelling
power, the artist's *enthusiasm*, is like a foreign force under which he
is bound and passive; the artistic *production* has on its part the form
of natural immediacy, it belongs to the *genius* or particular endow-
ment of the artist—and is at the same time a labour concerned with
technical cleverness and mechanical externalities. The work of art
therefore is just as much a work due to free option, and the artist is
the master of the God.

561

In work so inspired the reconciliation appears so obvious in its
initial stage that it is without more ado accomplished in the subjective

self-consciousness, which is thus self-confident and of good cheer, without the depth and without the sense of its antithesis to the absolute essence. On the further side of the perfection (which is reached in such reconciliation, in the beauty of *classical art*) lies the art of sublimity—*symbolic art,* in which the figuration suitable to the Idea is not yet found, and the thought as going forth and wrestling with the figure is exhibited as a negative attitude to it, and yet all the while toiling to work itself into it. The meaning or theme thus shows it has not yet reached the infinite form, is not yet known, not yet conscious of itself, as free spirit. The artist's theme only is as the abstract God of pure thought, or an effort towards him—a restless and unappeased effort which throws itself into shape after shape as it vainly tries to find its goal.

562

In another way the Idea and the sensuous figure it appears in are incompatible; and that is where the infinite form, subjectivity, is not as in the first extreme a mere superficial personality, but its inmost depth, and God is known not as only seeking his form or satisfying himself in an external form, but as only finding himself in himself, and thus giving himself his adequate figure in the spiritual world alone. *Romantic art* gives up the task of showing him as such in external form and by means of beauty; it presents him as only condescending to appearance, and the divine as the heart of hearts in an externality from which it always disengages itself. Thus the external can here appear as contingent towards its significance.

The Philosophy of Religion has to discover the logical necessity in the progress by which the Being, known as the Absolute, assumes fuller and firmer features; it has to note to what particular feature the kind of cultus corresponds—and then to see how the secular self-consciousness, the consciousness of what is the supreme vocation of man—in short how the nature of a nation's moral life, the principle of its law, of its actual liberty, and of its constitution, as well as of its art and science, corresponds to the principle which constitutes the substance of a religion. That all these elements of a nation's actuality constitute one systematic totality, that one spirit creates and informs them, is a truth on which follows the further truth that the history of religions coincides with the world-history.

As regards the close connection of art with the various religions it may be specially noted that *beautiful* art can only belong to those religions in which the spiritual principle, though concrete and intrinsically free, is not yet absolute. In religions where the Idea has not

yet been revealed and known in its free character, though the craving
for art is felt in order to bring in imaginative visibility to consciousness the idea of the supreme being, and though art is the sole organ
in which the abstract and radically indistinct content—a mixture from
natural and spiritual sources—can try to bring itself to consciousness;
still this art is defective; its form is defective because its subject-
matter and theme is so—for the defect in subject-matter comes from
the form not being immanent in it. The representations of this symbolic art keep a certain tastelessness and stolidity—for the principle
it embodies is itself stolid and dull, and hence has not the power
freely to transmute the external to significance and shape. Beautiful
art, on the contrary, has for its condition the self-consciousness of the
free spirit—the consciousness that compared with it the natural and
sensuous has no standing of its own; it makes the natural wholly into
the mere expression of spirit, which is thus the inner form that gives
utterance to itself alone.

But with a further and deeper study, we see that the advent of art,
in a religion still in the bonds of sensuous externality, shows that such
religion is on the decline. At the very time it seems to give religion
the supreme glorification, expression, and brilliancy, it has lifted the
religion away over its limitation. In the sublime divinity to which the
work of art succeeds in giving expression the artistic genius and the
spectator find themselves at home, with their personal sense and
feeling, satisfied and liberated: to them the vision and the consciousness of free spirit has been vouchsafed and attained. Beautiful art,
from its side, has thus performed the same service as philosophy: it
has purified the spirit from its thraldom. The older religion in which
the need of fine art, and just for that reason, is first generated, looks
up in its principle to an otherworld which is sensuous and unmean-
ing; the images adored by its devotees are hideous idols regarded as
wonder-working talismans, which point to the unspiritual objectivity
of that other world—and bones perform a similar or even a better
service than such images. But even fine art is only a grade of liberation, not the supreme liberation itself. The genuine objectivity, which
is only in the medium of thought—the medium in which alone the
pure spirit is for the spirit, and where the liberation is accompanied
with reverence—is still absent in the sensuous beauty of the work of
art, still more in that external, unbeautiful sensuousness.

563

Beautiful Art, like the religion peculiar to it, has its future in true
religion. The restricted value of the Idea passes utterly and naturally

into the universality identical with the infinite form; the vision in which consciousness has to depend upon the senses passes into a self-mediating knowledge, into an existence which is itself knowledge —into *revelation*. Thus the principle which gives the Idea its content is that it embody free intelligence, and as "absolute" *spirit it is for the spirit*.

Revealed Religion*

564

It lies essentially in the notion of religion,—the religion, i.e., whose content is absolute mind—that it be *revealed*, and, what is more, revealed *by God*. Knowledge (the principle by which the substance is mind) is a self-determining principle, as infinite self-realizing form— it therefore is manifestation out and out. The spirit is only spirit in so far as it is for the spirit, and in the absolute religion it is the absolute spirit which manifests no longer abstract elements of its being but itself.

The old conception—due to a one-sided survey of human life—of Nemesis, which made the divinity and its action in the world only a levelling power, dashing to pieces everything high and great—was confronted by Plato and Aristotle with the doctrine that God is not *envious*. The same answer may be given to the modern assertions that man cannot ascertain God. These assertions (and more than assertions they are not) are the more illogical, because made within a religion which is expressly called the revealed; for according to them it would rather be the religion in which nothing of God was revealed, in which he had not revealed himself, and those belonging to it would be the heathen "who know not God." If the word "God" is taken in earnest in religion at all, it is from Him, the theme and centre of religion, that the method of divine knowledge may and must begin; and if self-revelation is refused Him, then the only thing left to constitute His nature would be to ascribe envy to Him. But clearly if the word "Mind" is to have a meaning, it implies the revelation of Him.

If we recollect how intricate is the knowledge of the divine Mind for those who are not content with the homely pictures of faith but proceed to thought—at first only "rationalizing" reflection, but afterwards, as in duty bound, to speculative comprehension, it may almost create surprise that so many, and especially theologians whose vocation it is to deal with these Ideas, have tried to get off their task by

* *Die geoffenbarte Religion.*

gladly accepting anything offered them for this behoof. And nothing serves better to shirk it than to adopt the conclusion that man knows nothing of God. To know what God as spirit is—to apprehend this accurately and distinctly in thoughts—requires careful and thorough speculation. It includes, in its forefront, the propositions: God is God only so far as he knows himself; his self-knowledge is, further, a self-consciousness in man and man's knowledge *of* God, which proceeds to man's self-knowledge *in* God. See the profound elucidation of these propositions in the work from which they are taken: *Aphorisms on Knowing and Not-knowing, &c.,* by C.F.G—1.: Berlin 1829.

565

When the immediacy and sensuousness of shape and knowledge is superseded, God is, in point of content, the essential and actual spirit of nature and spirit, while in point of form he is, first of all, presented to consciousness as a mental representation. This quasipictorial representation gives to the elements of his content, on one hand, a separate being, making them presuppositions towards each other, and phenomena which succeed each other; their relationship it makes a series of events according to finite reflective categories. But, on the other hand, such a form of finite representationalism is also overcome and superseded in the faith which realizes one spirit and in the devotion of worship.

566

In this separating, the form parts from the content; and in the form the different functions of the notion part off into special spheres or media, in each of which the absolute spirit exhibits itself; (α) as eternal content, abiding self-centred, even in its manifestation; (β) as distinction of the eternal essence from its manifestation, which by this difference becomes the phenomenal world into which the content enters; (γ) as infinite return, and reconciliation with the eternal being, of the world it gave away—the withdrawal of the eternal from the phenomenal into the unity of its fullness.

567

(α) Under the "moment" of *Universality*—the sphere of pure thought or the abstract medium of essence—it is therefore the absolute spirit, which is at first the presupposed principle, not, however, staying aloof and inert, but (as underlying and essential power under the reflective category of causality) creator of heaven and earth; but yet in this eternal sphere rather only begetting himself as his *son*, with whom, though different, he still remains in original identity—just as, again, this differentiation of him from the universal essence eternally supersedes itself, and, through this mediating of a self-superseding mediation, the first substance is essentially as *concrete individuality* and subjectivity—is the *Spirit*.

568

(β) Under the "moment" of *particularity*, or of judgement, it is this concrete eternal being which is presupposed; its movement is the creation of the phenomenal world. The eternal "moment" of mediation—of the only Son—divides itself to become the antithesis of two separate worlds. On one hand is heaven and earth, the elemental and the concrete nature—on the other hand, standing in action and reaction with such nature, the spirit, which therefore is finite. That spirit, as the extreme of inherent negativity, completes its independence till it becomes wickedness, and is that extreme through its connection with a confronting nature and through its own naturalness thereby investing it. Yet, amid that naturalness, it is, when it thinks, directed towards the Eternal, though, for that reason, only standing to it in an external connection.

569

(γ) Under the "moment" of *individuality* as such—of subjectivity and the notion itself, in which the contrast of universal and particular has sunk to its identical ground, the place of presupposition (1) is taken by the *universal* substance, as actualized out of its abstraction into an *individual* self-consciousness. This individual, who as such is identified with the essence—(in the Eternal sphere he is called the Son)—is transplanted into the world of time, and in him wickedness is implicitly overcome. Further, this immediate, and thus sensuous, existence of the absolutely concrete is represented as putting himself in judgement and expiring in the pain of *negativity*, in which he, as infinite subjectivity, keeps himself unchanged, and thus, as absolute return from that negativity and as universal unity of universal and individual essentiality, has realized his being as the Idea of the spirit, eternal, but alive and present in the world.

570

(2) This objective totality of the divine man who is the Idea of the spirit is the implicit presupposition for the *finite* immediacy of the

single subject. For such subject therefore it is at first an Other, an object of contemplating vision—but the vision of implicit truth, through which witness of the spirit in him, he, on account of his immediate nature, at first characterized himself as nought and wicked. But, secondly, after the example of his truth, by means of the faith on the unity (in that example implicitly accomplished) of universal and individual essence, he is also the movement to throw off his immediacy, his natural man and self-will, to close himself in unity with that example (who is his implicit life) in the pain of negativity, and thus to know himself made one with the essential Being. Thus the Being of Beings (3) through this mediation brings about its own indwelling in self-consciousness, and is the actual presence of the essential and self-subsisting spirit who is all in all.

571

These three syllogisms, constituting the one syllogism of the absolute self-mediation of spirit, are the revelation of that spirit whose life is set out as a cycle of concrete shapes in pictorial thought. From this its separation into parts, with a temporal and external sequence, the unfolding of the mediation contracts itself in the result—where the spirit closes in unity with itself—not merely to the simplicity of faith and devotional feeling, but even to thought. In the immanent simplicity of thought the unfolding still has its expansion, yet is all the while known as an indivisible coherence of the universal, simple, and eternal spirit in itself. In this form of truth, truth is the object of *philosophy*.

If the result—the realized Spirit in which all mediation has superseded itself—is taken in a merely formal, contentless sense, so that the spirit is not also at the same time known as *implicitly* existent and objectively self-unfolding; then that infinite subjectivity is the merely formal self-consciousness, knowing itself in itself as absolute—Irony. Irony, which can make every objective reality nought and vain, is itself the emptiness and vanity, which from itself, and therefore by chance and its own good pleasure, gives itself direction and content, remains master over it, is not bound by it—and, with the assertion that it stands on the very summit of religion and philosophy, falls back rather into the vanity of wilfulness. It is only in proportion as the pure infinite form, the self-centred manifestation, throws off the one-sidedness of subjectivity in which it is the vanity of thought, that it is the free thought which has its infinite characteristic at the same time as essential and actual content, and has that content as an object in which it is also free. Thinking, so far, is only the formal aspect of the absolute content.

Philosophy

572

This science is the unity of Art and Religion. Whereas the vision-method of Art, external in point of form, is but subjective production and shivers the substantial content into many separate shapes, and whereas Religion, with its separation into parts, opens it out in mental picture, and mediates what is thus opened out; Philosophy not merely keeps them together to make a totality, but even unifies them into the simple spiritual vision, and then in that raises them to self-conscious thought. Such consciousness is thus the intelligible unity (cognized by thought) of art and religion, in which the diverse elements in the content are cognized as necessary, and this necessary as free.

573

Philosophy thus characterizes itself as a cognition of the necessity in the content of the absolute picture-idea, as also of the necessity in the two forms—on one hand, immediate vision and its poetry, and the objective and external revelation presupposed by representation—on the other hand, first the subjective retreat inwards, then the subjective movement of faith and its final identification with the presupposed object. This cognition is thus the *recognition* of this content and its form; it is the liberation from the one-sidedness of the forms, elevation of them into the absolute form, which determines itself to content, remains identical with it, and is in that the cognition of that essential and actual necessity. This movement, which philosophy is, finds itself already accomplished, when at the close it seizes its own notion—i.e., only *looks back* on its knowledge.

Here might seem to be the place to treat in a definite exposition of the reciprocal relations of philosophy and religion. The whole question turns entirely on the difference of the forms of speculative thought from the forms of mental representation and "reflecting" intellect. But it is the whole cycle of philosophy, and of logic in particular, which has not merely taught and made known this difference, but also criticized it, or rather has let its nature develop and judge itself by these very categories. It is only by an insight into the value of these forms that the true and needful conviction can be gained, that the content of religion and philosophy is the same—

leaving out, of course, the further details of external nature and finite mind which fall outside the range of religion. But religion is the truth *for all men:* faith rests on the witness of the spirit, which as witnessing is the spirit in man. This witness—the underlying essence in all humanity—takes, when driven to expound itself, its first definite form under those acquired habits of thought which his secular consciousness and intellect otherwise employs. In this way the truth becomes liable to the terms and conditions of finitude in general. This does not prevent the spirit, even in employing sensuous ideas and finite categories of thought, from retaining its content (which as religion is essentially speculative) with a tenacity which does violence to them, and acts *inconsistently* towards them. By this inconsistency it corrects their defects. Nothing easier therefore for the "Rationalist" than to point out contradictions in the exposition of the faith, and then to prepare triumphs for its principle of formal identity. If the spirit yields to this finite reflection, which has usurped the title of reason and philosophy—("Rationalism")—it strips religious truth of its infinity and makes it in reality nought. Religion in that case is completely in the right in guarding herself against such reason and philosophy and treating them as enemies. But it is another thing when religion sets herself against comprehending reason, and against philosophy in general, and specially against a philosophy of which the doctrine is speculative, and so religious. Such an opposition proceeds from failure to appreciate the difference indicated and the value of spiritual form in general, and particularly of the logical form; or, to be more precise still, from failure to note the distinction of the content—which may be in both the same—from these forms. It is on the ground of form that philosophy has been reproached and accused by the religious party; just as conversely its speculative content has brought the same changes upon it from a self-styled philosophy—and from a pithless orthodoxy. It had too little of God in it for the former; too much for the latter.

The charge of *Atheism,* which used often to be brought against philosophy (that it has *too little* of God), has grown rare; the more wide-spread grows the charge of Pantheism, that it has *too much* of him —so much so, that it is treated not so much as an imputation, but as a proved fact, or a sheer fact which needs no proof. Piety, in particular, which with its pious airs of superiority fancies itself free to dispense with proof, goes hand in hand with empty rationalism—which means to be so much opposed to it, though both repose really on the same habit of mind—in the wanton assertion, almost as if it merely mentioned a notorious fact, that Philosophy is the All-one doctrine, or Pantheism. It must be said that it was more to the credit of piety and theology when they accused a philosophical system (e.g., Spino-zism) of Atheism than of Pantheism, though the former imputation at the first glance looks more cruel and invidious. The imputation of Atheism presupposes a definite idea of a full and real God, and arises because the popular idea does not detect in the philosophical notion the peculiar form to which it is attached. Philosophy indeed can recognize its own forms in the categories of religious consciousness, and even its own teaching in the doctrine of religion—which there-fore it does not disparage. But the converse is not true; the religious consciousness does not apply the criticism of thought to itself, does not comprehend itself, and is therefore, as it stands, exclusive. To impute Pantheism instead of Atheism to Philosophy is part of the modern habit of mind—of the new piety and new theology. For them philosophy has too much of God—so much so, that, if we believe them, it asserts that God is everything and everything is God. This new theology, which makes religion only a subjective feeling and denies the knowledge of the divine nature, thus retains nothing more than a God in general without objective characteristics. Without in-terest of its own for the concrete, fulfilled notion of God, it treats it only as an interest which *others* once had, and hence treats what belongs to the doctrine of God's concrete nature as something merely historical. The indeterminate God is to be found in all reli-gions; every kind of piety—that of the Hindu to asses, cows or to dalai-lamas; that of the Egyptians to the ox—is always adoration of an object which, with all its absurdities, also contains the generic abstract, God in General. If this theory needs no more than such a God, so as to find God in everything called religion, it must at least find such a God recognized even in philosophy, and can no longer accuse it of Atheism. The mitigation of the reproach of Atheism into that of Pantheism has its ground therefore in the superficial idea to which this mildness has attenuated and emptied God. As that popular idea clings to its abstract universality, from which all definite quality is excluded, all such definiteness is only the non-divine, the secularity of things, thus left standing in fixed undisturbed substantiality. On such a presupposition, even after philosophy has maintained God's absolute universality, and the consequent untruth of the being of external things, the hearer clings as he did before to his belief that secular things still keep their being, and form all that is definite in the divine universality. He thus changes that universality into what he

calls the pantheistic: *Everything is* (empirical things, without distinction, whether higher or lower in the scale, *are*)—all possess substantiality; and so—thus he understands philosophy—each and every
secular thing is God. It is only his own stupidity, and the falsifications
due to such misconception, which generate the imagination and the
allegation of such pantheism.

But if those who give out that a certain philosophy is Pantheism,
are unable and unwilling to see this—for it is just to see the notion
that they refuse—they should before everything have verified the
alleged fact that *any one philosopher, or any one man,* had really ascribed
substantial or objective and inherent reality to *all* things and regarded them as God—that such an idea had ever come into the head
of anybody but themselves. This allegation I will further elucidate in
this exoteric discussion; and the only way to do so is to set down the
evidence. If we want to take so-called Pantheism in its most poetical,
most sublime, or if you will, its grossest shape, we must, as is well
known, consult the oriental poets; and the most copious delineations
of it are found in Hindu literature. Amongst the abundant resources
open to our disposal on this topic, I select—as the most authentic
statement accessible—the Bhagavat-Gita, and amongst its effusions,
prolix and reiterative *ad nauseam,* some of the most telling passages.
In the 10th Lesson (in Schlegel, p. 162) Krishna says of himself:[*] "I
am the self, seated in the hearts of all beings. I am the beginning and
the middle and the end also of all beings . . . I am the beaming sun
amongst the shining ones, and the moon among the lunar mansions.
. . . Amongst the Vedas I am the Sâma-Veda: I am mind amongst the
senses: I am consciousness in living beings. And I am Sankara (Siva)
among the Rudras . . . Meru among the high-topped mountains
. . . the Himalaya among the firmly-fixed (mountains). . . . Among
beasts I am the lord of beasts. . . . Among letters I am the letter A.
. . . I am the spring among the seasons. . . . I am also that which is
the seed of all things: there is nothing movable or immovable which
can exist without me."

Even in these totally sensuous delineations, Krishna (and we must
not suppose there is, besides Krishna, still God, or a God besides; as
he said before he was Siva, or Indra, so it is afterwards said that
Brahma too is in him) makes himself out to be—not everything, but
only—the most excellent of everything. Everywhere there is a distinc-

---

[*]The citation given by Hegel from Schlegel's translation is here replaced
by the version (in one or two points different) in the *Sacred Books of the East,*
vol. viii.

tion drawn between external, unessential existences, and one essential amongst them, which he is. Even when, at the beginning of the passage, he is said to be the beginning, middle, and end of living things, this totality is distinguished from the living things themselves as single existences. Even such a picture which extends deity far and wide in its existence cannot be called pantheism; we must rather say that in the infinitely multiple empirical world, everything is reduced to a limited number of essential existences, to a polytheism. But even what has been quoted shows that these very substantialities of the externally existent do not retain the independence entitling them to be named Gods; even Siva, Indra, etc., melt into the one Krishna.

This reduction is more expressly made in the following scene (7th Lesson, pp. 7 seqq.). Krishna says: "I am the producer and the destroyer of the whole universe. There is nothing else higher than myself; all this is woven upon me, like numbers of pearls upon a thread. I am the taste in water . . . I am the light of the sun and the moon; I am "Om" in all the Vedas. . . . I am life in all beings. . . . I am the discernment of the discerning ones. . . . I am also the strength of the strong." Then he adds: "The whole universe deluded by these three states of mind developed from the qualities [sc., goodness, passion, darkness] does not know me who am beyond them and inexhaustible: for this delusion of mine [even the Maya is *his*, nothing independent], developed from the qualities is divine and difficult to transcend. Those cross beyond this delusion who resort to me alone." Then the picture gathers itself up in a simple expression: "At the end of many lives, the man possessed of knowledge approaches me, (believing) that Vasudeva is everything. Such a high-souled mind is very hard to find. Those who are deprived of knowledge by various desires approach other divinities. . . Whichever form of deity one worships with faith, from it he obtains the beneficial things he desires really given by me. But the fruit thus obtained by those of little judgement is perishable. . . . The undiscerning ones, not knowing my transcendent and inexhaustible essence, than which there is nothing higher, think me who am unperceived to have become perceptible."

This "All," which Krishna calls himself, is not, any more than the Eleatic One, and the Spinozan Substance, the Everything. This everything, rather, the infinitely manifold sensuous manifold of the finite is in all these pictures, but defined as the "accidental," without essential being of its very own, but having its truth in the substance, the One which, as different from that accidental, is alone the divine and God. Hinduism, however, has the higher conception of Brahma, the pure unity of thought in itself, where the empirical everything of the world, as also those proximate substantialities, called Gods, vanish. On that account Colebrooke and many others have described the Hindu religion as at bottom a Monotheism. That this description is not incorrect is clear from these short citations. But so little concrete is this divine unity—spiritual as its idea of God is—so powerless its grip, so to speak—that Hinduism, with a monstrous inconsistency, is also the maddest of polytheisms. But the idolatry of the wretched Hindu, when he adores the ape, or other creature, is still a long way from that wretched fancy of a Pantheism, to which everything is God, and God everything. Hindu monotheism, moreover, is itself an example how little comes of mere monotheism, if the Idea of God is not deeply determinate in itself. For that unity, if it be intrinsically abstract and therefore empty, tends of itself to let whatever is concrete, outside it—be it as a lot of Gods or as secular, empirical individuals—keep its independence. That pantheism indeed—on the shallow conception of it—might with a show of logic as well be called a monotheism; for if God, as it says, is identical with the world, then as there is only one world there would be in that pantheism only one God. Perhaps the empty numerical unity must be predicated of the world; but such abstract predication of it has no further special interest; on the contrary, a mere numerical unity just means that its *content* is an infinite multeity and variety of finitudes. But it is that delusion with the empty unity, which alone makes possible and induces the wrong idea of pantheism. It is only the picture—floating in the indefinite blue—of the world as *one thing, the all*, that could ever be considered capable of combining with God; only on that assumption could philosophy be supposed to teach that God is the world; for if the world were taken as it is, as everything, as the endless lot of empirical existence, then it would hardly have been even held possible to suppose a pantheism which asserted of such stuff that it is God.

But to go back again to the question of fact. If we want to see the consciousness of the One—not as with the Hindus split between the featureless unity of abstract thought, on one hand, and on the other, the long-winded weary story of its particular detail, but—in its finest purity and sublimity, we must consult the Mohammedans. If, e.g., in the excellent Jelaleddin-Rumi in particular, we find the unity of the soul with the One set forth, and that unity described as love, this spiritual unity is an exaltation above the finite and vulgar, a transfiguration of the natural and the spiritual, in which the externalism and transitoriness of immediate nature, and of empirical secular spirit, is discarded and absorbed.*

*In order to give a clearer impression of it, I cannot refrain from quoting a few passages, which may at the same time give some indication of the marvellous skill of Rückert, from whom they are taken, as a translator. [For Rückert's verses a version is here substituted in which I have been kindly helped by Miss May Kendall.]

III

I saw but One through all heaven's starry spaces gleaming:
  I saw but One in all sea billows wildly streaming.
I looked into the heart, a waste of worlds, a sea,—
  I saw a thousand dreams,—yet One amid all dreaming.
And earth, air, water, fire, when thy decree is given,
  Are molten into One: against thee none hath striven.
There is no living heart but beats unfailingly
  In the one song of praise to thee, from earth and heaven.

V

As one ray of thy light appears the noonday sun,
But yet thy light and mine eternally are one.
As dust beneath thy feet the heaven that rolls on high:
Yet only one, and one for ever, thou and I.
The dust may turn to heaven, and heaven to dust decay;
Yet art thou one with me, and shalt be one for aye.
How may the words of life that fill heaven's utmost part
Rest in the narrow casket of one poor human heart?
How can the sun's own rays, a fairer gleam to fling,
Hide in a lowly husk, the jewel's covering?
How may the rose-grove all its glorious bloom unfold,
Drinking in mire and slime, and feeding on the mould?
How can the darksome shell that sips the salt sea stream
Fashion a shining pearl, the sunlight's joyous beam?
Oh, heart! should warm winds fan thee, should'st thou floods endure,
One element are wind and flood; but be thou pure.

IX

I'll tell thee how from out the dust God moulded man,—
Because the breath of Love He breathed into his clay:
I'll tell thee why the spheres their whirling paths began,—
They mirror to God's throne Love's glory day by day:
I'll tell thee why the morning winds blow o'er the grove,—
It is to bid Love's roses bloom abundantly:
I'll tell thee why the night broods deep the earth above,—
Love's bridal tent to deck with sacred canopy:
All riddles of the earth dost thou desire to prove?—
To every earthly riddle is Love alone the key.

XV

Life shrinks from Death in woe and fear,
  Though Death ends well Life's bitter need:
So shrinks the heart when Love draws near,
  As though 'twere Death in very deed:

I refrain from accumulating further examples of the religious and poetic conceptions which it is customary to call pantheistic. Of the philosophies to which that name is given, the Eleatic, or Spinozist, it has been remarked earlier (§ 50, note) that so far are they from identifying God with the world and making him finite, that in these systems this "everything" has no truth, and that we should rather call them monotheistic, or, in relation to the popular idea of the world, acosmical. They are most accurately called systems which apprehend the Absolute only as substance. Of the oriental, especially the Mohammedan, modes of envisaging God, we may rather say that they represent the Absolute as the utterly universal genus which dwells in the species or existences, but dwells so potently that these existences have no actual reality. The fault of all these modes of thought and systems is that they stop short of defining substance as subject and as mind.

These systems and modes of pictorial conception originate from the one need common to all philosophies and all religions of getting an idea of God, and, secondly, of the relationship of God and the world. (In philosophy it is specially made out that the determination

---

For wheresoever Love finds room,
   There Self, the sullen tyrant, dies.
So let him perish in the gloom,—
   Thou to the dawn of freedom rise.

In this poetry, which soars over all that is external and sensuous, who would recognize the prosaic ideas current about so-called pantheism—ideas which let the divine sink to the external and the sensuous? The copious extracts which Tholuck, in his work *Anthology from the Eastern Mystics*, gives us from the poems of Jelaleddin and others, are made from the very point of view now under discussion. In his Introduction, Herr Tholuck proves how profoundly his soul has caught the note of mysticism; and there, too, he points out the characteristic traits of its oriental phase, in distinction from that of the West and Christendom. With all their divergence, however, they have in common the mystical character. The conjunction of Mysticism with so-called Pantheism, as he says (p. 33), implies that inward quickening of soul and spirit which inevitably tends to annihilate that external *Everything*, which Pantheism is usually held to adore. But beyond that, Herr Tholuck leaves matters standing at the usual indistinct conception of Pantheism; a profounder discussion of it would have had, for the author's emotional Christianity, no direct interest; but we see that personally he is carried away by remarkable enthusiasm for a mysticism which, in the ordinary phrase, entirely deserves the epithet Pantheistic. Where, however, he tries philosophising (p. 12), he does not get beyond the standpoint of the "rationalist" metaphysic with its uncritical categories.

of God's nature determines his relations with the world.) The "reflective" understanding begins by rejecting all systems and modes of conception, which, whether they spring from heart, imagination or speculation, express the interconnection of God and the world: and in order to have God pure in faith or consciousness, he is as essence parted from appearance, as infinite from the finite. But, after this partition, the conviction arises also that the appearance has a relation to the essence, the finite to the infinite, and so on: and thus arises the question of reflection as to the nature of this relation. It is in the reflective form that the whole difficulty of the affair lies, and that causes this relation to be called incomprehensible by the agnostic. The close of philosophy is not the place, even in a general exoteric discussion, to waste a word on what a "notion" means. But as the view taken of this relation is closely connected with the view taken of philosophy generally and with all imputations against it, we may still add the remark that though philosophy certainly has to do with unity in general, it is not, however, with abstract unity, mere identity, and the empty absolute, but with concrete unity (the notion), and that in its whole course it has to do with nothing else—that each step in its advance is a peculiar term or phase of this concrete unity, and that the deepest and last expression of unity is the unity of absolute mind itself. Would-be judges and critics of philosophy might be recommended to familiarize themselves with these phases of unity and to take the trouble to get acquainted with them, at least to know so much that of these terms there are a great many, and that amongst them there is great variety. But they show so little acquaintance with them —and still less take trouble about it—that, when they hear of unity —and relation *ipso facto* implies unity—they rather stick fast at quite abstract indeterminate unity, and lose sight of the chief point of interest—the special mode in which the unity is qualified. Hence all they can say about philosophy is that dry identity is its principle and result, and that it is the system of identity. Sticking fast to the undigested thought of identity, they have laid hands on, not the concrete unity, the notion and content of philosophy, but rather its reverse. In the philosophical field they proceed, as in the physical field the physicist; who also is well aware that he has before him a variety of sensuous properties and matters—or usually matters alone (for the properties get transformed into matters also for the physicist)—and that these matters (elements) *also* stand in *relation* to one another. But the question is, Of what kind is this relation? Every peculiarity and the whole difference of natural things, inorganic and living, depend solely on the different modes of this unity. But instead of ascertaining these different modes, the ordinary physicist (chemist included) takes up only one, the most external and the worst, viz., *composition*, applies only it in the whole range of natural structures, which he thus renders for ever inexplicable.

The aforesaid shallow pantheism is an equally obvious inference from this shallow identity. All that those who employ this invention of their own to accuse philosophy gather from the study of God's *relation* to the world is that the one, but only the one factor of this category of relation—and that the factor of indeterminateness—is identity. Thereupon they stick fast in this half-perception, and assert —falsely as a fact—that philosophy teaches the identity of God and the world. And as in their judgement either of the two—the world as much as God—has the same solid substantiality as the other, they infer that in the philosophic Idea God is *composed* of God and the world. Such then is the idea they form of pantheism, and which they ascribe to philosophy. Unaccustomed in their own thinking and apprehending of thoughts to go beyond such categories, they import them into philosophy, where they are utterly unknown; they thus infect it with the disease against which they subsequently raise an outcry. If any difficulty emerge in comprehending God's relation to the world, they at once and very easily escape it by admitting that this relation contains for them an inexplicable contradiction; and that hence, they must stop at the vague conception of such relation, perhaps under the more familiar names of, e.g., omnipresence, providence, etc. Faith in their use of the term means no more than a refusal to define the conception, or to enter on a closer discussion of the problem. That men and classes of untrained intellect are satisfied with such indefiniteness, is what one expects; but when a trained intellect and an interest for reflective study is satisfied, in matters admitted to be of superior, if not even of supreme interest, with indefinite ideas, it is hard to decide whether the thinker is really in earnest with the subject. But if those who cling to this crude "rationalism" were in earnest, e.g., with God's omnipresence, so far as to realize their faith thereon in a definite mental idea, in what difficulties would they be involved by their belief in the true reality of the things of sense! They would hardly like, as Epicurus does, to let God dwell in the interspaces of things, i.e., in the pores of the physicists—said pores being the negative, something supposed to exist *beside* the material reality. This very "Beside" would give their pantheism its spatiality—their everything, conceived as the mutual exclusion of parts in space. But in ascribing to God, in his relation to the world, an action on and in the space thus filled on the world and in it, they would endlessly split up the divine actuality into infinite materiality. They would really thus have the misconception they call pantheism or all-one-doctrine, only as the necessary sequel of their misconceptions of God and the world. But to put that sort of thing, this stale gossip of oneness or identity, on the shoulders of philosophy, shows such recklessness about justice and truth that it can only be explained through the difficulty of getting into the head thoughts and notions, i.e., not abstract unity, but the many-shaped modes specified. If statements as to facts are put forward, and the facts in question are thoughts and notions, it is indispensable to get hold of their meaning. But even the fulfilment of this requirement has been rendered superfluous, now that it has long been a foregone conclusion that philosophy is pantheism, a system of identity, an All-one doctrine, and that the person therefore who might be unaware of this fact is treated either as merely unaware of a matter of common notoriety, or as prevaricating for a purpose. On account of this chorus of assertions, then, I have believed myself obliged to speak at more length and exoterically on the outward and inward untruth of this alleged fact; for exoteric discussion is the only method available in dealing with the external apprehension of notions as mere facts—by which notions are perverted into their opposite. The esoteric study of God and identity, as of cognitions, and notions, is philosophy itself.

574

This notion of philosophy is the self-thinking Idea, the truth aware of itself—the logical system, but with the signification that it is universality approved and certified in concrete content as in its actuality. In this way the science has gone back to its beginning; its result is the logical system but as a spiritual principle, out of the presupposing judgement, in which the notion was only implicit and the beginning an immediate—and thus out of the *appearance* which it had there—it has risen into its pure principle and thus also into its proper medium.

575

It is this appearing which originally gives the motive of the further development. The first appearance is formed by the syllogism, which is based on the Logical system as starting-point, with Nature for the middle term which couples the Mind with it. The Logical principle turns to Nature and Nature to Mind. Nature, standing between the

Mind and its essence, sunders itself, not indeed to extremes of finite abstraction, nor itself to something away from them and independent —which, as other than they, only serves as a link between them: for the syllogism is *in the Idea* and Nature is essentially defined as a transition-point and negative factor, and as implicitly the Idea. Still the mediation of the notion has the external form of *transition*, and the science of Nature presents itself as the course of necessity, so that it is only in the one extreme that the liberty of the notion is explicit as a self-amalgamation.

576

In the second syllogism this appearance is so far superseded, that that syllogism is the standpoint of the Mind itself, which—as the mediating agent in the process—presupposes Nature and couples it with the Logical principle. It is the syllogism where Mind reflects on itself in the Idea: philosophy appears as a subjective cognition, of which liberty is the aim, and which is itself the way to produce it.

577

The third syllogism is the Idea of philosophy, which has self-knowing reason, the absolutely universal, for its middle term: a middle, which divides itself into Mind and Nature, making the former its presupposition, as process of the Idea's subjective activity, and the latter its universal extreme, as process of the objectively and implicitly existing Idea. The self-judging of the Idea into its two appearances (§§ 575, 576) characterizes both as its (the self-knowing reason's) manifestations: and in it there is a unification of the two aspects —it is the nature of the fact, the notion, which causes the movement and development, yet this same movement is equally the action of cognition. The eternal Idea, in full fruition of its essence, eternally sets itself to work, engenders and enjoys itself as absolute Mind.

'Η δὲ νόησις ἡ καθ' αὑτὴν τοῦ καθ' αὑτὸ ἀρίστου, καὶ ἡ μάλιστα τοῦ μάλιστα. Αὑτὸν δὲ νοεῖ ὁ νοῦς κατὰ μετάληψιν τοῦ νοητοῦ· νοητὸς γὰρ γίγνεται θιγγάνων καὶ νοῶν, ὥστε ταὐτὸν νοῦς καὶ νοητόν. Τὸ γὰρ δεκτικὸν τοῦ νοητοῦ καὶ τῆς οὐσίας νοῦς. Ἐνεργεῖ δὲ ἔχων. "Ωστ' ἐκεῖνο μᾶλλον τούτου ὃ δοκεῖ ὁ νοῦς θεῖον ἔχειν, καὶ ἡ θεωρία τὸ ἥδιστον καὶ ἄριστον. Εἰ οὖν οὕτως εὖ ἔχει, ὡς ἡμεῖς ποτέ, ὁ θεὸς ἀεί, θαυμαστόν· εἰ δὲ μᾶλλον, ἔτι θαυμασιώτερον. "Εχει δὲ ὡδί. Καὶ ζωὴ δέ γε ὑπάρχει· ἡ γὰρ νοῦ ἐνέργεια ζωή, ἐκεῖνος δὲ ἡ ἐνέργεια·

ἐνέργεια δὲ ἡ καθ' αὑτὴν ἐκείνου ζωὴ ἀρίστη καὶ ἀΐδιος. Φαμὲν δὲ τὸν θεὸν εἶναι ζῷον ἀΐδιον ἄριστον, ὥστε ζωὴ καὶ αἰὼν συνεχὴς καὶ ἀΐδιος ὑπάρχει τῷ θεῷ· τοῦτο γὰρ ὁ θεός.

(Arist. Met. xii. 7.)

Annotated Bibliography

Works of Georg Wilhelm Friedrich Hegel in English Translation Not Listed under Abbreviations

On Art, Religion, Philosophy. Introductory Lectures to the Realm of Absolute Spirit. Edited and introduced by J. Glenn Gray. New York: Harper Torchbooks, 1970. Hegel's Introductions to his lectures on the philosophy of art, religion, and history of philosophy.

Early Theological Writings. Translated by T. M. Knox. Introduction and Fragments translated by Richard Kroner. Philadelphia: University of Pennsylvania Press, 1971. Published first by The University of Chicago Press, 1948, and reissued by Harper Torchbooks, 1961.

Hegel's Lectures on the History of Philosophy. Translated by E. S. Haldane and Frances H. Simson. 3 vols. New York: Humanities Press, 1892–1896. Another translation of the Introduction to Hegel's lectures of 1825–1826 appears in Quentin Lauer's *Hegel's Idea of Philosophy.* New York: Fordham University Press, 1971.

Hegel's Political Writings. Translated by T. M. Knox. Introduced by Z. A. Pelczynski. Oxford: At The Clarendon Press, 1964. The essays are (1) "The German Constitution"; (2) "On the Recent Domestic Affairs of Wurtemberg, especially on the Inadequacy of the Municipal Constitution"; (3) "Proceedings of the Wurtemberg Estates"; and (4) "The English Reform Bill."

Hegel's Science of Logic. Translated by W. H. Johnston and L. G. Struthers. 2 vols. New York: Macmillan, 1929.

[*Lectures on*] *The Philosophy of Fine Art.* Translated and edited by F.P.B.

Osmaston. 4 vols. London: G. Bell and Sons, 1920. Also translated by T. M. Knox. 2 vols. Oxford: Clarendon Press, 1975. Part of this translation appears in Frederick G. Weiss, ed., "Hegel in Comparative Literature," *Review of National Literatures* (St. John's University Press), 1:2 (1970). See also *Hegel on Tragedy*. Edited and introduced by Anne and Henry Paolucci. New York: Doubleday Anchor Books, 1962. Reprinted by Harper & Row, 1975.

[*Lectures on*] *The Philosophy of History*. Prefaces by Charles Hegel and the translator J. Sibree. Introduced by Carl J. Friedrich. New York: Dover, 1956. There have been many reprints of this translation which first appeared in 1857. Another translation of the Introduction to these lectures is *Reason in History*. Translated and introduced by Robert S. Hartman. Indianapolis: Bobbs-Merrill, 1953.

Lectures on the Philosophy of Religion, Together with a Work on the Proofs of the Existence of God. Translated by E. B. Speirs and J. B. Sanderson. 3 vols. London: Routledge & Kegan Paul, 1895.

The Phenomenology of Mind. Translated by J. B. Baillie. Paperback ed. New York: Harper Torchbooks, 1967. Another translation of the Preface to the *Phenomenology* appears in Walter Kaufmann's *Hegel: Texts and Commentary*. New York: Doubleday Anchor Books, 1966. A new translation by Kenley Dove of the Introduction to the *Phenomenology* appears in Martin Heidegger's *Hegel's Concept of Experience*. New York: Harper & Row, 1970.

Introductions and General Commentaries

Findlay, J. N. *Hegel: A Re-examination*. New York: Humanities Press, 1958. Reprinted by Collier Books, 1962. The book most responsible for the rebirth of Hegel scholarship in the English-speaking world. A paragraph-by-paragraph exposition of the system especially valuable for its treatment of the Logic and Philosophy of Nature.

Caird, Edward. *Hegel*. London: William Blackwood & Sons, 1883. Reprinted by Archon Books, 1968. The best brief treatment of Hegel's life and thought for nearly a century, by a British Hegelian.

Marcuse, Herbert. *Reason and Revolution: Hegel and the Rise of Social Theory*. New York: Oxford University Press, 1941. 2d ed. Humanities Press, 1954. Reprinted by Beacon Press, 1960. One of the fairest, most erudite, and comprehensive expositions of Hegel's thought by a Marxist.

Mure, G.R.G. *The Philosophy of Hegel.* London: Oxford University Press, 1965. An appreciative but not uncritical account of Hegel's thought. The best brief study of Hegel since that of Edward Caird.

Rosen, Stanley. *G. W. F. Hegel: An Introduction to the Science of Wisdom.* New Haven: Yale University Press, 1974. A valuable study of Hegel's thought in terms of its origins in the history of philosophy.

Stace, W. T. *The Philosophy of Hegel: A Systematic Exposition.* London: Macmillan, 1924. Reprinted by Dover, 1955. A simplified exposition for the beginner focusing on the *Encyclopaedia.*

Soll, Ivan. *An Introduction to Hegel's Metaphysics.* Chicago: University of Chicago Press, 1969. A brief and useful discussion of some of the key concepts of Hegel's epistemology and metaphysics against a background of the Kantian problematic.

Life and Development

Harris, H. S. *Hegel's Development: Toward the Sunlight, 1770–1801.* Oxford: At the Clarendon Press, 1972. A fascinating and scholarly study of Hegel's philosophical development through his *Lehrjahre* and *Wanderjahre* in Stuttgart and Tübingen, Bern and Frankfurt.

Kaufmann, Walter. *Hegel: Reinterpretation, Texts and Commentary.* Garden City, N. Y.: Doubleday, 1965. Paperback reprint. 2 vols. Garden City, N. Y.: Doubleday Anchor Books, 1966. A helpful study of Hegel's life and the historical background of his writings by a man who "disbelieves" both Hegel's method and its results.

Mueller, G. E. *Hegel: The Man, His Vision and Work.* New York: Pageant Press, 1968. An intimate and balanced presentation of Hegel's life and thought by a devotee, marred only by careless editing.

Wiedmann, Franz. *Hegel: An Illustrated Biography.* Translated from the German by Joachim Neugroschel. New York: Pegasus, 1968. A brief account of Hegel's life, most valuable for the many excerpts from the letters of Hegel and his contemporaries.

The Phenomenology

Kojève, Alexandre. *Introduction to the Reading of Hegel: Lectures on the Phenomenology of Spirit.* Assembled by Raymond Queneau, edited by Allan Bloom, translated by James H. Nichols, Jr. New York: Basic Books, 1969. An abridged translation of Kojève's 2d French edition of 1947. A markedly *unbalanced* series of commentaries for advanced students, where Hegel's philosophy is made out to be historicist and atheistic.

Loewenberg, Jacob. *Hegel's Phenomenology: Dialogues on the Life of Mind.* La Salle, Illinois: Open Court, 1965. The first (and at this point the only) full-length book in English on the *Phenomenology.* While in dialogue form and free of the usual scholarly apparatus, the author's style and language make for difficult reading.

Royce, Josiah. *Lectures on Modern Idealism.* New Haven: Yale University Press, 1919. Reprinted in paperback, 1964. An interpretation of Hegel's *Phenomenology* against the background of Kant, Fichte, Schelling.

While this bibliography is limited to works in English, an exception must be made to include: Hyppolite, Jean. *Genèse et Structure de la Phénoménologie de l'Esprit de Hegel.* 2 vols. Paris: Aubier, 1946. This monumental work is the best thus far in any language.

The Logic

Clark, Malcolm. *Logic and System: A Study of the Transition from "Vorstellung" to Thought in the Philosophy of Hegel.* The Hague: Martinus Nijhoff, 1971. An interesting evaluation of the place of the *Logic* in Hegel's system, and the relation of its categories to the forms of experience.

McTaggart, John. *A Commentary on Hegel's Logic.* Cambridge: At the University Press, 1910. Reprinted by Russell & Russell, 1964. A detailed, often critical account of the transitions from "Being" to the "Absolute Idea" in the *Larger Logic.*

Mure, G. R. G. *A Study of Hegel's Logic.* Oxford: Clarendon Press, 1950. A penetrating study by a deep student of Hegel, concentrating on the *Encyclopaedia Logic* (the *Lesser Logic*), and presupposing familiarity with Mure's earlier *Introduction to Hegel* (see p. 345).

Stirling, James Hutchison. *The Secret of Hegel, Being the Hegelian System in Origin, Principle, Form and Matter.* 2d edition. Edinburgh: Oliver & Boyd, 1898. Reprinted by William C. Brown Reprint Library, 1967. The book that introduced Hegel to England. Largely because of its antiquated style, it has been the butt of the undying joke that if Stirling had discovered Hegel's secret, he had kept it to himself. It is still a valuable treatment of Hegel's *Larger Logic,* and contains a translation and detailed commentary on the section on "Quality" therein.

Ethics and Political Philosophy

Avineri, Shlomo. *Hegel's Theory of the Modern State.* Cambridge: At the University Press, 1972. The first full-length study in English of Hegel's political philosophy. Avineri, an accomplished Marxian scholar, brings Hegel's early writings on politics and economics to bear upon his mature theory of the state.

Kaufmann, Walter, ed. *Hegel's Political Philosophy.* New York: Atherton Press, 1970. A series of debates and exchanges, collected from various journals, in which the meaning and implications of Hegel's "nationalism" are hotly disputed by T. M. Knox, E. F. Carritt, Sidney Hook, Shlomo Avineri, and Z. A. Pelczynski.

Pelczynski, Z. A., ed. *Hegel's Political Philosophy: Problems and Perspectives.* Cambridge: At the University Press, 1971. A balanced collection of new essays by both well-established and young scholars, which analyze his major moral and political concepts, and assess his contribution to the philosophy of morals, law, society, and history, his place in the tradition of modern political theory, and his relation to later thinkers such as Marx and Stirner.

Plant, Raymond. *Hegel.* Bloomington: Indiana University Press, 1973. A concise study of Hegel's political thought which establishes the relation between Hegel's political and metaphysical writings.

Reyburn, Hugh A. *The Ethical Theory of Hegel: A Study of the Philosophy of Right.* Oxford: At the Clarendon Press, 1921. Reprinted 1967. A faithful and sympathetic exposition of Hegel's major work on ethics and politics. The first half of the book is devoted to Hegel's general philosophical position, thus making it an excellent introduction to Hegel.

Walsh, W. H. *Hegelian Ethics.* New York: St. Martin's Press, 1969. A very brief sketch of Hegel's views on morality as contrasted with those of Kant.

Aesthetics

Hegel, G. W. F. *The Introduction to Hegel's Philosophy of Fine Art.* Translated by Bernard Bosanquet. London: K. Paul, Trench & Co., 1886. This translation, which is far better than Osmaston's (p. 339), is preceded by Bosanquet's essay "On the True Conception of Another World."

Kaminsky, Jack. *Hegel on Art. An Interpretation of Hegel's Aesthetics.* New York: State University of New York Press, 1962. A fair presentation of Hegel's philosophy of fine art sandwiched between two scabby criticisms of Hegel's metaphysics.

See also Paolucci's *Hegel on Tragedy* (p. 340), and my edition of *Hegel in Comparative Literature* (p. 340). The best work on Hegel's aesthetics is found in scattered journal articles and foreign books not listed here, and in the writings of such Hegelians as A. C. Bradley and Benedetto Croce.

Philosophy of Religion

Christensen, Darrel E., ed. *Hegel and the Philosophy of Religion: The Wofford Symposium.* The Hague: Martinus Nijhoff, 1970. The Proceedings of the first meeting of the Hegel Society of America. The excellent essays explore many facets of Hegel's philosophy of religion in its relationship to the system as a whole, the times, and other major thinkers such as Kant, Nietzsche, and Marx.

Fackenheim, Emil L. *The Religious Dimension in Hegel's Thought.* Bloomington: Indiana University Press, 1967. An impressive, erudite criticism which focuses the "failure" of Hegel's entire system in the philosophy of religion.

History of Philosophy

Easton, Loyd D. *Hegel's First American Followers. The Ohio Hegelians: John B. Stallo, Peter Kaufmann, Moncure Conway, and August Willich, with Key Writings.* Athens: Ohio University Press, 1966. A most interesting discussion of Hegel's influence in America in the middle of the nineteenth century.

Gray, J. Glenn. *Hegel and Greek Thought.* New York: Harper Torchbooks, 1968. A valuable statement of "Hegel's Hellenic Ideal," the title under which it was first published in 1941. Also valuable for Hegel's development.

Lauer, Quentin. *Hegel's Idea of Philosophy.* New York: Fordham University Press, 1971. A good text for the beginning student, containing a new translation by Lauer of Hegel's Introduction to his Berlin lectures of 1825–1826 on the history of philosophy, preceded by a lengthy essay on Hegel's system and a commentary on the text of the Introduction.

Mure, G. R. G. *An Introduction to Hegel.* Oxford: Clarendon Press, 1940. An introduction in name only. Mure brilliantly discusses the relationship of Hegel to Aristotle, Kant, and F. H. Bradley.

O'Malley, J. J.; Algozin, K. W.; Weiss, F. G.; eds. *Hegel and the History of Philosophy.* Proceedings of the 1972 Hegel Society of America Conference. The Hague: Martinus Nijhoff, 1974. A long overdue treatment of the subject, including studies of Hegel's relation to Plato, Descartes, Leibniz, Kant, Solovyov, and Peirce. Includes a lengthy bibliography.

Weiss, Frederick G. *Hegel's Critique of Aristotle's Philosophy of Mind.* The Hague: Martinus Nijhoff, 1969. A study of Hegel's detailed commentary on the *De Anima* in his *Lectures on the History of Philosophy*, preceded by an excellent and lengthy Preface by G. R. G. Mure on the general relation of Aristotle and Hegel.

Psychology

Greene, Murray. *Hegel on the Soul: A Speculative Anthropology.* The Hague: Martinus Nijhoff, 1972. The first full-length treatment of Hegel's Anthropology. An excellent introduction to Hegel's philosophy of Subjective Spirit, especially for the student familiar with Kant.

General Essays and Collections

MacIntyre, Alasdair, ed. *Hegel: A Collection of Critical Essays.* New York: Anchor Books, 1972. A useful assemblage of both new and previously published essays.

O'Malley, J. J. et al. *The Legacy of Hegel: Proceedings of the Marquette Hegel Symposium 1970.* The Hague: Martinus Nijhoff, 1973. A fine set of essays embracing specific topics of interest in contemporary Hegel studies and also the impact of Hegel's thought upon contemporary philosophical, political, and social problems.

Steinkraus, Warren E., *New Studies in Hegel's Philosophy.* New York: Holt, Rinehart and Winston, 1971. Mostly new essays, some of them excellent.

Travis, D. C., ed. *A Hegel Symposium.* Austin: University of Texas, 1962. Essays by Carl J. Friedrich, Sidney Hook, Helmut Motekat, Gustav E. Mueller, and Helmut Rehder.

Tulane Studies in Philosophy. vol. 9. *Studies in Hegel.* The Hague: Martinus Nijhoff, 1960. Essays by Alan Brinkley, J. K. Feibleman, M.

Franklin, Paul G. Morrison, Andrew Reck, R. C. Whittemore, and Edward Ballard.

Weiss, Frederick G., ed. *Beyond Epistemology: New Studies in the Philosophy of Hegel.* The Hague: Martinus Nijhoff, 1974. A comprehensive exposition of Hegel's philosophy as a systematic theory of truth; Hegel's relation to Phenomenology and Hermeneutics is also explored.

Journal Issues Devoted Wholly to Hegel

"Commemorative Issue, Hegel's 200th Birthday," *International Journal for the Philosophy of Religion* 1:3 (Fall 1970).

"G.W.F. Hegel, 1770–1970," *The Review of Metaphysics* 23:4 (June 1970).

"Hegel Today," *The Monist* 48:1 (January 1964).

Weiss, Frederick G., ed. "Hegel in Comparative Literature," *Review of National Literatures* 1:2 (Fall 1970).

Weiss, Frederick G., ed. *The Owl of Minerva.* Quarterly Journal of the Hegel Society of America 1:1 (1969–).

Bibliographies

The most comprehensive listing of *English* books on Hegel is to be found in Frederick G. Weiss, "Hegel: A Bibliography of Books in English, Arranged Chronologically," in *The Legacy of Hegel: Proceedings of the Marquette Hegel Symposium 1970.* The Hague: Martinus Nijhoff, 1973. In this volume, see also Frederick G. Weiss, "A Critical Survey of Hegel Scholarship in English, 1962–1969," in which can be found more detailed evaluations of many of the books in the present bibliography.

A lengthy, but dated, list of titles in many languages may be found in the German edition of Benedetto Croce's *What is Living and What is Dead of the Philosophy of Hegel.* Heidelberg, 1909. A good bibliography of English and foreign works may also be found in Harris' *Hegel's Development*, Steinkraus' *New Studies in Hegel's Philosophy*, (see "General Essays, Collections" above), and Kaufmann's *Hegel: Reinterpretation* (see "Life and Development").

9 780061 318313